THE CAMBRIDGE COMPANION

# ARISTOTLE'S *POLI*

One of the most influential works in the history of political theory, Aristotle's *Politics* is a treatise in practical philosophy, intended to inform legislators and to create the conditions for virtuous and self-sufficient lives for the citizens of a state. In this *Companion*, distinguished scholars offer new perspectives on the work and its themes. After an opening exploration of the relation between Aristotle's ethics and his politics, the central chapters follow the sequence of the eight books of the *Politics*, taking up questions such as the role of reason in legitimizing rule, the common good, justice, slavery, private property, citizenship, democracy and deliberation, unity, conflict, law and authority, and education. The closing chapters discuss the interaction between Aristotle's political thought and contemporary democratic theory. The volume will provide a valuable resource for those studying ancient philosophy, Classics, and the history of political thought.

MARGUERITE DESLAURIERS is Professor of Philosophy at McGill University. She is the author of *Aristotle on Definition* (2007).

PIERRE DESTRÉE is Associate Researcher at the Belgian FRS (Fonds de la Recherche Scientifique) and Associate Professor of Philosophy at the University of Louvain (Louvain-la-Neuve). He has edited several books, including *Akrasia in Greek Philosophy* (co-edited with Christopher Bobonich, 2007) and *Plato and the Poets* (co-edited with F.-G. Herrmann, 2011).

*Continued at the back of the book*

# The Cambridge Companion to
# ARISTOTLE'S
# POLITICS

Edited by

## Marguerite Deslauriers

*McGill University*

and

## Pierre Destrée

*University of Louvain*

# CAMBRIDGE
## UNIVERSITY PRESS

University Printing House, Cambridge CB2 8BS, United Kingdom

Published in the United States of America by Cambridge University Press, New York

Cambridge University Press is part of the University of Cambridge.

It furthers the University's mission by disseminating knowledge in the pursuit of education, learning and research at the highest international levels of excellence.

www.cambridge.org
Information on this title: www.cambridge.org/9780521181112

© Cambridge University Press, 2013

First published 2013

Printed in the United Kingdom by TJ International Ltd. Padstow Cornwall

*A catalogue record for this publication is available from the British Library*

*Library of Congress Cataloguing in Publication data*
The Cambridge companion to Aristotle's Politics / edited by Marguerite Deslauriers and Pierre Destrée.
    pages   cm
Includes bibliographical references and index.
ISBN 978-1-107-00468-9 (hardback)
1. Aristotle. Politics.   2. Political science – Early works to 1800.
I. Deslauriers, Marguerite, 1956–
JC71.A7C37   2013
320.1 – dc23      2013007955

ISBN 978-1-107-00468-9 Hardback
ISBN 978-0-521-18111-2 Paperback

# CONTENTS

# CONTRIBUTORS

MARGUERITE DESLAURIERS is Professor of Philosophy at McGill University. She is the author of *Aristotle on Definition* (2007).

PIERRE DESTRÉE is Associate Researcher at the Belgian FRS (Fonds de la Recherche Scientifique) and Associate Professor of Philosophy at the University of Louvain (Louvain-la-Neuve). He has edited several books, including *Akrasia in Greek Philosophy* (with Christopher Bobonich, 2007) and *Plato and the Poets* (with F.-G. Herrmann, 2011).

DOROTHEA FREDE is Emerita Professor of Philosophy at the University of Hamburg. She is the author of *Platon. Philebos. Übersetzung und Kommentar* (1997), and *Platons Phaidon. Der Traum von der Unsterblichkeit* (1999). She has also edited (with A. Laks) *Traditions of Theology: Studies in Hellenistic Theology, its Background and Aftermath* (2002), (with B. Inwood) *Language and Learning: Philosophy of Language in the Hellenistic Age* (2005), and (with B. Reis) *Body and Soul in Ancient Philosophy*.

BRYAN GARSTEN is Professor of Political Science at Yale University. He is the author of *Saving Persuasion: A Defense of Rhetoric and Judgment* (2006). He has edited *Rousseau, the Enlightenment, and Their Legacies* (2012).

ANTONY HATZISTAVROU is Lecturer in Philosophy at the University of Hull. He is the co-editor (with M. H. Kramer, C. Grant and B. Colburn) of *The Legacy of H. L. A. Hart: Legal, Political and Moral Philosophy* (2008).

ix

CHRISTOPH HORN is Professor of Philosophy at the University of Bonn. He is the author of several books, including *Antike Lebenskunst. Glück und Moral von Sokrates bis zu den Neuplatonikern* (1998), and *Einführung in die Politische Philosophie* (2003). He has co-edited (with N. Scarano) *Philosophie der Gerechtigkeit. Texte von der Antike bis zur Gegenwart* (2002), and (with A. Neschke) *Politischer Aristotelismus. Die Rezeption der aristotelischen 'Politik' von der Antike bis zum 19. Jahrhundert* (2008).

RICHARD KRAUT is Professor of Philosophy at Northwestern University. He is the author of numerous books, including *Aristotle on the Human Good* (1989), *Aristotle Politics Books VII and VIII: Translation with Commentary* (1997), *Aristotle: Political Philosophy* (2002), *What is Good and Why: the Ethics of Well-Being* (2007), and *Against Absolute Goodness* (2011). He is the editor of the *Cambridge Companion to Plato* (1992), *Plato's Republic: Critical Essays* (1997), *Aristotle's Politics: Critical Essays* (2005), and the *Blackwell Guide to Aristotle's Nicomachean Ethics* (2006).

MELISSA LANE is Professor of Politics at Princeton University. She is the author of *Method and Politics in Plato's Statesman* (1998), *Plato's Progeny: How Plato and Socrates Still Captivate the Modern Mind* (2001), and *Eco-Republic: What the Ancients Can Teach Us about Ethics, Virtue, and Sustainable Living* (2012). She is an associate editor of the *Cambridge History of Greek and Roman Political Thought* (2000) and co-editor of *A Poet's Reich: Politics and Culture in the George Circle* (2011) and *Politeia in Greek and Roman Philosophy* (2013).

THORNTON LOCKWOOD is Assistant Professor of Philosophy at Quinnipiac University.

FRED D. MILLER, JR. is Professor of Philosophy at Bowling Green State University. He is the author of *Nature, Justice and Rights in Aristotle's Politics* (1995), and co-editor of *A Companion to Aristotle's Politics* (1995).

DONALD MORRISON is Professor of Philosophy and Classics at Rice University. He has edited the *Cambridge Companion to Socrates* (2011).

KAREN MARGRETHE NIELSEN is Associate Professor of Philosophy at the University of Western Ontario. She has co-edited (with D. Henry) *Bridging the Gap between Aristotle's Science and Ethics* (forthcoming).

PIERRE PELLEGRIN is Directeur de Recherches Emérite au CNRS (Paris). He is the author of *Aristotle's Classification of Animals: Biology and the Conceptual Unity of the Aristotelian Corpus* (1986), and (with M. Crubellier) *Aristote le philosophe et les savoirs* (2002). He has co-edited several books, including (with D. Devereux) *Biologie, logique et métaphysique chez Aristote* (1990), and (with Mary Louise Gill) *A Companion to Ancient Philosophy* (2006). He is also the author of a number of French translations of Aristotle, including *Aristote, Les Politiques: introduction, traduction, notes et annexes* (1993).

ANDRÉS ROSLER is Professor of Philosophy of Law at the University of Buenos Aires and Associate Research Fellow at the National Council for Scientific and Technical Research, Argentina. He is the author of *Political Authority and Obligation in Aristotle* (2005).

MARCO ZINGANO is Professor of Philosophy at the University of Sao Paulo. He is the author of *Estudos de Etica Antiga* (2007), and *Aristoteles: Etica Nicomachea I 13–III 8. Tratado da Virtude Moral* (2008).

# ACKNOWLEDGEMENTS

Our first debt of gratitude is to the contributors to this volume. The substance of the work is theirs. We are especially grateful for the collaborative spirit the contributors brought to the project, and their willingness to present and to comment on work in progress.

We wish to thank Örsan K. Öymen who, both as the Founder and President of the Association of Philosophy, Art, and Science, and as the Founder and Director of Philosophy in Assos, very generously organized a conference at Assos, Turkey in June of 2010 at which versions of many of the chapters in this volume were first presented.

A second conference was held at McGill University in Montreal, Canada, in March 2011. The editors wish to thank the Departments of Philosophy and of Political Science, and the Research Group in Constitutional Studies at McGill for their support. We would also like to acknowledge the support of the Social Sciences and Humanities Research Council of Canada.

C. D. C. Reeve arranged with Hackett Publishing Company for permission to quote from his translation of the *Politics*; the editors wish to thank him and Hackett. We are also indebted to Thornton Lockwood for kind permission to include his topical bibliography on Aristotle's *Politics*.

For philosophical, editorial, and administrative help at various stages of the project, the editors would like to thank many colleagues and students: Joseph Burke, Andrea Falcon, Jacob Levy, Eric Lewis, Sara Magrin, Stephen Menn, Catherine Pakaluk, Michael Pakaluk, Esther Rogan, Geoffrey Sigalet, Marlene K. Sokolon, Brooks Sommerville, Natalie Stoljar, Daniel Weinstock, and Shiloh Whitney.

E. Zoli Filotas translated "Natural Slavery" by Pierre Pellegrin from the French, and assisted in the editorial process. His many philosophical and editorial suggestions amounted to an important contribution to the volume, and the editors wish to express special thanks to him.

Aristotle lived and worked for several years in Assos, which was at the time a city-state under the rule of the king Hermias. On the cover of this book the image of the temple of Athena – the goddess of science and the arts, as Aristotle himself tells us (*Politics* VIII 6, 1341b7–8) – commemorates his association, and ours, with Assos.

# ABBREVIATIONS

| | |
|---|---|
| *An. Post.* | *Posterior Analytics* |
| *Const. Ath.* | *Constitution of Athens* |
| *DA* | *On the Soul (de Anima)* |
| *EE* | *Eudemian Ethics* |
| *NE* | *Nicomachean Ethics* |
| *GA* | *Generation of Animals* |
| *HA* | *History of Animals* |
| *IA* | *Progression of Animals (de Incessu Animalium)* |
| *Met.* | *Metaphysics* |
| *MM* | *Magna Moralia* |
| *MA* | *Movement of Animals (de Motu Animalium)* |
| *Mund.* | *On the Universe (de Mundo)* |
| *PA* | *Parts of Animals* |
| *Phys.* | *Physics* |
| *Prob.* | *Problems* |
| *Pol.* | *Politics* |
| *Rhet.* | *Rhetoric* |
| *Top.* | *Topics* |

Note: Translations of Aristotle's *Politics* throughout the volume are from C. D. C. Reeve's *Aristotle*, Politics (Indianapolis, IN: Hackett, 1998) unless otherwise noted.

# Introduction

I

Aristotle's *Politics* is a classic in the history of political thought, a work that later philosophers (including Hobbes, Locke, Rousseau, and Marx) take to be fundamental to political theory. And yet the *Politics* is a work that many readers find both inaccessible and disagreeable. Two factors may explain this mixed response. First, the political entity that Aristotle viewed as the final and perfect form of political life, the *polis* (usually translated as "city-state"), was a small city together with its surrounding territory, more or less independent from other city-states, and nothing like a nation-state.[1] As an independent political structure it disappeared later in antiquity. So one might suppose the *Politics* to be only of historical interest, and its questions to have no bearing on our political lives. And indeed the *Politics* was largely neglected throughout antiquity – although the text was known to some, there seems to have been no ancient or medieval Byzantine Greek commentary on the work, and no translation into Arabic in the Abbasid period.[2] In the Western medieval period, philosophical interest in the treatise was renewed, in spite of the historical distance of the political structures that had given rise to it. The first Latin translation by Moerbeke (around 1260) allowed Albert the Great and Thomas Aquinas to write commentaries on the *Politics*, from which grew a Thomist tradition of Aristotelian political philosophy. Beginning in the sixteenth century, however, the interest aroused by the *Politics* was more often negative, particularly in the tradition of modern political thought established by Hobbes.[3]

Hobbes notoriously said that "scarce anything can be…more repugnant to government than much of that he [Aristotle] hath said in his *Politics*." This suggests the second factor that moves some to reject the book: not only is it concerned with a political world that is strange to us, but also it contains proposals that many modern readers find deplorable. Hobbes was no fan of any of Aristotle's works, but even those who do admire his moral philosophy or his natural philosophy may find themselves rejecting his political philosophy. At least one scholar has recently described Aristotle as a "totalitarian thinker."[4]

Aristotle certainly was a critic of the democracy of his time, which he understood to be demagogic and to lead necessarily to tyranny. He believed that some people were naturally suited to rule over others, and that the inhabitants of a city could be grouped according to their natural capacities, and natural entitlements, to rule. And so he defends male dominance, slavery, and cultural and linguistic racism, as well as strict limitations on citizenship. There is a growing body of scholarship on these issues in his political philosophy, most of which now seeks neither to defend nor to revile Aristotle for his views, but to situate those views in the context of ancient debates, and to understand the implications of his discussions for our own political lives. Most political communities, for example, do restrict citizenship; we can read Aristotle to understand what sorts of arguments might be made for such restrictions, to ask whether we agree with the premises of his arguments, and to consider the justice of, and the implications of, imposing or lifting such restrictions. Most women still lead lives that are different in important respects from those of the men in their communities; we can read Aristotle to see how a philosopher proceeds who sees that this is not simply a fact, but a political circumstance that requires explanation, to ask whether an explanation is a justification, and to think about the political implications of whatever differences there may be between men and women.

There are other, more positive, reasons to read Aristotle's *Politics*. Many of the political ideas that seemed important to him continue to hold interest for us: justice and the law; the status of the citizen; participation in the affairs of the political community as an obligation and a privilege; human flourishing or happiness; and public education. These remain subjects of political debate. And some recent reappraisals of Aristotle's political theory (for example, by Richard Kraut, Fred Miller, Josiah Ober, and Martha Nussbaum) have found value in certain of the themes of the *Politics*, especially the notion of human flourishing in a political context.[5]

Aristotle covers a great deal of ground in the *Politics*: he offers an account of human nature as political; distinguishes different kinds of people; describes, classifies, and evaluates a variety of constitutions; proposes how best to structure a political community; and investigates citizenship, wealth, conflict, and education, all the while arguing against some of his predecessors, instructing those who would legislate, and insisting on the continuity between moral and political issues. The *Politics* is an ambitious work that offers every reader an entry into reflection on political life by raising fundamental questions: What is the aim of political community? Why should some people govern others? Who should count as a citizen? Is war ever justified? Many of us will find ourselves in disagreement with Aristotle's answers, but the questions themselves demand reflection and discussion.

II

The title, *Politika*, under which the *Politics* has come down to us, was probably not Aristotle's own.[6] It does, however, reflect the central theme of the work, which is the nature of constitutions (*politeiai*), in the sense of the forms of government (*politeuma*) that a city-state might adopt.[7] When Aristotle wrote the *Politics*, a genre of writing on constitutions was already well established.[8] Plato's *Republic* (the Greek title is *Politeia*) is the most famous work in this tradition prior to Aristotle's *Politics*, but it was certainly not the only one, or the first.[9] Aristotle understood himself to be contributing to this tradition, and to be addressing especially those who were in a position to educate and train those who would become legislators. He accepts some of the assumptions of the genre, disputes others, but tries to meet many of its expectations. Among those expectations was, first, that the author would argue for the superiority of some particular constitution. Such an argument presupposed a classification of constitutions, and so a second expectation of writing on the *politeia* was that it should include such a classification.

Writing in the context of this tradition, Aristotle offers us in the *Politics* both a classification of constitutions, and several discussions of the best possible constitution. A constitution, Aristotle says, is "a certain organization of the inhabitants of a city-state" (III 1, 1274b38); more precisely, it is "an organization of a city-state's various offices" and especially of the office "that has authority over everything" (III 6, 1278b8–10). So, to write on constitutions is to discuss how a city-state should be organized, particularly with respect to rule and authority. The most basic political question is who should rule over others, and on what basis. Aristotle offers us two principles for distinguishing among different kinds of constitution: a moral principle, according to which a constitution is correct or legitimate if it looks "to the common benefit" and is organized "according to what is unqualifiedly just" and incorrect or deviant if it looks "only to the benefit of the rulers," in which case it will be unjust according to the standard of unqualified justice (III 6, 1279a17–20). The second principle of classification, which, like the first, had been employed by others before Aristotle, distinguishes constitutions according to the number of citizens who hold the most authoritative office: one, few, or many. These two principles allow Aristotle to set out six possible basic constitutions (kingship, aristocracy, polity, democracy, oligarchy, and tyranny). This schema is just the beginning; Aristotle gives a complex account of the different forms that several of the constitutions can take, and he seeks to explain how city-states can adopt constitutions that combine some mixture of elements.[10]

In keeping, again, with the tradition of writing on the *politeia*, Aristotle raises the question of which constitution is the best, although he qualifies the inquiry: "We propose to study which political community is best of all for people who are able to live as ideally as possible" (II 1, 1260b27–29). He offers no answer in Book II, but he does indicate in Book III that the best constitution is a kingship or aristocracy; then in Book IV he says that the best constitution for most cities, judged by "a life that most people can share and a constitution in which most city-states can participate" will be a "mixed constitution" which seems to be some mixture of aristocracy and polity (IV 11, 1295a29–31). Later, in Books VII–VIII, he describes the conditions for "the city of our dreams" (VII 4, 1325b36), in which all citizens rule. The relation between these different accounts of the best constitution, whether they can be reconciled, and how, is the subject of much scholarly debate.[11]

What is clear is that Aristotle believes a constitution must be suited to the character of the people who inhabit a city-state. In an important passage where he appears to offer the reader the program of the *Politics* as a whole (IV 1, 1288b10–20), he compares political science to the skill of an athletic trainer. The trainer must know what is appropriate for the best possible athletes, but also what is suitable for less gifted athletes. Similarly, a legislator must have knowledge both of the best possible constitution under ideal circumstances, and of the various constitutions that would suit less ideal circumstances. Aristotle contrasts his own approach to that of those who "seek only the constitution that is highest and requires a lot of resources," and others who "though they discuss a more attainable sort, do away with the constitutions actually in place" (IV 1, 1288b39–1289a1). Plato is (among others) the target of this remark, aimed at the best city, the Kallipolis described in his *Republic*, and the second best, more attainable, City of Magnesia, described at length in the *Laws*. In both cases these are ideal cities, not existing ones. Aristotle urges us to take an interest in existing city-states, "because it is no less a task to reform a constitution than to establish one actually in place...That is why, in addition to what has been just mentioned [i.e. the science of the best possible city], a statesman should also be able to help existing constitutions" (IV 1, 1289a3–7). He devotes so much effort to analyzing existing constitutions – oligarchies, aristocracies, and democracies – because he believes that one might improve existing constitutions, even bad ones. As he often says, practical sciences such as ethics and politics must aim at action, and not only at understanding (see e.g., *NE* X 9, 1179a35–b3).

One of the ways in which Aristotle imagines this improvement might be instituted is clear when we consider another point he emphasizes: that the aim of the city-state, indeed the aim of all communities, is to promote "living well" as opposing to "living" *tout court* (see e.g., II 9, 1280b10–12), contrary to what some sophists had already suggested, and contrary to what Hobbes and many modern political thinkers would later argue. Living "well" in this sense is living a truly human life, achieving *eudaimonia* (happiness or human flourishing), which is constituted by excellent activities (including the exercise of both moral and intellectual virtues). Aristotle acknowledges that people might come together in the first instance for the sake of protection and material benefits, but he insists that we would choose to live together in these ways even if we did not need, or expect to find, safety and material well-being together. This is part of what it means to say, as he does, that we are political animals (III 6, 1278b19–25). Only within political communities do we find what we need to flourish as human beings.

It follows from this that the task of those who formulate laws, and of those who govern, is to promote virtuous action among the citizens, and more broadly among the inhabitants, of the city-state. Promoting virtue will require a correct constitution, a just distribution of offices, good laws, and good education, as well as virtuous citizens. But Aristotle is very alive to the fragility of political structures, the sources of conflict that haunt every political community, and the difficulty of maintaining political stability. So he is concerned to reconcile certain political ideals with political realities as he sees them. We see this, for example, in the final chapters (14–16) of *Politics* IV, where he addresses the law-giver about different ways in which a state might combine various forms of legislative, executive, and judicial functions, without invoking any ethical principles.

### III

We have alluded to certain ongoing disagreements among scholars about the interpretation of the *Politics*. One source of these disagreements is that we cannot say with confidence how Aristotle intended to order the different books that constitute the work as we now have it. A review of the main themes of the eight books reveals that there is no evident organizing principle. Book I begins with some claims about the origins and final cause of the city-state, and proceeds to an analysis of household relations and management. Book II offers an often harsh appraisal of the best constitutions (both ideal and real) described by Socrates and others. Book III deals with some of the fundamental features of political life: citizenship, political virtue, and political justice; it also contains a classification of constitutions and a detailed analysis of kingship. The next three Books, IV through VI, concern themselves with more empirical issues. Book IV studies the existing regimes as well as certain possible constitutions that are good, although not ideal; Book V examines the sources of political conflict and how to save constitutions from dissolution; Book VI considers how constitutions are established. Finally, Books VII and VIII present the conditions for the best possible city, including a description of the education that such a city should provide to the young.

As this review demonstrates, there are four apparently independent sections of the *Politics*: Book I, Books II and VII–VIII, Book III, and Books IV to VI. Often no remark explicitly links one book to the next or the former, and when the text does include such remarks they are such that they might have been added by later editors. Moreover, the discrepancy in style and tone between the two largest sections is puzzling. Books II and VII–VIII, which treat of the best constitution, are emphatic in both their positive and negative assessments, and offer prescriptions for achieving happiness through political means. By contrast, Books IV–VI are generally coolly descriptive (they are often described as "sociological"), and seem to recommend preserving even bad constitutions rather than enduring political conflict. Moreover, there are discrepancies in content as well as tone. One discrepancy, mentioned above, is particularly important: Aristotle says in Book III that kingship and aristocracy (in which one or a few rule) are the best constitutions, but in Books VII–VIII he describes the best city we could wish for as one in which all the citizens rule because all are equally virtuous.

In the 1920s, Werner Jaeger argued that these discrepancies reflected changes in Aristotle's philosophical approach over the course of his life: Books VII–VIII (as well as III) were the product of his early, Platonizing, years, while Books IV–VI belonged to a later period in his life, when Aristotle approached phenomena from a more empirical point of view.[12] More recently, several scholars have suggested that the discrepancies might be explained by the difference in focus between Books VII–VIII, on the one hand, and Books III–VI on the other. On this interpretation, the city of Books VII–VIII is a utopia, an ideal constitution that would be possible only under ideal circumstances, whereas Books III and IV–VI deal mainly with existing constitutions, and offer judgments about the best possible constitutions in the real world.[13] It has also been suggested, as early as the fourteenth century, that we should re-order the books of the *Politics* by placing Books VII–VIII after Books I–III, so that Aristotle would describe the ideal city before returning, at the end of the treatise, to consider existing cities.[14] But none of the manuscripts we have follow this ordering, and Books VII–VIII do not seem at all concerned with the six-fold classification of III–VI, suggesting that they were not intended to follow Book III. Moreover, if we preserve the traditional ordering, we can understand the description of the best city in VII–VIII as the culmination of Aristotle's political philosophy, intended to follow after the description of non-ideal constitutions (actual and possible).[15]


IV

The essays in this volume take up some of the most important questions, philosophical and political, that Aristotle raises in the course of the *Politics*. They have been organized to follow, by and large, the order of the books, with two qualifications. First, the volume begins and ends with contributions that consider the relation between the *Politics* and some other work or works. "The political character of Aristotle's ethics" by Dorothea Frede concerns the relation between Aristotle's moral philosophy and his political philosophy; and both Bryan Garsten's "Deliberating and acting together" and Richard Kraut's "Aristotle and Rawls on the common good" evaluate the relationship between Aristotle's *Politics* and aspects of contemporary political philosophy – deliberative democracy and Rawls' liberalism, respectively. The other essays in this volume are organized to follow the themes of the books in sequence, but many discuss aspects of different books, reflecting the way in which certain themes resurface throughout the *Politics*. Five essays concern Books I and II: Fred D. Miller, Jr. sets out Aristotle's political anthropology and its basis in claims about reason; Pierre Pellegrin offers a new understanding of the relation between master and slave; Karen Nielsen addresses Aristotle's views on wealth (How much do we need? Is private property good?); and Marguerite Deslauriers argues that for Aristotle inequality is fundamental to political unity. Another five essays concern themselves with Books III through VI: Andrés Rosler, beginning with the gap between the virtuous person and the virtuous citizen, argues that Aristotle is more political, and less focused on what is morally good, than we might suppose. Christoph Horn develops an account of Aristotle as a political loyalist, by posing the question of obligation: Why should we obey laws imposed on us? Don Morrison offers an interpretation of the notion of "common good" so central to Aristotle's classification of the constitutions. Marco Zingano demonstrates that Aristotle's conception of natural justice is not opposed to political justice. Melissa Lane builds a new interpretation of Aristotle's account of democratic processes, especially deliberation and decision. Antony Hatzistavrou analyzes Aristotle's description of the sources of political conflict. Finally, Pierre Destrée's essay connects the aims of political life to the discussion of education that occupies Aristotle in Books VII and VIII.

Although the essays are, then, ordered to follow the structure of the *Politics* as we have it, certain themes recur in several contributions, and give the reader a sense of Aristotle's political preoccupations. The relation between politics and morality is clearly something Aristotle both embraces and worries about (see the essays by Frede, Miller, Rosler, Zingano, and Destrée). Commonality and the common good is another theme: What should we have in common, what does it mean to have it in common, and what will the political effects of common possession be? (Nielsen, Deslauriers, Morrison); how should we understand the common good? (Morrison, Kraut, Destrée). Political conflict – what it is, how to avoid it, and how to act when it does arise – is a third important theme (Rosler, Horn, Hatzistavrou). Reason, political deliberation, and decision-making make up a fourth theme (Horn, Lane, Garsten, Kraut), one that recalls the connection between Aristotle's moral psychology and his political philosophy.

Before leaving our readers to discover the essays in this volume – essays that aim both to introduce newcomers to Aristotle's political theory and to offer fresh perspectives to more seasoned readers – we conclude with two remarks. First, it is obvious to Aristotle that we cannot avoid being political, or that if we should manage to avoid it we would be incomplete as persons. In order to realize our political nature, we need to observe, analyze, and evaluate political possibilities; we need to participate in political reflection. Hence the importance of engaging with works such as Aristotle's *Politics*. But political reflection, however careful and comprehensive it might be, would be pointless were we not willing in some way or another to act to preserve, or to change, the political communities in which we live. Politics, for Aristotle, is a practical science, and so one that aims at truth in action.

Aristotle would say that how we organize ourselves politically is up to us, in the sense that it depends on our actions, but he would not allow that all forms of political life are equally good. It really does matter what we do. How to live in a political community is not a trivial question, and yet we may very well get it wrong. This brings us to the second remark. It is not only political life that we might get wrong; it is Aristotle himself. "About anyone as great as Shakespeare," T. S. Eliot once remarked, "it is probable that we can never be right; and if we can never be right, it is better that we should from time to time change our way of being wrong."[16] So, too, with Aristotle it is doubtful that we can ever offer a definitive interpretation, but this collection of essays is an attempt to help us change our ways of being wrong, if we cannot be certain of being right.

## WORKS CITED

Barnes, J. 1990. "Aristotle and political liberty." In *Aristoteles'* Politik, ed. G. Patzig. Göttingen: Vandenhoeck and Ruprecht. Reprinted in Kraut and Skultety 2005

Bordes, J. 1982. *Politeia dans la pensée grecque jusqu'à Aristote*. Paris: Les Belles Lettres

Cartledge, P. 2000. "Greek political thought: the historical context." In *The Cambridge History of Greek and Roman Political Thought*, eds. C. Rowe and M. Schofield. Cambridge University Press

Eliot, T. S. 1951. "Shakespeare and the Stoicism of Seneca." 1927. In his *Selected Essays*. London: Faber

Frank, J. 2005. *A Democracy of Distinction: Aristotle and the Work of Politics*. University of Chicago Press

Goodman, L. E. and Talisse, R. B., eds. 2007. *Aristotle's Politics Today*. Albany, NY: State University of New York Press

Horn, C. and Neschke-Hentschke, A., eds. 2008. *Politischer Aristotelismus. Die Rezeption der aristotelischen Politik von der Antike bis zum 19. Jahrhundert*. Stuttgart: Metzler

Jacoby, F. 1949. *Atthis: The Local Chronicles of Ancient Athens*. Oxford University Press

Jaeger, W. 1948 [1923]. *Aristotle: Fundamentals of the History of his Development*, trans. R. Robinson. 2nd rev. edn., Oxford University Press

Kahn, C. 1990. "The normative structure of Aristotle's *Politics*." In *Aristoteles'* Politik, ed. G. Patzig. Göttingen: Vandenhoeck and Ruprecht

Keyt, D. and Miller, F. D., eds. 1991. *A Companion to Aristotle's Politics*. Oxford: Blackwell

Kraut, R. 2002. *Aristotle: Political Philosophy*. Oxford University Press

Kraut, R. and Skultety, S., eds. 2005. *Aristotle's Politics: Critical Essays*. Lanham, MD: Rowman and Littlefield

Menn, S. 2005. "On Plato's Politeia." *Proceedings of the Boston Area Colloquium in Ancient Philosophy* XXI: 1–55

Miller, F. D. 1995. *Nature, Justice and Rights in Aristotle's Politics*. Oxford University Press

Newman, W. L. 1887–1902. *The Politics of Aristotle*. 4 vols, Oxford University Press

Nussbaum, M. 1988. "Nature, Function, and Capability: Aristotle on Political Distribution." *Oxford Studies in Ancient Philosophy*, Supplement: 145–84

Ober, J. 1998. " Political animals, actual citizens, and the best possible *polis*: Aristotle's *Politics*." In his *Political Dissent in Democratic Athens: Intellectual Critics of Popular Rule*. Princeton University Press

Pellegrin, P. 1987. "La *Politique* d'Aristote: unité et fractures. Éloge de la lecture sommaire." *Revue philosophique de la France et de l'Etranger* 177: 129–59

Rapp, C. 1994. "Was Aristotle a Communitarian?" *Graduate Faculty Philosophy Journal* 17(1–2): 333–49

Reeve, C. D. C. 1998. *Aristotle* Politics. Indianapolis, IN: Hackett

Rowe, C. J. 1989. "Reality and Utopia." *Elenchos* 10: 317–36

    1991 [1977]. "Aims and methods in Aristotle's *Politics*." In Keyt and Miller

    2000. "Aristotelian Constitutions." In *The Cambridge History of Greek and Roman Political Thought*, ed. C. Rowe and M. Schofield. Cambridge University Press

Schütrumpf, E. 1991–2005. *Aristoteles Politik*. 4 vols, Berlin: Akademie Verlag

Simpson, P. 1997. *The Politics of Aristotle*. Chapel Hill, NC: University of North Carolina Press

    1998. *A Philosophical Commentary on Aristotle's Politics*. Chapel Hill, NC: University of North Carolina Press

Susemihl, F. and Hicks, R. D. 1976 [1894]. *The Politics of Aristotle*. New York: Arno Press

NOTES

1. On this, and the historical context of the *Politics*, see Cartledge 2000.
2. Cicero seems to have had access to the *Politics* (which he refers to in his *De Finibus*), and the late Neoplatonist Proclus refers to Book II in his commentary on Plato's *Republic*. Moreover, some ancient

and byzantine Greek commentators on Aristotle's *Nicomachean Ethics* (Alexander of Aphrodisias, and Michael of Ephesus) did refer to the *Politics*, but do not seem to have written commentaries on it. The absence of an Arabic translation of the *Politics* during the Abbasid period is especially striking because translations of most of Aristotle's treatises (including the *Nicomachean Ethics*) were carried out at that time, and played an important role in the reception of Aristotle in the later medieval and Renaissance periods.

3. Even before Hobbes, Jean Bodin (whose *Les Livres de la République* appeared in French in 1576, and later in Latin) vigorously opposed Aristotle's *Politics*. See Horn and Neschke-Hentschke 2008 for the history of the reception of the *Politics*.

4. Barnes 1990.

5. For some recent assessments of Aristotle's political ideas that are at least in part positive, see Frank 2005, Kraut 2002, Miller 1995, Nussbaum 1988, and Kraut and Skultety 2005 (especially the essays by Keyt, Ober, and Waldron). See also the volume edited by Goodman and Talisse 2007. While Aristotle has sometimes been claimed as a forefather for communitarianism, see Rapp 1994 for an argument against such an interpretation.

6. In our manuscripts, *Politika* probably stands for *Politika biblia*, or "Political Books," each "book" corresponding to one papyrus roll. According to the list of Aristotle's works reported by Diogenes Laertius, the ancient title was "Lecture about politics (8 books)" (*Politikê akroasis*). In Aristotle's work, there is one mention of the *Politika* in his *Rhetoric* at I, 8, 1366a22, but it does not seem to be referring to the *Politics* as we have it.

7. The term *politeia* can also refer to a particular form of constitution, one in which "the multitude governs for the common benefit" (in which case it is usually translated as "constitutional government" or "polity"). A polity is distinguished from a democracy because in a democracy the multitude govern for their own benefit. In the same way, aristocracy is distinguished from oligarchy because aristocrats govern for the common benefit.

8. We do not know precisely when he wrote the treatise, and at any rate it is likely that it was written, re-arranged, and revised over time; it was probably not completed until some time between 336 BCE and Aristotle's death in 322.

9. For an account of the literature in this tradition prior to Aristotle, see Menn 2005 and Bordes 1982 (especially 127–227). For the claim that Aristotle invented a scientific form of writing on *politeiai* see Jacoby 1949: 211–15.

10. This classification of six constitutions is qualified later in the *Politics*, when, for example, Aristotle denies that tyranny is, properly speaking, a constitution.

11. For an excellent discussion of this debate, see Rowe 2000.

12. See Jaeger 1948. This explanation has largely been rejected because it cannot be confirmed or disconfirmed with the evidence we have. But Eckart Schütrumpf, in his commentary on the *Politics* (Schütrumpf 1991–2005), defends the idea that there is a radical discrepancy between the two approaches, the utopian and the empirical.

13. See Kraut 2002: 357–61 and Ober 1998: ch. 6.

14. Among modern editors, Susemihl and Hicks 1894, Newman 1887–1902, and more recently Peter Simpson in his translation and commentary (Simpson 1997 and 1998) adopt this view. This solution was apparently suggested by the first translator in any modern language, Nicole Oresme (1374), and was defended by the late Renaissance philosopher Scaino da Salo in his 1577 *Questions* on the *Politics*.

15. For recent in-depth discussions of the ordering of the books, and its impact on interpretations of the *Politics*, see especially Kahn 1990; Kraut 2002: chs. 5 and 10.1; Miller 1995: chs. 6–8; Pellegrin 1987; and Rowe 1989 and 1991.

16. Eliot 1951: 126.

# 1 The political character of Aristotle's ethics

## INTRODUCTION: THE IMPORTANCE OF POLITICAL SCIENCE

There is a short and a long answer to the question of the political character of Aristotle's ethics. The short answer confines itself to the fact that he indicates right at the outset of the *Nicomachean Ethics* that ethics forms part of politics. For, while the recognition of the right aim or *telos* of life is of the greatest importance for the individual, the order of the community represents a higher aim, because it concerns not just the good of the individual but that of the entire *polis* (*NE* I 2). The "most architectonic science" (*malista architektonikê*), that both studies and makes provisions for the overall conditions of the good life, is therefore political science (*politikê epistêmê*).[1] That this justification is not just a rhetorical device to emphasize the importance of ethics is confirmed by the fact that the political dimension of the investigation is never left entirely out of sight throughout the *Nicomachean Ethics*, even if its focus is largely on the conditions of the individual life and not on that of the community. As suggested by repeated remarks on the relevance of different aspects of the investigation for the politician, most particularly for the legislator,[2] Aristotle's audience did not just consist of philosophers but also attracted students with political ambitions, as did Plato's Academy. For this very reason Aristotle also sometimes indicates that there are limits to the extent to which students with special interest in politics need to penetrate the philosophical questions at issue.[3]

The short answer, that ethics is part of politics because the life of an entire community is a higher aim than the life of an individual,

14

has a deeper background and therefore requires a longer answer. This is indicated already in the initial specification of the task of political science. For it shows that politics concerns much more than the provision of what is necessary for the life of the community. The well-being of the community is not confined to economic security and to internal and external peace.[4] Its prime task is the care for the citizens' acquisition of knowledge and their moral conditioning. The very first elucidation of the aim of politics therefore indicates that Aristotle's statesman is no less an educator than Plato's.

There are two different points at issue in the education of the citizens. (i) Education must provide adequate instructions in the proficiencies that are essential for a functioning public life "for it is politics that ordains which of the sciences (epistêmai) should be studied in a state, and which each class of citizens should learn and up to what point they should learn them; and we see even the most highly esteemed of capacities fall under this, e.g. strategy, economics, rhetoric" (NE I 2, 1094a28–b5). (ii) Education also concerns the moral character and conduct of the citizens "since political science legislates as to what we are to do (prattein) and what we are to abstain from (apechesthai), the end of this science must include those of the others, so that this end must be the good for man" (NE I 2, 1094b5–7).[5] Because it serves the human good (t'anthrôpinon agathon) the second task is clearly the more important of the two, and its determination constitutes the longer and more pertinent answer to the question of the political character of Aristotle's ethics.

But given that this specification of the statesman's tasks comes right at the beginning of the Nicomachean Ethics, why should the answer to the question of the political character of the ethics be less conspicuous than the high rank assigned to political science would lead one to expect? The explanation lies in the fact that the statesman's responsibility for the ethical standard and the requisite education soon drops out of sight. From Chapter 3 on there is little mention of the statesman's involvement in that respect.[6] In the design of the good life as the actualization of the best virtues, in the distinction between virtues of character and virtues of the intellect, in the determination of the condition of human actions, and in the detailed analysis of the particular kinds of virtues and vices, the politician has all but disappeared, except as a beneficiary of

Aristotle's lectures. Hence it is easy to lose sight of the emphasis on political science's active role in the introduction.

## POLITICS AS THE REGULATOR OF THE GOOD LIFE

That the impression of the dispensability of statesmanship in ethical questions is mistaken emerges clearly in the closing chapter of the *Nicomachean Ethics*, which serves at the same time as the transition to the *Politics* (*NE* X 9). For at that point Aristotle emphasizes, once again, the crucial role of politics in the good life, not only of the community at large, but of every citizen as well. That Aristotle does not refer back to the beginning of the *Nicomachean Ethics* but re-introduces the statesman's central role in a rather circumspective way may be due to the fact that in the preceding chapters the life of the politician had been downgraded as "*ascholos*" (unleisurely) and as second best in comparison with the life of the philosopher (*NE* X 7, 1177b12–26). Thus, the final chapter represents an about-face that puts the focus, once again, on the practical aspect of the entire work and therefore gives a brief resumé of the conditions of the good life. This practical concern also explains why Aristotle affirms, once again, that words alone are insufficient to make people good, because only a proper conditioning of the affections (*pathê*) by the requisite practice will instill the love of what is noble and the hatred of what is base, and that it is hard, if not impossible, to reform ingrained bad character-traits (*NE* X 9, 1179b4–31).

The supreme authority over the citizens' proper upbringing and the guidance of their lives is prima facie not assigned here to the statesman but rather to the laws. Now, legal regulations had already been mentioned at the very beginning as the means of political science to ensure the proper conduct of the citizens (I 2, 1094b5). In his final conclusion of the *Nicomachean Ethics*, Aristotle attributes to the laws not only the supreme authority in education but also the respective executive power. The laws are both incentives to right action and powers that impose discipline (X 9, 1179b31–1180a4). That Aristotle, nevertheless, is no advocate of nomocracy emerges in what follows. For it turns out that the emphasis on the authority and importance of legal regulations serves as an introduction to the question of how to obtain competent lawgivers as the crucial prerequisite of legislation that supports a good constitution. Hence

the final question in the *Nicomachean Ethics* concerns the education of future legislators. This question not only re-affirms the close
connection between ethics and politics that Aristotle had postulated
at the beginning of the *Nicomachean Ethics*. It also makes explicit
what has been presupposed implicitly throughout that work's dis-
quisitions, that the right moral education is a public concern ("there
should be a public and proper care for such matters"; *NE* X 9,
1180a29). Aristotle's reason for taking up that issue by way of conclusion is that, with the exception of Sparta and Crete,[7] none of the
existing states make adequate provisions: parental command or that
of an individual alone has neither the authority nor the compelling
power of the laws, because the latter consist of rules that express
practical wisdom (*phronêsis*) and understanding (*nous*) as such.

The text at this point may appear somewhat indecisive as to
whether public education is really preferable to private education.
For, while Aristotle first rules out that every man should design his
own laws for his family as a relapse into an archaic state[8] (*NE* X
9, 1180a27–32), subsequently he seems to favor private over public education on the ground that private education is more adapt-
able to the individual's special needs. But a closer look shows that
there is actually no waffling on Aristotle's side: the laws are to provide the general rules of education "whether they are laws providing
for the education of individuals or of groups" (*NE* X 9, 1180b1). That
the father's authority may be more effective than public schooling
does not contradict this assessment. Aristotle is not here returning
to the Cyclops-like family-authority he had ruled out a few lines earlier. His point is, rather, that parental authority will be most apt to
impose the good laws of the community on children. What speaks
for private rather than for public education is not distrust in the
city's laws of education, but only the consideration, acknowledged
throughout the *Nicomachean Ethics*, that universal rules require
personal experience to adapt them to particular circumstances.

This is not the place to pursue any further Aristotle's more
detailed reflections on the advantages and disadvantages of private
and public institutions for the education of future politicians and legislators. The main point is that the standards of moral and political
education are treated as a public concern because a good community must be based on good laws, both written and unwritten.[9] Such
laws require universal knowledge of what is good for everyone, or at

least for a certain type of people (*NE* X 9, 1180b13–16). Aristotle here acknowledges, as he has done before, that personal experience has its value, but he gives priority to universal knowledge as the basis of legislation: "None the less, it will be agreed that if a man does wish to become master of an art or science he must go to the universal, and come to know it as well as possible, for, as we have said, it is with this that the sciences are concerned" (*NE* X 9, 1180b20–23).

Aristotle's more detailed considerations of how the right kind of knowledge of legislation is to be achieved (*NE* X 9, 1180b28–1181b12) can be only summed up here. He criticizes the same conditions in the existing states that Plato already had found fault with: that the active politicians do not pass on their political skills even to their own sons or close friends, while the self-professed teachers of political science, the sophists, have neither the necessary knowledge nor the experience. Collections of laws and constitutions of existing states (like those provided by Aristotle's analysis of the 158 city-states)[10] are of a certain use, but only if students already possess sound judgment of what is good and bad. Aristotle also deplores, somewhat to our surprise in view of Plato's *Laws*,[11] that his predecessors have left the subject of legislation unexamined. But while his complaints must simply be taken at face value here, it is of great importance for the relation of ethics to politics to note that Aristotle declares that the study of the constitution of the state is to "complete to the best of our ability our philosophy of human nature" (*NE* X 9, 1181b15: *hê peri ta anthrôpeia philosophia*). Ethics without politics, this lets us conclude, is only half the story.

References to the statesman and to his special kind of knowledge are actually not confined to the beginning and to the end of the *Nicomachean Ethics*. In his discussion of practical reason (*phronêsis*) in *NE* VI, Aristotle also comments on what is special about the politician in that respect. Though in principle the practical reason of the private person and that of the statesman are one and the same, outstanding politicians like Pericles are superior because their knowledge is not confined to their own good, but concerns what is good for human beings as such (*NE* VI 5, 1140b4–11). In addition, Aristotle emphasizes, once again, the special status of the legislator's knowledge as the "architectonic science" in politics (*NE* VI 8, 1141b23–33) and feels prompted, therefore, to explain the fact that everyday language does not do justice to the difference in function and quality among different types of politicians. The name *'politike'* is commonly not reserved for the special skill of legislators and superior statesmen but, rather, designates the skill of those who are actively engaged in public debates and decrees, although they are no more than "political handymen." Aristotle thereby indicates that he regards differentiations as necessary so that legislative and executive science should be kept apart, and the latter should be further subdivided into deliberative and judiciary science.[12] The inclusion of this differentiation in the discussion of practical reason is noteworthy, because it confirms that Aristotle never lost sight of the "master science" of human life in his discussion of the central aspects of ethics proper.

### THE PROBLEM OF THE IMPRECISION OF ETHICS

The dominant role assigned to the political master-science, in view of its responsibility for the moral education of the citizens and for the completion of the philosophy of human nature in general, speaks for a universalistic conception of ethics in Aristotle. For he repeatedly asserts that *eunomia* (good legislation) presupposes universal knowledge of the human good. It has a two-fold task: good order in the state and the appropriate education of the citizens.[13] But prima facie such a requirement of universal knowledge on the statesman's side seems not to agree with Aristotle's denial that ethics can be an exact science. This discord is all the more notable because his declaration that the principles of ethics can be no more than rules of thumb follows immediately after the introduction of political science as the master-science of life (*NE* I 3, 1094b11–27).[14] That the warning against the expectation of too much precision is not just an awkwardly inserted *obiter dictum* is confirmed by the fact that it is repeated several times at central places, so that it constitutes a serious challenge to universalistic interpretations of Aristotle's ethics.

The obvious move to counter this inconsistency would be to point out that legislation is by nature universal, while its application is not. Aristotle's own insistence on the need for equity in the discussion of justice (V 10) is a clear witness to his recognition that the very universality and inflexibility of the laws call for a flexible practice of adaptation to particular cases: the letter of the law does not always coincide with the spirit of the law. But before settling for such an easy solution for the ethics *in toto*, there should be a careful inspection of the reasons for Aristotle's denial of precision in ethics. He does not seem content with an adaptation of general rules to particular cases, but seems to question the very existence of general rules. And that fact must constitute a real difficulty. For the master-science of life is not just concerned with determining the letter of the law; it also incorporates its spirit by determining the citizen's moral character: "For legislators make the citizens good by forming habits in them, and this is the wish of every legislator, and those who do not effect it miss their mark, and it is in this that a good constitution differs from a bad one" (*NE* II 1, 1103b2–5).

Since the master-science extends, therefore, beyond legislation in the narrow sense, it is important to take a careful look at the kinds of restriction Aristotle imposes on the principles of ethics, for the very introduction of the restrictions makes clear that they directly concern the politician: "Now fine and just things, which political science investigates, admit of much variety and fluctuation of opinion, so that they may be thought of to exist only by convention, and not by nature" (*NE* I 3, 1094b14–16). Aristotle therefore concludes that "we must be content, then…to indicate the truth roughly and in outline, and in speaking about things which are only for the most part true and with premises of the same kind to reach conclusions that are no better" (*NE* I 3, 1094b19–22). And he expects his audience to agree: "For it is the mark of an educated person to look for precision in each class of things only so far as the nature of the subject admits."

The inclusive "we" and the extension of the reservations to the entire subject-matter should therefore preclude the solution that the vagueness concerns only the adaption to particular cases. Instead, it affects the very principles of the subject-matter. But if that is so, how can the master politician carry out the task of providing the right education and lifestyle for the citizens by providing the appropriate laws? The fact that Aristotle repeats his warning against the expectation of too much precision several times,[15] confirms that it concerns the fundamentals of his ethics. Thus, in *NE* II 2, 1103a35–1104a10 he seems to rule out precepts in ethics *tout court*, along with those in navigation and medicine. Decisions of what is appropriate for the occasion are left to the individual agent. But how can political authority be upheld if ethical questions allow for no more certainty than navigation and medical treatment? Is Aristotle's "ship of state,"[16] then, no more than a storm-tossed vessel whose captain sails by rules of thumb, always hoping for the best but also prepared for the worst?

There are three objections that speak against the seeming "anarchic" tendencies in Aristotle's ethics:

1.  In his outline of the basic conditions of ethics Aristotle makes no reservations. He shows, for instance, no hesitation in his determination of the human good *via* the "function-argument" that the good life presupposes the development and employment of the best human capacities. He equally shows no hesitation in his division of the soul into a rational and a nonrational part, or in the assignment of the relevant emotions to the nonrational part that is capable of listening to reason's decrees (*NE* I 13). This division lays the ground for the distinction between virtues of character, on the one side, and virtues of the intellect, on the other (*NE* II–V and *NE* VI). And Aristotle shows also no reservations in his depiction of the character-virtues as dispositions that consist in a mean between a vice of excess and a vice of deficiency. The same could be pointed out concerning his specifications of the factors that are involved in moral decision-making (*NE* III 1–5).

2.  Such sure-footedness is not limited to the philosophical groundwork, which might *eo ipso* be taken as exempt from reservations, because it is the fruit of Aristotle's reflections on the very possibility of ethics as a subject. But it is equally manifest in the discussion of the particular kinds of virtue and vice and of the respective actions and affections (*NE* III 6–V).

3.  Aristotle compares the presuppositions in ethics, that hold true only roughly and in outline with what holds "for the most part" (*NE* I 3, 1094b21: *hôs epi to polu*).[17]

It is therefore time to take a closer look at the reasons for the alleged vagueness of ethics and its conditions. The justification for the claim that "fine and just actions exhibit much variety and fluctuation" is that the so-called goods for certain people have harmful consequences, because "some have been undone because of their wealth and others by reason of their courage" (*NE* I 3, 1094b15–19). The problem seems therefore to concern the particular conditions of moral actions and the corresponding affections rather than the existence of standards and rules as such. To determine the extent to which the distinction between particular conditions and universal standards fits Aristotle's intentions requires a closer investigation of the way in which he presupposes moral education to work. For this will show what room there is for universal rules and standards, not only on the side of the master-scientist where they concern legislation, but also on the side of the individual moral agent where they play a somewhat different role, as will emerge in what follows.

## MORAL EDUCATION AND THE INDIVIDUAL

In *NE* II, the book dedicated to the development of his conception of the virtues of character, Aristotle is remarkably reticent about the question of how these virtues are acquired. This reticence causes uncertainty concerning two important points. (1) Though Aristotle makes clear right from the start that the virtues of character are dispositions to act and be affected in certain ways, acquired by habituation from early on, he gives just the barest indications as to how this habituation is supposed to work. (2) Because of the separation of the treatment of virtues of character and virtues of intellect, it remains unclear in what way moral education must incorporate both types of virtue. It may seem, therefore, that young people acquire their active and affective dispositions without explicit instruction concerning the requisite standards and rules. This impression is due in part to the contrast between the acquisition of intellectual virtue by instruction (*didaskalia*), that takes time and experience, and the acquisition of virtues of character that is the result of *habituation* (II 1, 1103a14–18: *ethizein*). And habituation, so it may seem at first sight, is no more than the frequent repetition of the same kind of exercise.[18]

Aristotle's exemplifications of "habituation," learning to play the kithara and to build houses, should give us pause when we equate habituation with a kind of mechanical drill. For, properly understood, neither of these two proficiencies is acquired by "mere habit." Greek musicians did not play from sheet music but had to be able to improvize. Learning to play the kithara, therefore, did not consist in mere finger-exercises but in mastering the entire complex system of

Greek harmonics, in addition to mastering the instrument. It goes without saying that analogous conditions apply to house-building. In Aristotle's time, architecture did not presuppose as much mathematics as it does nowadays, but its mastery was not confined to the acquisition of manual dexterity. Why, then, does Aristotle speak of habituation at all? The answer is very simple: these skills cannot be acquired by listening to a teacher or by reading instruction books only. It takes a lot of practice, not only to acquire the physical ability, but also the mental flexibility to cope with the multiple tasks required by such arts. As Plato has noted already, artists who merely follow established rules do mere hack-work.[19]

What, then, does habituation concerning the virtues of character consist in? The answer to this central question must remain sketchy because it would require a discussion of Aristotle's elucidations of the different types of virtue. Suffice it to say that it does not only consist in acquiring the disposition to be affected correctly in every particular situation,[20] but also the disposition to choose the right action. And both involve a good deal of thought. That this fact does not become immediately obvious is due to Aristotle's artifice of separating the intellectual and the moral virtues. That this is an artifice, designed to give the virtues of character primacy of place,[21] is indicated by the fact that the definition of moral virtue contains a reference to the requisite intellectual virtue: "Virtue is a disposition concerned with choice, lying in a mean relative to us, this being determined by reason (*logos*) and in the way the person of practical reason (*phronimos*) would determine it" (II 6, 1106b36–1107a2).

The reference to reason indicates, as one should have suspected anyway, that character-training does not consist simply of a habituation of one's feelings,[22] though a comprehensive "sentimental education" is an important part of it, but that it also involves judgment. Why should one have suspected that? The need for guidance by reason is already anticipated in the division of the faculties of the soul in I 13, 1102b28–1103a3, where Aristotle postulates that the non-rational, desiderative part of the soul follows reason's advice (*logos*) like that of a father or a friend. Character virtues are, then, dispositions that listen to such reasoning. Whichever of the many meanings of *logos* may be at stake in the definition of virtue of character, it stands to reason that the *logos* in II 6 is meant to refer back to the "advice" of the soul's rational part in I 13.

This leaves us with the difficulty of how to interpret the metaphor of "listening to reason's advice." At least in the case of grown-ups, no constant advising of the feelings by reason is likely to take place. Instead, practical reason must have transformed the affections so that there is no need for continued persuasion about the right course of action. Such is indeed the presupposition of interpretations that treat Aristotle as a moral particularist.[23] A morally well-trained individual will, quite naturally, respond to a given situation in the right way so that explicit processes of deliberation, invoking universal rules or standards, are unnecessary. This conclusion seems quite in harmony with Aristotle's warnings of undue expectations of precision, and also to accommodate his injunctions concerning particular actions: that the agent acts in the way she should (dei), to whom she should, by the means she should, when she should, etc.[24] Because these factors may vary from case to case, from individual to individual, there are no precise rules of how to act. What is an act of courage in the case of a physically strong person may be foolish rashness in the case of a weak one. What is an act of liberality towards a deserving friend in need may be a waste in the case of a gambler, and a small donation from a poor person may be magnanimous, while the same amount from a wealthy one would be niggardly. Given the right habituation, the agent will make the appropriate adjustments without much explicit reasoning. These considerations, that have to be kept at a minimum here, seem to speak for a particularist interpretation and to explain at the same time why Aristotle nowhere explicitly refers to universal rules and standards in his discussion of the virtues. For it seems that sufficient practice guarantees that the morally well-habituated person will act and react appropriately in life's many different situations.[25]

Such habituation of the affections and of the disposition to act should at the same time have to include the development of good judgment, i.e. the "advice" mentioned above that the desiderative part of the soul receives from the rational part. But the peculiar way in which Aristotle divides up the different rational capacities involved in moral actions makes it hard to determine how they cooperate. For he separates the wish for a good end from the deliberation concerning the ways and means needed for the realization of such an end in practice. It is these deliberations that finally lead to the decision of how to act. All these factors are discussed in Book III,

Chapters 2–5, in a systematic way. But despite that systematic procedure it is hard to assess the nature of the different rational capacities involved in moral decision-making and to determine whether a particularist or a universalist interpretation better fits the character of Aristotle's ethics.

## WISH, DELIBERATION, AND DECISION

Although wish comes last in Aristotle's discussion and receives only the briefest comments, it plays a crucial role because it determines the end of moral activities. How does it do that? Beforehand Aristotle has stated that the "ends" are not a matter of deliberation (*NE* III 3, 1112b12–19). As a justification for this somewhat surprising claim he refers to several analogues: Just as a doctor does not deliberate about whether he should heal, an orator whether he should convince, or a statesman whether he should produce good laws and order, so no one deliberates about the end of their actions. Instead they "posit" the end (*NE* III 3, 1112b15: *themenoi*). Now the problem with these analogues is that they refer to professions where the ends are settled quasi "*ex officio*." A doctor *qua* doctor will not deliberate about whether to cure a patient but only about the ways and means to do so, and the same applies to the other cases.[26] But how does this positing of ends work in the case of moral actions? The very short discussion of "wish" in III 4 tells us only that wish is for "the good," with the proviso that the good person's wish is for the truly good, while all others wish for what appears good to them. But beyond that we get little information about the determination of the good in that chapter.

This leaves the conception of the good underdetermined. For it is unclear whether "the good" refers to the overall good, i.e. the person's overall view of happiness, or whether it concerns specific ends, the goods attainable by particular moral actions. This question constitutes a fundamental divide between interpreters of Aristotle's ethics. On the one side there are the defenders of the "grand end view" who argue that what is excluded from deliberation is the ultimate good, because happiness is everyone's wish, whatever its conception may be. The specific ends, by contrast, are chosen in accordance with how they fit the overall end, and hence must be subject to deliberation.[27] The defenders of the specific end view regard the "grand end" as a mere formal concept that would leave the agent without guidance when it comes to making decisions. But whether the ultimate end is indeed only a formal or rather a rich concept with sufficient content, deliberations must be cumbersome processes, requiring considerable time, if they are to determine how a particular action fits into one's overall conception of happiness. How, for instance, could a soldier in battle come to a decision if his deliberating started with the question what course of actions would best fit his overall view of the good life? Or why should a person about to decide whether to indulge or abstain from a certain physical pleasure have to engage in such all-encompassing reflections?[28]

The advantages and disadvantages of the divergent views cannot be evaluated here in detail. Suffice it to say that, as argued in this article, there is no incompatibility, because at least the legislators must possess the "grand end view," while individuals can rely on their leader's knowledge. At any rate, Aristotle in III 4 seems to address not such global questions but the starting points of concrete decisions concerning different acts of virtue. For not only does he treat the "setting" of the end as a matter of judgment, but this judgment is determined by the respective virtue: "For each disposition has its own fine and good objects, and the good person differs most by seeing the truth in each of them, being, as it were, a norm and measure of them" (*NE* III 4, 1113a31–34).

That Aristotle is concerned here with specific ends, not with the overall conception of the happy life, follows naturally if the virtues of character are the determinants of human actions. For the different types of virtue would be quite idle if they did not provide the wish in question, such as the wish to achieve "the noble" in the danger of battle or the wish to do an act of magnanimity, and similarly in the case of other virtuous acts. The commitment to such specific ends is the result of good moral upbringing, for that is the main point of the development of the virtues of character: it makes us desirous of virtuous actions for the respective ends. These wishes are, in each case, the starting point of deliberation and determine the search for the appropriate ways to attain the good end. For deliberation is not just the calculation of what is effective in bringing about the desired end, it also considers whether a course of action fulfills the criteria required by the virtue in question, i.e. whether it is concerned with the person it should be, in the way it should be, when it should be, etc. Though Aristotle in the chapters dedicated to the elucidation of deliberation and choice (*NE* III 2, 3, and 7) does not point out that the "means" are not limited to morally neutral "instruments,"[29] reflection shows that deliberation must take care of the different deontic factors that Aristotle insists on.[30] For there is no other capacity to determine that the "what," the "how," the "to whom," the "when," etc. of the actions are as they should be.

Particularist interpreters of Aristotle's ethics have drawn the conclusion that since moral character, once acquired, is an integral part of the personality, explicit reflections on ends as well as on rules and standards of determining the means can be dispensed with. But a closer look shows that this view is short-sighted. The need to consider whether one acts as one should, when one should, the way one should, proves that these deontic factors are not settled without principled considerations, even in a well-brought-up person.[31] Though this may be unnecessary in routine cases, carried out a hundred times, it is required in critical decisions. That Aristotle was aware of that fact comes to the fore in his brief discussion of "mixed cases of voluntary actions" in *NE* III 1. They concern actions that no one would choose under normal circumstances, but may have to settle for under duress. As examples of such problem cases Aristotle cites coercion by a tyrant to choose between the life of one's parents or children and a shameful act, or the decision of a ship's captain in a storm to throw the cargo overboard to save the ship and the life of the passengers (*NE* III 1, 1110a4–26). That Aristotle rarely mentions such conflicts must be due to his concentration on the nature and function of the virtues of character, rather than on problems they may pose or on the casuistry necessary for their solution.[32] But it is important to note that he does not presuppose that decisions for the well-brought-up person come without effort. For that very reason he explains at some length the calculation involved in deliberation that starts with a fixed end and concludes with the decision to act, once the agent has reached her present situation.

As has been indicated above, the determination of the end is not due to deliberation, because it is settled by the person's character. But this does not mean that it involves no thought on the side of the agent but is fixed by her character. For, as Aristotle has it, the good person "judges rightly each kind of thing" (*NE* III 4, 1113a30). And given the broad spectrum of situations and possible actions within each kind of virtue, it is by no means obvious *a priori* what the noble end will be. Finding herself between a rock and a hard place, the good person cannot rely on her well-trained feelings and moral insights but has to reflect on the basic principles that determine whether a certain end is desirable, because it is the best one, all things considered. The question is, then, once again, what standards are in operation in such cases and where they come from.

## UNIVERSAL AND PARTICULAR KNOWLEDGE

Though there is a good deal that is "up to the individual," the principles that determine the wish for the good in question, on the one hand, and those that determine deliberation and choice, on the other, are neither self-created nor is the morally well-brought-up person self-taught. This brings us back to the question of moral education, because the moral and intellectual status of each individual depends on that. Where do the criteria of a good moral education come from? What is the basis of its standards? In good societies one may, no doubt, rely on tradition. But that merely pushes the question up to the next level, for the question now turns on the criteria that determine whether a certain tradition is good and provides good laws of education. The answer to this query is provided by Aristotle's own criteria for the good life: The quality of moral education depends on whether it provides the conditions determined by the *ergon*-argument. For, moral education must see to it that the members of a community develop both their moral and their intellectual potential in the best possible way. What that means is specified much more extensively in the case of the moral qualities than in the case of the intellectual virtues, because Aristotle takes great trouble to discuss the different kinds of character-virtues, the nature of the agents, the kinds of activities they are concerned with, and the way they are performed (*NE* III 5, 1115a4–5), while he gives no more than a summary of the nature and objects of the intellectual virtues.

A critical evaluation of Aristotle's system of character-virtues, its completeness, and suitability to constitute the best possible life would far exceed the limitations of this chapter. But there can be no doubt that Aristotle presupposes that at least in outline, his depiction of the good life contains all necessary elements. He would, then, in his own case lay claim to a "grand end" view of the good life in a substantial sense, i.e. of the ends to be pursued, their inter-connections, and of the requisite types of actions and affections. Otherwise his investigations could hardly pretend to provide deeper insights that are of use not only to the well-brought-up adult but also to the politician and especially to the legislator. That such is Aristotle's ambition emerges from his remarks concerning the pre-requisites of ethics and the benefits his lectures are to provide:

Hence anyone who is to listen intelligently to lectures about what is noble and just and, generally, about the subjects of political science must have been brought up in good habits. For the facts ["the that"] are the starting-point, and if they are sufficiently plain to him, he will not need the reason ["the why"] as well; and the man who has been well brought up has or can easily get the starting points. (NE I 4, 1095b3–8)

This pronouncement may suggest that very little is needed to com-plete the picture. This impression is strengthened by Aristotle's fur-ther admission that though his outline of the good life is a mere sketch, once the outline is well done the rest can easily be completed (NE I 7, 1098a20–25). This trust clearly rests on the assumption that the field is not *terra incognita* to either the political scientist or to the student of ethics in general. That, nevertheless, more than "a little help" (NE II 2, 1104a10f) is provided by his investigations of the theoretical underpinnings, emerges if we realize that these underpin-nings are to provide the necessary reflections concerning the con-ception of the happy, satisfactory life. Thus, a grand end view of the human good is one that is necessary not only for the philosopher, but also for the political scientist and for the well-brought-up indi-vidual with an interest in the foundations of the generally accepted standards and rules.

But how does this argument that speaks for a grand end view and for generally accepted standards and rules, at least for political sci-entists and enlightened citizens, fare in the face of the often repeated caveats that there can be no more than a rough outline of such rules and principles? For in the sequel to the passage quoted above Aris-totle repeats, once again, his warning of too much precision and emphasizes that if the facts are well established, the reason need not in all cases be required, because in some cases the starting points are grasped by induction, in others by perception, by habituation, or in some other way (*NE* I 7, 1098a26–b9). This seems to indicate that in the case of ethics there is no strict procedure but a variety of more or less stringent procedures. So what justifies the assumption that the grand end view can be more than a rough general outline that leaves all specific decisions to the individuals and their insights? What kind of privileged insights can be assigned to the political scientist?

To deal with this question, a closer look at the vagueness condition is necessary, as specified for ethics along with other disciplines that do not provide exact precepts, such as navigation and medicine. The emphatic tone of that denial (*NE* II 2, 1104a5–9) should not detract from the fact that Aristotle does not rule out the existence of general rules in medicine and in navigation. His point is, rather, that because the general account (*ho katholou logos*) of what is to be done cannot be overly precise, the particular one (*ho peri tôn kath hekaston logos*) is even less precise.[33] That particular cases "do not fall under any art or set of precepts" is no sign of total anarchy, but that the agent's decisions must be determined by the situation. There are, of course, rules of navigation that hold "for the most part," including what to do in a storm, when to throw the cargo overboard in order to save the ship. But when, exactly, that moment comes and under what conditions depends on the particular situation, and that is left to the captain's assessment, just as it is left to the doctor's judgment when to administer a certain drug to a particular patient and in what dosage. There cannot be precise precepts for all cases, not only because no manual could hold them all, but because not all eventualities can be foreseen.

In the case of moral decisions it is the individual's responsibility to determine what action fits the particular circumstances, i.e. what should be done, in what way, when, and so on. But the very fact that the responsibility concerns the adaptation of "the general account" to the particular circumstances confirms the existence of *ceteris paribus* rules, otherwise there would be nothing to adapt. Agents would be left entirely to their own devices. If such had been Aristotle's view he could have saved himself the trouble of giving detailed accounts of each virtue of character and the respective kinds of actions and affections. Moreover, the very idea of moral education through practice would be pointless. For practice of virtuous actions, e.g. by repeated acts of justice, presupposes two things: (1) the recognition of what is characteristic of acts of justice; and (2) the recognition of the conditions that make a particular act of justice an act of justice rather than of injustice. Education through practice must provide enlightenment of both types. That is why such practice is not a dumb show but presupposes verbal instruction and correction by praise and blame, punishment and reward. That Aristotle was fully aware of that fact is indicated in a passage in the *Politics* that explains why only humans are capable of citizenship: "But speech is for making clear what is beneficial and harmful, and therefore also what is just or unjust. For it is peculiar to human beings, in comparison to the other animals, that they alone have perception of what is good and bad, just and unjust, and the rest. And it is community in these that makes a household and a city-state" (I 2, 1253a14–19).

For these reasons the captain and the doctor must be able to justify *ex post facto* that theirs was the right decision, and experts will be able to confirm whether, given the situation, they did the right thing. The same is true in the case of moral actions. Even concerning a quite singular situation the justification must prove that the action was done by the person it should have, to whom it should have, and so on. This justifiability condition does not require that the agent must have acted with a "grand end" in view. In such cases it suffices that the determination of the end agrees with the virtue of character in question and that the means applied are no violation of the deontic conditions of the respective virtue.

The "grand end" does come in, however, if there is a conflict between several specific ends, and hence it is necessary to specify, at least in principle, the nature of and the need for such a comprehensive view. The particularist opponents of this view object to it because they regard it as a kind of "blueprint" of the good life as a whole that agents would have to consult in all decisions.[34] There are, however, different types of blueprints. Some contain only the overall design of a building, its different floors, rooms, doors, windows, etc. Others also include the interior decorator's plans for the furniture, drapery, pictures, vases, etc. And some over-eager architects' and decorators' blueprints even include precepts for their clients' use of those items. Given Aristotle's conviction of the need for an overall target in life, there can be little doubt that he has only a general blueprint in mind, a blueprint that leaves sufficient leeway for the agent's discretion. For that is what it is to be a moral agent: responsibility for one's own actions requires much more than the mere filling of blanks left by underspecified rules: it means the responsible active assessment of all circumstances. But the fact that a grand end view is not necessary for each particular moral decision does not mean that it is not required for the moral condition of the community and for the education of its members. For this reason not only the philosopher but also the statesman, the master-architect of human life, must possess such a view, if he is to make the laws that tell the citizens what to do and what to abstain from and that regulate their education.

### CONCLUSIONS: ARISTOTLE – AN ARCHITECTONIC SCIENTIST OF LIFE?

Given the importance of political science for ethics, Aristotle's readers may wonder whether he regarded himself as a political master-scientist, despite the fact that for most of his life his status as an alien resident debarred him from active engagement and therefore from the experience of a politician in legislation and in the education of the citizens of a community. Again, there is a short and a long answer to this question. The long answer would presuppose a careful evaluation of Aristotle's self-assessment as a political scientist. The short, and for the purposes of a conclusion preferable, answer must confine itself to clues concerning the task Aristotle set for himself in the *Nicomachean Ethics*. Thus, he asserts in *NE* II 2, 1104a26–31 that the purpose of his investigation is not just "theory" as in his other works, but "to make people good" – and that this requires an investigation of human actions, for otherwise it would be of no use. Another such clue is contained in the promise of "assistance" in view of the imprecision of ethics: "But though our present account is of that nature we must give what help we can." The ensuing help consists in nothing short of his entire theory of moral action and its basic conditions. Whether Aristotle's analysis of human nature and its *telos* are satisfactory according to our modern standards or not, he clearly regarded it as the foundation-stone of his ethics and therefore also of his politics, for it justifies at the same time his determination of the best possible constitution.

Further support that Aristotle saw himself as an "architectonic scientist" can be derived from the outline and execution of his *Politics*. That project includes, in the name of the best legislator, an outline of the best constitution in Book VII, and that outline ends with a plan for the citizens' education, a program that unfortunately is not carried out beyond the blueprint for the musical education of children. Whether Aristotle gave up his intention in view of the enormity of such a project, or whether the rest of the text has been lost, must remain an open question. But even its fragmentary state shows that Aristotle had been aware that such a program was, in principle, the legislator's obligation.

Against this necessarily short, affirmative answer, that Aristotle regarded himself as a master-scientist in politics, it may be objected that such a commitment does not fit well with his marked preference for the philosophical life in *NE* X. To deal adequately with this thorny problem would, again, exceed the limits of this chapter. Suffice it to say that his preference for pure *theôria* must be taken with more than a pinch of salt. Though Aristotle mentions this point only as an aside, he was fully aware that philosophy could not exist without a well-administered state, because it provides the opportunity to engage in philosophy.[35] Hence the exploration of the conditions of the typically human, second best life, in contradistinction to the superhuman theoretical life, is a task worth the philosopher's time. This may explain Aristotle's somewhat wistful reflections in the *Politics* on the philosopher's abstemiousness from politics that necessarily turns him into a kind of alien (*xenikos*).[36]

### WORKS CITED

Ackrill, J. L., 1980. "Aristotle on Eudaimonia." *In Essays on Aristotle's Ethics*, ed. A. O. Rorty. Berkeley, CA: University of California Press

Barnes, J., ed. 1984. *The Complete Works of Aristotle*. Princeton University Press

Bodéüs, R. 1993. "De quelques prémisses de la *Politique*." In *Aristote politique. Etudes sur la Politique d'Aristote*, eds. P. Aubenque and A. Tordesillas. Paris: PUF

Broadie, S. 1993. *Ethics with Aristotle*. Oxford University Press

Cooper, J. M. 1975. *Reason and Human Good in Aristotle*. Cambridge, MA: Harvard University Press

Kosman, A. 1980. "Being properly affected: virtues and feelings in Aristotle's ethics." In *Essays on Aristotle's Ethics*, ed. A. O. Rorty. Berkeley, CA: University of California Press

Kraut, R. 2002. *Aristotle: Political Philosophy*. Oxford University Press

McDowell, J. 1996. "Deliberation and moral development in Aristotle's ethics." In *Aristotle, Kant, and the Stoics: Rethinking Happiness and Duty*, eds. S. Engstrom and J. Whiting. Cambridge University Press

Miller, F. D. 1995. *Nature, Justice and Rights in Aristotle's Politics*. Oxford University Press

Ostwald, M. 1973. "Was there a concept *agraphos nomos* in Classical Greece?" In *Exegesis and Argument*, eds. E. N. Lee, A. P. D. Mourelatos and R. M. Rorty. Assen: Van Gorcum

Reeve, C. D. C. 1998. *Aristotle*, Politics. Indianapolis, IN: Hackett.

Roberts, J. 2009. "Excellence of the Citizen and the Individual." In *A Companion to Aristotle*, ed. G. Anagnostopoulos. Malden, MA/Oxford: Wiley-Blackwell

Schofield, M. 2006. "Aristotle's political ethics," In *The Blackwell Guide to Aristotle's Nicomachean Ethics*, ed. R. Kraut. Oxford: Blackwell

Striker, G. 2006. "Aristotle's ethics as political science." In *The Virtuous Life in Greek Ethics*, ed. B. Reis. Cambridge University Press

White, N. P. 2002. *Individual and Conflict in Greek Ethics*. Oxford University Press

NOTES

1. The topic here under discussion has therefore received quite some attention in the secondary literature. Cf. Bodéus 1993, Miller 1995; Kraut 2002; Striker 2006; Schofield 2006; Roberts 2009.

2. Such references are in fact quite frequent. Lawgivers (*nomothetai*) are mentioned twenty-four times, and there are even more references to political science (*politikê epistêmê*) or to the politician (*politikos*).

3. Cf. I 9, 1099b29–32; 13, 1102a7–25: on the importance of knowing the nature of virtue and therefore of the human soul "as far as that is important for the politician to know." Aristotle seems not to expect a politically interested audience to study the detailed analysis of the soul's faculties in the *De Anima*.

4. Cf. *Pol.* III 9, 1280a25–b6.

5. The translation of the *NE* follows, with some modifications (such as the reversion to "virtue" instead of "excellence"), that of W. D. Ross, revised by J. O. Urmson, in Barnes 1984.

6. There are, of course, some exceptions, cf. I 13, 1102a8–10: the true politician cares most about virtue because he wants to make the citizens good and obedient to the laws (cf. also *NE* III 3, 1112b14). The conception of justice in Book V requires good legislation, as witnessed especially in the discussion of universal justice (*NE* V 2, 1130b18–26), of natural justice (*NE* V 7, 1134b18–35), and the concept of equity (*NE* V 10).

7. Aristotle's approval of their legal systems concerns only the fact that they include detailed provisions for education, not their specific kind of education. Like Plato (*Laws* I 628c–e) he disapproves of their one-sided cultivation of the martial virtues and neglect of the virtues necessary for a life in peace (VII 4, 1333b11–1334a10).

8. Cf. Homer *Odyssey* (IX 114).

9. On written and unwritten laws cf. Ostwald 1973.

10. This collection is unfortunately lost, with the exception of a large part of *The State of the Athenians*.

11. The main justification for this complaint may be that Plato focuses on laws for his 'second best state', rather than on the principles of legislation as such.

12. The text in *NE* VI 8, 1141b23–1142a10 is very compressed and hard to penetrate. This is due to Aristotle's attempt to simultaneously explain the need for a differentiation concerning both *phronêsis* and political science.

13. On *eunomia*'s two-fold task cf. *NE* X 9, 1180a16–18; *Pol.* VII 4, 1326a29–31.

14. *NE* I 3, 1094b11–27; *NE* I 7, 1098a20–33.

15. Cf. *NE* I 7, 1098a26–33; *NE* II 2 1103b35–1104a11; *NE* III 5, 1114a35–b11; *NE* IX 2, 1164a27–30.

16. For the comparison of the organization of the state with that of a ship cf. *Pol.* III 4, 1276b20–29.

17. "Weak universality" of what happens only "for the most part" also applies to certain events in natural science (cf. *Phys.* II 5, 196b10–21 *et pass.*); but in nature the exceptions are due to accidental interferences, not to internal imprecision.

18. This impression owes a lot to Aristotle's explanation why a thing's nature cannot be changed by habituation: a stone will never be habituated to move upwards, no matter how often it is thrown up, while human nature is by nature apt to receive the virtues and be made perfect by repetition of the same activity (*NE* II 1, 1103a21–25).

19. *Phaedrus* 245a; similarly *Symposium* 203a.

20. On this issue cf. Kosman 1980.

21. A simultaneous treatment of both types of virtue might have detracted from Aristotle's innovation concerning the virtues of character or,

worse, made the character-virtues look like subordinate conditions as they are in Plato (cf. *Rep.* VII 518d–19a).

22. On the relevant *pathê* (usually translated by "feelings," "affections," "emotions," or "passions") cf. the list in *NE* II 5, 1105b21–23 and the fuller treatment in *Rhetoric* II 1–11.

23. Moral particularist interpeters of Aristotelian ethics deny both the need for and the possibility of universal rules concerning actions and affections. They deny the possibility because of Aristotle's warning against scientific precision in ethics. They deny the need because the habituation provides the individual with an ingrained tendency to act and react in the right way that requires no explicit reflection on general rules and standards. Universalists, by contrast, hold that though it may not always be necessary or even possible to recur to universal principles, they provide the ultimate criterion of right and wrong and the means of justification in case of disagreement and should therefore be specifiable.

24. The observation of these "deontic" conditions is the hallmark of Aristotelian virtue-ethics (cf. *NE* II 3, 1104b18–28 *et pass.*)

25. Cf. McDowell 1996: 26. "There is nothing for a correct conception of doing well to be apart from this capacity to read situations correctly...seeing them in the light of the correct conception of doing well."

26. Broadie 1993: 190–212 therefore treats the analogy with *technai* as highly misleading, because it insinuates a "grand end" view of ethics.

27. A representative of the "grand end view" is, for instance, Cooper 1975: 91–115.

28. For a defense of the specific end view cf. Broadie 1993, esp. ch. 4.

29. Cf. Ackrill 1980.

30. Aristotle, at *NE* III 3, 1112b17, confines himself to the indication that the means should be determined "in the finest possible way" (*kallista*) and mentions that if some impossibility is incurred the project will have to be given up (*NE* III 3, 1112b24–26). These impossibilities, no doubt, include not just the de facto impossible, but also morally inconceivable forms of action.

31. The remark in *NE* III 8, 1117a17–22 (cf. *EE* II 8, 1224a27–30) that actions done spontaneously in an unforeseen emergency may be a better sign of a courageous disposition than premeditated behavior does not show, as McDowell 1996: 25 would have it, that deliberative thought is unnecessary.

32. For a discussion of conflicts in Aristotle cf. White 2002: ch. 6.

33. Whether to translate *logos* by "account," "rule," or "prescription" is still very much a matter of debate. Since it concerns "what is to be done" the term has a normative component, but nothing hangs on the

terminology. "Account" is the most neutral and therefore the least offensive rendering.

34. Cf. Broadie 1993: 198–202; McDowell 1996: 21–22.
35. Cf. *NE* VI 13, 1145a6–11: political science does not give orders to philosophy but "provides for its coming into being."
36. *Pol.* VII 2, 1324a13–34.

# 2  The rule of reason

The *Politics* commences with an argument that the city-state is the most authoritative and inclusive community aiming at the highest good for its members. Aristotle then contends that this community requires a special kind of rule which is the subject of political science. He rejects Plato's claim that the skills of statesman, king, householder, and slave-master are the same.[1] This view assumes that the same science of ruling is merely applied to different *numbers* of subjects in different venues; there is no difference in kind. Aristotle complains that this is untrue, as he promises to show by means of his method of analysis, in which a compound such as the city-state is analyzed into incomposite elements (I 1, 1252a23). Not a few commentators have found this introduction puzzling.[2] Why does Aristotle place such emphasis on this particular disagreement with Plato, and why does he insist that different forms of association require different kinds of rule?

I shall argue that Aristotle's position is based on a deeper conviction: that different kinds of rule are appropriate for different *types* of rulers and subjects; more specifically, the kind of rule that is appropriate depends upon the extent and efficacy of their respective rational capabilities. In reconstructing Aristotle's argument, the first section examines the central place of the concept of ruling in his moral psychology and virtue ethics. The second section considers how he distinguishes the different psychological types and the forms of rule appropriate for them. The third section shows how he applies his articulated account of the rule of reason to pre-political forms of

I am grateful to David Keyt, Alexander Rosenberg, Nicholas Sars, and the editors for helpful comments on previous drafts.

social association in *Politics* Book I. The fourth section illustrates how he uses this account to answer problems of political science: Which constitution is the best possible for human beings, and which specific constitutional systems are appropriate for which actual city-states? It will become clear, in the process, how the first book of the *Politics* paves the way for the following books.

### MORAL PSYCHOLOGY AND VIRTUE ETHICS

Aristotle's political philosophy is founded on the following *principle of natural rule*:

[W]henever a number of constituents…are combined into one common thing, a ruling element and a subject element appear. These are present in living things, because this is how nature as a whole works. (I 5, 1254a28–33)[3]

Similarly, in the *Metaphysics* Aristotle compares the well-being of the universe to that of an army: the army's goodness is in its ordering and its goodness is also identical with its general. "And the general more so, since he does not depend on the ordering but it depends on him." The implication is that the cosmic order depends on a divine ruler (*Met.* XII 10, 1075a11–15). Moreover, *De Anima* identifies the soul as the ruler over the bodily elements, and the understanding as the ruling principle within the soul itself:

For the elements at least are like matter, and whatever it is which holds them together has the most authority. But it is impossible for anything to be stronger than, or ruling over, the soul; and it is even more impossible in the case of the understanding (*nous*). For it is reasonable to hold that the understanding is primordial or authoritative by nature. (*DA* I 5, 410b10–15)

Thus the principle of natural rule leads to the principle of *the rule of reason*.

Aristotle, so far, follows in Plato's footsteps. Plato maintained that a thing is in a good condition in so far as it exhibits the proper order or harmony (*Gorg.*, 506e2–4; *Rep.* IV, 443d). Moreover, a thing exhibits the proper order only if some part of it rules over the others according to nature, for example, the soul over the body (*Phaedo*, 79e–80a). Finally, the soul itself exhibits natural order only if the rational part rules over the spirited and appetitive parts (*Rep.* IV, 444d). The rule of reason underlies the tripartite psychology and political theory of the *Republic*, and in the *Laws* it supports a three-fold analogy of soul, city-state, and cosmos, each of which is in a good condition in so far as it is ruled by intelligence (*Laws* III, 689b; *Laws* X, 897b–d). When Aristotle rejects Plato's thesis that there is a single science of rule, his main point is that the kind of rule that is appropriate depends upon the respective psychologies of ruler and subject. It is not enough to distinguish between rational and nonrational capacities of the soul; it is also necessary to recognize that these capacities belong in different ways to different persons.

Aristotle remarks that the statesman "should legislate in a way that suits the parts of the soul and their actions" (VII 14, 1333a37–39). He distinguishes two main parts, one of which possesses reason (*logos*) intrinsically, while the other is nonrational (*alogon*) but capable of listening to reason; and he describes them, respectively, as desire and understanding (VII 14, 1333a16–18; VII 15, 1334b17–20). This corresponds to a division in the *Eudemian Ethics* between two parts of the soul that both partake of reason but do so in different ways: the one possesses reason and is able to issue orders, while the other is nonrational but able to obey, listen to, and follow the part that possesses reason (*EE* II 1, 1219b28–32; *EE* II 1, 1220a8–11).[4] Distinct from these two is another nonrational part that does not partake of reason at all, namely, the vegetative (cf. *EE* II 1, 1219b36–38). Aristotle views the rule of reason as a distinctive feature of the human soul: "If [a part belongs to a human being] *qua* human, there must be present in it reasoning (*logismos*), as a ruling principle (*archê*), and action; but reasoning does not rule over reasoning, but over desire and the affections; so [the human soul] must have those parts" (*EE* II 1, 1219b39–1220a2).[5]

Before proceeding, attention should be called to a distinction which Aristotle marks with two different verbs: "possess" (*echein*) and "partake" (*metechein* with genitive). This is, roughly, a distinction between having something fully and having it in only a partial sense, as in having a part of it or sharing it with others. When Aristotle says that one part of the soul possesses the capacity of reason he means that it has the complete repertoire of rational capabilities, including the ability to make inferences, calculate, deliberate, and so forth. When he says that another partakes of reason, this is consistent with it having only a more limited range of capabilities, such as "obeying, listening, and following" the conclusions reached at by the former part.

The *Nicomachean Ethics* offers a variant division of the soul. Once again, Aristotle divides the soul into a nonrational part and a part possessing reason (*NE* I 13, 1102a27–28), but then he further divides each part into two. On the nonrational side, one subpart, the vegetative or nutritive capacity, the cause of nutrition and growth, in no way shares in reason (*NE* I 13, 1102a32–33, b29–30), while the other fights or opposes reason (*NE* I 13, 1102b13–25). On the rational side, one subpart possesses reason in the authoritative sense and in itself (*NE* I 13, 1103a2), while the other possesses it in the sense that it in a way obeys or can listen to reason (*NE* I 13, 1103a3). This way of putting it is misleading, because the second nonrational subpart partakes of reason in a way (*NE* I 13, 1102b13–14, 25–26), and turns out to be identical with the second rational subpart (namely, the capacity for appetite and desire in general) since both are capable of obeying the rule (*peitharchikon*) of reason (cf. *NE* I 13, 1102b30–1103a3). But apart from this complication the *Nicomachean Ethics* is in basic accord with the *Eudemian Ethics* and *Politics*, where human souls include three parts: the rational faculty (or understanding) and two nonrational parts, the desiring faculty (capable of obeying reason) and the vegetative faculty (wholly unresponsive to reason).

There is an important addition to this scheme in *Nicomachean Ethics* Book VI, where the part possessing reason is subdivided into two subparts: "one by which we contemplate those beings whose principles cannot be otherwise, and one by which we contemplate things that can be otherwise." He calls them, respectively, the "epistemic" faculty and the "calculative" faculty, the latter being concerned with deliberation and calculation (*NE* VI 2, 1139a6–8, 11–13). He later calls the latter faculty "doxastic," that is, dealing with opinion (*doxa*) (*NE* VI 5, 1140b26–28; *NE* VI 13, 1144b14–17).[6] He also refers to the nutritive faculty as "the fourth part of the soul" (*NE* VI 12, 1144a9–10), where the other three are, presumably, the epistemic, calculative, and desiring faculties.

All the foregoing passages describe the psychological basis for Aristotle's virtue ethics. The *Eudemian Ethics* assigns intellectual virtues and moral virtues to different parts of the soul: "Since the intellectual virtues involve reason, they belong to the part possessing reason, which is capable of issuing orders to the soul in so far as it possesses reason, and the moral virtues belong to the nonrational part, which is naturally able to listen to the part possessing reason" (*EE* II 1, 1220a8–11). This basic distinction is followed by the *Politics* and Book I of the *Nicomachean Ethics* (VII 14, 1333a16–19; *NE* I 13, 1103a4–10), but Book VI of the *Nicomachean Ethics* distinguishes two classes of intellectual virtues corresponding to the two rational subfaculties distinguished in Book VI. The epistemic subfaculty exemplifies the virtues of knowledge (*epistêmê*) and theoretical wisdom (*sophia*), which are concerned with things that are unable to be otherwise – that is, with eternal, immutable objects. The calculative subfaculty exemplifies the virtue of practical wisdom (*phronêsis*), which involves deliberating about how to attain a good end, as well as cleverness (*deinotês*), which involves deliberating about how to attain any end whatsoever (cf. *NE* VI 2, 1119a26–31; VI 3,1119b19–26; VI 5, 1140b25–30).

Practical wisdom is described as "a true condition involving reason capable of acting concerning human goods" (*NE* VI 5, 1140b20–21). This intellectual virtue takes various forms, depending on whether it concerns the individual agent, the household, or the city-state: when it concerns the individual it is called "practical wisdom" in the narrow sense; other forms are called "household management," "legislation," and "politics" (exemplified by office holders), of which one part is deliberation and another adjudication. But it is in its legislative role that it is comparable to a ruling craft (*architektonikê*) (*NE* VI 8, 1141b23–33; cf. *NE* I 2, 1094b26–27). Practical wisdom is closely linked to deliberation: "Excellence in deliberation will be correctness with regard to what conduces to the end, of which practical wisdom is the true judgment" (*NE* VI 9, 1142b32–33). Practical wisdom is distinctive in that it is "capable of issuing orders; for its end is 'what ought to be done or not'" (*NE* VI 10, 1143a9–10). This implies that practical wisdom is the virtue by which the soul as a whole is ruled. This gives rise to a puzzle: How can practical wisdom, which is inferior to theoretical wisdom, have more authority than it, which seems implied by the fact that practical wisdom "rules and issues orders concerning each thing" (*NE* VI 12, 1143b33–35)? This would conflict with the view Aristotle defends in *Nicomachean Ethics* X 7–8, that theoretical wisdom has a higher status than practical wisdom. His solution is that the ultimate authority of practical wisdom does not extend to theoretical wisdom: "It does not have authority over theoretical wisdom – that is, over the better part – just as medicine does not have authority over health. For it does not use it but instead sees how to bring it about. Therefore, it issues orders for its sake but not to it. Further, [to assert that practical wisdom rules over theoretical wisdom] would be like saying that politics rules over the gods, because it issues orders about everything in the city-state" (VI 13, 1145a6–11).

It is noteworthy that Aristotle's descriptions of moral psychology and virtue theory are replete with the language of ruling and obeying. So far he follows Plato. But he goes on to insist that these parts themselves may manifest rationality in different ways, in which case different forms of ruling will be appropriate.

### BASIC FRAMEWORK: PSYCHOLOGICAL TYPES AND KINDS OF RULE

Aristotle begins his discussion of natural slavery by distinguishing between different kinds of rulers and subjects: "There are many kinds of rulers and ruled, and the better the ruled are, the better the rule over them always is; for example, rule over humans is better than rule over beasts. For a task performed by something better is a better task, and where one thing rules and another is ruled, they have a certain task" (I 5, 1254a24–28).[7] Aristotle is especially interested in the distinction between natural and unnatural rule. He illustrates this distinction within an individual animal in the following intriguing passage:

Soul and body are the basic constituents of an animal: the soul is the natural ruler; the body is the natural subject . . . [I]t is, as I say, in an animal that we can first observe both despotic rule and political rule. For the soul rules the body with a despotic rule, whereas the understanding rules desire with a political or kingly rule. In these cases it is evident that it is natural and beneficial for the body to be ruled by the soul, and for the affective part to be ruled by understanding (the part that possesses reason), and that it would be harmful to everything if the reverse held, or if these elements were equal. (I 5, 1254a33–35, b3–9)

This passage states a corollary of the principle of natural rule: a thing is in a natural condition only if its natural ruling part in fact rules over its natural ruled part; it is in an unnatural condition if the natural ruling element is ruled by the natural ruled part or if they are on an equal footing. The corollary applies to two cases: within an animal the soul is natural ruler over the body, and within a human soul it is understanding that is natural ruler over desire. Moreover, Aristotle distinguishes between two kinds of natural rule: despotic rule in the soul–body case, and political or royal rule in the understanding–desire case.[8]

Next Aristotle shifts to the social arena and makes a perfunctory attempt to justify rule by men over slaves, beasts, and women. A natural slave, he claims, is a human being "who shares in reason to the extent of perceiving it, but does not possess it himself" (I 5, 1254b22–23). It is unclear how a natural slave can perceive reason but not possess it. Can a slave recognize a command and follow instructions? Some beasts can do so as well. Of course, slaves can also interpret instructions and adapt them to variable circumstances, converse with their masters and ask for clarification, anticipate their wishes, and so forth. In what sense, then, does Aristotle think that slaves fail to *possess* reason even if they can *partake of* it? Aristotle also declares peremptorily, "The relation of male to female is that of natural superior to natural inferior, and that of ruler to ruled" (I 5, 1254b13–14). Are we to infer that women are less rational than men?

Aristotle does not let matters rest here, however. Later on, in *Politics* I 13, he distinguishes different types of natural subjects based on *comparative moral psychology*. He contends that different sorts of humans are capable of different sorts of virtue:

Consideration of the soul leads immediately to this view. The soul by nature contains a part that rules and a part that is ruled, and we say that each of them has a different virtue, that is to say, one belongs to the part that possesses reason and one to the nonrational part. It is clear, then, that the same holds for the other cases as well [e.g. slaves, children, and women], so that most instances of ruling and being ruled are natural. For free rules slaves, male rules female, and man rules child in different ways, because, while the parts of the soul are present in all these people, they are present in different ways. The slave possesses no deliberative faculty [*bouleutikon*] at all, while the woman possesses it but it lacks authority; a child possesses it but it is incompletely developed. (I 13, 1260a4–14)

This argument may be understood in terms of the aforementioned distinction between possessing reason and merely partaking of it. In the present passage, completely developed human beings possess the deliberative faculty because they have a full repertoire of capabilities, including recognizing the good life as an end, deliberating about how to achieve it, and carrying out the results of deliberation in action. But imperfect human beings, Aristotle asserts, are unable to deliberate for themselves, so that they cannot be said to possess the deliberative faculty. Even so, they can be said to partake of or share in (*koinônein*) reason in so far as they are capable of perceiving the conclusions of others' deliberations and of obeying them (I 5, 1254b22–3). Moreover, this passage grants that women and children possess the deliberative capacity, which suggests that they have certain key capabilities but which they are unable to exercise fully and efficaciously. Only free (i.e. completely developed) adult men enjoy a full panoply of developed effective deliberative capabilities. (The implications of these claims are explored in the following section.) The upshot of this argument is that human beings are capable of moral virtue only to the extent that they possess the deliberative faculty. Hence, only free adult men are capable of virtue fully and without qualification. Women, children, and slaves are capable of only an inferior kind of virtue. Now, it goes without saying that nearly all modern philosophers regard Aristotle's arguments about slaves and women as unconvincing and his conclusions as highly objectionable.[9] Still, his arguments offer insights into the place of the rule of reason in his constitutional theory. It will be instructive to focus first on a more abstract question: *If* a person's rational capabilities *were* lacking or limited in certain ways, what would this imply about the manner in which it would be appropriate for such a person to rule over others or to be ruled by others?

Based on *Politics* Book I it is possible to reconstruct a provisional list of psychological types in terms of their rational capabilities:

> Type 0: vegetative faculty only, e.g. plants
> Type 1: vegetative, perceptive, and desiring faculties only, e.g. beasts[10]
> Type 2: capability of obeying reason but no deliberative capacity (or only defective deliberative capacity), e.g. many barbarians

Type 3: deliberative capacity which is developed but lacking authority, e.g. adult Greek women

Type 4: incompletely developed deliberative capacity, e.g. free Greek boys

Type 5: completely developed effective deliberative capacity, e.g. free adult Greek men

*No rule* is possible in the case of Type 0, because it is incapable of perceiving and following a ruler's commands. The higher-order types can become subject to rule because they are all in some manner or other responsive to reason. There are, then, five different levels of natural rule corresponding to the five psychological types of subject, assuming a Type 5 ruler with developed effective deliberative capability:

Rule over Type 1, e.g. pastoral rule over beasts
Rule over Type 2, e.g. despotic rule over barbarians
Rule over Type 3, e.g. marital rule over wives
Rule over Type 4, e.g. paternal rule over sons
Rule over Type 5, e.g. fraternal rule over brothers

Given Aristotle's aforementioned thesis that natural rule over better subjects is better (I 5, 1254a24–28), it may be inferred that the above ordering reflects a hierarchy of natural rule from worse to better, assuming that the numbering of psychological types reflects their relative position in the *scala naturae*.[11] But, in any case, we may derive the following general definition:

*Definition of natural ruler*: *x* is a natural ruler over *y* if, and only if, *both x* is of Type 5, with a completely developed efficacious deliberative capacity, *and y* is of a lower type than *x*.

Given this definition, there can be no natural ruler if the *subject* is also of Type 5. Aristotle implies, however, that ordinary political rule involves rulers and subjects of the same type. Because "they tend by nature to be on an equal footing and to differ in nothing," they take turns at ruling and being ruled. Although such rulers are not superior by nature, they are elevated by means of various conventions including titles, bearing, and trappings, as was the gold footbath of Amasis (I 12, 1259b4–9). Taking this into account we can set forth a comprehensive principle:

*Principle of rule of reason*: x ought to rule over y if, and only if, *either* (I) x is the natural ruler over y, *or* (II) x and y are both Type (5), with a completely developed efficacious deliberative capacity, and they share rule in a manner that is appropriately equal.

Aristotle also implies that the natural ruler is subject to a normative requirement mentioned in connection with slavery: "If something is capable of rational foresight, it is a natural ruler and master, whereas whatever can use its body to labor is ruled and is a natural slave. That is why the same thing is beneficial for both master and slave" (I 2, 1252a26–34). The *common-advantage requirement*, that natural rule should be advantageous to subject as well as ruler, is thus an important corollary to the rule of reason.[12] It is violated in the case of those who are not masters and slaves by nature but stand in this relation based on law and force (I 6, 1255b12–15). The principle of the rule of reason and the common-advantage requirement together constitute a basic theoretical framework within which Aristotle analyzes and evaluates various modes of rule. The next section will examine his treatment of the various modes of pre-political rule within this framework.

### THE RULE OF REASON IN PRE-POLITICAL ASSOCIATIONS

This section will discuss Aristotle's account of the five distinct ruling relationships which can precede the formation of a city-state: pastoral, despotic, marital, paternal, and fraternal.

*Pastoral rule*: Human beings, alone among animals, are capable of reasoning (I 2, 1253a9–10; VII 13, 1332b5; *NE* I 7, 1097b33–1098a5). "The other [sc. nonhuman] animals do not perceive reason but obey their passions" (I 5, 1254b23–24).[13] Beasts have a Type 1 psychology, so that they are in a relation of permanent natural subordination to humans. However, "the other [i.e. nonhuman] animals mostly live under the guidance of nature alone, although some are guided a little by habit" (VII 13, 1332b3–4). Unlike instincts (innate invariable traits), habits must be acquired by first exercising the relevant action: "The things we have to learn before we can do, we learn by doing" (*NE* II 1, 1103a20–33). For instance, humans learn to become lyre-players by playing a lyre. The fact that animals too can form habits makes them tractable and more responsive to rational guidance by humans. Aristotle observes, "Some animals share in learning and teaching, in some cases from each other and in other cases from human beings, and these include animals that have the power of hearing, not only hearing sounds but also discerning the differences between signs" (*HA* IX 1, 608a17–21). It is this higher-order capability that distinguishes tame animals such as elephants from wild animals (*HA* IX 46).

Aristotle also claims "tame animals are by nature better than wild ones, and it is better for all of them to be ruled by human beings, since this will secure their safety" (I 5, 1254b10–13, cf. *Prob.* X 45, 896a2–3). Pastoral rule thus satisfies the common-advantage requirement, though in a weak sense, because the interests of humans take precedence over those of other animals: "Plants are for the sake of animals, and the other animals for the sake of human beings, tame ones both for using and eating, and most but not all wild ones for food and other kinds of support, so that clothes and the other tools may be got from them. If then nature does nothing incomplete or pointless, it must have made all of them for the sake of human beings" (I 8, 1256b15–22).

*Despotic rule*: The rule of master over slave is natural according to Aristotle when the two parties have complementary bodies and souls: the natural ruler can exercise rational foresight for their mutual survival, while the natural slave can use its body to carry out orders (see I 2, 1252a26–34, cited above). Aristotle argues that slaves are natural subjects by analogy with beasts: "Those people who are as different from others as body is from soul or beast from human, and people whose task, that is to say, the best thing to come from them, is to use their bodies are in this condition – those people are natural slaves" (I 5, 1254b16–19). Natural slaves are "naturally suited for being ruled" (I 8, 1256b25), because, allegedly, they lack the rational capability to govern themselves. Natural slaves, however, are capable of understanding, following, and even anticipating instructions: "A slave shares in reason to the extent of perceiving it, but does not possess it himself" (I 5, 1254b22–23). But, according to Aristotle's comparative moral psychology, "the slave possesses no deliberative faculty at all" (I 13, 1260a12). Natural slaves thus possess a Type 2 psychology, which explains why they are not genuine agents but merely tools for agents of a higher type (cf. I 4, 1253b30–1254a17).

In the case of despotic rule (even more explicitly than in that of pastoral rule) Aristotle affirms the common-advantage requirement:

For the same thing is beneficial for both part and whole, body and soul; and a slave is a sort of part of his master – a sort of living but separate part of his body. Hence, there is a certain mutual benefit and mutual friendship for such masters and slaves as deserve to be by nature so related. When their relationship is not that way, however, but is based on law, and they have been subjected to force, the opposite holds. (I 6, 1255b10–15; cf. I 2, 1252a34)

Aristotle holds that a natural master is subject to certain norms. Slaves, in so far as they share in reason, are capable of virtue, and they should acquire as much of it as they can, even if it is not much (I 13, 1260a17–20). Therefore, the master ought to be responsible for his slaves' virtue and not merely teach them to perform menial tasks. "Those who deny reason to slaves, but tell us to give them orders only, are mistaken; for slaves should be admonished more than children" (I 13, 1260b5–7).[14] Aristotle here assumes that natural slaves partake of reason in the sense of having some limited rational capabilities but not the full range of capabilities possessed by other adults. Thus, even natural slaves are corrigible and to some extent educable.

Aristotle later, in *Politics* III, qualifies his claim that natural despotic rule satisfies the common-advantage requirement: "[R]ule by a master, although in truth the same thing is beneficial for both natural masters and natural slaves, is nevertheless rule exercised for the sake of the master's own benefit, and only coincidentally for that of the slave. For rule by a master cannot be preserved if the slave is destroyed" (III 6, 1278b32–37). Arguably, however, this is not a great departure from his earlier account in Book I, where he has asserted that the slave is analogous to a bodily part of the master with a function subordinate to the master's. Despotic rule will seek to promote the slave's interests only so far as is necessary to advance the master's.[15]

*Marital rule*: Aristotle views the marital unit as a basic form of human association: "Those who cannot exist without each other necessarily form a couple, as female and male do for the sake of procreation (they do not do so from deliberate choice, but, like other animals and plants, because the urge to leave behind something of the same kind as themselves is natural" (I 2, 1252a26–30). Aristotle says that "the relation of the male to the female is that of natural superior to natural inferior, and that of ruler to ruled" (I 5, 1254b13–14), for "a male, unless he is somehow constituted contrary to nature, is naturally more fitted to lead than a female" (I 12, 1259b1–3). This argument is evidently based on Aristotle's claim that the woman is of Type 3, possessing a deliberative faculty which "lacks authority" (akuron) (I 13, 1260a13). The precise meaning of this laconic remark is a matter of controversy, but it possibly points to an alleged deficiency in the female psyche whereby her desires are not fully under the control of her understanding. The History of Animals contains the observation that in most animal species the female is less spirited and courageous than the male. Consequently, the female tends to be more cunning and impulsive but less courageous than the male, differences which Aristotle finds most pronounced in human beings (HA IX 1, 608a33–b4). Again, Aristotle's assertion of male superiority follows shortly after the remark that "understanding rules desire with a kingly and political rule" (I 5, 1254b5–6). These remarks lend support to the interpretation that, although women possess a complete deliberative capacity, they are less capable than men of carrying out and standing by their conclusions, especially in the face of threats, because their spirit (thumos) is weaker. Consequently, their rational faculty lacks the efficacy required for decisive action, especially in times of crisis and danger, so that they need male guidance.[16]

The common-advantage requirement is much stronger for marital rule than despotic rule, because women, like children, are naturally free (I 12, 1259a39–40). Rule over free persons differs from rule over slaves in that it aims primarily at the well-being of the subjects themselves (VII 14, 1333a3–6). This point is made explicitly in Book III: "Rule over children, wife, and the household generally, which we call household management, is either for the sake of the ruled, or for the sake of something common to both. Essentially, it is for the sake of the ruled ... but coincidentally it might be for the sake of the rulers as well" (III 6, 1278b37–1279a2). An important implication is that the household manager should be concerned with the virtue of all those under his authority, including his wife (I 13, 1260a17–20). Female virtues, though inferior to male virtues, are still superior to the servile virtues which are all that slaves can muster (I 13, 1260a20–24; cf. II 5, 1264b5). The husband should encourage and respect his wife's virtues, including temperance, courage, and justice, albeit in their appropriate form.

What does all this imply about the proper form of marital rule? Aristotle answers this question twice, once in *Politics* I and once in his ethical works. The *Politics* is less precise: marital rule is *political*, but not in the ordinary sense in which the ruler and subject take turns because they are natural equals, since the husband always stands as natural ruler over his wife (I 12, 1259b1, 4–10). Aristotle does not explain here this special sense of "political" rule, and in the ethical works he describes marital rule instead as *aristocratic*.[17] "The association of man and wife appears aristocratic; for the man rules in accordance with merit and in those matters in which a man ought to rule; but the matters that are fitting for a woman he gives over to her" (*NE* VIII 10, 1160b32–35; cf. *EE* VII 9, 1241b30 and *Pol.* III 4, 1277b24–25). The husband should respect the wife's domain, the sphere in which she is worthy of exercising authority, doubtless including internal household management. Aristotle adds that incorrect marital rule is *oligarchical*, which takes two forms: "If the man exercises authority over everything it changes into oligarchy. For he acts contrary to merit and not in so far as it is better. But sometimes the wives rule because they are heiresses. Hence their rule does not occur on account of virtue but due to wealth and power, just as in oligarchies" (*NE* VIII 10, 1160b35–1161a3). For instance, Aristotle criticizes Sparta for permitting an unnatural gynecocracy in which the women have become the de facto rulers (II 9, 1269b22–1270a11).

*Paternal rule*: The parental association represents the natural fulfilment of the marital association, which exists for the sake of reproduction (I 2, 1252a27–28). Paternal rule, like marital, is grounded in the natural superiority of one of the parties. In this case "someone older and completely developed is naturally more fitted to lead than someone younger and incompletely developed" (I 12, 1259b1–4). Once again, Aristotle explains this in terms of his comparative psychology: children have a Type 4 deliberative faculty that is "incompletely developed" (I 13, 1260a14). Aristotle elaborates this view in connection with education under the ideal constitution. Rehearsing the familiar bipartition of animal and soul, he continues:

And just as the development of the body is prior to that of the soul, so the nonrational part is prior to the rational. This too is evident. For spirit, wish, and appetite are present in children right from birth, whereas reasoning and understanding naturally develop as they grow older. That is why supervision of the body comes first and precedes that of the soul; then comes supervision of appetite or desire. But supervision of desire should be for the sake of understanding, and that of the body for the sake of the soul. (VII 15, 1334b17–28)

"The supervision of desire" means instilling in children proper habits of desiring and feeling, which they must have before they are receptive to the guidance of reason. As he remarks in the *Nicomachean Ethics*, "[R]eason and teaching are not effective in most persons, but the soul of the student must be worked on beforehand by means of habits for noble enjoyment and hatred, like earth which will nourish the seed" (*NE* X 9, 1179b23–26). Even when children have good aims and the right sorts of impulses to be courageous or just (i.e. "natural virtue"), they will go astray if they lack understanding (*nous*), like a strong body that stumbles badly due to the lack of sight. Only when they acquire understanding do they attain to genuine moral virtue (*NE* VI 13, 1144b8–14).[18]

Paternal rule, like marital rule, is exercised over free persons and is properly exercised for the sake of the children who are the subjects (III 6, 1278b37–1279a2; VII 14, 1333a3–6). Thus, paternal rule is a form of *kingly* rule: "a parent rules on the basis of both age and affection, and this is a type of kingly rule. Hence Homer did well to address Zeus, who is the king of them all, as 'Father of gods and men.' For a king should have a natural superiority, but be the same in stock as his subjects; and this is the condition of older in relation to younger and father in relation to child" (I 12, 1259b10–17; cf. *NE* VIII 10, 1160b24–27; *EE* VII 9, 1241b29–30). The deviation from kingship is tyranny: the tyrant aims at his own advantage, while the king aims at that of his subjects (*NE* VIII 10, 1160a34–b3). Aristotle remarks that paternal rule as practiced by the Persians is not kingly but tyrannical, because the father treats his sons as slaves. Such tyrannical rule is "despotic" in a deviant or mistaken sense, because it is exercised over an inappropriate psychological type (see *NE* VIII 10, 1160b27–32). Despotic rule is appropriate for rule over subjects lacking deliberative capability (Type 2) but not for subjects with more or less fully developed deliberative capabilities (Types 3, 4, and 5).

*Fraternal rule*: Aristotle discusses fraternal rule briefly in his ethical works in connection with friendship, where he describes it

alternately as a form of polity (*EE* VII 9, 1241b30–31) or timocracy
(*NE* VIII 10, 1161a2–3): "The friendship of brothers is like that of
comrades. For they are equal and of like age, and such persons are
for the most part alike in their feelings and their characters. Like
this, too, is the friendship appropriate to timocracy; for the citizens
tend to be equal and decent; hence they rule by taking turns and
do so equally; and the friendship here will be like this" (*NE* VIII
11, 1161a25–30). Although Aristotle does not mention fraternal rule
in *Politics* I he creates the logical space for it when he mentions
the ordinary form of political rule that is appropriate for persons
who "tend by nature to be on an equal footing" (I 12, 1259b1, 4–
10). Likewise, when brothers are all of psychological Type 5 and possess a fully developed rational capacity, some sort of power-sharing
arrangement is appropriate. The deviation from timocracy or polity
is democracy, which Aristotle likens to domestic anarchy: "Democracy is especially present in masterless households (for everybody
there is on an equal footing), and in those where the ruler is weak
and everybody has liberty" (*NE* VIII 10, 1161a6–9; cf. *Met.* XII 10,
1075a19–22).

*Transition to constitutions*: *Politics* Book I distinguishes different
kinds of pre-political rule corresponding to different psychological
types and offers a rationale for such rule based on the rule of reason. Domestic rule can have correct or mistaken forms, depending
on whether or not it aims at the common advantage. The *Eudemian
Ethics* points out the parallel with the six political constitutions distinguished in *Politics* III 7: "All the constitutions are present within
households, both the correct and the deviant ones... That of the parent is kingly, that of husband and wife is aristocratic, and that of
brothers is a polity; and the deviations from these are tyranny, oligarchy, and democracy" (*EE* VII 9, 1241b27–32). More guardedly, the
*Nicomachean Ethics* describes the domestic forms of rule as "like-
nesses" or "patterns" of the political constitutions (VIII 10, 1160b22–
1161a9). These parallels lead one to expect the rule of reason to continue to play an important role when Aristotle turns to political constitutions in the *Politics*.

## THE RULE OF REASON IN POLITICAL CONSTITUTIONS

Aristotle makes an analogy between political science and the art of
gymnastics. Gymnastics should concern itself not only with what

sort of training would benefit the best-endowed body (for example, that of an Olympic champion) but also more generally with what sorts of regimen would be advantageous for which sorts of inferior bodies. Likewise, political science should study not only the ideal constitution, but also inferior kinds of constitutions which are suitable for various actually existing city-states (IV 1, 1289a10–35). Hence, a legislator should take into account the population's psychological profile, which will determine to what extent and in what manner it is amenable to the rule of reason. This will depend on various factors, including ethnic, generational, and socio-economic differences.

*Ethnic differences*: There cannot be a city-state composed of natural slaves, any more than of brutes, because neither of them possess the deliberative faculty or capacity for deliberate choice necessary for a good life (III 8, 1280a32–34; cf. *NE* III 3, 1113a10–12). Aristotle also claims that barbarians "do not have anything that naturally rules; rather their community consists of a male and female slave" (I 2, 1252b5–8). It might be supposed that by "barbarians" he simply means natural slaves. His view of barbarians is more nuanced, however, as may be gathered from a passage in which he contrasts the Greeks with other nationalities:

The nations in cold regions, particularly Europe, are full of spirit but somewhat deficient in intelligence [*dianoia*] and craft knowledge. That is precisely why they remain comparatively free, but are apolitical and incapable of ruling their neighbors. Those in Asia, on the other hand, have souls endowed with intelligence and craft knowledge, but they lack spirit [*thumos*]. That is precisely why they are ruled and enslaved. The Greek race, however, occupies an intermediate position geographically, and so partakes of both sets of characteristics. For it is both spirited and intelligent. That is precisely why it remains free, governed in the best way, and capable, if it chances upon a single constitution, of ruling all the others. (VII 7, 1327b23–33)

This passage can be interpreted in terms of the psychological types distinguished above. The Europeans have a Type 2 psychology because they do not possess the deliberative faculty required for natural rule, while the Asians have a Type 3 psychology because their deliberative capability is inefficacious and unsupported by spirit. In order for reason to rule it must be supported by spirit, which is "both imperious and indomitable" (VII 7, 1328a6–7). In contrast the Greeks (i.e. adult, male Greeks) have the Type 5 psychology – completely developed and effective deliberative capability – required for political rule.[19]

Interestingly, Aristotle goes on to point out similar differences in intelligence and spiritedness among the Greek nations themselves: "Some have a nature that is one-sided, whereas in others both of these capacities are well blended. It is evident, then, that both spirit and intelligence should be present in the natures of people if they are to be easily guided to virtue by the legislator" (VII 7, 1327b33–38). Aristotle tactfully refrains from naming the Greek nations with lopsided natures,[20] but he does frequently point out differences among various city-states, especially in *Politics* IV–VI. The rest of this section concerns differences between various groups *within* the city-state that bear on their ability to share in the rule of reason.

*Generational differences*: Aristotle observes that the things that are possible and fitting for citizens are "determined by one's stage of life" (VIII 7, 1342b18–20). Because boys have a Type 4 psychology, with an incompletely developed deliberative capability, they are not ready to achieve the level of practical wisdom and moral virtue required for a citizen participating in political rule. They are only "incomplete" citizens (III 5, 1278a4–6; cf. III 1, 1275a14–18). Maturation is a gradual process by which males reach their physical prime between the ages of thirty and thirty-five and mental prime at about forty-nine, after which they sink gradually into senescence (*Rhet.* II 14, 1390b9–11; cf. *Pol.* VII 16, 1335a29, 33). Aristotle describes the differences between the generations in the *Rhetoric*. The younger tend to be more spirited and confident, which enables them to behave more courageously (*Rhet.* II 12, 1389a25–29). They are also more inclined to rely on virtuous habits rather than calculation (*logismos*), so that they choose noble deeds over useful activities (*Rhet.* II 12, 1389a34–36). These traits are reversed when they reach old age. Their spirit wanes and they live more by calculation than character; they grow less concerned with noble acts than with advantageous ones, especially those which will extend their lives and preserve their wealth (*Rhet.* II 13, 1390a16–18). They tend to be more skeptical and cynical in judgment and more diffident in action. Only those in their prime will have the right blend of spirit and calculation, so that they do not aim at nobility or advantage exclusively, but at both (*Rhet.* II 14, 1390a34–b1).

Such generational distinctions underlie Aristotle's proposal that the ideal constitution should distinguish two tiers of citizen, a military class and an administrative class: "The constitution [should] assign both tasks to the same people, but not at the same time. Instead, since it is natural for physical strength to be found among younger men and practical wisdom among older ones, it is beneficial and just to assign the tasks to each group on the basis of age, since this division is based on merit" (VII 9, 1329a13–17). By obeying their elders and being educated, the younger warriors will acquire the practical wisdom required for them to become rulers themselves when they have reached the appropriate age (cf. III 4, 1277b7–13).[21] Along similar lines, those who become too old to carry out administrative duties should be relieved of them and made priests (VII 9, 1329a31–34; III 1, 1275a14–18). Aristotle argues that this arrangement is natural as well as just: "Nature itself settled the choice by making part of the same species younger and part older, the former fit to be ruled and the latter to rule" (VII 14, 1332b35–38).

*Socio-economic differences*: Aristotle frequently explains the diversity of constitutions in terms of class differences (IV 4, 1290b23–24, 38–39; cf. II 2, 1261a22–24; III 1, 1274b39–40; III 4, 1277a5–12; IV 3, 1289b27–28). These classes display many cultural and socio-economic differences, the most pronounced being the gap between the rich and the poor. Focusing on the latter Aristotle rejects the conventional definition of democracy and oligarchy as, respectively, rule by the many and rule by the few (cf. *Politics* III 7 and Plato *Statesman* 291d–e). He argues instead that "a democracy exists when the free are in authority and an oligarchy when the rich are; but it happens that the former are many and the latter few, since many are free but few are rich" (IV 4, 1290b1–3). *Politics* IV and V document how the enmity between rich and the poor leads to injustices perpetrated by those in power, to civil wars and revolutions in which opposing factions struggle for dominance, and to conflicting alliances of democratic and oligarchic city-states culminating in cataclysms such as the Peloponnesian War. However, Aristotle also emphasizes that the mere division between rich and poor does not explain why there are different forms of democracy and oligarchy. Classes are also distinguished in terms of occupation as well as habit, upbringing, education, and virtue. Nine classes are listed in *Politics* IV 4: farmers, artisans, merchants, laborers, soldiers, judges, counselors, wealthy benefactors, and officials.[22] Among these Aristotle distinguishes between upper (administrative) and lower (productive) classes:

Yet even in those communities of four (or however many) classes, there must be someone to assign and decide what is just. So if indeed one should regard the soul as a more important part of an animal than the body, then, in the case of city-states too, one should regard things of the following sort to be parts, rather than those dealing with our necessary needs: the warriors; those who participate in administering judicial justice; and also those who deliberate, since deliberation is a task for political understanding. (IV 4, 1291a24–28; cf. III 4, 1277a5–12)

Aristotle uses this class analysis to explain why democracies and oligarchies alike take different forms ranging from moderate to extreme, where the extreme forms are not subject to the rule of law and resemble tyrannies (IV 4–6). He is more detailed and clear in applying this analysis to democracy. Within the people (*dêmos*) generally he distinguishes farmers, artisans, merchants, sailors, wage-earning laborers, and so forth (IV 4, 1291b17–28), and the different kinds of democracy are dominated by different classes: "If the multitude of farmers is predominant, it will be the first [i.e. moderate] kind of democracy; if the vulgar craftsmen and wage earners are, the last [extreme] kind; and similarly for the others in between these" (IV 12, 1296b28–31; cf. VI 4, 1319a24–28). In general, democracies become more extreme as lower classes are enfranchised: "There is a multitude of farmers, that of vulgar craftsmen, and that of laborers. And when the first of these is added to the second, and the third again to the both of them, it not only affects the quality of the democracy for better or worse, it also changes its kind" (VI 1, 1317a22–29).

The different types of democracy are better or worse because the corresponding social classes have occupations and lifestyles which not only limit the amount of wealth and leisure available to the practitioners but which also corrupt their souls and their capacity for virtue. In the case of farmers:

because they do have much property, they lack leisure and cannot attend meetings of the assembly frequently. And because they do not have the necessities, they are busy at their tasks and do not desire other people's property. Indeed, they find working more pleasant than engaging in politics and holding office, where no great profit is to be had from office, since the many seek money more than honor. (VI 4, 1318b11–17; cf. IV 6, 1292b27–29; VII 9, 1328b41–1329a2)

Whatever their shortcomings, the farmers are superior to even lower classes, such as the vulgar craftsmen, who make necessary goods and luxurious or beautiful commodities (IV 4, 1291a1–4). The vulgar (*banausoi*) are so called because of the degrading effect of their work: "Any task, craft, or branch of learning should be considered vulgar if it renders the body or mind of free people useless for the practices and activities of virtue. That is why the crafts that put the body into a worse condition and work done for wages are called vulgar; for they debase the mind and deprive it of leisure" (VIII 2, 1337b8–15). The vulgar have "souls that are distorted from their natural state" (VIII 7, 1342a22–23). Even more degrading is the profession of merchants, who are motivated by the desire for profit and for unlimited desires. "[T]hey are preoccupied with living, not with living well. And since their appetite for life is unlimited, they also want an unlimited amount of what sustains it [i.e. wealth]" (I 9, 1257b41–1258a2). Those with such excessive appetites are prone to injustice (II 7, 1267a2–6).

Aristotle also attributes the different kinds of oligarchies to different kinds of so-called notables (*gnôrimoi*), "who are distinguished by wealth, good birth, virtue, education, and the other characteristics that are ascribed to them on the basis of the same sort of difference" (IV 4, 1291b17–18, 28–30).[23] Beyond this vague description Aristotle's treatment of the classes inclined to oligarchy is much sketchier that of those inclined to democracy. Sometimes he distinguishes them merely in terms of how much wealth they possess. For example, the best form of oligarchy is composed of citizens "who own property, but a smaller amount – not too much." They comprise a large enough multitude of citizens that they "consent to having the law rule and not themselves." However, as greater wealth is concentrated in fewer hands, more extreme forms of oligarchy arise which reject the rule of law (IV 6, 1293a17–34). Sometimes, however, Aristotle hints at types of notables distinguished by virtue or vice. He remarks that wealth alone can lead to greed, arrogance, and self-indulgence (V 7, 1307a19–20; cf. IV 11, 1295b8–9; IV 12, 1297a9; IV 13, 1297b9–10; V 9, 1310a23–24).[24] In contrast, notables who are "cultivated and possess understanding (*nous*)" will share oversight of the poor and help them to begin productive lives (VI 5, 1320b7–9). Presumably, these cultivated notables are the sort who possess virtue and education in addition to wealth.

Aristotle also describes a "middle constitution," which he contends is superior to democracy and oligarchy:

> In all city-states, there are three parts of the city-state: the very rich, the very poor, and, third, those in between these. So, since it is agreed that what is moderate and in a mean is best, it is evident that a middle amount of the goods of luck is also best. For it most readily obeys the rule of reason, whereas whatever is exceedingly beautiful, strong, well born, or wealthy, or conversely whatever is exceedingly poor, weak, or lacking in honor, has a hard time following reason. For the former sort tend more toward arrogance and major vice, whereas the latter tend too much toward malice and petty vice; and wrongdoing is caused in the one case by arrogance and in the other by malice. (IV 11, 1295b1–12)

This argument regarding socio-economic differences parallels the previous arguments based on ethnic and generational differences. Because the middle class avoids the extreme tendencies of the very rich and very poor, it is better able to follow the rule of reason (*tôi logôi pethairchein*).[25] The moderately affluent are less inclined to become embroiled in class warfare and pursue their special interests at public expense (IV 11, 1295b28–33, 1296a35–38). Consequently, Aristotle claims that the constitution dominated by the middle class is the best constitution for city-states which do not enjoy the advantages of education, prosperity, and leisure required for the ideal constitution. The middle constitution thus serves as a standard for evaluating various forms of democracy and oligarchy: "The one nearest to this must of necessity always be better and one further from the middle worse – provided one is not judging them on the basis of certain assumptions [e.g. about what might benefit certain special interests]" (IV 11, 1296b7–9).

*The rule of reason: elitist or popular?* Most of the applications of the principle of the rule of reason so far suggest an authoritarian bias. But, in fact, Aristotle leaves it open whether reason should rule from the top down (i.e. via an elite class of rulers) or from the bottom up (via a self-governing multitude of citizens). In one passage he grants that the argument that the multitude or people (*dêmos*) are more qualified to rule than the virtuous few, though puzzling, may contain some truth (III 11, 1281a39–42; cf. III 11, 1281b16, 1282a28).[26] Each of the inferior many possesses "some part" of virtue and practical wisdom; and, when they all come together, the multitude resembles a single human being possessing their aggregate states of character and thought, just like an army that has many legs, arms, and perceptions (III 11, 1281b4–5). In such a case the multitude can display greater wisdom than the virtuous few. A body of citizens deliberating together resembles a panel of art critics who can do a better job than a single expert at judging musical and poetical works, because different persons judge different parts and everybody judges everything (III 11, 1281b7–10). Hence, each of the multitude "may be a worse judge than those who know, but a better or no worse one when they all come together" (III 11, 1282a15–17). Hence, it can be argued that it is just for the multitude to have authority over some important matters even if not over all political decisions.

This argument for popular rule rests on two crucial premises. The first is that each of the many inferior citizens possesses at least "some part of virtue and practical wisdom." This presupposes in turn that free adult men can possess different amounts of developed rational capability, probably due to a complex of variable innate factors (e.g. age and pedigree) and cultural factors (e.g. experience, education, and occupation). This makes more explicit an idea already implicit in the arguments based on generational and socio-economic differences: namely, that what we have been calling psychological Type 5 (developed efficacious deliberative capability) covers in fact a spectrum of cases in which the deliberative faculty is developed to a greater or less extent. The second premise is that when the inferior come together, their combined practical wisdom and virtue exceeds that of the superior few. This assumes that the practical wisdom and virtue of the many, even if partial, is *commensurable* with that of the one or few. This second premise comes under scrutiny when Aristotle turns to the case for absolute kingship.

The argument for absolute kingship rests on the supposition that "there is one person or more than one (though not enough to make up a complete city-state) who is so outstanding by reason of his superior virtue that neither the virtue nor the political power of all the others is commensurable with his (if there is only one) or theirs (if there are a number of them)" (III 13, 1284a3–8). By "not commensurable" Aristotle implies not merely that this exceptional individual's virtue exceeds the virtue of each ordinary person considered as an individual, but that his virtue exceeds theirs even when they are all combined.[27] He should not be treated as a mere part of the city, and it would be unjust to accord him the political rights of a mere citizen equal to others (III 17, 1288a26–29). For this exceptional individual should rule perpetually and not take turns with others (III 17, 1288a28–29; cf. III 13, 1284b28–34). This explains why Aristotle regards kingship as "the first and most divine": this constitution exhibits the rule of reason to the highest degree, when the king is so superior to ordinary citizens that he "would reasonably be regarded as a god among human beings" (IV 2, 1289a40; III 13, 1284a10–11). This remarkable argument assumes *a new psychological Type 6*: with a rational capacity that is incommensurably superior to that of normal human beings!

The consideration of whether absolute kingship is better than a popular constitution leads to the question of whether it is better to be ruled by law or by a good king. This issue naturally arises because for the absolute king "there is no law, since they themselves are law," and "anyone who attempted to legislate for them would be ridiculous" (III 13, 1284a13–15). In contrast, popular rule requires a legal order enabling many people to share in governance, an idea expressed in the formula, "Order [*taxis*] is law" (III 16, 1287a18–20). Aristotle contends that if ordinary rulers are not constrained by law they are more likely to act from emotion, rather than deliberative reason: "Anyone who instructs law to rule would seem to be asking god and the understanding alone to rule; whereas someone who asks a human being asks a wild beast as well. For appetite is like a wild beast, and spirit perverts rulers even when they are the best men. That is precisely why law is understanding (*nous*) without desire" (III 16, 1287a28–30). The rule of law is thus for ordinary human beings the most reliable embodiment of the rule of reason. But things would be different if there were an extraordinary individual with "godlike" virtue and practical wisdom: "Whenever it happens, then, that there is a whole family, or even some one individual among the rest, whose virtue is so superior as to exceed that of all the others, it is just for this family to be the kingly family and to control everything, and for this one individual to be king" (III 17, 1288a15–19). Aristotle seems, however, to regard this as only a remote possibility which has no application to his own ideal constitution, for which one must not assume impossible conditions (cf. VII 4, 1325b39; II 6, 1265a17–18). If the rulers differed from the ruled "as much as gods and heroes are believed to differ from human beings, if the former were so greatly superior, first in body and then in soul, that their superiority was indisputable and manifest to those they ruled – it would clearly be altogether better if the same people always ruled and the others were always ruled." But, Aristotle finds no evidence that there are such superior individuals. Hence, "it is necessary for all to share alike way in ruling and being ruled in turn. For equality consists in giving the same to those who are alike, and it is difficult for a constitution to last if its organization is contrary to justice" (VII 14, 1332b16–29). The implication is that, even in Aristotle's ideal constitution, the rule of reason must be exercised by all of the citizens together according to the rule of law.

## CONCLUSION

The rule of reason is a principle based on Aristotle's moral psychology and virtue ethics which has far-reaching ramifications for his political theory. It explains the naturalness of the pre-political associations out of which political life emerges, and it provides a norm for political legislation itself, in that constitutions are more just to the extent that they ensure that political rule is exercised in a rational manner. An important theme throughout Aristotle's *Politics* is that the rule of reason takes different forms depending on the rational capabilities of the rulers and subjects in question. Unfortunately, Aristotle's applications of this principle often rely on opinions about the relative capabilities of various groups which are today rejected as empirically mistaken and morally objectionable. This includes his views that women are intellectually and ethically inferior to men, as are barbarians to Greeks, and productive workers to the notables. Apart from such misapplications, however, Aristotle's principle is of continuing interest. As he recognized, it implies that shared governance is warranted when citizens in fact have comparable rational capabilities. His argument for the wisdom of the multitude implies that the citizens may through collective action exercise a type of rationality which exceeds that of an elite class. Related to this is his argument that public choice may become more rational if it is restrained by the rule of law. If these arguments have validity, the rule of reason may still have relevance to modern democratic politics.

WORKS CITED

Bar On, B.-A., ed. 1994. *Engendering Origins: Critical Feminist Readings in Plato and Aristotle*. Albany, NY: SUNY Press

Cole, E. B. 1994. "Women, slaves, and 'love of toil' in Aristotle's moral psychology." In *Engendering Origins: Critical Feminist Readings in Plato and Aristotle*, ed. B.-A. Bar On. Albany, NY: SUNY Press

Fortenbaugh, W. W. 1977. "Aristotle on slaves and women." In *Aristotle on Aristotle*, vol. II, eds. J. Barnes, M. Schofield and R. Sorabji. London: Duckworth

Keyt, D. 1991. "Aristotle's theory of distributive justice." In *A Companion to Aristotle's Politics*, eds. D. Keyt and F. D. Miller. Oxford: Blackwell

Lord, C. 1984. *Aristotle, The Politics*. University of Chicago Press

Mayhew, R. 2004. *The Female in Aristotle's Biology: Reason or Rationalization*. University of Chicago Press

2009. "Rulers and ruled." In *A Companion to Aristotle*, ed. G. Anagnostopoulos. Malden, MA and Oxford: Wiley-Blackwell

Modrak, D. 1994. "Aristotle, women, deliberation, and nature." In *Engendering Origins: Critical Feminist Readings in Plato and Aristotle*, ed. B.-A. Bar On. Albany, NY: SUNY Press

Newman, W. L. 1887–1902. *The politics of Aristotle*. 4 vols, Oxford University Press

Reeve, C. D. C. 1998. *Aristotle*, Politics. Indianapolis, IN: Hackett.

Schofield, M. 1990. "Ideology and philosophy in Aristotle's theory of slavery." In *Aristoteles' politik*, ed. G. Patzig. Göttingen: Vandenhoeck and Ruprecht

Smith, N. D. 1983. "Plato and Aristotle on the Nature of Women." *Journal of the History of Philosophy* 21: 467–78

1991. "Aristotle's theory of natural slavery." In *A Companion to Aristotle's Politics*, eds. D. Keyt and F. D. Miller. Oxford: Blackwell

Woods, M. 1992. *Aristotle Eudemian Ethics Books I, II, and VIII*. Oxford: Clarendon Press

NOTES

1. The Eleatic Stranger in *Statesman* 258e–59d is the implicit target, although Aristotle only refers to "those who believe" this.
2. An exception is Mayhew 2009, which sheds valuable light on Aristotle's distinction between kinds of rule. Mayhew's essay, however, has a

different focus from mine, which is on the psychological underpinnings of Aristotle's distinction.

3. Translations of the *Politics* are by C. D. Reeve, with occasional alterations for the sake of consistency. Translations of other works by Aristotle are by the author.

4. The verb *peithesthai* is translated "obey," but note that it is the active form *peithein*, which is translated "persuade." The association between *peithesthai* and *akouein* is also closer than that between "obey" and "listen" in English. The *Magna Moralia* (of disputed authorship) similarly divides the soul into two parts: the one rational and the other nonrational but subordinate to the part possessing reason (*MM* I 5, 1185b3–13).

5. This follows the textual construal, though not the translation, of Woods 1992.

6. The rational part is also subdivided in *MM* I 34, 1196b15–33. Elsewhere Aristotle distinguishes between "contemplative" and "practical" understanding: *DA* III 9, 432b26–27, *DA* III 10, 433a14–16; cf. *NE* VI 2, 1139a26–27.

7. This is followed by the passage (I 5, 1254a27–36), quoted at the beginning of the previous section, in which Aristotle promulgates the principle of natural rule.

8. The Greek *politikon* is translated "political" throughout (sometimes departing from Reeve, who here translates it as "rule of a statesman"). At I 12, 1259b4–10 Aristotle distinguishes "political" in the strict sense in which citizens (*politai*) take turns ruling and being ruled, from a broader sense in which marital rule is "political" (i.e. "constitutional"). Perhaps the broader sense is also intended at I 5, 1254b5–6.

9. See Schofield 1990: 1–27.

10. Aristotle is concerned here with the fact that nonhuman animals possess desire but not reason. In *On the Soul*, animals are distinguished from plants primarily by possessing perception (*DA* II 2, 413b2). However, whatever has the perceptive faculty also has the desiring faculty (*DA* II 3, 414b1–6). Further, many animals also possess imagination (*DA* III 10, 433a9–10).

11. Aristotle is not explicit about the relative ordering of boys and their mothers. However, he would presumably hold that if an actual man is superior to an actual woman, then a potential man is also superior to an actual woman. (Analogously, a potential man is superior to an actual horse.) It is also suggestive (though not decisive) that in both *Politics* I 12 and 13 he considers the three cases of inferior subjects in the same order: slaves, women, boys.

12. Although see Pierre Pellegrin, Chapter 4.

13. Reading with the $\Pi^2$ group of manuscripts (departing from Reeve's translation, which follows the $\Pi^1$ group and Ross's deletion of *aisthanomena*). The $\Pi^2$ reading makes clearer the psychological difference between animals and natural slaves, as noted in Lord 1984: 248 n. 16.

14. Aristotle here disagrees with Plato's *Laws* VI, 777e–78a.

15. *Nicomachean Ethics* VIII 11, 1161b5–8 qualifies this even further: There can be justice and friendship with a slave but only *qua* human, not *qua* slave. On the difficulties of reconciling Aristotle's different claims, see Smith 1991.

16. Aristotle's controversial claims about female psychology have inspired a wide range of interpretations, including Fortenbaugh 1977; Smith 1983; Modrak 1994 (found in Bar On 1994, a collection including other relevant essays); and Mayhew 2004.

17. See above note 8 on this sense of "political."

18. Unfortunately we do not have Aristotle's fuller account of the education of children, promised at I 13, 1260b8–13 and VII 16, 1335b4.

19. Some non-Greeks do have the psychological requisites for politics. Aristotle remarks that the Carthaginians are believed to govern themselves well, and he adds that their constitution has many fine arrangements, so that they have avoided factional conflict and tyranny (II 11, 1272b24–33). Presumably the Macedonians, who had recently conquered much of Greece, would be another exception.

20. The overly spirited Greeks may include the Arcadians and Aetolians, and the dispirited some of the Ionians in Asia Minor, as conjectured by Newman 1887–1902, vol. 3: 366.

21. In his discussion of civic virtue, Aristotle maintains that in the best constitution the rulers must have practical wisdom, while the subjects need only true belief (III 4, 1277b25–29). Later he argues that those who excel in virtue and practical wisdom make the greatest contribution to the political community and have a greater just claim to political rights (III 9, 1281a4–8; III 12, 1283a1–3).

22. Contrast the list in VII 8 where the ideal city-state has six classes, excluding laborers (presumed to be slaves) and merchants (presumed to be metics), combining judges, counselors, and officials into a single class, and adding priests (superannuated citizens).

23. Cf. VI 2, 1317b38–41 which states that "oligarchy is defined by birth and wealth and education." However, the sentence seems to be out of place and is deleted by Susemihl, Dreizehnter, and Keyt.

24. An apparent exception is IV 8, 1293b38–40: "The rich are believed (*dokousin*) to possess already what unjust people commit injustice to get, which is why the rich are referred to as noble-and-good men, and as

notables." But the passages cited in the main text make clear that Aristotle does not share the belief that the rich are virtuous merely because they already possess an abundance of goods which they do not have to take from others.

25. Compare the use of *peitharchein* at *NE* I 13, 1102b26, 31, quoted above. My translation of this phrase departs from Reeve.

26. Although Aristotle mentions the people (*dêmos*) he is probably considering an argument not for democracy as he understands it, but for a republican form of government with elected magistrates in addition to popular courts and deliberative bodies, like Solon's constitution of Athens: see III 11, 1282a29–36.

27. On the interpretation of "not commensurable" see Keyt 1991: 275.

# 3    Economy and private property

In the *Nicomachean Ethics*, Aristotle defines the happy person as "the one whose activities accord with complete virtue, with an adequate supply of external goods, in a complete life" (*NE* I 10, 1101a15–17).[1] Since happiness consists in virtuous activity, Aristotle classifies happiness as a good of the soul (*NE* I 8, 1098b13–18). Bodily goods (such as health and beauty) and external goods (such as wealth, friends, and political power) are not constituents of the highest good, though they are beneficial if used well. In so far as they are up to us, we should pursue them only to the extent that they contribute to our self-sufficiency and happiness. Aristotle sees two roles for external goods in the happy life. First, an adequate (*hikanôs*) supply of external goods is a material precondition for virtuous activity. We "cannot, or cannot easily, do fine actions if we lack the resources" (*NE* I 8, 1099a31–b1). In many virtuous acts, we use wealth, friends, and political power as instruments. Second, a rich supply of external goods adds "adornment" to our life, making it more blessed (*NE* I 10, 1100b26). Deprivation of certain external goods, such as "good birth, good children, and beauty," mars our blessedness. "For we do not altogether have the character of happiness if we look utterly repulsive or are ill-born, solitary, or childless; and we have it even less, presumably, if our children and friends are totally bad, or were good but have died" (*NE* I 8, 1099b2–6). Frequently, such misfortunes are just that – misfortunes – and hence not up to us (*eph'hêmin*). But wealth acquisition seems to depend on our own efforts, since we can deliberate well or badly about how to *acquire* wealth (cf. *NE* III 1, 1110b19). We may also deliberate well or badly about how to *use* wealth once it has been acquired, for instance, what we should give to whom in what circumstances. Since an adequate supply of wealth is a precondition for leisure (scholê) and the excellent activities that make it up, legislators, who wish to promote happiness and self-sufficiency in the city, need to determine how wealth should be acquired, who should own it, and how it can best be put to use. They do so, not because they are concerned with preserving life, but because they are concerned with the good life, since we don't live for the sake of living, but for the sake of living well.[2]

How much wealth is "adequate" to lead a life of excellent activity of the part of soul that has reason? And what are appropriate sources of wealth? Should wealth be owned privately by each citizen or publicly by the community? And who should decide how wealth is used: individual citizens or the citizens as holders of deliberative and judicial office?

These questions receive little explicit attention in the *Ethics*, but they are at the forefront of Aristotle's thought in the *Politics*. Aristotle's neglect of these questions in the *Nicomachean Ethics* could potentially be explained with reference to his claim in Book X that the life of study is the best life. The contemplative life doesn't have external goods as its subject matter – indeed, wealth and friends may even be impediments to contemplation (*empodia*; *NE* X 8, 1178b4) if they extend beyond the necessary. Aristotle recommends the contemplative life for each person able to enjoy it, urging us to be "pro-immortal" and to "go to all lengths to live a life in accord with our supreme element" (*nous*) (*NE* X 7, 1177b35–36). But even if he succeeds in making himself pro-immortal, the wise man is still a human being, and hence "lives together with other human beings" and "chooses to do the actions that accord with virtue" (*NE* X 8, 1178b5–7). He will therefore need external goods for living a human life, and he will need to participate in politics (IV 1, 1288b22–27). Only in a city governed by good laws will virtuous activity – and hence happiness – be attainable for individuals.[3] Aristotle's remarks in *NE* X therefore do not entail that self-sufficiency is attainable without wealth or outside a political community. Indeed, in claiming that the wise man "chooses to do the acts in accord with virtue," he indicates that political activity is intrinsically valuable.

My aim in this chapter is to examine Aristotle's account of household management (*oikonomia*) and the art of acquisition in *Politics* I 3–13 with a view to determining what role Aristotle sees for wealth in the well-governed city, and why he prefers that wealth be owned by private citizens ("household managers"). Aristotle defines household management as the science concerned with rule of free male citizens over slaves, wife, and children.[4] He notes that a fourth part, the art called "wealth acquisition" (*chrêmatistikê*), is sometimes identified with household management *simpliciter*, or treated as its largest component. Aristotle asks whether it is a part of *oikonomikê technê* at all, or merely an auxiliary instrument (*hupêretikê*) (I 8, 1256a3–5). His answer is that it is a part, but a part with a specific role. Though I will return to Aristotle's discussion of childrearing in the final section of the chapter, my main focus will be Aristotle's account of economy in the narrow sense (wealth acquisition and use) and his defense of private property rights. In particular, I will examine his description of the natural type of wealth acquisition that is part of household management, as well as his critique of commercial money-making as an "unnatural" form of wealth acquisition. Why, apart from prejudice, does Aristotle disparage money-making through commerce? I will then turn to Aristotle's argument for a system of "private ownership, common use." My aim is to decide how and to what extent Aristotle agrees with the Greek proverb "friends have everything in common" (II 5, 1263a30; *Rep.* IV, 423e–424a; *Rep.* V, 449c–66d). Plato and Aristotle both treat this kind of sharing as an ideal, but they disagree over how to effect it.

Aristotle is often celebrated as the patron saint of private property rights. But his defense of private ownership in *Politics* II 5–7 is not unqualified. While ownership should be private, he recommends public use. What does Aristotle's provision for "private ownership, public use" entail? Critics have mostly been stumped on this point, sometimes supplying their own conjectures to fill in Aristotle's unfinished sketch.[5] This has led one critic, C. D. C. Reeve, to argue that Aristotle's prescription for property in the ideal constitution is "not much more than a notional variant of a system of public ownership" that Plato defends in the *Republic*.[6] I will argue that Reeve misrepresents Aristotle's model for common use of private property, but that the model itself, as exemplified in Aristotle's discussion of magnificence (*megaloprepeia*) and liturgy (*leitourgia*) in *Nicomachean Ethics* IV 2, was already under strain when Aristotle wrote the *Ethics* and *Politics*. Aristotle's model of "private ownership, public use" requires that rich citizens be willing to volunteer their wealth for the common good, but such citizens were in short supply in fourth-century Athens. Thus, history seems to bear out Reeve's claim that "the system of property adopted in [Aristotle's] ideal constitution ... does not seem to be the best from the point of view of maximizing the citizens' happiness ... many other systems seem much more preferable, for example, fair taxation on private property and income, with the proceeds going to maintain public property and provide public services."[7]

By arguing that property is made common through "virtue" and "good laws," Aristotle shifts the burden of proof over on his provisions for moral education. If Aristotle's ideal constitution can ensure that citizens are raised with good characters, ready to share with their citizen friends through voluntary acts of generosity and magnificence, then Aristotle's model of "private property, common use" may be workable. But if such education is insufficient, then we may have reason to reconsider Aristotle's rationale for adopting the principle "private ownership, common use." In the final part of the chapter, I will argue that Aristotle's reasons for making moral habituation a task for legislators and statesmen rather than private citizens are strangely at odds with his arguments for keeping property private. Aristotle maintains that "correct habituation distinguishes a good political system from a bad one" (*NE* II 2, 1103b6–7). But he fails to note that his reasons for favoring public over private moral education may equally be adduced in support of a system that makes *property* publicly rather than privately owned. If we have reason to think that the ills that plague the Platonic model of common ownership also plague Aristotle's system of public moral education, then we have reason to doubt that public education will ensure that the citizens of Aristotle's state will volunteer to use their wealth for the common good.[8]

### NATURAL AND UNNATURAL ACQUISITION

Before we can even consider how property should be owned, we need to establish that there is such a thing as "property" in the first place. This is a question Aristotle explicitly considers in *Politics* I 8. Though his affirmative answer is perhaps unsurprising, the reason he gives is not, for Aristotle appears to introduce a global teleological order of a kind that he elsewhere appears to eschew.[9] In defending the "natural" status of property, Aristotle rests his case on observations about natural teleology in the development of embryos. All animals are equipped with property from the moment of conception:

It is evident that nature herself gives such property to all living things, both right from the beginning, when they are first conceived, and similarly when they have reached complete maturity. (a) Animals that produce larvae or eggs produce their offspring together with enough food to last them until they can provide for themselves. Animals that give birth to live offspring carry food for their offspring in their own bodies for a certain period, namely, the natural substance we call milk. (b) Clearly, then we must suppose in the case of fully developed things, too, that plants are for the sake of animals, and that the other animals are for the sake of human beings, domestic ones both for using and eating, and most but not all wild ones for food and other kinds of support, so that clothes and other tools may be got from them. If then nature makes nothing incomplete or pointless, it must have made all of them for the sake of human beings. (I 8, 1256a7–22)

The transition from (a) to (b) is surprising. It presupposes a move from the teleology of individual substances to a "global" teleology according to which organisms lower down in the scale of nature are "for the sake of" organisms higher up in the scale of nature. In so far as human beings are the most perfect animals, all other living things exist for our sake.[10] If this is "natural," as Aristotle insists, then it would be contrary to nature for us not to help ourselves to nature's bounty, for plants and other animals exist for our sakes, as material for food, tools, and shelter. Aristotle thus posits a natural teleological hierarchy where plants and lower creatures are instruments that exist for the sake of human *eudaimonia*. In helping ourselves to natural resources, we are acting in accordance with a natural order.

The argument for the existence of property as yet tells us nothing about just distribution or proportionate equality as a principle of dividing up property among members of a political community.[11] Still, Aristotle takes unlimited acquisitiveness to be unnatural, for it lacks a proper end:

One kind of property acquisition is a natural part of household management, then, in that a store of the goods that are necessary for life and useful to the community of city-state or household either must be available to start with, or household management must arrange to make it available. At any rate, true wealth seems to consist in such goods. For the amount of this sort of property that one needs for the self-sufficiency that promotes the good life is not unlimited, though Solon in his poetry says it is: "No boundary to wealth has been established for human beings." But such a limit or boundary has been established, just as in the other crafts. For none has any tool unlimited in size or number, and wealth is a collection of tools belonging to statesmen and household managers. (I 8, 1256b27–37)

Aristotle typically cites Solon with approval (cf. *NE* X, 1179a9–14; *NE* I 10, 1100a11–15; *EE* II 1, 1219b6; and *Pol.* IV 11, 1296a18–21). His departure in *Pol.* 1 8 is unique (see Natali 1990). In so far as wealth is an instrument, wealth has a natural limit, and that limit is whatever is needed to ensure the self-sufficiency of a community. It follows that self-sufficiency cannot *itself* be measured in wealth; self-sufficiency is rather the end that determines how much wealth we need. As Aristotle states in the *Ethics*, "we regard something as self-sufficient when all by itself it makes a life choice-worthy and lacking in nothing; and this is what we think happiness does" (*NE* 7, 1097b14–16). Because fine actions are the content of happiness, and wealth is an instrument for fine actions, we should only pursue wealth to the extent that it enables us to act finely, either as individual household managers or as a political community. It is what kind of life you can lead with your wealth – what kind of activity it enables – that determines whether it is beneficial or harmful. Human beings should therefore not use nature imprudently, to satisfy desires that are inflated beyond what is appropriate for a good and self-sufficient life. Nor should they neglect their own needs so they lack an adequate supply of external goods. Excess and deficiency impede *eudaimonia*.

Aristotle distinguishes four sources of acquisition in decreasing order of naturalness: (a) direct from nature; (b) through direct exchange of goods between two parties without the use of money (barter); (c) exchange of goods for money between two parties; and (d) money-making through trade, banking or wage labor. Of these, the household manager should supervise the first kind, including (1) livestock rearing, (2) farming of fruit and vegetables; and perhaps (3) beekeeping and the rearing of other useful animals. These are natural modes of acquisition. Logging and mining also extract useful things from the earth, but in this case, the product needs to be bartered or sold for a profit, and hence the craft is less natural.

Initially, says Aristotle, villagers traded "real things of use for real things of use" (shoes against food, or wine against corn). But since it is sometimes useful to postpone acquisition, coinage was introduced as a guarantee of future purchases, which simplified trade. Foreign imports and exports made this particularly useful, since "not every natural necessity is easily carried" (I 9, 1257a35). In commercial trades, goods are no longer used in a way that is "proper" to the thing – a shoe is not used as a shoe, and a house is not used as a house. Instead they are traded for the sake of accumulating wealth. Aristotle divides the commercial part of wealth acquisition into three: (4) trade, with the subcategories of ship-owning, transport, and marketing; (5) money-lending; and (6) wage-earning, itself subdivided into that of vulgar craftsmen and manual laborers. Of these three parts of commerce, money-lending and wage earning are the least honorable and least natural. While Aristotle thinks that a well-governed city-state will trade with other states, the reputable household manager will leave trade to foreigners and wage labor to people unsuited for participation in political deliberation. Aristotle reserves special spite for money-lenders, for their profit does not correspond to a specific quantity of flour or shoes, but rather to the other's needs and to time:

usury is very justifiably detested, since it gets its wealth from money itself, rather than from the very thing money was devised to facilitate. For money was introduced to facilitate exchange, but interest makes money itself grow bigger. (That is how it gets its name; for offspring (tokos) resemble their parents, and interest (tokos) is money that comes from money.) Hence of all kinds of wealth acquisition, this one is the most unnatural. (I 10, 1258b1–7)

Aristotle here applies a standard of "naturalness" to measure the worth of different kinds of acquisition. The very point of the money-maker's efforts is to add yet another quantity of coin to his wealth, so that the sum can be augmented – there is no further end. Aristotle concludes that money-makers fail to give the proper shape to their lives, for they chase an ever-moving target:

The reason they are so disposed, however, is that they are preoccupied with living (to zên), not with living well (alla mê to eu zên). And since their appetite for life is unlimited, they also want an unlimited amount of what sustains it. (I 9, 1257b41–1258a2)

When money-makers *do* refer their activities to an overarching end, they tend to identify living well with experiencing maximum physical gratification. And since this seems to depend on having property, they spend all their time acquiring wealth. Aristotle thinks that the second kind of wealth acquisition arose because of this: "For since their gratification lies in excess, they seek the craft that produces the excess needed for gratification...These people make [all the virtues] into forms of wealth acquisition in the belief that acquiring wealth is the end, and that everything ought to promote the end" (I 9, 1258a6–14).

A virtuous household manager, by contrast, procures what his household needs because he understands that wealth is essentially an instrument for fine action. And he knows that he can act finely with modest resources. What matters is not how much money he possesses, but that he uses his resources well.[12] In Aristotle's economic theory, there is thus an intimate connection between (1) the happy life; (2) the self-sufficient life; and (3) the naturalness of a mode of acquisition. A mode of acquisition is natural if it promotes the self-sufficiency of a state or a household, and it promotes the self-sufficiency of a state or household if it promotes virtuous activity and hence happiness. True wealth (alêthinos ploutos; I 8, 1256b30) is whatever a household manager needs to run his household virtuously and whatever the statesman needs to run the state virtuously; it does not consist in material possessions per se. This allows Aristotle to distinguish between two senses of "the art of acquisition," or "chrêmatistikê technê." The name may be applied to commercial activity that aims to increase the merchant's wealth, where wealth is either treated as an end in itself, or as a means to physical gratification. This is unnatural activity. First, it lacks a proper end. Second, it uses the resources that nature supplies (grain, oil, wool) not as nature intended, to satisfy human needs, but as commodities that can be traded to increase the merchant's wealth. It is precisely because Aristotle thinks that it is nature's business to furnish food to living creatures (I 10, 1258a35–38) that commercial trade subverts the global teleological order that Aristotle posits as the first principle of property. Whether an economic activity is natural or not, then, depends on the extent to which its aims coincide with nature's aims in equipping living creatures, and human beings in particular, with what they need to flourish as the kinds of beings that they are.

We must therefore distinguish the natural and necessary art of acquisition that serves the needs of the household and the city from the unnatural and unnecessary practice whereby the pursuit of ever-increasing quantities of wealth becomes an end in itself (*chrêmatistikê* in the derogatory sense, sometimes referred to by Aristotle as "*kapêlikê*," or commerce). Many household managers confuse the two, for they think that the art of household management just is the art of increasing the wealth of the household, or at least keeping it stable.[13] In so far as every art has a limit (I 8, 1256b34), the "art" of breeding money from money is really just a knack based on experience (*empeiria*) – it cannot be a real art (*technê*) since it always aims at more and more without any regard for its virtuous use. And it is virtuous activity, whether private or political, that is the end of the natural and necessary art of acquisition.

### "FRIENDS HAVE EVERYTHING IN COMMON"

To most of Aristotle's contemporaries, the existence of private households would have seemed an unalterable fact of life. In the *Republic*, Plato challenges received opinion when he recommends the abolition of the household as a constituent of the ideal state. Inspired by arrangements in Sparta and Crete, he recommends that the ruling classes lead a communal life without private property or families of their own. Private kinship bonds and private wealth threaten the stability and *eudaimonia* of the city. Aristotle defends the private household against Plato's objections in *Politics* II 1–5. Private kinship bonds and private property are *preconditions* for happy and well-ordered states, claims Aristotle, not impediments.

It is tempting to overestimate the distance that separates Aristotle's "householdism" from Platonic communism. First, Aristotle's critique of Plato should not be read as an unqualified defense of private property rights, for Aristotle denies that private ownership should be extended to all members of a household or a city. Though nature makes nothing in vain, equipping each species with the necessities of life, it does not follow that property should belong to each member of the species individually, and that the right to own property is therefore universal. Tellingly, Aristotle rejects Plato's proposal for community of women in the section devoted to *private property* in *Politics* II 5. Some members of the household *just are* pieces of property (a natural slave is, as he notoriously notes, "a tool with a soul" (*empsuchon organon*; I 4, 1253b32; *NE* VIII 11, 1161b4). Children have not yet developed the requisite practical reason; female children never will. While a woman should aim to preserve her husband's possessions, she should not be allowed to *own* either land or slaves, for she lacks the psychological resources to manage property virtuously.

Second, we should not overlook Aristotle's distinction between private ownership and public use. Aristotle is surely right when he notes that the family and the right to own private property are recognized even by city-states that impose strict limits on the *use* of private wealth, such as Sparta, where citizens are obliged to place their slaves, dogs, and horses at the disposal of others, and travelers may take whatever provisions they need from the fields (II 5, 1263a33–35). Every real city-state is constituted from households, but they organize the use of property differently. The burden of proof therefore rests squarely on Plato to show that his constitution is superior to existing ones, including the ones that make provisions for public use.

To Plato's mind, private possessions – things we call our own (*ta oikeia*) – stand in the way of concord, and hence of happiness. In a just city, where each class of citizens does its own work, rulers will not be concerned with private wealth or distracted by private kinship bonds. If they were to retain private households, the guardians would be performing multiple functions at once, functions that are at cross-purposes. Plato therefore decrees that his guardian rulers give up their private possessions, only mate at state-appointed times with state-appointed partners, and abandon their offspring to public nurses, all in the interest of keeping children's identities hidden to their parents, and parents' to their children (*Rep.* V, 459d–61e). These policies remove the opportunity to overreach (*pleonektein*), since the guardians will say "mine and not mine" about the same things. If "friends possess everything in common" (*Rep.* IV, 423e–24a; *Rep.* V, 449c–66d), questions of equitable distribution of burdens and benefits won't arise. No citizen can treat their own kin preferentially in Plato's system of "double blind" procreation, nor will they fight with relatives over property and inheritance, for they have none. They also lack the means to fan the flames of their appetitive desires.

The abolition of the household is really less punitive than the alternative, Plato maintains. If the guardians are permitted to acquire private land (*gên idian*), houses (*oikias*), and currency (*nomismata*) themselves:

> [T]hey will be household managers (*oikonomoi*) and farmers (*geôrgoi*) instead of guardians – hostile masters of the other citizens instead of their allies. They'll spend their whole lives hating and being hated, and plotting and being plotted against, more afraid of internal than external enemies, and they'll hasten both themselves and the whole city to almost immediate ruin. (*Rep.* III, 417a–b)

In so far as they will lead a communal life in communal dwellings, eating together from their communal storehouses and treating each fellow guardian as a friend and brother, Plato's guardians will not need to possess the art of household management, since their "household" coincides with the state. They will deal with non-guardians much in the way that Greeks according to Aristotle should deal with non-Greeks: as people of inferior rationality who benefit from the beneficent rule of the fully rational (I 2, 1252b4–8). Although the traditional household is preserved for the producing and money-making classes, the state, as Plato envisions it, is not a union of households, entities that comprise individuals bound together by bonds of kinship or servitude, but a union of individual citizens, unmediated by private associations like the household. Therefore, no art of household management is needed to bridge the gap between individual virtue and political science. Political science need not concern itself with household management traditionally construed, for the only house that the guardians are required to keep in order is the state.

### ARISTOTLE'S QUESTIONS FOR PLATO

Aristotle admits that the end that Plato promotes in eliminating the household is admirable:

> Such legislation may seem attractive, and might seem to display a love of humanity (*philanthropia*). For anyone who hears it accepts it gladly, thinking that all will have an amazing friendship for all, particularly when someone blames the evils now existing in constitutions on property's not being communal. (I mean lawsuits brought against one another over contracts, perjury trials, and flattery of the rich.) Yet none of these evils is caused

by property not being communal but by vice. For we see that those who own and share communal property have far more disagreements than those whose property is separate... Furthermore, it would be fair to mention not only how many evils people will lose through sharing, but also how many good things. The life they would lead seems to be totally impossible. (II 5, 1263b15–29)

Aristotle here identifies three questions that must be answered in the affirmative before we accept Plato's proposal:

1.  Is Plato's city possible?
2.  Will the abolition of family and private property solve the problems Plato has identified?
3.  Supposing that it does solve these problems, will the benefits outweigh the costs?

Aristotle is convinced that each of these questions must be answered with a definite "no."

Most fundamentally, Aristotle objects that Plato's city is a metaphysical impossibility. It suffers from "excessive unity." A city as Aristotle understands it is "by nature a mass of people; as it becomes more and more unified, first the city will turn into a household, and then the household will turn into just one person" (II 2, 1261a17–19). If Platonic *philanthropia* were even possible, the result would not be a well-ordered city, but a fused entity like Aristophanes' lovers.

Turning to the second question, Plato is also wrong to assume that common ownership and the dissolution of families will make us less prone to quarrel. Blaming property for vicious behavior is as misplaced as blaming the tool for the craftsman's mistakes. It is vice, not private property, that makes citizens quarrel. If citizens are just and equitable, private property will not be an obstacle to political friendship.

As Aristotle explains in the *Nicomachean Ethics*:

concord (*homonoia*), then, is apparently political friendship (*politikê philia*), as indeed it is said to be; for it is concerned with advantage and with what affects life [as a whole]. This sort of concord is found *in decent people* [emphasis added]. For they are in concord with themselves and with each other, since they are practically of the same mind; for their wishes are stable, not flowing back and forth like a tidal strait. They wish for what is just and advantageous, and also seek it in common. Base people, however, cannot be in concord, except to a slight degree, just as they can be friends only to a slight degree; for they seek to overreach (*pleonexias ephiemenous*) on benefits [to themselves], and shirk labors and public service (*tais leitourgiais*). And since each wishes this for himself, he interrogates and obstructs his neighbour; for when people do not look out for the common good, it is ruined. The result is that they are in conflict, trying to compel one another to do what is just, but not wishing to do it themselves. (*NE* IX 7, 1167b2–16)[14]

Abolishing private property will do nothing to cure the selfish impulse that causes civic discord. The right approach is not to blame these ills on private property and private kinship bonds; they spring from improper *use* of private wealth rather than from wealth itself.

Why, then, might we nevertheless be drawn to Plato's ideal state? Aristotle explains the appeal of Plato's constitution by exposing an equivocation in his use of personal pronouns. Plato claims that citizens in an ideal state will say "mine" and "not mine" about the same things, but his proposal only seems attractive because this can be interpreted in two incompatible ways. It can either mean that all the city's children, wives, and property belong to each one of them individually, in which case the result according to Aristotle would be "fine, but not possible." Alternatively, they may say "mine" and "not mine" about the same things, indicating that they own it as a collective (not "each taken one at a time," as Aristotle puts it). But in that case, "it contributes nothing to concord," as Aristotle notes. For they would then need to decide who looks after what, and what a just distribution of rights and duties would be, thereby re-introducing the old quarrels that they were supposed to get rid of.

This leads us to overlook the Achilles' heel of Platonic communism, the negative impact it will have on care and concern. Aristotle pinpoints the phenomenon known as the "tragedy of the commons" when he remarks that:

What is held in common by the largest number of people also receives the least care. For people give most attention to their own property, less to what is communal, or only as much as it falls to them to give. For apart from anything else, the thought that someone else is attending to it makes them neglect it more (just as a large number of household servants sometimes gives worse service than a few). (II 3, 1261b33–37)

Responsibility evaporates where private ownership and private attachments have been abolished. If every child under a certain age is my "son" or my "daughter," I will care about them not as if they were actual sons or daughters, but as distant relatives. Sharing of wives and children will make friendship in the city "watery," Aristotle maintains. "Better to have a cousin of one's own than a son in the way Socrates describes" (II 3, 1262a13–14). In Socrates' city "each citizen will have a thousand sons, but not sons of each taken one at a time; any given son will be the son of this father no more than any other, and so all the fathers alike will care little about them" (II 3, 1261b37–40). The same applies to property.

Communal ownership also eliminates the benefits associated with private ownership. Aristotle emphasizes that private property and private kinship bonds have beneficial consequences when tempered by "good habits and good laws." The existing system of privately owned households and intimate bonds between parents and children will increase the city's eudaimonic self-sufficiency *provided that* the citizens can be made virtuous, and this is a task for the legislator. Virtuous citizens will aid one another willingly and act with friendly feelings whenever they cannot succeed on their own. Voluntary acts of generosity and helpfulness are therefore better at achieving the aims that Plato wants to promote through common ownership, Aristotle maintains. There will be more acts of generosity and more friendly relations in a city run on Aristotle's principles than one run by Plato's ideal constitution. As Aristotle puts it, "virtue will make friends' possessions common for their use" (II 5, 1263a29–30). Aristotle therefore infers that, "evidently, it is better if we own possessions privately, but make them common by our use of them. And it is the legislator's proper task to see that the right sort of people develop" (II 5, 1263a39–41).

In addition, Aristotle is convinced that Plato's constitution removes an important source of pleasure from the guardians' lives:

To regard something as one's own makes an enormous difference to one's pleasure ... Moreover, it is very pleasant to help one's friends, guests, or companions, or do them favors, as one can if one has property of one's own. (II 5, 1263b1–7)

Aristotle distinguishes between a proper kind of self-love and the deformed version that is called selfishness. The pleasure we take in calling something our own should not be confused with selfishness, for unlike selfishness, it is natural. In a state run by Plato's principles, we would be cut off from the pleasures of two distinct virtues, temperance and generosity, since we could not even *practice* these virtues in their usual domains. In particular, we cannot be generous unless we have private property to confer on our friends, and men cannot be sexually temperate if every woman is shared (II 5, 1263b9–13). If generosity has its function in the use of possessions, then I cannot do acts of generosity if the supposed beneficiary already owns the gift as much as I do. And if I cannot perform acts of generosity, then I cannot develop the character disposition that results from habitual performance of generous acts. The same applies to sexual temperance. Therefore, the citizens in Plato's *Republic* will be less than perfectly virtuous, contrary to Plato's stated objective, and they will not experience the pleasures unique to the exercise of these virtues.

Aristotle has maintained that, "evidently, it is better if we own possessions privately, but make them common by our use of them. And it is the legislator's proper task to see that the right sort of people develop" (II 5, 1263a39–41). But even if we are sympathetic to Aristotle's criticisms of Plato, we may wonder whether Aristotle gives sufficient weight to the potential downsides of investing such broad powers in individual citizens and household managers. He may certainly be right that *virtuous* men will care for their households and the common good. But the unsavory flavor of Aristotle's patriarchal model of the household still persists. And it is hard to see how Aristotle can avoid veering into ideal theory when he presumes that the right legislation will suffice to make male citizens virtuous.

Is Aristotle right to assume that autonomous household managers will produce better outcomes than alternative models? Take his argument from virtue. Aristotle holds that since:

1.  generosity and temperance in the use of possessions presupposes private ownership; and
2.  generous and temperate acts are necessary preconditions for happiness;
3.  all citizens should be equipped with private possessions (a household).

But even if we accept the first premise (by itself a contentious claim), and insist that such acts are part of the happy life, it does not follow that the city as a whole will be better off if all male citizens (average as well as exemplary) are equipped with private property. If the citizens aren't *already* temperate or *already* generous (not prone to neglecting their families in the manner of Socrates or drinking in the manner of Alcibiades), how can the state ensure that they won't squander their property, maltreat their wives and slaves, and lay waste to their households?

And regarding premise (1), is private ownership really a precondition for generosity? If children can learn generosity and temperance by doing generous and temperate acts without *owning* their food or the things they give away (a flower, a funny nut), then why not adults? Why should we assume that owning something privately is a precondition for taking pleasure in it or even taking pleasure in using it well? These questions all come down to this: If we subtract the potential costs of private ownership in the real world from its potential benefits, and compare the result with those of Plato's ideal, do Aristotle's policy recommendations seem superior for a community of *actual* people? The answer to this question will depend, in part, on the appropriateness of their respective assumptions about human psychology, the power of laws to shape people's characters, and exactly what form private ownership is supposed to take in a state governed by Aristotle's ideal, but realistic, constitution.

## COMMON USE: PLATONISM BY ANOTHER NAME?

In this section, I will address the last question. It is far from clear what Aristotle's insistence on "private property, common use" entails, and scholars have offered widely different interpretations. Until we understand the fundamentals of Aristotle's proposal, we are not in position to assess its merits relative to Plato's.

While Aristotle certainly champions private ownership, he does not reduce the question of property management to that of ownership. For as I noted, we must also examine whether private property should be privately or commonly *used*. The provision for "common use" complicates the notion of "property" at play in the *Politics*, though it has received little attention. In the *Rhetoric*, Aristotle defines property ownership as "having the power to alienate or dispose of it [property] through either gift or sale" (*Rhet.* I 5, 1361a21–22). How, then, is Aristotle's model of "private ownership, public use" even coherent? If others have a just claim to *use* what I own, then my ownership seems less than robust – at least until the law lays down specific rules for the kind of use that I and others may make of my property. In a city adhering to the principle of "private ownership, public use," I may own a field and the crops that grow in it, but not have exclusive claim to the use of either field or crops. If the use-right of others is identical to my own, then it seems that we are faced with exactly the same evil that private ownership was supposed to combat, namely, neglect through dissolution of care. Why should I care to cultivate my crops if any citizen can help himself to the fruits of my labor? Aristotle speaks favorably of the arrangements in Sparta that allow citizens to enjoy common meals and use of resources when they travel, but it is not clear to what extent and in what specific ways this practice should be implemented.

Taking "public use" to apply indiscriminately to all property, C. D. C. Reeve objects that Aristotle's principle of "private ownership, public use" fails to tackle the problems inherent in Plato's model. The reason is that it simply *is* another version of a system of communal ownership. After all, ownership, by Aristotle's lights, is *defined* with reference to *use*, namely, the (presumably exclusive) right to alienate or dispose of possessions. It would seem to follow that communal use *entails* communal ownership, in which case the familiar problems ensue. On Reeve's interpretation, Aristotle's principle of "private property, public use" is simply Platonism by another name, neither worse nor better equipped to tackle "the present evils in political communities" than the original proposal.

I think it is possible to come to Aristotle's partial defense here. Though underdeveloped, Aristotle's concept of "communal use" does not give blanket permission to any old citizen to use just any of your belongings in just any circumstance, contrary to what Reeve assumes. Nor does Aristotle explain the conception of common use as a *right*, but rather as a privilege bestowed voluntarily by the owner. In defending his model, Aristotle maintains that:

The present practice, provided it was enhanced by virtuous character (*kai epikosmêthen ethesi*) and a system of correct laws (*kai taxei nomôn orthôn*), would be much superior [to communal ownership]. For it would have the good of both – by "of both" I mean of the common ownership of property and of private ownership. For while property should be in one way communal, in general it should be private. For when care for property is divided up, it leads not to those mutual accusations, but rather to greater care being given, as each will be attending to what is his own. *But where use is concerned, virtue will ensure that it is governed by the proverb "friends share everything in common."* (II 5, 1263a22–30, emphasis added)

Aristotle's proposal is that friends and fellow citizens, provided they are virtuous, will allow each other the use of their property through acts of generosity. This could be either small-scale acts, like lending your neighbor a tool, or larger-scale acts, like the major public expenditures undertaken by citizens with the Aristotelian virtue of magnificence (*megaloprepeia*; *NE* IV 2). While Plato quotes the proverb as saying that "friends possess everything in common" (*Rep.* IV, 423e–24a; *Rep.* V, 449c–66d), Aristotle emphasizes that only *virtue* will make this the case (*di'aretên*), and that it only applies to use (*pros to chrêsthai*). It is precisely because the gift belonged to me in the first place that I have the power to alienate or dispose of it. The proposal, then, is not that just any private citizen can help himself to anything in any circumstances, but that virtuous citizens will permit common use of resources in appropriate circumstances through voluntary acts. And that is a far cry from Reeve's free-for-all. It does not, for instance, demand that a citizen give up his possessions in circumstances where his own family will suffer gravely as a consequence. Nor does it allow expropriation of his wealth for any purpose whatsoever. In a state where such use is enshrined in the laws, citizens will still have reason to care for their land and their crops even if the city may demand some of it some of the time. Citizens may even come to realize that "common use" is in their interest as political animals, and contribute willingly.

Why should Aristotle insist that the use of property in a well-ordered state should be common? At this point, we may offer a conjecture. In a well-ordered state, citizens are bound together by a common conception of the good. They promote it through political activity, which realizes their political nature. In participating in political deliberation, they engage in collective agency. Citizens are not individuals negotiating with each other about the distribution of burdens and benefits, for their aim should not be to maximize their private interests, but to promote the common good. But just as individual agents need external goods as the material of virtuous activity, collective agents need external goods as the material for *eupraxia*. If each citizen individually had full discretion over his own property, there could be no political action. Aristotle thinks that political activity is part of a happy life, and so citizens have reason to provide whatever materials are needed for it.

### LITURGIES AND THE PRACTICE OF PHILANTHROPY

Even if we reject Reeve's interpretation, Aristotle's proposal for "common use" is still underdetermined as far as the "voluntary" or "compulsory" nature of contributions is concerned. We may still worry that my "willing" contribution is simply the virtuous acquiescence in what the law anyway requires. Aristotle appears to face a dilemma. Either:

(a) he is proposing voluntary acts of generosity; or

(b) he is proposing non-negotiable "taxes" (contributions to the community required by law) that I may or may not contribute willingly (in the sense of "gladly" or "with pleasure").

If (a), then common use results from voluntary acts of generosity, with no legal repercussions for dodgers. The institution of common use would then be charity writ large. Here, we may turn Reeve's worry on its head: "if private property, public use" boils down to the view that virtuous citizens will provide what the city needs out of the goodness of their hearts, then it seems that we will have no recourse if our fellow citizens are less than virtuous and refuse to provide what the city needs to prosper. In a city ruled by Aristotle's ideal law-giver, citizens would act for the common good, but Aristotle cannot simply stipulate that citizens be generous, for he is in the business of developing laws that take people's real motivations into account. Even well-governed cities include the occasional miser.

Alternatively, (b), we may take Aristotle to mean that the laws mandate that I give up what the city needs, and that the virtue requirement simply points to my willingness to do what I am legally required to do *with pleasure*. Thus, I assent with approval to giving the city what it needs, although it is not really up to me to bestow it as a gift.

If this is Aristotle's view, then it seems that the citizen's virtue is *unnecessary* to ensure that use is common – provided that the city has effective enforcement mechanisms. In such a state, where taxes are mandatory rather than voluntary gifts, a rich household manager might conceivably say to himself, "Next year, I'll be less diligent in my fields, since city officials will apply the profits to public projects anyway, and the rest of my property I will hide" – as Reeve worries. But he may also rest content with retaining a proportion of his surplus. If he has been habituated correctly, he will not display this unjust attitude. He will also realize that by promoting the common good, he is promoting his own greater good as a citizen. Thus, the apparent conflict between private interest and public good rests on a misunderstanding. But Aristotle should not simply assume that habituation will suffice to make a large number of citizens sufficiently virtuous that they will be eager to volunteer for the common good. That, arguably, would be veering too far into ideal theory.

It is not clear, however, whether the principle of "private ownership, public use" that Aristotle defends supports (a) or (b).

Aristotle's ambiguity on this point likely tracks historical developments in Greek city-states in the fourth century BC. The strains that ultimately undid the institution of liturgies in Athens in the fourth century BC illustrate the problems inherent in Aristotle's proposal.[15] Originally, wealthy Athenians were obliged to finance and supervise essential state services, such as equipping and training a chorus (*choregia*) or supervising young men training for torch races (*gymnasiarchia*). They could also be selected for military liturgies, for instance equipping and supervising a warship (a trireme). Benefactors in Athens were picked from a list of "volunteers" by the city's magistrates. Whoever the magistrates thought most able to pay was chosen. The list of "volunteers" contained the names of proper volunteers (self-nominators), as well as names proposed by private citizens or by representatives of the Athenian tribes. If we trust the work of the orators, citizens frequently attempted to evade the view of the magistrates, either because they were in fact unable to fund such costly projects, or because they were unwilling to do so. Many concealed their wealth to avoid having their names included on the list of "volunteers."[16]

Matthew Christ describes the liturgy system as "compulsory philanthropy," remarking that:

Although the model bearer of liturgy was an eager volunteer (*ethelontês*), by the fourth century many, if not most, wealthy men performed liturgies only after being nominated for them. Speakers thus sometimes boast that they not only carried out public service, but even volunteered to do so. Such a claim is intelligible only if a popular audience deemed volunteerism exceptional. The standard terminology that the wealthy employ to refer to public service also suggests that it was in essence regarded as obligatory: to perform a liturgy was to comply with the city's orders (*ta prostattomena*) and to act in accordance with its laws (*nomoi*). [17]

Aristotle's model for "private ownership, public use" takes its cue from the institution of liturgies. But it also inherits the ambiguities inherent in it. Proper enforcement mechanisms would seem better suited for ensuring that wealthy citizens contribute to public projects than a model resting on voluntary acts of beneficence. But once contributions become mandatory, the virtue requirement seems dispensable: whether I pay what I owe depends not on my inherent generosity, but on my being a citizen with certain duties, independent of my pleasure or pain at having to contribute to the public good. Granted, law-givers may still want to instill a sense of civic duty in taxpayers, since the system of taxation would break down in the face of general non-compliance. Threats of punishment lose their power in such a climate. But it still seems that in such a system, it is not virtue that makes property common, but rather the law, aided, perhaps, by virtue. In the *Nicomachean Ethics*, Aristotle praises the magnificent person, who spends large amounts of wealth "gladly and readily" for the sake of the fine, and adds that such expenses include "those that provoke a good competition for honor, for the common good" (*NE* IV 2, 1122b23). At the time Aristotle wrote, the ideal of voluntary public service that Aristotle praises was practically obsolete, about to be replaced by a system of compulsory contributions. It is not uncharitable, then, to read Aristotle's recommendations for "public use" as another example of Aristotle's political theory as the owl of Minerva – he is, in effect, praising a political arrangement that has outlived its role.

Perhaps, however, Aristotle can defend the old arrangement by falling back on his claim that the laws will make citizens virtuous, and argue that the problems in current states are due to their neglect of habituation. This strategy is not without dangers, however. In the *Ethics* and *Politics*, Aristotle recommends that *legislators*, not private citizens, ensure that the citizens receive the right education. To leave such matters in the hands of private citizens would be imprudent, says Aristotle: "Only a Cyclops" – a creature incapable of political community – "lives as he wishes, 'laying down the rules for his children and wife'" (*NE* X 9, 1180a29). To Aristotle's mind it "is difficult for someone to be trained correctly for virtue from his youth unless he has been brought up under correct laws" (*NE* X 9, 1179b32–33). A father's instruction lacks the power to prevail and compel, but the law has this power. Identifying correct laws is the task of political science (*NE* X 9, 1180a21–24). But if Aristotle is right to fear the tragedy of the commons with respect to property, it seems that he has every reason to fear it with respect to education. Why should we think that the city is any better at promoting virtue than it is at owning property? Parity of argument would seem to suggest that the tragedy of the commons is no less a threat when it comes to public education than it is when it comes to public ownership, and this spells trouble for Aristotle's ideal but realistic state.

## WORKS CITED

Annas, J. 1990. "Comments on J. Cooper." In *Aristoteles' Politik*, ed. G. Patzig. Göttingen: Vandenhoeck and Ruprecht

Barnes, J. 1990. "Aristotle and political liberty." In *Aristoteles' Politik*, ed. G. Patzig. Göttingen: Vandenhoeck and Ruprecht

Christ, M. R. 1990. "Liturgy Avoidance and Antidosis in Classical Athens." *Transactions of the American Philological Association* 120: 147–69

   2007. "The Evolution of the eisphora in Classical Athens." *Classical Quarterly* 57: 57–69

Cooper, J. M. 1990. "Political animals and civic friendship." In *Aristoteles' Politik*, ed. G. Patzig. Göttingen: Vandenhoeck and Ruprecht

Dobbs, D. 1985. "Aristotle's Anticommunism." *American Journal of Political Science* 29: 29–46

Finley, M. I. 1977. "Aristotle and economic analysis." In *Aristotle on Aristotle*, vol. II, eds. J. Barnes, M. Schofield and R. Sorabji. London: Duckworth

Foxall, L. 1989. "Household, Gender and Property in Classical Athens." *Classical Quarterly* 39: 22–44

Irwin, T. H. 1988. *Aristotle's First Principles*. Oxford University Press

   1990. "The good of political activity." In *Aristoteles' Politik*, ed. G. Patzig. Göttingen: Vandenhoeck and Ruprecht

   1991. "Aristotle's defense of private property." In *A Companion to Aristotle's Politics*, eds. D. Keyt and F. D. Miller. Oxford: Blackwell

Judson, L. 1997. "Aristotle on Fair Exchange." *Oxford Studies in Ancient Philosophy* 13: 147–75

Mayhew, R. 1993. "Aristotle on Property." *Review of Metaphysics* 46: 802–31

McNeill, D. 1990. "Alternative Interpretations of Aristotle on Exchange and Reciprocity." *Public Affairs Quarterly* 4: 55–68

Meikle, S. 1991. "Aristotle and exchange value." In *A Companion to Aristotle's Politics*, eds. D. Keyt and F. D. Miller. Oxford: Blackwell
    1995. *Aristotle's Economic Thought*. Oxford University Press

Miller, F. D. 1998. "Was Aristotle the First Economist?" *Apeiron* 31: 387–98
    2005. "Property rights in Aristotle." In *Aristotle's Politics: Critical Essays*, eds. R. Kraut and S. Skultety. Lanham, MD: Rowman and Littlefield

Nagle, D. B. 2006. *The household as the foundation of Aristotle's Polis*. Cambridge University Press

Natali, C. 1990. "Aristote et la chrémastique." In *Aristoteles' Politik*, ed. G. Patzig. Göttingen: Vandenhoeck and Ruprecht

Pellegrin, P. 1982. "Monnaie et chrematistique: Remarques sur le mouvement et le contenu de deux textes d'Aristote à l'occasion d'un livre récent." *Revue Philosophique* 4: 631–44

Pomeroy, S. B. 1994. *Xenophon Oeconomicus: A Social and Historical Commentary*. Oxford: Clarendon Press

Reeve, C. D. C. 1998. *Aristotle*, Politics. Indianapolis, IN: Hackett

Saunders, T. J. 1995. *Aristotle*, Politics, *Books I and II, translated with a commentary*. Oxford: Clarendon Press

Schaps, D. 1975. "Women in Greek Inheritance Law." *Classical Quarterly* 25: 53–57

Sedley, D. 1991. "Is Aristotle's Teleology Anthropocentric?" *Phronesis* 2: 179–96

Sorabji, R. 1987. "Comments on J. Barnes." In *Aristoteles' Politik*, ed. G. Patzig. Göttingen: Vandenhoeck and Ruprecht

Stalley, R. F. 1991. "Aristotle's criticism of Plato's Republic." In *A Companion to Aristotle's Politics*, eds. D. Keyt and F. D. Miller. Oxford: Blackwell

NOTES

1. I quote T. H. Irwin's translation of the *Nicomachean Ethics* throughout.
2. Aristotle rejects menial occupations as inappropriate for freeborn men. A leisurely life cannot be preoccupied with necessities, since such activities lack the nobility characteristic of virtue. In the *Eudemian Ethics* (I 5, 1215b26–29), Aristotle states that death is preferable to a life devoted to procuring necessities.
3. Conversely, a city cannot be happy unless the citizens are also happy. "Citizens" here refers to "unqualified" citizens, the subset of men

eligible to participate in deliberative and judicial office (III 1, 1275b17–18). Aristotle criticizes Socrates in the *Republic* for presuming that the city can be happy if the guardians must sacrifice some of their happiness.

4. He divides up the branches of household science with reference to the parts that constitute the household: (1) "mastership" (*despotikê*) is the art of governing slaves; (2) "marital" science (*gamikê*) concerns a husband's rule over his wife; and (3) "procreative" science (*teknopoiêtikê*) concerns the production and rearing of children (I 3). Aristotle recommends that each household have two plots of land, one close to the city and one close to the frontier (VII 10, 1330a10–17). He denies that citizens will be actively engaged in farming – slaves and non-Greek subject-peoples should see to this (VII 9, 1329a25). The well-governed city will also have communal land farmed by communally owned slaves that provides food for the citizens' messes – poor citizens are unlikely to contribute to the messes, but none should go without sustenance. The common lots also produce what is needed for public service to the gods. It follows that Aristotle's model combines the principles "private ownership, common use" and "common ownership, common use" for different parts of property (VII 10, 1330a2–13). For a discussion of Aristotle's conception of the household, see Nagle 2006.

5. See Barnes 1990: 252, who writes, "A clear account of the concept of property is needed in many parts of political theory – not least in Aristotle's own defense of slavery. But Aristotle's view is vague: 'It is better for holdings to be private and for us to make them common in their use' (1263a38; cf. H 10, 1329b41–1330a2). In what sense is this Victoria plum tree my private holding if anyone may use its fruit? Property, as the Romans put it, consists in the right to 'use and abuse' (cf. Pl., *Euthd.* 301E). It is hard to see how private ownership can consist with common use...But Aristotle's remarks in the *Politica* are too nebulous to sustain any serious discussion." Barnes' assessment is echoed by Sorabji 1987: 256, though Sorabji thinks Aristotle is deliberately vague because he does not want to pick out only *one* way in which a plum tree can be private, but its use public: "Given a certain type of community and constitution, the owner might be asked to surrender a *tithe* of his plums for common use."

6. Reeve 1998: lxxviii.

7. Reeve 1998: xxviii.

8. See Irwin 1988: para. 251 for a succinct statement of the problem.

9. See the discussion in Sedley 1991.

10. The passage introduces anthropocentric teleology. Elsewhere, Aristotle typically posits finality in the internal structure and functioning of

individual organisms, but not between organisms. For a controversial defense of other instances of global, anthropocentric teleology in Aristotle, see Sedley 1991.

11. Questions of fair distribution and fair exchange are ethical rather than economic questions; Aristotle treats them in connection with justice in *NE* V. See the discussion in Judson 1997.

12. Though Aristotle recognizes that happiness is unattainable without life's necessities (*aneu gar tôn anankaiôn adunaton kai zên kai eu zên*; I 4, 1253b24–25), he places the bar fairly low: "a truly good and prudent person, we suppose, will bear strokes of fortune suitably, and from his resources at any time will do the finest actions, just as a good general will make the best use of his forces in war and a good shoemaker will make the finest shoe from the hides given to him, and similarly for other craftsmen" (*NE* I 10, 1101a1–7).

13. Witness the merchant Cephalus in *Republic* I, "As for me, I'm satisfied to leave my sons here not less but a little more than I inherited" (330b); see also the discussion in Natali 1990.

14. I do not here have the space to go into the debate between Cooper 1990 and Annas 1990 on the role of friendship in political communities. I find myself sympathetic to Cooper's interpretation.

15. For an account of the institution of liturgies in Athens, see Christ 1990. For an account of developments in the Athenian institution of "*eisphora*," taxes levied on wealthy citizens for specific purposes, see Christ 2007: 57–69.

16. Liturgy avoidance was dissuaded through the institution of "*antidosis*," an appeal procedure through which individual citizens picked for liturgies could decline by demonstrating that the wealth of another citizen exceeded theirs.

17. Christ 1990: 156.

# 4 Natural slavery

Slavery is one of the most widespread social realities in human history. It clearly comes in highly varied forms, as historical anthropologists have found that slaves existed even in stateless societies. But, underlying this diversity, there are three unchangeable properties that define the concept itself: a slave is a forced worker who is his master's *property*; he is *merchandise*; and he is *foreign* to the people who harbor him. The fact that these three characteristics can be found more or less explicitly in the Aristotelian concept of "natural slavery" shows that, however significant the differences between the kind of slavery Aristotle advocates and the kind actually practiced in his time, he is indeed talking about a genuine type of slavery. Thus, it would be inappropriate to try to exonerate Aristotle of all the sins that seem to us to come with slavery, an institution which he well and truly supports. Aristotle was able to observe around him a massive system of slavery, as very many of the inhabitants of Greek cities belonged to the servile class, both in the city and in the surrounding countryside, at least on major farms and within households.[1] This system of slavery was quite deeply integrated into the Greek understanding of the world, as can be seen in the omnipresence of slaves in the cultural products of the time – literary works, visual images, and so on. This did not, however, keep the legitimacy of slavery from becoming the object of a debate about which Aristotle's *Politics* provides some of the most important testimony.

Two preliminary remarks are in order before we begin our study of the Aristotelian conception of slavery itself. Both remarks are based on an article by Malcolm Schofield.[2] I have said elsewhere that I find it obvious that Aristotle's position is *ideological* in the Marxist sense. Schofield objects that Aristotelian doctrine does not meet all of the requirements of an ideology. This, he argues, is because for a theory, belief, or idea to be ideological, it is not enough for it to be in a false relationship to reality, and in the interests of some social group. It is also necessary that the people who accept such mental constructs do not do so on the basis of rational considerations. And Schofield claims that the Aristotelian theory of slavery is built on the internal requirements of Aristotle's philosophy. This disagreement may be largely verbal, but we must nevertheless remember that the Aristotelian theory of slavery is indeed profoundly linked to the rest of Aristotle's philosophy, particularly his ethics and politics – even though, as Schofield emphasizes, his conception of slavery is also sometimes hard to reconcile with other aspects of his work.

This brings us to the second remark. I have argued elsewhere that it is astonishing that Aristotle's analysis of slavery should be more or less the only ancient attempt to give a theoretical treatment of such an important social practice.[3] But I should have added, as indeed Schofield does, that the "treatise on slavery" made up by Chapters 3 to 7 of Book I of the *Politics* does not offer a freestanding analysis of slavery, but rather an auxiliary study meant to shed light on things other than the properties and the nature of servitude. For Aristotle, it amounts mainly to a critique of the view of the Platonists, for whom the city is a big family, and also of the "many people" who think that all power is by nature despotic (VII 2, 1324b32). Indeed, Aristotle insists from the first chapter of the *Politics* onward, that the statesman, the king, the master of slaves, and the head of a family exercise different forms of rule and that they do not differ just because of the number of people ruled, but because they are different *in kind*. The ultimate goal of all of this is to identify an object that is as paradoxical as it is essential to the political philosopher, namely, "a kind of rule exercised over those who are equal and free" (III 4, 1277b7). Slavery, then, acts in the *Politics* as a kind of theoretical foil for the work's central question, the question of *political power*.[4]

As I have said, the text of Book I of the *Politics* clearly bears the traces of an earlier debate on the legitimacy of slavery, one that was no doubt ongoing in Aristotle's time. Without naming names, Aristotle frames this debate with two extreme positions: according to one all slavery is unjust because it deprives humans of their liberty; according to the other, since might makes right, it is always just to enslave those weaker than oneself. The Aristotelian theory of natural slavery certainly provides a way to take a position in this debate, but Aristotle does not by any means offer an objective and/or normative analysis of the kind of slavery that existed in his time. This means that after reading his "treatise on slavery," we still do not really know what Aristotle thinks about the slavery of his time: which forms of it are more and which less acceptable, how slaves should be treated, and so on.[5] This is not to say that Aristotle is unaware of the problems he would have to address in order to treat slavery on its own terms. Such a study would require a distinction between several kinds of slaves (III 4, 1277a37), just as studies of constitutions require sorting those into several kinds. Finally, we should observe that the Aristotelian analysis sometimes enlarges the field of slavery. It does so, for example, when it explains that for barbarians all relations of power are relations of servitude (I 2, 1252b6), or that the climate in Asia inclines people to slavery (VII 7, 1327b28). The concepts of the slave and of slavery are therefore diluted, and no longer contain the essential characteristics of the slave which we saw at the beginning of this chapter. This is what many philosophers did after Aristotle, and no doubt before him too, for example in discussing the moral slavery of the vicious.

CONCEPT OF SLAVERY

In a well-known article, Victor Goldschmidt shows that in Book I of the *Politics*, far from starting with observations about the phenomenon of slavery, Aristotle first develops the concept of slavery (in Chapter 4), and only later asks (at the beginning of Chapter 5) "whether anyone is really like that by nature or not" (I 5, 1254a17).[6] It is in the following chapter that Aristotle turns to the debate that was taking place in his time on the legitimacy of slavery, before moving on, in Chapter 7, to the question of the "art of rule" (if any) that the master should possess in order to be a master. Finally, he comes back to slavery in the last chapter of Book I, where he asks about the *virtue* of each of the members of the various relationships of subordination that constitute the family, that is, the relationship between husband and wife, father and child, and master and slave. We would expect Aristotle to start with a survey of the views of his predecessors on the problem he is examining, especially since he himself acknowledges in Chapter 6 that these opinions exist. This departure from Aristotle's standard practice may be a kind of confirmation that he doesn't think of himself as taking up the question of slavery, properly speaking, nor of addressing it in the way he addresses questions when he considers them in earnest.

Before he even starts to develop his conception of slavery, Aristotle makes theoretical room for the concept, starting from the three relationships that make up the family. Chapter 3 comes back to the results of the preceding chapter, which is one of the most famous texts in the Aristotelian corpus. One of the main points in that text (Chapter 2) is that the most basic natural community is the *family* (*oikia*), which exists for the sake of satisfying two fundamental needs, namely, reproduction and preservation. Now, the satisfaction of these needs presupposes a relationship between certain agents who, first, "cannot exist without each other" (I 2, 1252a26) and, second, have hierarchical relationships – that is, relationships of rule. The domination of a slave by a master in natural slavery is just one instance of a hierarchical structure that embraces "nature as a whole" (I 5, 1254a31), the functioning of which requires the cooperation of elements hierarchically ordered with respect to each other, a pattern that extends even to non-natural phenomena like harmony. In reproduction, which individuals experience as necessary because "the urge to leave behind something of the same kind as themselves is natural" (I 2, 1252a29), the relevant hierarchical relationship is that between a man and a woman. As for "preservation" (*sôtêria*), this presupposes the cooperation of a ruler and a person who is ruled, and that cooperation is required by nature. On reading Chapter 2, we get the impression that the only hierarchical relationship needed to account for preservation is that between master and slave (cf. I 2, 1252a30–34).

This point, while it might seem minor, is in fact important. It is obvious that in fact many other factors contribute to preservation, but as some commentators have pointed out, in offering the account of the birth of the city Aristotle is not engaged in a historical study, nor does he describe any socio-historical reality. Rather, he delivers a conceptual analysis, as Rousseau would do later when he described a state of nature which he doubted had ever existed, or ever would. Clearing theoretical space for the concept of the slave amounts to the following: not *describing* the factors that can contribute to the preservation of the family, which are necessarily diverse and disparate, but showing that nature, which "does nothing in vain," has foreseen a special relationship to satisfy this need. Within this description of natural dependence which contributes to mutual preservation, which Aristotle already refers to as the relationship between master and slave (I 2, 1252a32, 34), he gradually adds content to the notion of the "slave." Thus, lines 1252a30–34 explain that mastery and slavery are naturally just when they are based on distinct, complementary natural capacities. The power of the master, when he is a natural master, belongs to him because he is naturally suited to "foresee in thought" the tasks that the slave is naturally capable of performing. From this *natural* complementarity, there follows one of the most important properties belonging to the relationship between master and slave, a property that is a consequence of the naturalness of the relationship and at the same time reveals that naturalness, namely, that servitude is advantageous to both parties.

To upset this hierarchy is to cause harm. Likewise, in many people the emotional part of the soul rules the intellectual part, or is equal with it; in these cases, Aristotle says, this equality or reversal is "harmful to all the parts of the soul" (I 5, 1254b9). But are such reversals of equality even possible in relationships of servitude? The slave certainly cannot take the master's place, since he is unable to plan the work that must be done. As for the master, he certainly is not incapable of doing the work, but it would be harmful to him for several reasons of varying importance. First, it would divert him from the activities that necessarily fall to him, namely, philosophy and politics (a point to which we will return); this risks damaging him ethically, since virtue springs from practice (cf. VIII 2, 1337b11–14). Second, and more importantly, we must bear in mind the link that Aristotle establishes between the relationship of slavery and the goals of nature (as we will again recall this link when we get to the crucial question of common advantage). The relationship of servitude is the structure destined by nature to "preserve" the family, and it is not appropriate that a function should be accomplished by something that is not naturally designed to accomplish it, or that a natural capacity should remain unused. A passage from Book III of the *Politics* (III 4, 1277b3) is instructive about this point of view, even if its interpretation remains controversial: manual work, Aristotle says, "should not be learned by a good person, nor by a statesman, nor by a good citizen, except perhaps to satisfy some personal need of his own (for then it is no longer a case of one person becoming master and the other slave)." This undoubtedly means, for example, that when we work with our hands to meet our immediate needs or for pleasure, the distinction between master and slave is no longer relevant. But this brings us some distance from the "preservation" of the family. An activity is thus not naturally servile *in itself*, but only when it is inserted into the relationship between master and natural slave with regard to a certain goal, namely, preservation. Thus "it is noble even for free young men to perform many of the tasks that are held to be appropriate for slaves. For the difference between noble and shameful actions does not lie so much in the acts themselves as in their ends, on that for the sake of which they are performed" (VII 14, 1333a7).

The concept of the slave, as it is developed in Chapter 4 of Book I of the *Politics*, is constructed in several stages, which in the end yield a text that is hard to understand. The slave is immediately defined as a living tool that is one of the goods necessary for the life of a family. Aristotle ends this passage with the comment, which has been the object of much discussion, that slavery is necessary because shuttles do not weave by themselves, nor do picks play the lyre alone. Here, Aristotle seems to take a position that might be shared by all slave-holders, and that treats slavery as a necessary evil. Some have suggested that, for Aristotle, it is possible to imagine, at least at the level of fiction, alternatives to slavery: technological inventions that could reduce, if not eliminate, the need for slaves.[7] This is contrary to the Aristotelian approach, for even in a completely automated society, there would nevertheless remain natural masters and slaves, each with an interest in slavery that is not merely economic but, as we will see, ethical.

This instrumental approach to slavery is all the more inadequate, if not fallacious, considering that Aristotle immediately goes on to an analysis denying slaves the status of tools, properly speaking. The line of thought behind this argument can be formalized with two syllogisms: (Ia) "a piece of property is a tool for maintaining life" (I 4, 1253b31); (Ib) "a slave is a piece of animate property" (I 4, 1253b32); (Ic) the slave is a tool for maintaining life (implicit conclusion); (IIa) = (Ic), (IIb) "life consists in *praxis*" (I 4, 1254a7), (IIc) slaves "are assistants in the class of things having to do with action"

(I 4, 1254a8). Moreover, since Aristotle opposes production and *praxis* in this chapter, thereby refusing to make the slave an instrument of production, some have suggested that he thinks the slave is what we call a "domestic servant," dedicated to "household chores."[8] In fact, Aristotle's position is both stronger and more unusual than this, at least from a contemporary perspective.

The difference between action (*praxis*) and production (*poiêsis*) is precisely that the latter produces something "beyond the use of it" (I, 1254a2), and the tools dedicated to these two activities therefore differ in the same way. For example, a shuttle is a tool dedicated to production, but from a coat or a bed we draw nothing except its use. The things Aristotle calls *ktêmata* (a term poorly rendered as "possessions") are goods that allow us to carry out our lives within the family; they belong, he says, to the sphere of action. The slave is one of those things. All of these arguments converge on a quasi-biological approach to the slave characterized as *part* of his master, admittedly "a sort of living but separate part of his body" (I, 1255b11), but a part nevertheless. Let us note that this strongly (re)integrates the slave into the family, since the other relationships that make up the family also exhibit this characteristic of fused life. This holds as much for marriage, in which the partners make up "a single flesh," as for the relationship between a father and the children who are "flesh of his flesh." From this point of view, my jacket is also part of me in so far as it, unlike a shuttle, extends my body. The slave is therefore a *practical* and not a productive agent, because he belongs as an organ (and here it is certainly better to translate *organon* as "organ" than as "tool") to the life of his master. In this, he is like all the other members of the family, who are in a sense parts of a single body. This in no way means that the slave cannot have a productive function: a hand can have one too, and it is likely that "preservation" as Aristotle conceives it involves slaves taking charge of many productive tasks.

This gives the *possession* of a slave a distinctive character. We have seen that the fact that the slave is the property of another man is one of the defining traits of slavery. And from this point of view as well, Aristotle's natural slavery is a true form of slavery. At I 4, 1254a14, he announces that anyone who "is by nature not his own but someone else's is a natural slave; and he is someone else's when, in spite of being human, he is a piece of property." He repeats this claim at I 5, 1254b21 by saying that the slave is "he who belongs to someone else."[9] In fact, this "piece of property" is not only closely linked to its owner, but the latter cannot do without him, without being at risk of losing his status as the head of a family. Indeed, later on we will see that the master needs the slave rather more than the slave does the master. Under these circumstances, we might ask if it is possible for the master to *sell* his slave, one of the essential prerogatives of actual systems of slavery. If we set aside the easy case of a vicious and disobedient slave from whom the master receives no benefit, it seems that it would be more difficult for the master to sell his natural slave in the system of natural slavery as Aristotle conceived it than it was in the system that existed in Greece. Nevertheless, it remains that in insisting that the slave is a *separate* part of his master, Aristotle retained the possibility that he might be sold. Moreover, Aristotle refers to the commercialization of slaves by means of an allusion to a slave market where "well-born" people might be found if slavery were grounded in force (I 6, 1255a28), and in his failure to develop this idea, there is no doubt further proof that he does not mean to address the question of slavery in itself, at least not as a historian or a sociologist.

Two conditions must therefore be in place if natural slavery is to exist. For one, the master and slave must "deserve" their stations (I 6, 1255b14; VII 14, 1333b40), and we will see below what that means for the slave. So far, we have established that a person who is "capable of rational foresight" is not a natural slave. But he obviously can be a slave in the Greek system of slavery, a system founded on the risk of capture. For another, master and slave must have a "shared life" (I 13, 1260a40), and this relationship cannot exist with other subordinates. Thus, for Aristotle, there is no slavery outside the family, since that is the only place where this "fusion" is possible. At III 5, 1278a11, he introduces this distinction: "those who perform necessary tasks for an individual are slaves; those who perform them for a community are vulgar craftsmen and hired labourers." This runs counter to the social practice attested by public slaves. The immediate sequel to the passage from I 13 that was just cited goes even further, for Aristotle says there that a free worker experiences a sort of "delimited slavery" (I, 1260b1), and he makes the following astonishing remark: "virtue pertains to him to just the same extent that slavery does" (I 13, 1260a40). This means that when he is in a position to collaborate with someone who foresees for him, the worker ultimately has the status of a slave – even if this is to a lesser degree, since he lacks the intimacy that develops between the master and the slave who live together continuously, which allows Aristotle to attribute *friendship* to them. Thus, working for others confers on the manual worker a *virtue* that he does not possess when he is not in this servile state. It follows that for Aristotle, it is better to be a slave than a manual worker, because as a slave a person can exercise a certain excellence full-time, by participating in a natural task which the free laborer only undertakes in his working hours. Thus, the laborer is unable to "engage in virtuous pursuits" (III 5, 1278a20) by himself. And in Aristotle's eyes the fact that manual labor can bring about wealth – "most craftsmen become rich" (III 5, 1278a24) – does nothing to make up for this; quite the opposite, since this class of wealthy people who do not deserve to be free uses its freedom to exercise undue power in the city, forming a politically dangerous private interest group.

Aristotle's distinctive way of restricting slavery to the domestic sphere radically distinguishes his conception from the system of slavery that existed in the Greece of his time, even though a large majority of the slaves there were owned by the heads of families, and even though a non-negligible number of them had their activities restricted to the home. Aristotle's conception might be closer to what anthropologists call "lineage slavery."[10] Against the claims of Marxist-style history, which finds the true origin of oppression in the simultaneous birth of antagonistic social classes and a state apparatus ruling in the interests of the dominant class, these anthropologists have shown that in fact even stateless societies contain the extreme form of exploitation of man by man that is slavery. Foreigners, having been captured, or more often sold by their people for penal reasons, are assigned to lineages that use them as workers while keeping them apart from normal lineage relationships. Their servile status is marked in several ways that distinguish it from other kinds of dependence: they have no access to legitimate marriage (which by no means suggests that their sexual relations, including relations outside of their class, are not tolerated; indeed, toleration of such relationships allows them to have descendents, among other things); they have symbolic names indicating their subjection; they are excluded from political and religious life; they incur distinct and generally degrading forms of punishment; and after death, their bodies are not treated in the same way or buried in the same places as those of the free. In such systems, there are only small numbers of slaves relative to the free population, which prevents slavery from being the main source of tension in the society that harbors it.[11] Moreover, lineage slavery uses a process that assimilates slaves into the heart of the lineages that own them, as the children of slaves may be integrated into these lineages by taking part in the legitimate marriage that was forbidden to their parents and grandparents.[12]

It must be repeated that this kind of lineage slavery is a genuine form of slavery, even if it seems "gentler" than certain other forms that servility takes in slave-based modes of production – we might think, for example, of the lives of the forced workers in the true death-by-work camps that were the mines of Laurion. For lineage slavery is a social system in which human beings, reduced to the condition of merchandise, are appropriated so that the fruits of their labor may be taken from them. Indeed, Aristotle recognizes that the form of slavery that he declares "natural" rests on force: "the art of acquiring slaves ... is a kind of warfare or hunting" (I 7, 1255b37). The legislator must even take steps to train citizens in war so that they may become "masters of those who deserve to be slaves" (VII 14, 1333b37). In fact, the differences between lineage slavery as a historical reality and Aristotle's natural slavery are more revealing than their similarities. The most important of these differences is that in the lineage system, slavery develops within lineages because there is no state to organize and control the phenomenon; by contrast, in Aristotle's system, slavery is *kept outside of the institutions of the state* for one powerful reason, the same one we have been considering: that the relationship of power between master and slave is not based on political power, which is fundamentally power exercised by and over equals. A second difference is that in Aristotelian slavery, even if the descendents of slaves may also be called into their lineage as free members, this will be for *ethical* reasons, and not only because of the passage of time. We will see, however, that on closer examination this second difference loses some of its bite.

Once he has developed the concept of the slave – as a human being who can, and therefore should, be annexed to a master because both share the common task of "preservation," to which each brings to bear different natural capacities – Aristotle states that there exist people who instantiate this concept. At this point, the debate on the legitimacy of *the principle* of slavery, which Aristotle himself reports took place in his time, is settled:

There is a certain mutual benefit and mutual friendship for such masters and slaves as deserve to be by nature so related. When their relationship is not that way, however, but is based on law, and they have been subjected to force, the opposite holds. (I 6, 1255b13)

We must, then, identify the characteristics which cause an individual to *deserve* the status of a slave. These characteristics are, on the one hand, natural and unrelated to circumstance, since the people who are natural slaves are so "right from birth" (I 5, 1254a23), and not, for example, as a result of imprudence (as in capture by pirates) or bad behavior (as when a person is sold because of his debts). But they are also, on the other hand, based on psychological characteristics in the Aristotelian sense, which is to say traits that are related to *ethical* properties. Consider several passages from Book I of the *Politics*.

In what seems to us a very harsh passage, Aristotle declares that "in the use of them" there is not much difference between slaves and domestic animals (I 5, 1254b24). The difference between slaves and animals is a matter of rationality, in that animals "obey not reason but feelings" (I 5, 1254b23).[13] As for the natural slave – and Aristotle certainly seems to treat this characteristic as a distinctive trait of natural slavery – he "shares in reason to the extent of understanding it, but he does not have it himself" (I 5,1254b22). To understand the significance of this difficult passage, which deserves extended commentary, we must recall one of Aristotle's characteristic theoretical habits, which consists of bringing to bear only the theoretical apparatus required by his topic. Several times in the *Politics*, Aristotle refers to a summary description of the human soul that has led some commentators to assign those texts to an early period, before Aristotle developed the complex psychology of his "maturity."[14] That slaves "do not possess reason" must be understood with some qualifications, since Aristotle makes strictly the opposite claim in Chapter 13: "Those who deny reason to slaves, but tell us to give them orders only, are mistaken" (I 13, 1260b5).

The solution to this distinctly Aristotelian aporia – slaves do not have reason in one sense, but they do have it in another – is provided in Chapter 13 of *Politics* I. Aristotle expresses his solution as follows: when it comes to the subordinate members of the various relationships that make up the family, namely, the woman, the child, and the slave, "while the parts of the soul [i.e. those present in free adult men] are present in all these people, they are present in different ways" (I 13, 1260a10). This means that, like all animals, the slave obviously has the vegetative, sensitive, and moving parts of the soul; but he also has the rational part, although this may lack certain functions present in the perfect human being, and have certain other functions otherwise disposed, or in a less developed state than the latter. Thus, "the deliberative part of the soul is entirely missing from a slave; a woman has it, but it lacks authority; a child has it but it is incompletely developed" (I 13, 1260a12). In due course, we will return to this fundamental point. Crucially, the result of this situation is that everyone, including slaves, has a share of the ethical virtues, but in different ways, considering that only he who is naturally suited to command, and who is therefore *a fortiori* a free, male adult, possesses "virtue of character complete" (I 13, 1260a17). We must therefore understand that there are versions of temperance, courage, and justice proper to the slave just as there are versions proper to women (I 13, 1260a20), and that these virtues are those that allow the slave, and also the woman and the child, the excellent performance of the task that falls to each of them.

As Schofield points out, it is hard to reconcile Aristotle's theory of slavery with certain well-established Aristotelian doctrines. He points out the following contradiction: How can we designate one and the same person both as "human" and as a "slave"? A different point will be especially important to us: How can we attribute *virtue* to someone to whom we deny the faculty of deliberation? We must first of all refuse to answer in terms of quasi-homonymy. Even if he seems to suggest this approach when he declares that the slave "needs only a small amount of virtue – just so much as will prevent him from inadequately performing his tasks" (I 13, 1260a35), Aristotle is not here considering the possibility that a slave has virtue in the same way as a horse or a knife; rather, in this text, the virtue in question is *ethical virtue*. That a child has only a potential virtue, and that a woman only has it without "authority" (whatever that might mean) does not prevent them from developing ethical virtue, but how is this possible for someone who in no way (*hólos*; I 13,

1260a1) has that faculty? It is true that we can infer that the slave does not have ethical goodness in the "strong sense" (*kuriôs*) of those with practical wisdom (*NE* VI 13, 1144b31; cf. below), but that does not really answer the question. He who is unable to deliberate is therefore unable to decide, which effectively bars him from ethical life.[15] This, finally, is what Aristotle is recognizing when he declares that slaves have no part in happiness, which is the end of the ethical life: there exists no city made up of slaves or animals "because these share neither in happiness nor in a life guided by deliberative choice" (III 9, 1280a32; cf. *NE* X 6,1177a8).

In fact, Aristotle briefly but clearly answers the question of the ethical virtue of slaves. At I 13, 1260a32–33, he announces that the virtue distinctive of the slave is relative not to him but to his master. This analysis must be combined with the claims considered earlier according to which the slave is a part of his master and participates in reason only in so far as he perceives it in his master. The master and the slave have a division of psychological and ethical labor. It is this that allows Aristotle to say several times that the relationship between master and slave is analogous to that between soul and body.[16] Furthermore, "the soul rules the body with the rule of a master" (I 5, 1254b4). Like all ethical beings, the slave (to use the superficial psychology that we find in the *Politics*) does indeed submit his inclinations to the rule of reason, but he submits them *to the reason of his master*. What it means to follow the admonitions of the master (cf. I 13, 1260b6) is precisely to comply with the reason of the master, in the sense that "the cause of such virtue in a slave must be the master" (I 13, 1260b3). The same goes for the slave's lack of a deliberative faculty. Unable to deliberate on his own, the slave is unable to choose; in particular, he is unable to choose what is good for him. As a result, he needs someone to do this for him. It must be added that, unlike children, who must learn to deliberate – because they possess an "imperfect" deliberative faculty, which is to say one that is at the moment not yet developed – the slave must get assistance all his life from someone who decides for him. If, as Aristotle says several times, "it is not possible to be good in the strict sense without practical wisdom (*phronêsis*), nor practically wise without moral virtue" (*NE* VI 13, 1144b31, trans. Ross), then Marguerite Deslauriers is correct to write that "natural subjects acquire virtue by borrowing the *phronêsis* of a natural ruler."[17] Here, then, we find that

Aristotle understands servile relations as the organic unity of master and slave, taken to the extreme length that allows the one to lend reason to the other. Granted the irredeemable imperfection of his nature, the presence of a master who deliberates and decides in his place is therefore beneficial to the slave. Most interpreters think that for the slave this is a matter of survival.

### SLAVERY IS ADVANTAGEOUS FOR THE MASTER AS WELL AS THE SLAVE

Even without re-introducing the problem of whether or not Aristotle's theory of natural slavery is ideological, we can hardly avoid noticing that it is a constant of ideological discourse to claim that the oppressed ultimately have an interest in their own oppression. Aristotle, in any case, mostly avoids this tendency by recognizing without difficulty that the relationship between master and slave is for the advantage of the master "and only coincidentally for that of the slave" (III 6, 1278b35). And the comparison he develops after this passage is illuminating: unlike a master, a father exercises his power essentially (*kath'hauto*; III 6, 1278b39) for the sake of his child, just as doctors essentially practice their art to benefit their patients, and only accidentally benefit from it themselves. But what exactly does it mean that the relationship of servitude is only *accidentally* beneficial to the slave?

In the rightly constituted city, as Aristotle conceives it, the family must perform certain functions necessary for the city, and in the interest of the city. This is a fundamental disagreement with Plato, who wanted to re-absorb the domestic sphere into the political sphere. Here too, we may find the essential difference between Plato and Aristotle indicated earlier: the relationships between fellow citizens and those between the members of a family are not governed by the same kind of rule. Furthermore, recognition of this distinction must work in both directions – it is just as much contrary to nature to want to govern the city like a (big) family as it is to want to have political power over one's wife, children, and slaves. The family must maintain its own logic, on the condition that its goals do not overcome those of the city. The hierarchical relationships that structure the family have consequences, two of which are particularly important for the city. First, the family is the place where future citizens are produced, and even if, according to Aristotle, the city has something to say about the education of children, there is no question of its taking the family's place in performing this task. Second, the economic organization of the family tends to satisfy the needs of its members while relieving its most eminent members, namely, the citizens, of material tasks. The *Politics* even advises that the head of the family should delegate responsibility for directing slaves to a steward so that he can devote himself to the activities worthy of him, politics and philosophy (I 7, 1255b35).

To fulfill these executive functions, which free citizens from work that is superfluous for them, slavery is legitimate, just so long as there exist human beings who are ethically such that they may be considered natural slaves. And it turns out that such beings exist, and will undoubtedly exist forever. On this topic, there is a well-known chapter of the *Politics* (VII 7) that offers a theory of climate that is anything but original. The idea that a region's climate moulds the character of the people who live there seems to have been shared by many Greeks, and we can find versions in Plato as well as in the Hippocratic treatise *On Water, Air, and Places*. Aristotle uses this theory to show that only the Greeks can hope to live in cities, for the barbarians of the West, who are brave but stupid because of their cold environment, and the barbarians of the East, who are clever but cowardly because they live in warmer climates, cannot do so. Indeed, intelligence is not enough to protect one from slavery, for "people who are unable to face danger courageously are the slaves of their attackers" (VII 15, 1334a21). What Aristotle here presents as a *fact* takes on considerable theoretical significance. This is, first of all, because the Aristotelian theory of natural slavery is inscribed into an understanding of the universe that is itself also Aristotelian. In effect, the organization of the world presented in this chapter of the *Politics* shows that in placing human beings unable to live in cities on the peripheries of the Greek world, nature in its goodness created, in a certain way, reservoirs of natural slaves. The text then gives us the resources to cast some light on what has been said above about the inferiority of natural slaves. Book VII, Chapter 7 of the *Politics* also leads us to another conclusion, namely, that the slave, whether he is stupid or cowardly, will little by little lose his characteristics once he is removed from his original climate (or if he does not, his descendants will). Thus, we may find in Aristotle's theory of slavery a feature of lineage slavery, namely, its tendency to integrate the descendants of slaves into their lineage after a certain period of time. But for Aristotle this is because time has ethical effects.

We must certainly suppose that the determinism of climate invoked here is not strict, for Aristotle surely does not think that all the inhabitants of Asia Minor are natural slaves, to say nothing of the *Greeks* living in Asia Minor. This chapter gives one of the causes of the natural tendency these people have for being slaves. Even though Aristotle's analysis of the concept of slavery does not include the characteristic of not being Greek, it can be seen that nature itself, in its great wisdom, tends to ensure by means of climate that natural slaves are barbarians, thus restoring to Aristotelian slavery one of the characteristics of all slavery, namely, that it reduces foreigners to servitude, as we saw at the beginning.[18] At the same time, we may observe that the inability to deliberate characteristic of slaves is not necessarily an effect of stupidity. When Aristotle writes that Asians "have souls endowed with intelligence and craft knowledge" (*dianoêtika kai technika tên psychên*; VII 7, 1327b26), we must certainly give these terms their full meaning. After all, Aristotle was not at all unaware of the scientific and technical accomplishments of certain barbarian peoples, and the Greek collective memory was likewise full of their military exploits.[19] Moreover, he would have had to recognize that at least the Asian, and perhaps also Western, barbarians had the ability to reason and to foresee, and even, no doubt, to display some kind of *phronêsis*, even though the texts do not say so. After all, Aristotle attributes a form of *phronêsis* to certain animals.[20] More generally, there is no shortage of texts in which Aristotle denies reason to animals, denies them ethical virtue and, *a fortiori*, denies them practical wisdom,[21] but it is a no less well-established position of Aristotle's that animals nevertheless have "traces" (*ichnê*) of human rational and ethical states.[22] But as Jean-Louis Labarrière says in an article on this topic, in spite of all the shared features of human and animal *phronêsis*, especially a certain relationship to experience and to time, since animal *phronêsis* cannot rely on either judgment or deliberation, "it does not preside over any *praxis*."[23]

This brings us back once more to the relationship between slaves and deliberation.[24] For Aristotle, the two main aspects of deliberation are, first, that it bears on things that depend on us (we do not deliberate about the orbit of heavenly bodies) and, second, that it determines means to a given end. But as Aristotle himself says several times, it is not the same thing for a person to deliberate about "what is good and expedient for himself, not in some particular respect, e.g. about what sorts of thing conduce to health or to strength," as it is to deliberate about "what sorts of thing conduce to the good life in general" (*NE* VI 5, 1140a25, trans. Ross). Here we encounter the opposition between technical deliberation, which is a capacity for reasoning, and the ethical form of deliberation that is not restricted to finding the means to an end but also directs those means toward an ethical good. We may ask ourselves how best to conduct a military campaign both at the general level of the commander as well as at the level of the ordinary solider, but the virtuous deliberation of the brave has a different nature than either of these, since brave people act in view of the good – courage is a good – and this end is dictated to them by their virtue itself.[25] Heath very rightly notes that in this regard there is a difference between children and slaves: children are incapable of all deliberation; but the slave, unless he is unable to deliberate as the result of a mental defect that prevents him from grasping the means needed to achieve an end, is capable of technical but not ethical deliberation. It is this latter kind of deliberation that is, in fact, true deliberation for Aristotle, and it is what allows him to say that while he can foresee, the slave "in no way" (*holôs*; I 13, 1260a12) has the ability to deliberate, as we have seen. However intelligent and capable he may be, natural slaves therefore lack the ability to *choose* – it must be remembered that choice depends on deliberation – actions that might direct him toward an ethically good life. As Aristotle says in the passage from the *Nicomachean Ethics* cited above, this incapacity is ultimately caused by the lack of a virtuous *hexis* in the natural slave.[26]

But there remains a crucial point to consider. Is it true, as all commentators say, that the slave has an interest in his servile condition because he would not survive if he were left to his own devices, which seems to be the case for children? We must now show that this approach is certainly wrong.

Indeed, it seems that for Aristotle it is the master who cannot survive without his slave. After the passage from *Politics* III 6 cited earlier, in which he recognizes that the relationship between master and slave is essentially for the benefit of the master, Aristotle adds:

"rule by a master cannot be preserved if the slave is destroyed" (III 6, 1278b36). This seems to mean that the master needs the slave to live his master's life, which is only the case because, indeed, shuttles do not weave by themselves. But how much does the slave need the master? We must therefore address this crucial question: Could the slave survive without his master?

When Schofield, in agreement with practically all other interpreters, writes that "they [slaves] need someone else to deliberate on their behalf if they are to survive," he expresses a claim that, if it were true, would also lead to a contradiction with other Aristotelian positions.[27] After giving as an example the hierarchical relationship, beneficial to both parties, that holds between the passionate part of the soul and the intellect, Aristotle gives a second example: it is better for animals to be ruled by human beings, which means that "domestic animals are by nature better than wild ones, and it is better for all of them to be ruled by human beings, since this will preserve their safety (sôtêria)" (I 5, 1254b10–13). It is worth noting that Aristotle does not restrict his remarks to tame, domesticated animals, but says that for the others too (that is, for wild animals) it is better to be ruled by human beings. But it might well seem that the less humans interfere with wild animals, the better they are, since in Aristotle's time there was no need to try to protect species from human activity by making them reproduce in captivity. Moreover, it is not true that domesticated animals need humans to survive, since, as we learn in the *History of Animals* (I 1, 488a30, trans. Thompson), "whenever a race of animals is found domesticated, the same is always to be found in a wild condition; as we find to be the case with horses, swine, men, sheep, goats, and dogs." I have argued elsewhere that in his biological works Aristotle analyzes the perfection of a living organism in two ways.[28] Each animal species bears within itself the conditions for its own perfection, which ensure that it will survive eternally, granted appropriate living conditions. Thus, it is part of the camel's perfection that it has a hard palate, since the food to which it has access is spiny (*PA* III 14, 674b2). We might imagine that in the case of domesticated animals, their submission to human goals is part of their nature, and perhaps that is the main reason that their nature is said to be "better" than that of wild beasts (I 5, 1254b10). By contrast, it is doubtful that Aristotle thinks that submission to human ends is part of the nature of wild animals that are impossible to tame. But there is also a kind of perfection of animals that is determined by the degree to which they resemble the most perfect among them, the human being. Indeed, Aristotle declares, the human being is "natural in a higher degree than the other animals" (*IA* 4, 706a19, trans. Farquharson; cf. 5, 706b10). It is undoubtedly this kind of perfection which is at play in the passage from *Politics* I 5, which cannot be fully understood unless we go one step further. When we consider the shared work of a natural ruler and a natural subordinate who, together, make up an organic unity – even one built out of separate members, as in the relationship of slavery – whatever might be to the *individual* advantage of the ruled part dissolves, as it were, into the advantage of the whole. This can be seen clearly in the passage from *Politics* I 5 that discusses the relationship between the soul and the body. If it is true that "it is natural and beneficial for the body to be ruled by the soul" (I 5, 1254b6), we have left behind the direct advantage of the body (which is, let's say, pleasure) and, therefore, the advantage in question belongs to the whole made up of soul and body, which is in the end the advantage of the soul.

It is the sequel to the passage from the *Eudemian Ethics* cited earlier that expresses this situation most clearly. In the relations between master and slave, as in those between soul and body, master and slave "are not two, but the former is one and the latter a part of that one, not one itself; nor is the good divisible between them, but that of both belongs to the one for whose sake they exist" (VII 9, 1241b20, trans. Rackham). To be naturally ruled is also, for the party who is ruled, to achieve a kind of perfection other than the perfection that belongs to its own nature, by participating in a task that belongs to whatever rules it. Aristotle goes even further, saying that the perfection proper to the thing ruled participates in the perfection of the relationship of rule: "the better the ruled are, the better the rule over them always is; for example, rule over humans is better than rule over beasts" (I 5, 1254a25). It is therefore in the ruler's interest that the thing or person ruled should be as good as possible. That is – since here we are dealing with relative perfection – what is ruled must, in ethical value, be as much like the ruler as possible. So we cannot say that for an animal it is naturally better to serve human ends than to serve its own ends, except from two points of view: from the point of view of the "user" – it is natural for human beings to use the tools that they find in nature, and especially animals, in order to satisfy their needs – and from the point of view of nature as a whole rather than the animal's particular nature. The same goes for slaves.

The fact that the inferior is naturally in the position of an organ in relation to the superior, which is the case for the natural slave, even when this situation is not inscribed in its own nature, has several consequences. First, there are degrees of naturalness such that human goals are "more natural" than the goals of other animals, and that the goals of a virtuous person are "more natural" than those of his slave. This allows us to interpret Aristotle's brief remarks at 1254b22–24: animals do not have reason, but they can act rationally, at least in a sense, when they follow the rational prescriptions of human beings. We have seen that the same thing goes for slaves, about whom we may say that they possess reason in a sense because it has been delegated to them. This rational conduct caused by another is therefore "more natural." Next, this double-norm of perfection – with regard to oneself and with regard to nature as a whole – illuminates the famous passage in the *Politics* that is often taken to reveal a "providentialist" position in Aristotle: "We must suppose ... that plants are for the sake of animals, and that the other animals are for the sake of human beings" (I 8, 1256b16). It is natural for tigers to eat people, and because of this, *and from the tiger's point of view*, "people exist for tigers." But from the point of view of human nature and nature as a whole (in which human beings are "more according to nature" than tigers) tigers exist for the sake of human beings.

At last, we may be better equipped to return to the problem of *preservation*. It seems doubtful that Aristotle could maintain that human beings naturally suited to servitude would need masters for survival, as children, for example, need their parents. After all, barbarians are servile by nature (cf. I 2, 1252b6; VII 7, 1327b28), and they survive perfectly well. What is preserved in the relation of slavery is the community of master and slave, and it is this that is advantageous to both parties. For the master, the benefit is not hard to see. For the slave, the benefit is to take part, by means of capacities that he does not possess by himself – namely, the reason that the master in a sense lends to him, and especially the complete ethical virtue of the master – in a task whose performance exceeds his own excellence. This is the source of a modest correction that we can bring to the claim that slaves have no access to happiness: "No one assigns to a slave a share in happiness – unless he assigns to him also a share in human life" (NE X 6, 1177a8, trans. Ross), the "life" in question undoubtedly being best understood as the ethical life of a free man. Thus, in the relation of slavery, the slave takes part in this life indirectly.

We saw that some animals even have the same capacity to foresee, which leads Aristotle to describe them as "practically wise." What goes for animals certainly goes for slaves, and if Aristotle addressed this problem in the one case and not the other, this is certainly because, as Schofield has rightly emphasized, slavery does not interest him in itself, but only as a means for understanding the various kinds of rule. By contrast, animals are the subject of a detailed study by Aristotle. From this, it seems to follow that the slave cannot deliberate or foresee when it comes to the work he shares with his master, for when it comes to this work only the master has a vision of the whole and, above all, only he can provide his actions and the actions of his slave with an ethical horizon. But nothing in Aristotle's text allows us to suppose that he thinks that slaves left to themselves outside of the relation of slavery would be unable to set goals for themselves – eating, finding shelter, reproducing – and to survive by reasoning about what is to their advantage. Under these circumstances, then, they would evidently not be natural slaves.

CONCLUSION

Aristotle's theory of natural slavery allows us to think that slavery as it was practiced in his time did not have Aristotle's support. He did not necessarily condemn its violent and "ethnic" character, since he thought capture was justified, assimilating it to hunting and war; and he explains that in a way it is natural for barbarians to be slaves. But Aristotle held that slavery as it was practiced, since it was not built on an ethical foundation, deserved serious reproach for two reasons. First, since it rested only on force, it could reduce to slavery people who were not destined by nature to be slaves. This is the tale of Plato kidnapped by pirates and sold as a slave. Second, in failing to situate slavery within the enlarged family, Aristotle's contemporaries made it impossible for the slave to exercise his virtue, and thus to develop ethically. Indeed, there is no reason, even beyond the beneficial effects of the Greek climate which would mostly be reflected in their descendants, that slaves, like other human beings, could not develop in virtue. The virtues unfold and take root through the repetition of good actions, for the free as for slaves. Still, it is true that Aristotle not only legitimates the use of force to reduce to slavery those "who deserve it," but, in the chapter of the *Politics* that he dedicates to opposing claims about slavery (I 6), he declares that only two of those claims should be preserved, since the others "have neither force nor anything else to persuade us" (I 6, 1255a20). Even though they disagree about the nature of virtue, they both recognize that those who are superior in virtue have a right to rule, by force if necessary.

There remains a point that has scarcely been mentioned, namely, the friendship between a slave and his master. A passage cited earlier (I 6, 1255b13) mentions their reciprocal friendship, while the *Nicomachean Ethics* clearly states that there can be no more friendship or justice with a slave than with a tool, a horse, or a cow (VIII 11, 1161b1). But Aristotle adds the following: "there can be no friendship with a slave as slave, though there can be as human being" (*NE* VIII 11, 1161b5, trans. Rackham). This impossibility of friendship with a slave rests on two very different, even opposite, foundations, only the first of which has been noticed by interpreters. On the one hand, there is too great a heterogeneity between the two parties: we cannot be friends with those who belong to us, because friendship requires reciprocity. But there is also the extreme fusion presupposed by the natural relation of servitude, which makes of the slave "something that is not even one," as in the passage from the *Eudemian Ethics* cited earlier. Thus, one is not friends with one's hand. In order to have the friendship of one's slave, one must remove him from his servile condition and see the human being in him, particularly by giving to him, or restoring to him, some kind of ethical autonomy.

WORKS CITED

Aubonnet, J. 1960–1989. *Aristote: Politique.* 5 vols., Paris: Les Belles Lettres
    I: 20–31
Brunschwig, J. 1979. "L'esclavage chez Aristote." *Cahiers philosophiques* 1:
    20–31

Deslauriers, M. 2003. "Aristotle on the Virtues of Slaves and Women." *Oxford Studies in Ancient Philosophy* 25: 213–31

Finley, M. 1980. *Ancient Slavery and Modern Ideology*. Harmondworth: Penguin

Goldschmidt, V. 1973. "La théorie aristotélicienne de l'esclavage et sa méthode." In *Zetesis: Mélanges E. de Strycker*. Antwerp/Utrecht: De Nederlandsche Boekhandel

Heath, M. 2008. "Aristotle on Natural Slavery." *Phronesis* 53: 243–70

Labarrière, J.-L. 1990. "De la phronèsis animale" In *Biologie, logique, et métaphysique chez Aristote*, ed. D. Deveureux and P. Pellegrin. Paris: Éditions du Centre National de la Recherche Scientifique

Meillassoux, C. 1991. *The Anthropology of Slavery*. University of Chicago Press

Memel-Fotê, H. 2007. *L'esclavage dans les sociétés lignagères de la forêt ivoirienne*. Abidjan/Paris: Les Editions du CERAP

Miers, S. and Kopytoff, I., eds. 1977. *Slavery in Africa: Historical and Anthropological Perspectives*. Madison, WI: University of Wisconsin Press

Nuyens, F. 1948. *L'Évolution de la psychologie d'Aristote*. Louvain-la-Neuve: Peeters

Pellegrin, P. 1982. "La théorie aristotélicienne de l'eslavage: tendances actuelles de l'interprétation." *Revue Philosophique de la France et de l'Étranger* 172: 345–57

    1990. "Naturalité, excellence, diversité. Politique et biologie chez Aristote." In *Aristoteles' Politik*, ed. G. Patzig. Göttingen: Vandenhoeck and Ruprecht

    2001. "Hausverwaltung und Sklaverei." In *Aristoteles'* Politik, ed. O. Höffe. Berlin: Akademie Verlag

Reeve, C. D. C. 1998. *Aristotle*, Politics. Indianapolis, IN: Hackett

Schofield, M. 1990. "Ideology and philosophy in Aristotle's theory of slavery." In *Aristoteles'* Politik, ed. G. Patzig. Göttingen: Vandenhoeck and Ruprecht

Smith, N. 1991 [1983]. "Aristotle's theory of natural slavery." In *A Companion to Aristotle's Politics*, eds. D. Keyt and F. Miller. Oxford: Blackwell

NOTES

1. The best discussion of ancient slavery may still be that of Moses Finley, in *Ancient Slavery and Modern Ideology*, 1980. See pp. 73–77 for the definition of the slave.

2. Schofield 1990: 1–27.

3. See e.g., Pellegrin 2001: 38.

4. This *contra*, e.g. the introductory comments of Nicholas Smith's article on slavery: "In Book I of the *Politics*, Aristotle develops a theory
   of natural slavery that is intended to serve two purposes: to secure the
   morality of enslaving certain human beings and to provide a foundation
   for the uses of slaves that he advocates in later books." Smith 1991: 142.

5. The treatise in Aristotle's corpus entitled the *Oeconomica* does have
   something to say about this last point, but it is not by Aristotle.

6. Goldschmidt 1973.

7. Cf. Jean Aubonnet's comment in his (French) translation of the *Politics*,
   in a note on the passage in question: "In the fourth century, only Aristotle seems to have been able to guess that the solution to the problem
   of manual labor and slavery lay in the development of the machine."
   Aubonnet 1960: 114.

8. This was maintained in Brunschwig 1979.

9. Aristotle's phrasing is curious: "He who can belong to someone else
   (and that is why he actually does belong to someone else)...is a natural
   slave." We must surely understand this as follows: "belonging to someone else" is at least a distinctive property of a slave (even if it is not the
   definition of a slave), and this is true even before they come to belong
   to someone.

10. Cf. among recent publications, Harris Memel-Fotê's survey (2007).

11. H. Memel-Fotê reports that in 1904 slaves accounted for between 2.5
    percent and 4.8 percent of the total population in land of the Adjoukrou
    (in Southern Cote d'Ivoire), according to colonial statistics. Memel-Fotê
    2007: 435.

12. This is a fundamental point for several reasons. For example, in the sys-
    tems of slavery in state societies, historians have observed that mas-
    ters have great difficulty ensuring that their slaves reproduce by natural
    means. This is the source of slave societies' need to engage in endless
    wars for the purpose of enslavement, and of the problems these systems
    run into when their sources dry up, as they did for the southern United
    States in the nineteenth century. (Cf. Meillassoux 1991: Part III, Ch.
    5: "To buy or to breed?") Lineage slavery does not seem to have run
    into this problem, which has led to incredible theoretical confusion.
    For example, in a landmark work on slavery in Africa, editors Suzanne
    Miers and Igor Kopytoff think they can establish that the distinctive
    feature of African slavery is that it extends to foreigners the kinds of
    dependence that normally apply to women and children (Miers and
    Koptytoff 1977: esp. 22–24). Did Miers and Kopytoff realize that they
    were adopting an anti-Aristotelian, *Platonic* position?

13. There is an important discrepancy in the ms. at 1254b23. I adopt *logou*, the reading that is best established paleographically, rather than *logôi*, which would yield the meaning "animals, while they perceive it, do not obey reason but rather feelings" (Ross, Dreizehnter).

14. Cf. for example, Nuyens 1948: 197.

15. Cf. *NE* III 2, 1112a15: decision presupposes deliberation.

16. Cf. "The relationship between master and slave being the same as that between body and soul, or the worker and his tool" (*EE* VII 9, 1241b17); and in the *Politics*, "the same thing is beneficial for both part and whole, body and soul; and a slave is a sort of part of his master" (I 6, 1255b10).

17. Deslauriers 2003: 216.

18. There is a very interesting passage to this effect at I 6: those who say that slaves are people captured by force are unwilling to accept the consequences of this claim (that someone "well-born" could be a slave), and add that this applies only to barbarians. Aristotle replies that "in saying this, they are seeking precisely the natural slave . . . For they have to say that some people are slaves everywhere, whereas others are slaves nowhere" (I 6, 1255a30).

19. It is hard to say what Aristotle understands by "the barbarians of Asia." Were Egyptians, to whom Aristotle attributes the invention of arithmetic, filed under this heading? As for the triumphs of the Medes or the Persians, on the one hand, these were insufficient to allow them to defeat Greeks, but on the other, they illustrate the probabilistic character of climate determinism, which means, for example, that some soldiers can love war even among the Asians.

20. Cf. *NE* VI 7, 1141a26, trans. Ross: "we say that some even of the lower animals have practical wisdom, viz. those which are found to have a power of foresight (*dynamis pronoêtikê*) with regard to their own life."

21. *NE* VI 13, 1144b; VII 3, 1147b3; VII 6, 1149b31.

22. See especially *HA* VIII 1, 588a16.

23. Labarrière 1990: 415.

24. This question has been dealt with very well in Heath 2008, which I agree with on many points.

25. Cf. *NE* III 7, 1151b20, trans. Ross: "The end of every activity is conformity to the corresponding state of character."

26. See above note 25.

27. Schofield 1990: 14.

28. Pellegrin 1990: 124–51.

# 5  Political unity and inequality

## INTRODUCTION

*Politics* II is dominated by questions of commonality – what we should have in common in the best city-state, but also what we should not share.[1] What we have in common makes us the same in some respect, and what we do not have in common makes us different. Since, for Aristotle, equality and inequality track sameness and difference, what we have in common makes us equal (in some respect) and what we do not have in common makes us unequal. Aristotle views political unity as beneficial, and believes that it is promoted when we exchange goods (which need not be material). To create unity we must therefore have different goods for exchange, which means that we will not have all things in common. Since what we do not share in (or share less in) makes us different and unequal, we must enter into relations of exchange as unequals in some respects (*NE* V 5, 1133a16–18). If, for example, we do not share equally in wealth, we will be economically unequal, and if we do not share equally in virtue we will be morally unequal. While Aristotle believes that some forms of inequality lead to faction and endanger unity (see e.g., III 1 1301b26–29), here in Book II he argues for the preservation of certain inequalities.

The aim of this chapter is to show that Aristotle advocates creating political unity through inequalities, and in particular through the inequalities of virtue that he ascribes to those who rule and those who are ruled. Three questions focus the discussion: (i) What kind

I'd like to thank the participants at two workshops, in Assos and Montreal, who offered helpful comments on earlier versions of this chapter. I am especially grateful to Fred Miller and E. Zoli Filotas for their detailed comments.

of unity does Aristotle think is advantageous to a political community? (ii) Why does he think that a city should have a lesser degree of unity than a household or an individual person? (iii) What kind of inequalities should serve as the foundation of political unity on Aristotle's view?

I begin, in the next section, with an examination of the notion of *koinônia* (community or association), which is connected with the idea of having something in common.[2] The stated aim of *Politics* II is to determine the best form of political life by considering not only constitutions in use in cities, but also any other constitutions that are reputed to be good. Aristotle takes as his guiding question: Should the members of a city-state have everything in common or only some things? That they should have nothing in common he takes to be impossible; they must at least share a common place. So the very existence of a city-state, and especially its unity, depends on establishing what people will have in common. According to Aristotle, a political community is characterized by its origin in shared moral perceptions and affection, its aim of living well, and its practice of exchange.[3]

In the third section I consider Aristotle's criticisms of Socrates and Plato, since those criticisms shape the argument of Book II, bringing into focus the relation between what we have in common and the unity of the city-state. Although Aristotle is severely critical of the Socratic ideal constitution, he makes use of certain key ideas presented by Socrates in order to criticize that ideal. This makes more pressing the question why exactly Aristotle finds the Socratic city-state wanting. Of the proposals put forward by Socrates, those concerning the possession of women and children in common are of the greatest interest to Aristotle, because the most original or unusual; according to him, no one else had suggested anything similar. In elaborating his objections to these arrangements Aristotle develops his own argument for the importance of difference and inequality for enduring unity in the city-state, for a certain kind and degree of unity in the city-state, and also for the role of affection in promoting unity. That there should be different kinds of people in the city is necessary in order to secure unity, and also to secure self-sufficiency in a precise sense. But the question remains: What kind of differences among people will promote rather than undermine unity, allow for self-sufficiency, and hence be built into the best constitution?

In the fourth section I turn to that question. The differences in kind, I argue, must be differences between those who rule and those who are ruled; and they must be differences in virtue. Aristotle certainly thinks that a city must be self-sufficient in an economic sense, and that will require differences in skills and professions among the inhabitants. But the unity of the city and the capacity of a city to allow its inhabitants to live well will depend on differences in virtue between those who rule and those who are ruled.

My argument connects exchange, inequality, and unity. Political community requires exchange, in order for the parts of the community to be unified. Exchange requires differences between those who exchange, and those differences constitute inequalities. So political community requires inequalities and differences. Quite different features might differentiate groups of people (wealth, strength, virtue) and quite different things might be exchanged – and, indeed, will be exchanged in any political community – to equalize those differences (property, money, honor) depending on what people have, or fail to have, in common. But the unity of the community, and hence the community itself, requires that differences among groups (ruler and ruled) be established by virtue, and that the exchange be an exchange of honor, on the one hand, and benefits on the other.[4]

## COMMUNITY (*KOINÔNIA*) AND COMMONALITY

Aristotle introduces the project of Book II:

> We must begin, however, at the natural starting point of this investigation. For all citizens must share (*koinônein*) everything, or nothing, or some things but not others. It is evidently impossible for them to share nothing. For a constitution is a sort of community (*koinônia*), and so they must, in the first instance, share their location; for one city-state occupies one location, and citizens share that one city-state. But is it better for a city-state that is to be well managed to share everything possible? Or is it better to share some things but not others? (II 1, 1260b36–1261a4)

We see in this passage that the notion of having something in common or sharing something is linked linguistically to the idea of a community or association. The questions that govern Aristotle's analysis and evaluation of the proposed and actual constitutions surveyed in Book II are, then: What do the citizens of this community have in common? Given what they have in common, how good is their constitution? This suggests that what, and how much, is shared by citizens is a measure of the quality of the political community in which they live, and a measure of the quality of the constitution that governs that community.

Now, it is clear that a city-state is one form of community or association. Aristotle says: "A city-state is a sort of association, an association of citizens of a constitution." In the most general sense, an association is a composite whole, one made up of parts (e.g. at III 3, 1276b7; *EE* VII 9, 1241b19), and this will certainly hold true of the city. But in the *Politics* Aristotle makes more precise the claim that "the constitution (*politeia*) is some association (*koinônia*)," by specifying the aim of the association that is a city. That aim is living well in the sense of performing noble actions:

[There is a city-state] only when households and families (*genera*) live well as a community whose end is a complete and self-sufficient life...And a city-state is the community of families and villages in a complete and self-sufficient life, which we say is living happily and nobly. So political communities must be taken to exist for the sake of noble actions, and not for the sake of living together. (III 9, 1280b33–1281a4)[5]

In general, Aristotle takes it that any association or community functions for the sake of some benefit or advantage to the parts of the association.[6] The benefit in the case of political community is noble action. The question about what the citizens should have in common is, then, the question: What do they need to have in common in order to promote noble actions? And this, in fact, is the measure Aristotle uses in evaluating the success of different arrangements of common possessions, as we will see. The political association which takes as its aim the promotion of virtue and of virtuous acts is then the best association, with the best constitution. Aristotle insists on this:

Hence it is quite evident that the city-state (at any rate, the one truly so called and not just for the sake of argument) must be concerned with virtue. For otherwise the community becomes an alliance that differs only in location from other alliances in which the allies live far apart. (III 9, 1280b6–10)

So, a city is an association structured in such a way as to produce noble or virtuous acts, and hence to promote living well, and the best city will be the one that best promotes virtuous action. If Aristotle distinguishes the city from other forms of association according to its aim, he also distinguishes it according to its origin. The origin of a political community is a decision to live together that Aristotle recognizes as a form of affection, connects with the aim of living well, and takes to be distinctive of political communities. Affection or friendship (*philia*) characterizes the true city, because people are unwilling to form communities with their enemies (IV 11, 1295b24).[7] Marriage connections, clans, festivals, and the pastimes of living together arise in cities because "things of this sort are the result of friendship, since the deliberative choice of living together constitutes friendship. The end of the city-state is living well, then, but these other things are for the sake of the end" (III 9, 1280b38–40).[8] Aristotle characterizes affection here as a kind of choice to flag the difference between the association that is a city, and other forms of association. That is, he says, slaves and non-human animals also form "associations" in some sense, but their associations do not involve shared happiness and they do not choose to live together (because neither slaves nor animals have a capacity for choice in the strict sense (III 9, 1280a31–34; see also III 9, 1281a3)). Affection, then, indicates in this context the intentional choice of living together, rather than an emotion, and this choice is one of the features Aristotle expects to find among the citizens of a constitution that is well structured.

Moreover, this choice to live together, and the way that choice distinguishes political communities among free men from associations of slaves or animals, is based on shared perceptions of moral qualities. At *Politics* I 2, 1253a15–18, Aristotle specifies that a city, as well as a household, is a community in a particular sense: "For it is peculiar to human beings, in comparison to the other animals, that they alone have perception of what is good or bad, just or unjust, and the rest. And it is community in these that makes a household and a city-state." A city is, then, an association distinguished by its aim – living well – and its origin – a decision to live together for the sake of living well, based on shared perceptions of right and wrong.

Finally, in many passages Aristotle insists that a political community involves and requires exchange (see e.g., *NE* V 5, 1132b31; V 5, 1133a17–b15; IX 1, 1164a20; *Politics* II 2, 1261a31). The function of this exchange is to equalize the differences between the parts, which a city must have because every association is a whole made up of parts. In a political community these parts are rulers and ruled (VII 14, 1332b12). And in the *Eudemian Ethics* Aristotle says that the exchange is an exchange of services for honor: "Equality must then be restored and proportion created by some other means [i.e. other than an exchange of money or services]; and this means is honor, which by nature belongs to a ruler or god in relation to a subject. The profit and the honor must be equated" (*EE* VII 10, 1242b18–21, trans. Solomon in Barnes 1984). That is, those who are ruled will profit from the community, and those who rule will be honored in the community.[9]

I will say more about this exchange below. Consider first some of Aristotle's objections to the Kallipolis, or ideal city, proposed by Socrates in the *Republic*. We will see that Aristotle is critical of Socrates for failing to distinguish the right kind and degree of unity appropriate to the association that is a city, and also for proposing mechanisms to ensure unity that will, in Aristotle's view, be ineffective.

UNITY

The end or aim of the city is, as we have seen, living well, and living well in an enduring way – since it is difficult to live well with a threat of faction.[10] Unity is what is required among the parts of the city in order to avoid faction, and so unity becomes a clear political good for Aristotle. He approaches the question of what people should have in common with this question: What do the citizens need to have in common in order to promote unity, and thus create the conditions for living well? More particularly, as he surveys both actual and ideal constitutions, he asks in each case: What is shared among inhabitants in this political community that is not shared under other constitutions? Will such sharing promote or undermine unity?

The novel element in Plato's political philosophy is the suggestion that women and children in the guardian class should be shared, or "held in common." In *Republic* V, Socrates returns to two contentious assertions and proposals that he has made earlier (objections to which he refers to as "waves"), in formulating the plan for an ideal city. The first is that women and men are the same by nature in all important respects, and so should have the same education and perform the same work (*Rep.* V, 454d–e). The second is that women are to be held in common – that is, that they should not live privately with individual men.

SOCRATES: I suppose that the following law goes along with the last one and the others that preceded it.

GLAUCON: Which one?

SOCRATES: That all these women are to belong in common to all the men, that none are to live privately with any man, and that the children, too, are to be possessed in common, so that no parent will know his own offspring or any child his parent. (*Republic* V 457c–d) [11]

This second proposal has as a corollary that there will be no households among the guardians. [12]

The question Aristotle poses in *Politics* II 1 is: Would it be better to keep "things as they are now" (i.e. to retain differentiated roles for men and women, and private households) or to adopt the law laid down in the *Republic* with respect to having wives and children, as well as property, in common (II 1, 1261a8–9)? Asking whether it would be better is asking whether it would promote unity; this becomes clear as Aristotle formulates his objections to the proposals. There are two objections:

1.    The object (final cause) for the sake of which Socrates recommends holding women in common evidently is not borne out (i.e. not proved to be a desirable object) by his arguments (II 2, 1261a10–12). That is, Socrates believes that these arrangements would promote unity; but his arguments do not demonstrate that making the city as unified as possible is good.

2.    As a means to the end (unity) the possession of women in common is not practicable (II 2, 1261a13–14). So, even if we assume that unity is a good thing in a city, the common possession of women would not lead to unity. [13]

As Aristotle elaborates these objections he makes clear that he believes that only a certain kind and degree of unity is good for the city, and so he disagrees with Socrates, who suggests that unity *as such* is good for the city. In formulating objection (1), Aristotle asserts that the unity appropriate to a city is the unity of parts different in kind. He argues that a city should be made up not only of a number of persons, but of persons different in kind, because a unity must be made up of elements that are different in kind:

A city-state consists not only of a number of people, but of people of different kinds (*eidei diapherontôn*), since a city-state does not come from people who are alike. For a city-state is different from a military alliance. An alliance is useful because of the weight of numbers, even if they are all of the same kind, since the natural aim of a military alliance is the sort of mutual assistance that a heavier weight provides if placed on a scales.[14] A nation (*ethnous*) will also differ from a city-state in this sort of way, provided the multitude is not separated into villages, but is like the Arcadians. But things from which a unity must come to be differ in kind. (II 2, 1261a22–30)[15]

This is a point Aristotle made first in Book I (I 13, 1259b37). Because a city-state is made up of different kinds of people, it is distinct both from a military alliance (where greater numbers make the whole better) and from the Arcadian way of life (where there might be the same number of people as in a city-state, but no structure organizing those people). Moreover, the different kinds of people are necessary for exchange and reciprocal equality, a principle which Aristotle holds to be necessary for political life, as we saw above. Indeed, the differentiation of elements in a city-state is so important that it is imitated even when it is not strictly possible (because of "natural equality"):

That is why reciprocal equality preserves city-states, as we said earlier in the *Ethics*, since this must exist even among people who are free and equal. For they cannot all rule at the same time, but each can rule for a year or some other period. As a result they all rule, just as all would be shoemakers and carpenters if they changed places, instead of the same people always being shoemakers and the others always carpenters. But since it is better to have the latter [i.e. to have people with specialized skills, as with carpenters and shoemakers] also where a political community is concerned, it is clearly better, where possible, for the same people always to rule. But among those where it is not possible, because all are naturally equal, and where it is at the same time just for all to share the benefits or burdens of ruling, it is at least possible to imitate this [i.e. to imitate the case where the same people always rule] if those who are equal take turns and are similar when out of office. For they rule and are ruled in turn, just as if they had become other people. (II 2, 1261a30–b5)[16]

So, a city is not by nature a unity in that sense affirmed by some people (including Socrates) – that is, its unity does not depend on the sameness of the people that constitute it, but to the contrary, on the differences that mark them off from one another.[17] So important are these differences that if they do not appear naturally, they must be imitated or agreed upon by convention.

If Socrates is mistaken in trying to create the wrong *kind* of unity, by eliminating the differences among people (at least within the guardian class), he is also mistaken in aiming for a high *degree* of unity in the city. A city may be too unified, because too much unity destroys it. The claim, more precisely, is that a city that is too unified is no longer a city, but a more elementary social unit:

And yet it is evident that the more of a unity a city-state becomes, the less of a city-state it will be. For a city-state naturally consists of a certain multitude (*plêthos*); and as it becomes more of a unity, it will turn from a city-state into a household, and from a household into a human being. For we would surely say that a household is more of a unity than a city-state and an individual human being than a household. Hence, even if someone could achieve this, it should not be done, since it will destroy the city-state. (II 2, 1261a16–22)

This passage suggests that there are degrees of unity along some continuum on which the individual, the household, and the city are situated – a continuum of social wholes. Aristotle believes that there is a single kind of unity appropriate to these social wholes, a kind that distinguishes them from wholes in which the parts are all the same. Social wholes should have the kind of unity that organisms have – the unity of, say, a wolf, which depends on differences in kind in the parts; they should not have the unity of, say, wine, which depends on the parts being identical in kind. At the same time, Aristotle thinks that the degree of unity appropriate for each of these social wholes is different – so a city should be less unified than a household, which in turn should be less unified than an individual. Why should it be less unified? Among other reasons, because certain opportunities to perform virtuous actions are lost if we make the city too unified (II 5, 1263b5–14). Both temperance with respect to women, and liberality with respect to property, are virtues that are lost in cities that are excessively unified. And excessive unification is the circumstance in which everything, rather than some things, is held in common:

> One has to think that the reason Socrates goes astray is that his assumption is incorrect. For a household and a city-state must indeed be a unity up to a point, but not totally so. For there is a point at which it will, as it goes on, not be a city-state, and another at which it will be a worse city because it is close to not being a city. It is as if one were to reduce a harmony to a unison, or a rhythm to a single beat. But a city-state consists of a multitude, as we said before, and should be unified and made into a community by means of education. (II 5, 1263b29–37)[18]

The mistaken assumption is that unity in all ways in the city is, without qualification, a political good. In fact, promoting virtues and virtuous acts among the inhabitants of the city-state is the unqualified political good – unity, and affection, are to be cultivated in the service of, and for the sake of, virtue.[19]

So much for Aristotle's first objection to the Socratic proposals. In *Politics* II 3, Aristotle starts to elaborate his second objection (2) that Socrates' proposal will not in practice bring about the unity of the city-state. This second objection reinforces the point of the first (that there is a particular kind and degree of unity suitable for a city) by showing that the mechanisms Socrates proposes for holding women and children in common will not in fact produce the right kind and degree of political unity. We have seen that while Aristotle agrees with Socrates that a city must be a unity, he disagrees about the kind and the degree of that unity. Aristotle agrees with Socrates on two further points: (a) that the citizens of a city should be of one mind; and (b) that the citizens should have affection for one another. But he objects that the strategies Socrates proposes to cultivate like-mindedness and affection among the inhabitants of a city will not produce the *right* like-mindedness or the *right* affection. The right kinds will be those that promote the right kind of unity.

In formulating the second objection, Aristotle's first point (2.a) is that Socrates does not make clear what he means by "having in common": "That 'all say the same thing' is in one way fine, though impossible, while in another way it does not make them of one mind [*homonoêtikon*]" (II 3, 1261b30–32, trans. Lord, adapted).[20] If the citizens all say "mine" of the same things, that might mean either one of two things: (i) that each thinks of the object to be possessed as belonging to him individually (the distributive sense); or (ii) that each acknowledges the object to be possessed as a common possession (the collective sense). Aristotle clearly thinks that it is the former sense Socrates intends (he says "If it means 'each individually', perhaps this would be closer to what Socrates wants to do"), and that it is that sense one would need in order to be of one mind, but that it is the latter that people would be likely to use if in fact they possessed women and children in common. But speaking in the collective sense about women and children will not in fact promote the unity based on shared moral perceptions that is the foundation of political community. Being of one mind, we know from the *Nicomachean Ethics* at IX 6, 1167a26–28, is a question of sharing judgments about what is beneficial, and choosing the same things. And, as we have seen, Aristotle believes that the choice to live together in a political community, and so the very origin of that community, is based on a shared perception of good and bad, right and wrong (I 2, 1253a15–18) – and this is what it means to say that two or more people are *homonoêtikon*: that they are in agreement. So Aristotle agrees with Socrates that the unity of shared purposes and moral perceptions is a political good. His objection in II 3 is that Socrates' proposals would not be an effective strategy for bringing about *this* unity, because saying "mine" of the same things will not entail that people agree about what is good and bad.[21]

Let us turn now to the question of affection in the city (2.b). Aristotle agrees again, in principle, with Socrates, that affection is politically good, but argues that the proposed mechanisms will not bring about the right *kind* of affection among the right citizens. At II 4, 1262b7–14, Aristotle says that Socrates advocates the unity of the city-state through affection (*philia*), and this is the kind of unity attributed to the lovers in "the erotic speeches," where Aristophanes says that the lovers, because of an excess of affection, desire to grow together and to become a double one from being two; but then of necessity one or both will die (see *Symposium* 191a–b). Aristotle has two objections: first, that the kind of affection pursued and exhibited by Aristophanes' halved creatures is an unhealthy model for political affection, because it promotes a unity in which the parts are no longer distinct (he does not think that the parts that form the city-state should merge; rather, they should remain distinct) (II 4,

1262b12–14); and second, that at any rate the affection pursued by the halved creatures is an intense and passionate bond, and this is not the affection that would in fact be promoted by the possession of women and children in common (II 4, 1262b14–16). The objection, then, is that these proposals will not aim to promote affection of the right kind (where the right kind would preserve differences and avoid passion), and that at any rate they will not be effective. The proposals aim to produce the erotic affection Aristophanes describes, but they will not effectively produce it; nor, however, will they produce true political affection.

Socrates' proposals are also mistaken in advocating holding women and children in common among the guardians, rather than among the farmers. Remember that holding women and children in common breeds the "collective" sense rather than the "distributive" sense of common possession, and the collective sense produces less unity in the sense of a shared purpose or perception of good. If, then, the farming class preserves private households while the guardian class shares women and children, the guardian class will be less unified than the farming class. Aristotle argues that the farming class should be less unified than the guardian class, since less unity among the farmers would make them more susceptible to rule, and that would be a good thing: "But it is the *ruled* who should be like that [i.e. without much affection for one another] in order to promote obedience and prevent rebellion" (II 4, 1262b2–3). In general Aristotle associates affection or friendship with unity ("For we regard friendship (*philia*) as the greatest of goods for city-states, since in this condition people are least likely to engage in factional conflict. And Socrates himself particularly praises unity in a city-state, something that is held to be, and that he himself says is, the result of friendship" (II 4, 1262b7–10)). But affection, like unity, is a qualified good. So Aristotle does not think we should promote every kind of affection among all citizens, precisely because, as we have seen, the appropriate unity for the city-state will require differences among groups of people. One important difference will be how bound together different groups are by affection; the greater the affection among them, the stronger they will be as a group, and that is a good thing if they are ruling – but if they are a group to be ruled, then affection is not something we should encourage among them, since it will not cultivate in them the virtue of obedience to authority.[22]

Aristotle makes, then, two points about affection in objecting to Socrates' proposals on women and children: (i) the affection that a political community should promote is political affection (the decision to live together based on shared moral perceptions) and not erotic affection; and (ii) that political affection should be promoted to the highest degree among the members of the ruling class.

Let me now summarize the two points about unity that emerge from the objections Aristotle lodges against Socrates' proposals on holding women and children in common. Together these points make clear that Aristotle believes that the city as a whole, and its various parts, should exemplify unity in different ways and in different degrees. (i) The first point is that the kind of unity that Aristotle thinks is beneficial to cities (and also to households and individuals) is the kind that belongs to any organic entity, where the parts of the unified whole are non-identical. Socrates may well have agreed with this point; indeed, his division of the city into distinct classes suggests that he understood the importance of difference to unity. Aristotle's objection, however, is that the mechanisms Socrates proposes, purportedly to promote unity, will in fact lead to the unity appropriate to military alliances or bodies of water or wine, but not to the organic unity appropriate to political entities. (ii) The second point is that this organic unity can (and should) be had to a greater or lesser degree in different social units, and the lesser degree is appropriate to a city-state. That is, the right kind of unity must also obtain in the right degree in the city-state (or it becomes a household). Socrates promotes an extreme degree of unity – excessive unity for a city – and that excessive unity threatens to turn the political community into a household. In what follows I explore this second point further, by examining the relation between the right degree of unity and the right degree of self-sufficiency.

How does the unity of the political community differ from the unity of the household? The answer to that question concerns self-sufficiency, a notion that I will introduce here, and consider further in the next section. Aristotle offers as a rationale for the claim that the city-state should be less unified, that it will be *more* self-sufficing if it is *less* unified:

It is also evident on other grounds that to try to make a city-state too much a unity is not a better policy. For a household is more self-sufficient than

a single person, and a city-state than a household; and a city-state tends
to come about as soon as a community's population is large enough to be
fully self-sufficient. So, since what is more self-sufficient is more choiceworthy, what is less a unity is more choiceworthy than what is more so. (II
2, 1261b10–15)[23]

This has to mean that a unified city will be less unified than a household or individual, and that the degree of unity in a social entity
corresponds inversely to the degree of self-sufficiency – so the more
self-sufficient, the less unified it will be.[24] The differences in degrees
of unity and corresponding differences in degrees of self-sufficiency
mark important differences beyond differences in size: a city-state is
not simply a very large household (Aristotle has disparaged that view
at I 1, 1252a12–13). Individual, household, and city-state are different precisely because of the degree of unity and of self-sufficiency
that they ideally exhibit.

What does this mean in practice? That is, how will these differences in unity and in self-sufficiency be exhibited in the individual, the household, and the city? The notion of self-sufficiency
suggests a diversity of professions, and a pragmatic concern for satisfying the physical needs of the inhabitants, and it will be true that
the city more than the household will include and require a diversity
of professional skills. This is not, however, all that Aristotle intends
to include in the notion of self-sufficiency which, on his account,
extends beyond living per se to living well.[25] We are self-sufficient as
people not when our material needs are met – although of course they
must be met – but when we have a context in which to exercise fully
our capacity for virtue.[26] It is only in the city that we have that context, and hence the city is more self-sufficient than the household,
which in turn is more self-sufficient than the individual, since even
the household affords more opportunity for virtuous action than does
solitude. This account of self-sufficiency confirms the interpretation
offered above of the argument at II 2, 1261a16–22, in which Aristotle
claims that, although both a city and a household are organic uni-
ties, the city should be less unified than a household. We saw that
it should be less unified in order that it might provide more opportunities to exercise virtue, and here we see that Aristotle links the
lesser degree of unity with a greater degree of self-sufficiency in the
sense of a larger context for virtuous action.

Aristotle suggests also that we can distinguish the degrees of unity in social wholes according to how natural the differences in rule are among the parts of that whole. The individual, the household, and the city will all have different parts, and each will have parts that rule other parts. The rule of soul over body is natural in the strongest sense, and the unity of body and soul is the highest degree of unity; the rule of free men over women, children, and slaves in the household is natural but less so than the rule of soul over body, and so the degree of unity of the household is somewhat less than the degree of unity in individuals. And while the differences in kind in the parts of the city might be natural – natural rulers might emerge – they might not occur naturally (say, in a *politeia*), in which case, as we have seen, they will have to be imitated. This produces the lowest degree of unity.

Consider again the passage at *Politics* II 2, 1261a29–b5, where Aristotle discusses the principle of reciprocity. It suggests that households are more unified because their parts are more *naturally* distinct. That is, if reciprocity is reciprocity of rule, in the individual there is no question but that reason should rule over the other parts of the soul, and in the household there is no question but that men should rule over women and free men over slaves. It is only in the city-state that Aristotle allows that there will sometimes be only designated (as opposed to natural) rulers and subjects (see II 2, 1261a30–35 and I 12, 1259b7–9), in the case of a body of citizens who are free men and equals. So in the city the parts that are different in kind are not always *naturally* different in kind. The unity of the city-state is less than that of household or individual because while all three constitute wholes for Aristotle, the parts of the whole that is the household or the individual are naturally created as subjects and rulers, whereas in the city the parts are not (usually) naturally different. In most cities the citizens are likely to be naturally equal and similar, but in some city there might be an incomparably superior individual who deserves to be an absolute king, in which case the city-state will resemble more closely a household with a single ruler.

## INEQUALITIES AND DIFFERENCES

I have already remarked on the importance of inequality for the structure of the good city, demonstrated by Aristotle's insistence (in the passage at II 2, 1261a22–26, cited above) that the elements of the city should be different. That there should be different kinds of people in the city is necessary in order to secure unity, and also in order to secure self-sufficiency.

What are the differences among people that will constitute the different parts of the city-state and provide for unity and self-sufficiency? Some commentators believe that the differences in question (the differences among "kinds of people") is a difference in professions.[27] There is evidence for this in Aristotle's claim that greater unity is bad because it diminishes self-sufficiency (II 2 1261b10–15), assuming that the self-sufficiency of a state is produced by the variety of professions practiced by its citizens (that certainly seems to be Aristotle's meaning). But, as I have said above, differences in profession cannot exhaust the differences Aristotle has in mind, since his claim is that the differences are necessary for a self-sufficiency that is moral as well as economic – for living well, and not just for living. Moreover, Aristotle is critical of Socrates' Kallipolis with respect precisely to the notion of self-sufficiency on which it is built, a notion according to which self-sufficiency is provided by having sufficient diversity of "necessary things":

That is why what is said in the *Republic*, though sophisticated, is not adequate. For Socrates says that a city-state is constituted out of four absolutely necessary classes, and these, he says, are weavers, farmers, shoe-makers, and house builders. Then, on the grounds that these are not self-sufficient, he adds blacksmiths, people to look after the necessary livestock, and those engaged in retail trade and commerce. All these become the full complement of his first city-state – as if every city-state were constituted for the sake of providing the necessities, not for the sake of what is noble, and had equal need of both shoemakers and farmers. (IV 4, 1291a10–19)

This passage makes clear that unity and self-sufficiency require differences other than the differences of shoemakers and farmers. Let us consider how, beyond differences in profession, Aristotle thinks the parts of a city should, ideally, differ in order to guarantee unity and self-sufficiency. As we have seen, it would be best if these differences existed by nature, but they can, if necessary, be instituted through political practices; it is so important that there should be different kinds of people, that these differences must be created if they do not occur naturally. I contend that the fundamental difference Aristotle advocates is a difference in virtue, which can, on his view, be produced artificially if it does not exist naturally.

First, there is some evidence that the differences in kind must be differences between those who rule and those who are ruled in Aristotle's criticisms of Socrates in the *Republic*, and of Plato in the *Laws*. One of his objections to Plato's *Laws* is precisely that Plato has failed to elaborate or give content to the differences between rulers and subjects: "Also omitted in the *Laws* is the matter of the rulers, and how they will differ from the ruled. For he asserts that just as the warp is made of a different kind of wool from the woof, so the rulers should stand with respect to the ruled" (II 6, 1265b18–21, trans. Lord 1984). And in criticizing the *Republic*, Aristotle is concerned that Socrates has not specified just how the citizens who are not guardians will differ from those who are guardians with respect to what they have in common:

If all is to be common to all in the same way, how will they differ from the guardians? And how will they benefit from submitting to their rule? Or what on earth will prompt them to submit to it – unless the guardians adopt some clever stratagem like that of the Cretans? For the Cretans allow their slaves to have the same other things as themselves, and forbid them only the gymnasia and the possession of weapons. (II 5, 1264a17–22)

Notice two points in this passage. First, Aristotle acknowledges that one might structure a city through differences in kind where those differences are simply differences in physical power or practical force. But if one *were* to structure the city in that way, then the unity gained through inequality would be vulnerable to circumstance – should the weak become strong, or the unarmed obtain arms. Aristotle understands that keeping the lower classes in a state of incapacity will prevent revolt, and that this is one way of producing a kind of unity among the parts of the city. But his concern is how to structure the city-state so that the lower classes do not wish to revolt, so that the principle upon which they submit to be ruled is something better than a recognition of their circumstantial incapacity. The second and more general point is that inequalities are not all equally good ways of ensuring unity; one has to structure a political community around certain precise inequalities in order to give those who are ruled an enduring motive to agree to be ruled and

to give those who rule a legitimate basis on which to assert authority. Aristotle acknowledges, then, that it makes a great difference
whether one structures the city around an inequality of brute force
or an inequality of virtue; the difference it makes is in the motives
one provides to both ruler and ruled to assent to the arrangement.

Which differences, then, should distinguish those who rule from
those who are ruled? There is evidence that those who rule and
those who are ruled should be unequal with respect to virtue. In
Book III Aristotle associates sameness and difference with equality
and inequality in a passage that introduces his claims for virtue as a
politically salient measure of worth:

> For they all grasp justice of a sort, but they go only to a certain point and
> do not discuss the whole of what is just in the most authoritative sense. For
> example, justice seems to be equality, and it is, but not for everyone, only
> for equals. Justice also seems to be inequality, since indeed it is, but not for
> everyone, only for unequals. They disregard the "for whom," however, and
> judge badly . . . So since what is just is just for certain people, and consists in
> dividing things and people in the same way (as we said earlier in the *Ethics*),
> they agree about what constitutes equality in the thing but disagree about it
> in the people. This is largely because . . . they think they are speaking about
> what is unqualifiedly just. For one lot thinks that if they are unequal in one
> respect (wealth, say) they are wholly unequal, whereas the other lot thinks
> that if they are equal in one respect (freedom, say) they are wholly equal.
> But about the most authoritative considerations [i.e. living well] they do
> not speak. (III 9, 1280a9–25)[28]

The general point this passage emphasizes is that justice involves
giving to people who are equal (in some specified respect) the same
amount of some good, and giving to those who are not equals (in
the same specified respect) different amounts of some good. At the
same time, Aristotle insists here that we cannot extrapolate from
difference or sameness in one respect to difference or sameness in
every respect. So, for example, should some number of people be
equal with respect to freedom, or with respect to property, it does
not follow that they will be equal in other respects. Most political commentators have got it wrong by focusing on some respect
in which people are indeed the same or different, but which is not
the important respect for political structures or decisions; they focus
on property, or on freedom, when they should focus on living well,
i.e. virtuous action. This means that the differences most important

for creating unity in a city-state are differences in virtue. This is not, of course, to say that some people should be virtuous and others not. It is rather to say that some people should have the virtues of rulers and others the virtues of the ruled. And if this does not occur naturally, then it should be imitated, because, as we have seen, even when everyone is equal in their nature, ruler and ruled must imitate natural differences (II 2, 1261a30–b5).

Further evidence that the difference between those who rule and those who are ruled is a difference in virtue is found in Aristotle's discussion of the virtues of ruler and ruled, and the relation between the good person and the good citizen, where he draws an analogy, famously, between the sailors on a ship and the citizens in a city:

Just as a sailor is one of a number of members of a community, so, we say, is a citizen. And though sailors differ in their capacities (for one is an oarsman, another a captain, another a lookout, and others have other sorts of titles), it is clear both that the most exact account of the virtue of each sort of sailor will be peculiar to him, and similarly that there will also be some common account that fits them all. For the safety of the voyage is a task of all of them, since this is what each of the sailors strives for. In the same way, then, the citizens, too, even though they are dissimilar (*anhomoiôn*), have the safety of the community as their task. But the community is the constitution. So the virtue of a citizen must be for his constitution. (III 4, 1276b20–31)

In this analogy Aristotle is comparing the different virtues of different sailors, to the different virtues of different citizens. The comparison is intended to make a point about virtue, and not a point about trades or skills. This is confirmed later in the chapter, when Aristotle, while claiming that the virtues of the ruler and the virtues of the ruled are sometimes found in the same person, says that they are nonetheless different (III 4, 1277b13). Moreover, in a passage we've already considered at II 2, 1261a29–b5, Aristotle mentions the importance of different professions to the political community to make a point about the difference between those who rule and those who are ruled, not the difference between carpenters and shoemakers. That is, Aristotle is claiming that those who rule are different from, not the same as, those who are ruled; and if they are not, in fact, different, they must "imitate" the difference between natural rulers and natural subjects. That the difference is not simply one of skill is made clear by the remark that in the case of this imitation it is as if the rulers become "other persons" when they take a turn at being ruled.

Now, one reason that differences in profession might seem to be the differences in kind that Aristotle alludes to as necessary for unity and self-sufficiency is the emphasis that he places on relations of exchange in establishing political unity. In the first line of a passage we have looked at (II 2, 1261a29–b5), Aristotle states the principle of reciprocal equality, and refers us to the *Nicomachean Ethics* for its original formulation:

In communities for exchange, however, this way of being just, reciprocity that is proportionate rather than equal, holds people together; for a city is maintained by proportionate reciprocity. For people seek to return either evil for evil, since otherwise [their condition] seems to be slavery, or good for good, since otherwise there is no exchange; and they are maintained [in a community] by exchange . . . For no community is formed from two doctors. It is formed from a doctor and a farmer, and, in general, from people who are different and unequal and who must be equalized. (*NE* V 5, 1132b33– 1133a20, trans. Irwin 1999)

These differences in virtue between ruler and ruled do not preclude the relations of exchange that Aristotle thinks are so vital to unity in the city. The exchanges between, say, doctors and farmers in the city clearly are necessary in order to provide it with "necessary things," but they are not enough to provide it with the conditions for self-sufficiency in the moral sense. Ruler and ruled must also be different in kind in order to form a community, the basis of which is always exchange. Exchange arises from having different possessions, or skills, or moral qualities – and not from having these in common (or not from having all of them in common). Just, then, as the doctor and farmer engage in an exchange of goods and services, so too the ruler and the ruled engage in exchange, but the currency of their exchange is somewhat different. As we saw at the outset, in the passage at *EE* VII 10, 1242b18–20, the exchange between ruler and ruled is one of honor for benefits. This is the exchange that is necessary for political unity, because it provides those who are ruled with a motive to agree to be ruled that is enduring and invulnerable to circumstance. And it is the exchange necessary for the self-sufficiency that allows for the full exercise of human virtue.

We might wonder why Aristotle objects so strongly to Socrates' proposals on women in the context of a discussion of political unity – what it is and how it might be promoted. He clearly believes that his own proposals for the treatment of women, outlined in Book I, and largely consistent with contemporary Athenian practice, will be more in harmony with the unity of the city.[29] When Socrates proposes that we should "hold women in common" this is in conjunction with proposing that we should educate women to be the same as men. So Socrates is in fact arguing for the abolition of the household and the leveling of sexual difference. He is turning the household into a community of equals; this is what Aristotle objects to.

In formulating that objection, Aristotle insists that there are certain natural differences between the sexes, differences which constitute inequalities, and should be reflected in the treatment of women, and in the structure of the city-state, rather than suppressed or minimized. Here, a very brief account of these differences will suffice to show the contrast between Socrates and Aristotle. In the political realm the most important difference between men and women is a difference in their deliberative capacities; Aristotle claims that the deliberative faculty in women is "without authority" (I 13, 1260a13). He means that women, while capable of deliberation (unlike natural slaves), must allow their deliberations and especially their decisions to be determined by the male head of the household.[30] The lack of authority of the deliberative faculty in women leads to a difference in kind, and not only in degree, in their virtues: women, while they have all the moral virtues that men do (with the possible exception of courage (andreia)) have a different kind of (for example) temperance, or justice. The virtues of women are the virtues of the ruled, rather than the virtues of rulers.

We know that these sexual differences constitute inequalities for Aristotle; the authority that free men enjoy with respect to deliberation is a superiority in virtue, and that superiority is precisely what justifies his rule over others. Moreover, while the relation between men and their wives can, Aristotle tells us in the *Nicomachean Ethics*, constitute a friendship, it will be a friendship of unequals (NE VIII 7, 1158b12–14). "For the excellence and the function of each of these [husband and wife] is different, and so are the reasons for which they love; the love and the friendship are therefore different also. Each party, then, neither gets the same from the other, nor ought to seek it" (*NE* VIII 7, 1158b17–20). The inequality between men and women, like other inequalities, promotes a kind of exchange, in which each gives the other something different in kind. They also exchange different amounts of love: "In all friendships implying inequality the love also should be proportional, i.e. the better should be more loved than he loves" (*NE* VIII 7, 1158b24–25). This exchange, like others, requires the differences between men and women. If they were the same, they would have less to offer one another in exchange.

We might suppose that Socrates and Aristotle in this debate are treating women and children simply as a form of property, so that the arguments against holding women in common are just an instance of the arguments against abolishing private property. But one reason to suppose that Aristotle does not treat women as a form of property is that he allows that affection or friendship occurs, indeed should occur, between men and women, and parents and children, in the household. Aristotle is not concerned only with affection between equal citizens, but also with affection between those who rule and those who are ruled, and the ways in which affection might equalize people who are naturally unequal. This means, I think, that the arguments about private property are concerned only with the effect of private property on free men – do two men who share property feel more united, or more affectionate, than those who do not? The arguments about women, on the other hand, are not only about the effects of holding women privately or in common on the relationships between men, but also about the effects on the relationships between men and women. If women are held in common, and that makes women less different than men, then it eliminates the important difference between ruler and ruled on which political unity depends, loosens the unions and lessens the unity of the household, and also interferes with the bonds of affection and unity between men.

## CONCLUSION

I have argued that living well on Aristotle's view requires political unity, and that unity requires differences or inequalities among people. This is because the kind of unity Aristotle believes is necessary to a city-state is the organic unity of a whole, the parts of which perform different tasks, all of which contribute to some overall aim. And the degree of unity that Aristotle advocates for the city-state is minimal, because a higher degree of unity would make the city less self-sufficient. I have said that the self-sufficiency in question is a kind of moral self-sufficiency, which allows the citizens and other inhabitants of the city to exercise every human virtue. This moral self-sufficiency depends on differences in virtue between those who rule and those who are ruled, and so those differences should be imitated if they do not occur by nature.

As Aristotle formulates his objections to Socrates and Plato in Book II, he illuminates some of the important claims of Book I. He returns to the notion that the individual, the household, and the city-state are different, and not only different in size. With the claim that there are differences in self-sufficiency in these social wholes, we can see that the context they afford for the exercise of virtue is quite different. And we can understand better why Aristotle in Book I claims that different kinds of people in the household must be different with respect to the kind, and not only with respect to the degree, of virtue that they possess. These differences are necessary for the unity of the household, just as the moral differences between ruler and ruled are necessary for the unity of the city-state.

### WORKS CITED

Aubonnet, J. 1960–1989. *Aristote: Politique*. 3 vols, Paris: Les Belles Lettres

Barnes, J., ed. 1984. *The Complete Works of Aristotle*. Princeton University Press

Charles, D. 1988. "Moral Perfectionism: Reply to Nussbaum." *Oxford Studies in Ancient Philosophy* Supplemental vol.: 184–206

Cooper, J. M., ed. 1997. *Plato: Complete Works*. Indianapolis, IN: Hackett

Deslauriers, M. 2003. "Aristotle on the Virtues of Slaves and Women." *Oxford Studies in Ancient Philosophy* 25: 213–31

Dobbs, D. 1985. "Aristotle's Anticommunism." *American Journal of Political Science* 29: 29–46

1996. "Family Matters: Aristotle's Appreciation of Women and the Plural Structure of Society." *American Political Science Review* 90: 74–89

Höffe, O., ed. 2001. *Aristoteles Politik*. Berlin: Akademie Verlag

Kraut, R. 2001. "Aristotle's critique of false utopias (*Pol.* II.1–12)." In Höffe, 2001

Lord, C. 1984. *Aristotle, The Politics*. University of Chicago Press

Newman, W. L. 1887–1902. *The Politics of Aristotle*. 4 vols, Oxford University Press

Nussbaum. M. C. 1988. "Nature, Function and Capability: Aristotle on Political Distribution." *Oxford Studies in Ancient Philosophy* Supplemental vol.: 145–84

Reeve, C. D. C. 1998. *Aristotle*, Politics. Indianapolis, IN: Hackett

Saunders, T. J. 1996. *Politics, Books I and II*. Oxford: Clarendon

Saxonhouse. A. W. 1982. "Family, Polity, and Unity: Aristotle on Socrates' Community of Wives." *Polity* 15: 202–19

Simpson, P. 1991. "Aristotle's Criticism of Socrates' Communism of Wives and Children." *Apeiron* 24: 99–114

NOTES

1. I generally use the term "city-state" to translate *polis* throughout; in some instances I have instead used the term "city" to avoid repetition.

2. The noun *koinônia* and its cognates I have translated variously as "community" or "association," and occasionally as "partnership," depending on the context. The verb *koinein* I have translated as "to share."

3. The term *philia* is translated here, and frequently below, as "affection." It also means "friendship," and I adopt that term in some instances.

4. I am assuming that Book II is, as it stands, a unity and that the review of "ideal" or "utopian" constitutions and the review of well-regarded contemporary constitutions are parts of the same endeavor – to identify what is best in those constitutions, particularly with respect to what is common. Aristotle himself says at the beginning of Book II, "Since we propose to study which political community is best of all for people who are able to live as ideally as possible, we must investigate other constitutions too, both some of those used in city-states that are said to be well governed, and any others described by anyone that are held to be good" (II 1, 1260b27–32). (See also Saunders, who says "This coupling makes sense; for all the constitutions Aristotle will consider have some claim to a principled superiority independent of the rival merits of the four traditional constitutions [kingship, aristocracy, oligarchy, and democracy], which were the staple of normal partisan political controversy, and indeed of Aristotle's own discussion in III-VI" (Saunders 1996: 104).) See Aubonnet 1960 (vol. 1) for a helpful summary of the issues around the structure of the *Politics* as a whole.

5. The notion of "living well" is introduced at I 2, 1252b27–30, where Aristotle describes the city-state as a community with the aim of living well.

6. See e.g., *NE* V 6, 1134a26; *NE* VIII 9, 1160a9–11.

7. Aristotle here and at VII 8, 1328a36 seems to say that friends are equals, which might suggest that friendship will be limited to political equals. But in other passages he allows that friendships between unequals are possible, so long as the inequality is addressed.

8. At III 6, 1278b16–23, Aristotle suggests that we want to live together just because we are political animals (recalling his claim at I 2, 1253a1–4), and so we want to live together even when we do not need one another's help (although of course it will also be convenient when we do need help).

9. In at least two passages, Aristotle seems to understand the relation of parts in a *koinônia* as active and passive. So, at *De anima* I 3, 407b18, in speaking of the relation of body to soul, he says "Because of community the one acts and the other is affected, and the one moves and the other is moved." And at *NE* V 5, 1133a14–17, in an aside during the discussion of proportionate reciprocity, Aristotle draws an analogy between an unfair bargain, in which work of different qualities is exchanged, and "the other arts also; for they would have been destroyed if what the patient suffered had not been just what the agent did, and of the same amount and kind."

10. For Aristotle's advice on preserving the stability of political constitutions, and avoiding faction, see especially V 8.

11. Trans. Grube, revised by Reeve, in Cooper 1997.

12. These proposals are summarized at *Timaeus* 18c.

13. In setting out these objections I have largely used the language of Newman 1888, vol. I: 229. One might think that there is a third objection: (3) It is unclear how we are to interpret the sense of "possessed in common" Socrates intends (II 2, 1261a13–14). Aristotle certainly says this; the question is whether it is a distinct objection. I have interpreted it as part of (2). See Simpson 1991: 100–3 for a discussion of other ways in which one might distinguish the objections.

14. There are different ways to read this phrase, but either way the import remains the same. See Newman 1887: 231.

15. Reeve trans., adapted. For a discussion of the sense of *ethnos* in this passage, and the reference to Arcadia, see Newman 1887: 231–3.

16. Reeve trans., adapted. The reference in this passage to the *Ethics* can be found at *NE* V 5, 1132b32–1133a30, *NE* IX 1, 1163b32–1164a2 and at *EE* VII 10, 1242b1–21, 1243b29–36. I will have more to say about this passage below.

17. See below p. 132 and note 27.

18. Reeve trans., adapted.

19. Kraut 2001 makes this point well.

20. This passage takes up an objection first voiced at II 2, 1261a13–14. One issue that Aristotle himself raises, and many commentators subsequently have noted, is that Plato does not make clear whether his proposals for women are confined to the guardian class, or intended to obtain in each of the classes in the Kallipolis.

21. The debate between David Charles (1988) and Martha Nussbaum (1988) concerns this point.

22. It is worth noting that Aristotle considers the advantages of affection not only for fellow-citizens but for the constitution itself: In II 8, 1268a23–25 he asks how, in the city proposed by Hippodamus, people who do not share in the constitution/regime will be able to have affection for the constitution/regime. This implies that affection *for the politeia* is a form of affection that we should cultivate among every group in the city; but that is consistent with cultivating affection for one another only among certain groups of citizens. The suggestion is that without generalized affection for the *politeia*, the city is subject to conflict and revolt.

23. See also *Politics* I 2, 1252b28–30.

24. The progression Aristotle suggests, from the extreme unity of the individual, to the reduced unity of the household, and the still further reduced unity of the city-state, is not unexpected in the context of the *Politics*. In *Politics* I he has suggested that a city-state is, if not the historical culmination of groupings of individuals into households, and households into villages, at least an entity that can be analyzed into households (I 2, 1252b13–1253a1). And he reiterates this claim in *Politics* III 9, at 1280b33–4 and 1280b40–1281a1.

25. Differences in profession cannot exhaust the differences Aristotle has in mind since, as many commentators have pointed out, Socrates proposed a division of labor in the Kallipolis of the *Republic*.

26. Dobbs says that Aristotle objects to Plato's 'communism' not because it is economically inefficient (i.e. not because the Platonic city-state will not be economically self-sufficient) but because it destroys the city-state as a place in which to cultivate virtue (Dobbs 1985: 35). But the question we need to address is: Why exactly would the sameness of elements to which Aristotle objects destroy the city-state in this sense?

27. See e.g., Saunders 1996: 110. Newman takes the "likes" in the passage at II 2, 1261a29–b5 to be people with the same profession (e.g. shoemakers); see Newman 1887: 233.

28. See *NE* V 3.

29. For an interesting discussion of Book II and its concern with women, see Saxonhouse 1982. While I disagree with her interpretation of Aristotle's aims (she says, "Aristotle rejects Socrates' position not because he

wishes to preserve the family's sexual hierarchy which Socrates would discard" (203); I think he clearly does wish to preserve the family's sexual hierarchy), Saxonhouse points out that Aristotle "raises the crucial political question of how one transfers the love of oneself to the love of what is common" (214).

30. See Deslauriers 2003 for a defense of this interpretation.

# 6 Civic virtue: citizenship, ostracism, and war

## INTRODUCTION

At the time of its reception in medieval and early-modern Europe, Aristotle's *Politics* was considered to be the flagship for the autonomy of politics. It was taken to embody the idea that "political philosophy constitutes an independent discipline worthy of study in its own right," and it helped to put into currency the very concept of "politics" (*politica*) for the first time.[1] If Aristotelian politics was envisaged as a branch of moral philosophy, it was envisaged as a *distinct* branch of moral philosophy.[2]

Things have changed. Very distinguished voices in contemporary liberal political philosophy have claimed that Aristotle understands politics to be but "the continuation of ethics," and that he fails to make any distinctions between moral and political philosophy since he holds "that there is but one ... conception [of the good] to be recognized by all citizens who are fully reasonable and rational."[3] Aristotle's account of civic virtue and the common good is seen hence as a textbook case of politics as an application of ethics, as nothing short of an attempt to give ethical solutions to political problems.

A similar thought underlies the recent decision made by no less distinguished representatives of contemporary republicanism to cut loose the ship of the republic from any Aristotelian moorings it might have had in the past. Because republicanism distinctively relies on civic virtue as a key ingredient of political life, and because

I am very grateful to Marguerite Deslauriers for her several insightful comments on prior versions of this chapter: They have improved it a great deal. My thanks also to Antony Hatzistavrou for sharing with me his comments on the last-but-one version of this chapter.

Aristotle takes civic virtue very seriously, it had been only natural to hail him as the founding father of republicanism.[4] Nowadays, however, this view has been vigorously challenged on the ground that the pedigree of republicanism is Roman rather than Greek, and, as a result, Aristotle himself is no longer counted as a republican. Moreover, neo-roman republicans claim that Aristotle's robust theory of the human good commits him to the belief that there are some ends shared by all citizens. On this interpretation, then, Aristotle's political theory is far too ethical to accommodate the possibility of political conflict – viz. the distinctively republican tenet that in political debate it is always possible to argue on both sides of a case.[5]

In this chapter I argue that understanding Aristotle's *Politics* as an application of his moral philosophy does not do justice to his treatment of civic virtue (political virtue) in its entirety: Aristotle is much more political a thinker than is often acknowledged. In what follows I shall first set out Aristotle's account of civic virtue, beginning with the specific tasks citizens are expected to fulfill, and moving to the vexed question of the relation between the good man and the good citizen, and the possibility that they are not the same. An examination of what might be called the very "principle of citizenship" will show that in Aristotle's eyes it is conceptually linked to some kind of exclusion that is not necessarily moral in nature. We shall then move on to discuss the tension between Aristotle's two conceptions of civic virtue – to say this in Rawlsian parlance, the "comprehensive" account of *Pol.* VII–VIII and the "political" account of *Pol.* III 9–13.

In a second section I discuss Aristotle's wholeheartedly political justification of the practice of ostracizing law-abiding (and even morally upright) citizens. The case of ostracism demonstrates that Aristotle allows purely political considerations – considerations independent of morality – to be invoked in case of constitutional dire straits.

Finally, to complicate this picture, in the third section I discuss the civic virtue of performing courageous actions in war in the service of the best political community, and the relation of that virtue to Aristotle's justification of war. War seems to represent an exception to the political approach to civic virtue, because Aristotle subjects its political aims to moral assessment. But his account of war, ethical as it is, cannot at times avoid getting political in the pejorative sense of the word, as he seeks to rationalize enslavement and hegemony as compelling reasons for wars.

## CIVIC VIRTUE

### *That thing you do: the tasks of a citizen*

In general, by the noun *virtue* Aristotle refers to some excellence a person may display in a particular role. Were we to apply Aristotle's functional theory of virtue to his account of citizenship, a virtuous citizen would be someone who performs his function as a citizen well.[6] Now Aristotle distinguishes between "peaceful" and "warlike" civic functions (I 6, 1254b31–32). It is actually noteworthy that the first civic function to appear in the list of parts of the *polis* set out in *Pol.* IV 4 belongs to the warlike genre: the "military" (*to propoleméson*).[7] The rest of the list refers to peaceful civic activities: the part regarding "those who participate in administering judicial justice"; "those who deliberate" about common affairs; "the rich" or "those who perform public service by means of their property," and finally "the civil servants, those who serve in connection with the various offices" (IV 4, 1291a7, 27–28, 33–34, 35).

When it comes to how citizens should act as they fulfill their civic duties, Aristotle mentions three qualities that those who hold office are expected to possess: "first, friendship for the established constitution; next, the greatest capacity for the tasks of office; third, in each constitution the sort of virtue or justice that is suited to the constitution" (V 9, 1309a33–39). As far as most constitutions are concerned, instead of requiring patriotism of citizens, Aristotle says only that citizens should be "well disposed toward the constitution." And he is actually willing to settle for citizens who "at least [do] not regard those in authority as their enemies" (VI 5, 1320a14–17).

Regarding the capacity for the tasks of office, certain specific roles, such as military or financial functions, will require some particular technical expertise or special resources, but most will not. There are, however, certain ethical shortcomings that affect all forms of civic activity in so far as they stand in the way of any meaningful and efficient participation in a common enterprise such as political life. As Aristotle explains, a citizen must have at the very least a "shred of courage, temperance, justice, or practical wisdom"; he cannot be "afraid of the flies buzzing around him"; and he must not be someone who will "stop at nothing to gratify his appetite for food or drink, betray his dearest friends for a pittance, and have a mind as foolish and prone to error as a child's or a madman's" (VII 1, 1323a28–34). Although this description appears in Aristotle's discussion of the best constitution, it describes a modicum of self-control and intellectual skill which would be useful in any constitution.[8]

### An officer and a gentleman? The good citizen and the good person

Aristotle's discussion of the third quality expected of citizens – virtue that is suited to the constitution – raises the vexed question of the relation between the excellent man and the good citizen, viz. whether they should be regarded as the same or not (III 4, 1276b17). It is clear that Aristotle claims that ethical virtue and civic virtue are not necessarily the same (III 4, 1276b34–35). The only issue is why he comes to that conclusion.

A first and *inter*-constitutional argument for the claim that ethical and civic virtue are distinct (I will call this "the separation thesis") derives from the role-related nature of civic virtue itself. Aristotle claims that "it is clear that there cannot be a single virtue that is the virtue – the complete virtue – of a good citizen," "if indeed there are several kinds of constitutions." In effect, only the good man "does express a single virtue: the complete one. Evidently then, it is possible for someone to be a good citizen without having acquired the virtue expressed by a good man" (III 4, 1276b30–34). This conclusion is borne out by what Aristotle asserts elsewhere on aristocracy: "Only here is it unqualifiedly the case that the same person is a good man and a good citizen. But those who are good in other constitutions are so relative to their constitutions" (IV 7, 1293b5–7; see also V 9, 1309a38–39).

A second and *intra*-constitutional argument for the separation thesis is provided by the nautical analogy employed by Aristotle in *Pol.* III 4 to illustrate the nature of political virtue. The analogy not only brings out the fact that sailors share in the common task of preserving the ship, but also points out the different tasks assigned to them: "One is an oarsman, another a captain, another a lookout, and others have other sorts of titles" (III 4, 1276b22–24). Thus, although some civic duties will be easily met by all citizens, other civic tasks will only be fulfilled by citizens with some particular ethical and intellectual skills. For instance, while oarsmen and lookouts do not need to know where they are heading or why in order to perform their duty, the captain does need to possess the ethical and intellectual wherewithal to coordinate the different activities of the crew, keep the ship going, and ensure the safe arrival of the ship at the port of destination. So one might be excellent at performing some civic functions without being a virtuous person.

It is in a similar spirit that Aristotle draws a difference in virtue between rulers and subjects. Only the "excellent ruler is good and possesses practical wisdom," not the citizen (III 4, 1277a14–16). This is why "[the virtue of] a ruler and that of a citizen would not be the same' (III 4, 1277a23): while practical wisdom is peculiar to the ruler ("practical wisdom is not the virtue of one who is ruled, but true opinion is"), the other virtues "must be common to both rulers and ruled" (III 4, 1277b25–29).

Aristotle claims that this intra-constitutional point applies even to the best regime (III 4, 1276b35–37).[9] At first sight it must strike us as odd that Aristotle claims that it is impossible for his best regime to be composed entirely of good men (III 4, 1276b37–38), since in his own ruminations on the best city he claims that *all* its citizens will be good men (VII 13, 1332a34–35). A first and rather implicit way of dealing with this discrepancy would be to distinguish between the best constitution of Book III and its counterpart in Books VII and VIII, on two grounds.

First of all, whereas Book III envisages both kingship and aristocracy as tokens of the best constitution, in Book VII there is no talk of kingship as the best constitution. Second, whereas in Book VII Aristotle seems to have a colonial setting in mind,[10] in Book III Aristotle is not so much interested in proposing a new political system as he is in assessing traditional ones, so that no fresh start or major political overhaul is in view. If Aristotle is trying to make do with the civic material he has at hand, we can assume that there will be some hierarchy of merits and hence of authority in the best city by the standards of Book III.[11] These citizens would be ruled to the extent that, e.g. they obey the king, but they may well share in ruling themselves as they occupy offices under the king.

There is a second and rather straightforward way in which Aristotle might resolve the discrepancy between the claim that the best regime cannot be composed entirely of good men and the claim that all the citizens will be good men in the best city. Although for his best regime in Book VII Aristotle sticks to the principle that all who are parts of the constitution should "share alike in ruling and being ruled in turn," for "equality consists in giving the same to those who are alike" (VII 14, 1332b26–27), he meets this standard in a rather idiosyncratic way. Indeed, Aristotle divides the political class (to politikon) into "two parts, the military and the deliberative" (VII 9, 1329a30–31) and he distributes these offices consecutively to different age groups, for two reasons. On the one hand, there is the functional-cum-ethical consideration that "since the best time for each of these tasks is different, in that one requires practical wisdom and the other physical strength, they should be assigned to different people" (VII 9, 1329a7–9), since "nature itself settled the choice by making part of the same species younger and part older, the former fit to be ruled and the latter to rule" (VII 14, 1332b35–38). On the other hand, there is the realistic awareness that "since those capable of using and resisting force cannot possibly tolerate being ruled continuously, for this reason the two tasks [using force and ruling] should be assigned to the same people. For those who control the weapons also control whether a constitution will survive or not" (VII 9, 1329a9–14). All in all, Aristotle's division of the political class into two parts allows him to claim that all citizens in the best city will be good men though they will reach the top of their civic game at different times.

### Nice work if you can get it: Who can display civic virtue?

Citizenship is not only a functional notion but also an ascriptive one: it refers both to *what* is to be done and to *who* is permitted to do it.[12] Aristotle recommends leaving aside the practices of extant *poleis* as models for assigning citizenship when he rules out the definition usual at the time according to which a citizen is "someone who comes from citizens on both sides" (III 2, 1275b22–23). He is also apprehensive about the case of "those who are made citizens" (III 1, 1275a6), i.e. "those who come to participate in a constitution after a revolution, such as the citizens created in Athens by Cleisthenes after the expulsion of the tyrants (for he enrolled many foreigners and alien slaves in the tribes)" (III 2, 1275b35–37; cf. VI 4, 1319b19–27). Although Aristotle is happy to acknowledge that these people are citizens in a sense, he is not prepared to admit that they are rightly so (III 2, 1275b37–38).

Aristotle's reservations regarding existing standards for ascriptive citizenship stem from their failure to derive the assignment of political tasks from the standards of "distributive justice" (see *NE* V 2, 1130b30–1131a1), according to which a distribution is just if and only if there is an equality of ratios between the good being distributed and the persons obtaining that good.[13] More precisely, there ought to be a proportion between the worth (*axia*) of the receiver (*NE* V 3, 1131a24–26) and the value of what is received. As far as Aristotle is concerned, worth can only be measured by the capacity to lead the life of the fullest virtuous activity supplied with the necessary equipment (VII 1, 1323b46–1324a2). Hence, Aristotle's favored conception of citizenship assignment is mainly ethical in nature, as shown by his discussion of citizenship in the best regime (e.g. VII 9, 1329a2–5, 35–39).

We may well find fault with Aristotle's emphasis on a level of ethical excellence or achievement as a standard of citizenship. We might want all those who are interested in the job to have the same opportunities, and hence to be eligible for citizenship. Many who may have wanted to lead the good life Aristotle expects of his best citizens would have been ineligible – let us recall, e.g. Aristotle's defense of natural slavery.[14]

Nevertheless, we should pause to observe that our own political culture is not so distant from Aristotle's as we may believe, when we read that "the truth is that not everyone without whom there would not be a city-state is to be regarded as a citizen" (III 5, 1278a2–3). Not even modern states bestow citizenship on all the people on whom they depend, often excluding those who live outside the country, and sometimes even some of those who live inside it, e.g. as "guest-workers." Hence, although it is very likely we shall find Aristotle's handling of political exclusion not to our taste, it cannot be its exclusionary nature *as such* that offends us but rather the *moral* standard of political exclusion that Aristotle employs. Finding a correct standard of political exclusion, however, may well turn out to be much trickier than it appears.

Indeed, at the very root of a political community there seems to lie a formative exclusion that functions as a principle of citizenship: by the very fact of saying that X is a citizen of political community Y we are saying not only that X is a member of Y (and hence defining a group inclusively, in terms of who its members are), but also thereby excluding some people from membership in that group. We can imagine a political community pursuing such an open-house approach to immigration that citizenship may well turn out to be everyone's for the taking. But that kind of policy would still exclude those unable and/or unwilling to apply for citizenship. And, as a matter of historical record, "Not even a Commonwealth was ever found so popular, but that those who were very poor, or Strangers, the Women and young Folks, were excluded from publick Councils."[15]

The only way to do away with the exclusion that accompanies this principle of citizenship would be to embrace cosmopolitan citizenship: if the entire world were one political community or literal *cosmopolis*, no individual would be left out. This is an option that Aristotle openly discards, as we shall see at the end of this chapter. In the meantime we should keep in mind that Aristotle is not without very good company in defending political particularism. Most people in liberal democracies prefer to be free and equal within their own nation, rather than to be free and equal cosmopolitan citizens, because cosmopolitan citizenship would make it hard for them to live and work in their own language and culture. The preference for particular nations holds even though it prevents people from having the freedom to work and vote elsewhere and makes it hard for those who are not citizens of a liberal country to live and work in it.[16]

Aristotle's ethical standard of citizenship might actually be preferable to the liberal standard in that the latter defers to factors such as culture (at best) and violence (at worst) and, as a result, those who are included in a liberal political community do not differ in any morally relevant sense from those who are excluded from it. This is why Aristotle could claim that moral virtue seems to fare rather well as a means of determining citizenship in comparison to standards such as having being born south or north of liberal state borders. After all, moral reasons for action are those that cannot be justifiably denied by anybody.[17]

## Two conceptions of citizenship: comprehensive civic virtue and political civic virtue

Aristotle, in Book VII of his *Politics*, seems to assume a high standard of ethical excellence in his discussion of who gets to be a citizen, and hence who gets to exercise civic virtue. He, however, expects the best moral agents that money can(not) buy to attend an assembly to decide what to do together as a political community (see VII 4, 1326b6). Indeed, instead of assuming that his excellent agents will all agree on what is to be done regarding public affairs as a result of perfect individual ethical reasoning, Aristotle seems to expect them, excellent as they are, to engage in collective deliberation on the assumption that in public affairs it is always possible to argue both sides of a case. This is why political issues even in the best regime are finally resolved by public deliberation and decision. And the need for public deliberation and decision implies that politics has a considerable degree of autonomy from moral reasoning and virtue.

The political awareness that underlies Aristotle's institutional design in his best *polis* seems to come to the surface as we approach Book III 9–13, where he adopts a straightforward political tack on the question of who gets to exercise civic virtue on the assumption that no moral argument will carry the day in a discussion on public affairs, particularly with respect to the question of who gets to be a citizen. Aristotle here is interested in standards that are likely to attract agreement from all the parties to political disagreement, even if for different reasons.

As he discusses political virtue in *Pol.* III 9 in terms of its contribution to the genuine aim of a political community, although he does not entirely forsake the principle that "political communities must be taken to exist for the sake of noble actions, and not for the sake of living together" (III 9, 1281a2–4), Aristotle defends the rather nuanced claim that "those who contribute most to this sort of community have a *larger* share in the city-state than those who are equal or superior in freedom or family but inferior in political virtue, and those who surpass in wealth but are surpassed in virtue" (III 9, 1281a5–8).[18] Hence, instead of treating freedom and wealth as significant only insofar as they contribute to virtue, Aristotle upgrades them to factors separately eligible for consideration in their own right as a standard of political distribution.

Thus, whereas *Pol.* VII delivers what Rawlsians today would call a "comprehensive" theory of civic virtue since it is based exclusively upon Aristotle's conception of the human good, *Pol.* III 9–13 offers what Rawlsians would call a "political" or free-standing conception of civic virtue that can be endorsed by different comprehensive doctrines and for different reasons.[19]

At any rate, those who, were they to be judged by the standards of Book VII, would be ineligible for citizenship – and might even be slaves – would be fit to display political virtue themselves, if judged by the standards of *Pol.* III 9. In *Pol.* III 10 Aristotle expands his political horizon to the extent of adding tyrants to the list of possible recipients of political authority together with the rich, the multitude, and the virtuous (III 10, 1281a11–13). More than that, when he raises the issue of whether virtuous people should "rule and have authority over everything," he suggests that an answer in the affirmative would bring about the puzzling result that "everyone else must be deprived of honors by being excluded from political office" (III 10, 1281a28–30).[20]

Moreover, in *Pol.* III 12 in the context of his discussion of political justice and equality, Aristotle concedes that the appropriate standard for assigning political office "must be based on the things from which a city-state is constituted" (III 12, 1283a14–15) and no longer insists on the ethical goal of the city as the exclusive standard. Aristotle's conclusion is astonishing if seen from the viewpoint of Book VII: "Hence the well-born, the free, and the rich reasonably lay claim to office. For there must be both free people and those with assessed property, since a city-state cannot consist entirely of poor people, any more than of slaves" (III 12, 1283a16–19). In *Pol.* III 13 he even raises the issue of how to resolve the dispute as to who should rule in case "the good, the rich, the well-born, and a political multitude in addition" were all present in a *polis* (III 13, 1283b1–2).

Thus, it looks as though when Aristotle got to tackle the issue of political virtue in Book III his idea in Book VII of reserving citizenship for practitioners of his ethical theory only was abandoned. As far as Book III is concerned, any free Greek adult man could make a good citizen.

OSTRACISM

*It had to be you*

As we have seen, in Book III Aristotle is clearly willing to invoke political considerations to determine who should be included in the citizen body, and hence who should be allowed to display civic virtue. He also seems to advocate ostracism, namely, the practice of excluding – if only temporarily – a law-abiding and possibly morally virtuous citizen from the civic community for purely political reasons, in order to preserve the constitution.[21]

Aristotle gets off to a rather moralizing start that seems incompatible with justifications of ostracism when he claims that in the case of "one person or more than one (though not enough to make up a complete city-state)" who "is so outstanding by reason of his superior virtue that neither the virtue nor the political power of all the others is commensurable with his (if there is only one) or theirs (if there are a number of them)," "then such men" of incommensurably superior virtue "can no longer be regarded as part of the city-state" (III 13, 1284a3–8). Furthermore, he adds that "it is clear that legislation ... must be concerned with those who are equals both in birth and in power" and that for those who are outstandingly unequal in virtue "there is no law, since they themselves are law" (III 13, 1284a11–14). In fact, "anyone of that sort would reasonably be regarded as a god among human beings" (III 13, 1284a10–11).[22]

We should bear in mind that the kind of virtue that Aristotle has in view at this juncture, the kind that seems to be the target of ostracism, is not just ethical excellence but ethical superiority of a godlike, incommensurable, or absolute kind. In the case of ordinary ethical excellence, X's superiority in virtue to Y calls for a proportional distribution of political power between X and Y – let us call this "comparable" or "relative" superiority. In the case of godlike ethical excellence, X's superiority in virtue over Y is such that X and Y cannot be said to be different parts of the same whole since X is a whole for himself, and hence all power should go to X – let us call this "incomparable" or "absolute" superiority.[23] Aristotle's point seems to be that beyond a certain threshold quantity transforms into quality.

Having described the type of virtue at stake, Aristotle concludes precisely that those who "are so unequal in virtue and political power would be treated unjustly if they were thought to merit equal shares" (III 13, 1284a9–10). As he refers to the best constitution Aristotle comments that "surely people would not say that such a person should be expelled or banished, but neither would they say that they should rule over him," for "that would be like claiming that they deserved to rule over Zeus, dividing the offices. The remaining possibility – and it seems to be the natural one – is for everyone to obey such a person gladly, so that those like him will be permanent kings in their city-states" (III 14, 1284a29–34; see also III 17, 1288a24–29). Not only, then, should the person of absolute virtue not be ostracized, he should be cheerfully obeyed.

What is striking at this point is that Aristotle not only reports that deviant regimes (democracy, oligarchy, tyranny) turn to ostracism but even seems to put in a good word for ostracism itself, as he adds that "those who criticize tyranny" for turning to ostracism "should not be considered to be unqualifiedly correct in their censure" (III 13, 1284a27). According to Aristotle, "the problem" of ostracism "is a general one that concerns *all* constitutions, even the correct ones. For though the deviant constitutions use methods with an eye to the private benefit, the position is the same with those that aim at the common good" (III 13, 1284b3–7).[24]

Indeed, Aristotle adds that even monarchs would be "in harmony with the *polis* they rule when they resort to this sort of practice, provided their rule benefits their city-states" (III 13, 1284b13–15). Thus, Aristotle, unlike modern scholars, does not only recognize the practice of ostracism in Athenian democracy but also argues that ostracism is a handy institution for *any* right constitution. And it is significant that it is immediately after making the point on kingship that Aristotle concludes that "where acknowledged sorts of superiority are concerned, then, there is some political justice to the argument in favor of ostracism" (III 13, 1284b15–17; cf. *NE* V 6, 1134a25–26).[25]

Now Aristotle's endorsement of the pursuit of civic equality by means of ostracism may be far less surprising than it seems once we realize that its real target is not necessarily absolute moral virtue. First of all, Aristotle's comparison between ostracism and exile tips us off that their targets are "*outstanding* people" (*tous huperechontas*) (III 13, 1284a36–37),[26] an expression which may well refer *both* to absolute and to relative superiority. The same applies to a considerable degree to the "crafts and sciences" analogy used by Aristotle in defense of ostracism. Whereas the reference to the chorus master seems to strike an absolute chord as he is said to be unwilling to tolerate "a member of the chorus who has a louder and more beautiful voice than the *entire* chorus" (III 13, 1284b8–13),[27] painters and shipbuilders seem to have relative superiority in mind as they are said to be unwilling to allow a part to "exceed the symmetry" (*huperballonta . . . tēs summetrias*) of their work even if this part were "different in beauty" (*diapheroi to kallos*) from all others.[28]

Secondly, the cases used by Aristotle to illustrate ostracism suggest that the moral starting-point for his discussion of ostracism may well turn out to be a red herring for political purposes. Indeed, on Aristotle's view, the citizens who are fair game for ostracism are "those held to be outstandingly powerful" in terms of garden-variety political goods necessary for the exercise of civic virtue such as "wealth, . . . many friends, or any other source of political power" (III 13, 1284a20–21). Thus, ostracism is just in so far as it promotes the common good since its point is to expel for a fixed period of time a citizen who does not excel absolutely in moral virtue but whose absolute or relative superiority in external goods may well turn out to be a menace to the constitution. Absolute moral superiority being out of the question,[29] comparable moral superiority as a rule should not be a cause for ostracism except in the rather unlikely case of an agent who relatively excels others in moral virtue *and* has acquired too much political power for himself – even if unintentionally – in terms of friends, wealth, or strength, to the extent of becoming a danger for political stability.

To be sure, Aristotle is confident that a good legislator – who is a craftsman of sorts after all (e.g. VII 4, 1326a35–38) – would be able to establish the constitution from the get-go so that it would have "no need for such a remedy" (III 13, 1284b17–19; see also V 3, 1302b15–21 and V 8, 1308b16–19), and presumably that will be the situation described by Book VII. But failing that, "the next best thing is" for the political craftsman "to try to fix the constitution, should the need arise, with a corrective of this sort" (III 14, 1284b19–20).

Now the fact remains that ostracism seems to be fundamentally unjust in that it is designed to target individuals who are law-abiding citizens. Indeed, "it would seem to involve punishing a person who has not violated the rights of anyone else. It is hard to see how this can be justified on the basis of corrective justice."[30] Actually, the ostracized citizen seems to suffer harm without having acted at all. Even those who speak in its favor grant that ostracism does not consist in punishing a crime actually committed by the ostracized person but in assessing "what hurt he would do."[31] While punishment belongs to corrective justice in the strict sense and thus is essentially backward-looking in so far as a criminal is sanctioned on the grounds of his past wrongdoing, ostracism belongs to "political justice" (III 13, 1284b16) and thus is forward-looking in that potential enemies of the constitution are anticipated as they are expected to harm the regime.

Aristotle's reply might thus be that corrective justice in terms of punishment does not exhaust the entire field of justice. He seems to be of the view that:

(a)  sometimes it is very difficult (if not impossible) to harmonize the interests of those who are parties to a political conflict by implementing common rules at no one's expense – as we have seen, Aristotle is aware that political communities may well be *formed* at the expense of morally impeccable agents; and

(b)  constitutions should not only encompass the quotidian smooth operation of institutional structures that deal with the needs of peaceful and stable times and that follow the backward-looking guidelines of corrective justice, but should also, regrettably, include some extraordinary measures called for in rare times of deep constitutional crises under the forward-looking guidelines of political justice precisely in order to *preserve* the constitution. It is this two-track system that allows for the regular functioning of the constitution and its defense in exceptional cases.[32]

WAR

## Peace or pacifism: peace as the aim of war

In the first section of this chapter, I set out the concept of civic virtue, distinguished it from ethical virtue, and related it to two conceptions of citizenship. In the second section, we saw that Aristotle allows that the political community may sometimes be justified in excluding some of its citizens, even citizens who display ethical virtue. All of this indicates that Aristotle's treatment of civic virtue is much more political than suggested by the interpretation according to which it is nothing but an application of ethical virtue.

One might object that the moral treatment Aristotle gives to the civic virtue of the courage displayed in war in the service of the best political community stands in contrast to the political tenor of his account of civic virtue and ostracism, and there is some truth to that claim. We shall see, nonetheless, that even Aristotle's avowedly moral account of civic courage in war has certain nasty political overtones.

There is no question but that Aristotle thinks highly of military service and war in ethical terms as he claims that the finest "deaths are deaths in war; for then the danger is greatest and finest" (*NE* III 6, 1115a30–31). Moreover, he seems to understand war as an opportunity for virtue.[33] Whereas "the enjoyment of good luck and the leisure that accompanies peace tend to make them arrogant," war "compels people to be just and temperate" (VII 15, 1334a26–28). This emphasis on war as an opportunity for virtue has been an easy target for those who claim that there are other activities that "equally involve risk of death and injury, solidarity with comrades, vigorous competition, and so on." Indeed, the only feature distinctive of war seems to be "that you get the opportunity to maim and kill and to be maimed and killed by other human beings; even if this is in a good cause, it can hardly add to the moral value of war compared to its peaceful counterparts."[34]

Now although Aristotle is more than willing to "let slip the dogs of war" he is also adamant that they are to be kept on a short normative leash. Surely Aristotle's best citizens will behave as the courageous person is depicted at *NE* III 7, 1115b19–20: "the courageous person feels and acts as the occasion merits, and follows the correct prescription, however it may direct him." The correct prescription will be that "War must be chosen for the sake of peace" (VII 14, 1333a35; cf. I 6, 1255a25). This does not seem to be a promising start since making war for the sake of peace seems to be like having sex for the sake of chastity. Aristotle might reply to this objection that this line of argument can only be taken by extreme pacifists, viz. those who entertain the view that every war is a crime, so much so that war *as such* should be outlawed – including wars of self-defense – and hence that the most unjust peace would be preferable to the justest of wars.

Aristotle, on the contrary, seems to take war to be like other cases of justified violence such as "just retributions and punishments," which certainly "spring from virtue, but are necessary uses of it, and are noble only in a necessary way, since it would be more choiceworthy if no individual or city-state needed such things" (VII 13, 1332a12–15).[35] Aristotle thus can be said to be committed to a rather moderate brand of pacifism which instead of outlawing war altogether is nothing but the reverse side of a theory of justified war. According to moderate pacifism, the formula "for the sake of" should be understood in causal terms, so that war could be made at time $T_n$ for peace to take place at a posterior $T_{n+1}$. This is very much in keeping with the old slogan: "if you want peace, get ready for war."[36] Nevertheless, Aristotle's commitment to causal pacifism does not go to the length of claiming that there is a war capable of achieving perpetual peace, viz. a war capable of ending war once and for all.

At any rate, Aristotle's moderate pacifism quarters three reasons (what nowadays is called the *jus ad bellum*) why morally wrong actions like killing, destruction, and capture can be transmuted into justified belligerent acts, viz. into courageous actions performed in the service of the best political community.

## Freedom fighters: war justified as self-defense

The first justification for war brought up by Aristotle is self-defense: war is permissible "to avoid becoming enslaved to others" (VII 14, 1333b40–41).[37] Aristotle illustrates his first argument for war by saying that "as the proverb says, there is no leisure for slaves, and people who are unable to face danger courageously are the slaves of their attackers" (VII 15, 1334a20–22).[38] This is why Aristotle's own best regime counted among its constituent parts those who carry weapons (*hopla*) in order to deal with invaders (VII 8, 1328b2–4, 7–10). This is in keeping with the serious thought given by Aristotle to the possibility of an isolated life for his best *polis* (VII 3, 1325b23–27): a contemplative, i.e. isolated life led by the best *polis* would require only defensive arrangements.

There seem to be at least two grounds for being skeptical about understanding this first argument as an appeal to national self-defense, at least as this notion is understood nowadays.[39] First of all, Aristotle seems to be referring to a justified response in the face of unjustified violence, but on the part of individual citizens rather than the *polis* itself. Second, by a war of self-defense we usually understand a justified violent response to an "aggression," viz. "[e]very violation of the territorial integrity or political sovereignty of an independent state."[40] But, whereas our contemporary understanding of self-defense proceeds on the assumption that there is a nation-state with its attendant homeland, Aristotle does not seem to set great store by territorial integrity. According to Aristotle, "the most important thing citizens have in common is the goal of leading...[the best possible] life, and anything else that is common to them – their land, education, rulers, and so on – must be shared because it is needed to promote such a life," as Richard Kraut has pointed out. This is why Aristotle is taken to be "fundamentally opposed to nationalism," according to which "territorial...affinities" are among "the most significant similarities that tie people together into a political community...rather than their perfectibility as human beings."[41] A particular geography seems to play no inherent role in the Aristotelian political script.

Regarding the first objection, it may well turn out to be an asset for Aristotle. Indeed, national defense is usually seen as "simply an application, *en masse*, of the familiar right of individuals to protect themselves and others from unjust lethal attack" riding on the back of what is usually called the "domestic analogy." If this is the case, then "national defense" would be "something of a misnomer," "for there would be no independent right to use lethal force in defense of the state or the nation, as such, only the rights of individuals to defend their own lives, and those of others."[42] So Aristotle may not be susceptible to this objection. The individualist flavor of our passage is, however, clearly offset by Aristotle's explanation elsewhere of the reason why defensive warriors (*to propolemêson*) are precisely a necessary part of *poleis*: they are "no less necessary" than the other parts "if the inhabitants are not to become the slaves of any aggressor (*epiousin*). For no city-state that is naturally slavish can possibly deserve to be called a city-state at all; for a city-state is self-sufficient, whereas something that is slavish is not self-sufficient" (IV 4, 1291a6–10). It is the freedom of the city itself, then, that is on the line, and not just the freedom of its citizens.

When it comes to the second objection, it is undeniable that according to Aristotle the territory, being one of the things that are common to the best citizens, is valuable only because it is needed to promote the best possible life for them. Territory then is not a "part" of the *polis* in Aristotle's rather demanding sense of the term but simply belongs to "the things that are necessary for the existence of a city-state" (VII 8, 1328a22–23, 28); it is just one of the "conditions (*hupotheseis*) that should be presupposed to exist" by the *polis* (VII 4, 1325b35–36).

The force of this objection may, however, turn out to be weaker than it seems to be, especially if we bring Aristotle and nationalism closer together by deflating somewhat the notion of nationalism. We could claim that nationalists may well be interested only in showing that if human beings want to live together as a political community, they will need to control *a* piece of land rather than *this particular* territory. This weaker notion of nationalism can easily be attributed to Aristotle. Although he does seem to have in mind, *malgré lui* perhaps, a particular culture or kind of people for his best *polis* (VII 7, 1327b29–31), he does not seem to be particular about the land his best citizens will inhabit to the extent that it meets some general requirements (VII 5–6).[43]

### Slavery fighters: war justified on the basis of natural slavery

No one acquainted with Aristotle's views on natural slavery would be surprised to learn that Aristotle's endorsement of self-defense against foreign enslavement is not based on the principled rejection of slavery as such. Indeed, in Aristotle's view the pursuit of an aggressive war of enslavement against those who, according to his analysis of slavery, deserve to be slaves is a second reason for waging justified war (VII 14, 1334a2).[44]

Thus, although the first justification for waging war was fairly close to our contemporary understanding of war, this second one could not possibly be further from our moral beliefs. First of all, while we would be reluctant to lump self-defense and enslavement together as rationales to justify war, Aristotle seems to treat them as the defensive and the aggressive sides of the same coin. Indeed, his endorsement of civic freedom seems to go hand in hand with his conception of natural slavery as a central piece of his political philosophy, not only as a conceptual and normative matter but also and essentially as an ontological possibility, to the extent that he seems to believe that if slavery were abolished it would also cut the ground from under the feet of freedom. Thus, on this view, you could only believe in freedom and literally fight for it if you were also to believe in slavery and to pursue the mastery "of those who deserve to be slaves" (VII 14, 1334a2).[45]

Second, we would surely feel ourselves estranged from the very idea of an aggressive war as a justified option. The contemporary understanding of aggression as a purely derogatory term would make the question of the justification of aggression as such impossible in the first place, since it would be tantamount to stating a contradiction in terms. This is precisely why our current understanding of aggression as a crime has caught the eye of a distinguished Aristotelian: "The present-day conception of 'aggression,' like so many influential conceptions, is a bad one. Why *must* it be wrong to strike the first blow in a struggle? The only question is, who is in the right, if anyone is."[46]

Thirdly, those who are the target of an aggressive war of enslavement happen to be non-Greeks. Aristotle actually reports without disapproving that "our poets say that 'it is proper for Greeks to rule non-Greeks', implying that non-Greek and slave are in nature the same" (I 2, 1252b8–9). And by means of an idiom which proved to be extremely popular with the entire Western just war tradition, he claims that "the science of warfare...ought to be used not only against wild beasts but also against those human beings who are unwilling to be ruled, but naturally suited for it, as this sort of warfare is naturally just (*phusei dikaion touton onta ton polemon*)" (I 8, 1256b23–26; cf. I 6, 1255a24–25).[47]

Hence, those who turn out to be the target of a naturally just war of enslavement would surely object that just war theories seem to rationalize political goals as moral justifications for war, so that the very idea of demanding a just cause to wage war is actually either (a) "something self-evident, if it means that war can be risked only against a real enemy"; or (b) "it is a hidden political aspiration" to wrest from the target of a just war its right to fight back so that "it is no longer a...free people and is absorbed into another political system."[48]

### Follow the leader: war justified as a benefit

Even if in our eyes these first two reasons for waging a just war – self-defense and enslavement – are poles apart from each other in

moral terms, they both bring to mind a clearly asymmetrical relation in which some form of wrong-righting is at stake: self-defense
against someone who is about to commit a *wrongful* act or aggression (VII 8, 1328b9), enslavement of someone who *deserves* to be
a slave (VII 14, 1334a2) arguably by way of "ethical correction."[49]
Things seem to change as we approach the remaining reason why
the best *polis* could be at war, since it involves the pursuit of "a
position of leadership (*hêgemonian*) in order to benefit the ruled"
(VII 14, 1333b41–34a1).[50] This take on war is very much in keeping
with Aristotle's reference to the "political life" – in opposition to
a purely "theoretical life" – of his best regime, namely, the life of a
*polis* pursuing a rather hearty international agenda (VII 2, 1325a5–14;
cf. II 6, 1265a18–25) but arguably mainly amidst a Greek context.

Leaving aside our contemporary ingrained disgust for aggressive
wars, what sounds odd right off the bat is that, as Aristotle himself points out, this "position of leadership" goes hand in hand with
political rule, i.e. a kind of rule entirely at odds with mastery of
neighbors (VII 2, 1324b22–28; cf. VII 3, 1325a24–30) since it is exercised over free and willing people. Actually it is in this context that
Aristotle says that it would be "absurd" for a statesman to "study
ways to rule or master his neighbors, whether they are willing or
not" (VII 2, 1324b25–26). Thus, the talk of benefiting the ruled could
not make up for the unwillingness of the ruled.

The fact that the neighbors Aristotle has in mind when he refers
to the "political life" of the best *polis* are precisely Greek makes
things even more difficult for him. Indeed, political rule not only
requires that those subject to it be free and benefit from it but also
calls for ruling in turns under some description (e.g. I 1, 1252a15–
16; I 12, 1259b4–5), and then again it is precisely in this context
that Aristotle rejects the view that "someone who has the power
to rule should not surrender it to his neighbor but take it away from
him" (VII 3, 1325a37–38). Aristotle would also have some difficulty
defending the foreign policy of his best regime against his own criticism regarding what "each of those who achieved leadership in
Greece" did – (namely, Athens and Sparta) as they have looked "to
their own constitutions... aiming not at the benefit of these city-
states but at their own" (IV 12, 1296a32–36; see VI 7, 1307b19–24).

Against this background, and in spite of Aristotle's distinction
between hegemony and despotic rule (VII 14, 1333b41–1334a1), it

would be only natural for those *poleis* being attacked allegedly for their own good to experience the policy of hegemony of Aristotle's best *polis* as nothing but a façade of well-meaning leadership and thus as a form of what we would nowadays call outright imperialism. They will also probably share the misgivings concerning just war of those who happen to be the target of wars of natural enslavement and they might as well turn to Aristotle's argument on self-defense vis-à-vis slavery against the imperialistic foreign policy of Aristotelian best regime itself. As it turns out, the best regime's slogan seems to be something like "if you want peace, slaves, and hegemony, get ready for war."

Two roads seem to be open to Aristotle to deal with this ancient Greek "tension between the will to leadership...and the ideal of self-sufficiency that no city could renounce without denying its very nature":[51] he may awkwardly claim that those who are to benefit from political rule as subjects should consent to being attacked, or claim that the war is waged not as an acquisitive project but as a defensive enterprise against a third party. After all, Aristotle's wording leaves the passage at VII 14, 1333b41–34a1 open to two radically different readings: it concerns either (a) wars waged literally *against* those who are to benefit from the leadership of his best regime; or (b) wars waged simply *on the occasion of* the pursuit of leadership over willing *poleis* and on their behalf against third parties – this reading may well accommodate Aristotle's claim that "a city-state should be formidable on both land and sea, able to defend not just itself but some of its neighbors as well" (VII 6, 1327a41–b3).[52]

A third and rather drastic alternative would be to eliminate the moral distinction between wars of aggression and wars of defense altogether and go with an approach to war that does not so much care about *what* is fought over as about *who* does the fighting, so that both sides in a war face each other in full agonistic equipoise if they meet some formal standards.[53] Since, much like tango, it takes two to agonize, this position may be a difficult one for Aristotle to adopt if his best *polis* will be not only "well-ordered"[54] (VII 4, 1326a30) and thus in possession of the normative high ground, but also the *only* well-ordered possessor of the normative high ground. After all, it was surely this assumption that shored up Aristotle's best *polis*'s claim to be the occasional leader of other Greek civic communities in the first place.

It is noteworthy nevertheless that elsewhere in the *Politics* Aristotle is no stranger to this agonistic model of war. Indeed, in Book III he describes without disapproving the Greek practice of signing agreements according to which neither of the signatories should act "unjustly toward the other" (III 9, 1280b4–5) or the practice of signing "treaties about refraining from harming each other (*adikein*)" (III 9, 1280a39–40).[55] At IV 14, 1297b41–98a7, Aristotle refers to that part of the constitution that "deliberates about public affairs" and "has authority in relation to war and peace" and "the making and breaking of alliances" (a5),[56] as though war were the continuation of politics by other means.

Indeed, to allow for some normative space for this way of dealing with war is to assume that those who sign a treaty have the mutual liberty to do precisely what they commit themselves to refrain from doing. The point of this kind of treaty, then, is for two or more *poleis* to pull themselves out of what would be otherwise a legitimate and fully symmetrical warlike condition. Seen from the viewpoint of a just war model, such treaties of mutual restraint of violent behavior would be normatively redundant, since according to the just war model *poleis* have a duty to refrain from acting unjustly anyway.

The picture seems to be essentially the same if we bring into it treaties of an offensive and defensive alliance so that the participating *poleis* were to "have the same friends and enemies."[57] This formula only makes sense if *poleis* do have the normative liberty of committing themselves to alliances in advance of who their enemies are and more importantly what they are fighting for.

What seems to underlie Aristotle's political approach to war at the very least in *Politics* III thus is the ancient Greek understanding of war as an *agôn* (see also, e.g. *NE* 1116b13–14), a kind of violent activity between consenting adults – or at least adults afraid of dishonor (*NE* III 8, 1116a21), a legitimate though violent rule-bound mechanism for conflict resolution: "a ritualistic collision, head-on, with the spears of their enemy to end the whole business quickly and efficiently." In effect, the very circumstances of Greek hoplitic warfare made it the case that "once the invader arrived in the spring, the entire 'war', if that is the proper word, usually consisted of an hour's worth of hard fighting between consenting, courageous hoplite[s]."[58]

Even if we were not convinced by the consensual approach to war – Aristotle himself was not entirely happy with it (*NE* III 8,

1116a30) – our own discussion of political virtue as a role-related concept has already set the stage for deriving the normative symmetry of hoplites from a different source. Citizens of different regimes are expected to fight as a patriot or *philopolis* for their *poleis* and thus what is sauce for the goose is sauce for the gander – particularly if geese are reared in the rather stressful environment of warlike poultry farms. This moral equality of soldiers no matter what they are fighting for – precisely what Aristotle refers to as "civic courage" (*NE* III 8, 1116a17) – has actually become part and parcel at least of the Western way of war down to our own days.[59]

Some remarks of Aristotle on the law of war prevailing at his time seem to confirm that he is no stranger to an embryonic form of *jus in bello*. Indeed, Aristotle takes *nomos* or (international) law to task for being "a sort of agreement by which what is conquered in war is said to belong to the victors" (I 6, 1255a6–7) and claims that "no one would say that someone is a slave if he did not deserve to be one; otherwise, those regarded as the best born would be slaves or the children of slaves, if any of them were taken captive and sold" (I 6, 1255a25–28). In his *Nicomachean Ethics* he even includes the ransom for prisoners of war within political justice as a practice regulated by legal justice (*NE* V 7, 1134b23).

Thus, according to Aristotle those who find themselves on either side of an inter-Greek war might find comfort of sorts in knowing that they are not, by definition, natural slaves, but naturally free Greek citizen-soldiers fighting for their country. Although they may be lawfully killed in a pitched battle just like those who are the object of a war of enslavement, unlike slaves they are entitled to fight back (see *NE* V 5, 1133a1) and once the battle is over they may be said to fall under the protection of a set of intra-cultural regulations of war and thus they will be secured against enslavement.[60]

### If I ruled the world? Aristotle's rejection of cosmopolitanism

It remains to address the strong suspicions of worldwide imperialism raised by Aristotle's claims that "the Greek race," unlike its European and Asian counterparts, "is both spirited and intelligent" and that "that is precisely why it remains free, governed in the best way, and capable, if it chances upon a single constitution, of ruling all others" (VII 7, 1327b31–33; cf. II 10, 1271b32–34).[61] Actually Aristotle is also said by Plutarch to have given Alexander the following advice: "Treat Greeks hegemonically, barbarians despotically."[62] On top of this, at *De mundo* 400b27 Aristotle even speaks of "that greater city, the universe."[63] Taken together, these remarks seem to conflate the slavist and the hegemonic arguments for war into a justification for world rule.

This conflation of arguments may be said to kill two birds with one stone as it would allow Aristotle's best *polis* to exercise political rule over other *poleis* of the same ethnic stock, and also to cash in on pan-Hellenism to bring together the Greek nation in a war of enslavement against barbarians.[64] If taken to the extreme, this scenario would lead to something akin to the literally international conflagration depicted by Albrecht Altdorfer in his painting *The Battle of Issus* (1529), namely a situation in which two cultures in their entirety – the Greek Occident against non-Greek Orient – represented by the armies of Alexander the Great and Darius respectively, oppose each other in a battle of cosmic proportions. For all its aesthetic attributes this is not, on many grounds, a pretty picture.

However, Aristotle's own political theory is not without resources to counteract this explosive cocktail of ethnocentrism, just war theory, and world rule. To start with, his prejudiced views on non-Greek culture did not prevent him from doing justice to at least some non-Greek political systems. Indeed, Aristotle has rather kind words to say on Carthage and actually thought it deserved to be counted among the reputed well-ordered constitutions of his time (II 11), its barbarian nature notwithstanding. Second, Aristotle does not favor a world order based on Macedonian rule under one man, let alone that according to 1324b9–17 Macedonia is a barbarous *ethnos* but at most an alliance of Greek *poleis* against barbarians.[65] Third, Aristotle's remarks on the natural qualities of people are not as culturally biased as they seem, since he is open-minded enough to bring them to bear upon Greeks themselves: he claims that the "Greek nations also differ from one another in these ways" (VII 7, 1327b30–33), viz. some Greeks will fail to be "both spirited and intelligent."[66]

Fourth, by Aristotle's own standards, a literal *cosmopolis* would be ungovernable due to its extension and population: only a "divine power, the sort that holds the entire universe together" could handle such a task (VII 4, 1326a32–33; cf. *NE* IX 10, 1170b31–33). Other than that, in Aristotle's eyes such a "cosmopolitan" system would be nothing but "a nation [*ethnos*], not a *polis*" (VII 4, 1326b4–5; cf. III 3, 1276a28–29). As for Aristotle's reference at *De mundo* 400b27 to that "greater city, the universe," it may well have been simply a metaphor. Finally, we should always recall that Aristotle finishes off his eulogy of Greek culture with a conditional which refers in turn to a mere chance: the Greek race is "capable . . . of ruling all others" "*if it chances upon* a single constitution." This is so big an if that it could never be met by Aristotle's own standards.[67]

To be sure, Aristotle shared in the Greek distinction between a "thin" and a "thick" conception of foreignness reflected linguistically by the terms *xenoi* or Greek from a different *polis* (e.g. VII 4, 1326a20; VII 4, 1326b20; V 11, 1314a10–11) and, as we have seen, *barbaroi* or a fully foreign non-Greek. But he fell far short of making the Platonic point that any inter-Greek warlike activity whatsoever should be considered *eo ipso* civil war or domestic conflict (*stasis*), and hence that the concept of war as such (*polemos*) should be reserved for "enmity of the foreign."[68] Although Aristotle does envisage a war of enslavement against barbarians, he does not explicitly recommend it as an alternative to war among Greeks.

We have seen that Aristotle's account of war, ethical as it is, cannot at times avoid getting political in the pejorative sense of the word as he seeks to rationalize enslavement and hegemony as compelling reasons for wars. However, for all his willingness to countenance wars of enslavement and hegemony, Aristotle remains true to his commitment to political particularism.[69] He understands the sphere of politics as what a distinguished Aristotelian has called the "sphere of the *highest concrete universality*,"[70] namely, as an activity that can only be embodied in the pluralistic context of several equally independent civic communities, which occasionally get together for the sake of defense without making up a new political community (III 9, 1280b26–28) – or indulging in world rule for that matter.

### WORKS CITED

Annas, J. 1996. "Aristotle on Human Nature and Political Virtue." *Review of Metaphysics* 49: 731–53

Anscombe, E. 1981. "War and murder." In *Ethics, Religion and Politics*. Oxford: Blackwell

Atkins, E. M. and Griffin, M. T., eds. 1991. *Cicero: On Duties*. Cambridge University Press

Barnes, J., ed. 1984. *The Complete Works of Aristotle*. Princeton University Press

Broadie, S. and Rowe, Ch., eds. 2002. *Aristotle: Nichomachean Ethics*. Oxford University Press

Coady, C. A. J. 2008. *Morality and Political Violence*. Cambridge University Press

Covarrubias, D. de 2006. "De iustitia belli adversus Indos." In *Kann Krieg erlaubt sein? Ein Quellensammlung zur politischen Ethik der Spanischen Spätscholastik*, eds. H.-G. Justenhoven and J. Stüben. Stuttgart: Kohlhammer Verlag

Defourny, M. 1977. "The aim of the state: peace." In *Articles on Aristotle II: Ethics and Politics*, eds. J. Barnes, M. Schofield, and R. Sorabji. London: Duckworth

Everson, S., ed. 1988. *Aristotle: The Politics*. Cambridge University Press

Frede, D. 2001. "Staatsverfassung und Staatsbürger." In *Aristoteles' Politik*, ed. O. Höffe. Berlin: Akademie Verlag

Gentili, A. 1612. *De iure belli*. Hanau

Geuna, M. 2006. "Skinner, pre-humanist rhetorical culture and Machiavelli." In *Rethinking the Foundations of Modern Political Thought*, eds. A. Brett and J. Tully. Cambridge University Press

Grotius, H. 2005. *The Rights of War and Peace*, ed. Richard Tuck, trans. John Morrice. 3 vols., Indianapolis, In: Liberty Fund

Habermas, J. 1973. *Theory and Praxis*, trans. J. Viertel. Boston, NJ: Beacon Press

Hanson, V. D. 1989. *The Western Way of War: Infantry Battle in Classical Greece*. New York: Oxford University Press

Hegel, G. W. F. 1991. *Elements of the Philosophy of Right*, ed. A. W. Wood, trans. H. B. Nisbet. Cambridge University Press

Hobbes, T. 1991. *Leviathan*, ed. R. Tuck. Cambridge University Press

Keyt, D. 1991. "Aristotle's Theory of Distributive Justice." In *A Companion to Aristotle's* Politics, eds. D. Keyt and F. Miller. Oxford: Blackwell

  2007. "The Good Man and the Upright Citizen in Aristotle's Ethics and Politics." *Social Philosophy and Policy* 24: 220–40

Kraut, R. 1997. *Aristotle Politics, Books VII and VIII*. Oxford University Press

  2002. *Aristotle: Political Philosophy*. Oxford University Press

Kymlicka, W. 1995. *Multicultural Citizenship*. Oxford University Press

Meister, R. 1915. "Aristoteles als ethischer Beurteiler des Krieges." *Neue Jahrbücher für Pädagogik* 18: 481–94

Miller, F. D. 1995. *Nature, Justice and Rights in Aristotle's Politics*. Oxford University Press

Neff, S. C. 2005. *War and the Law of Nations: A General History*. Cambridge University Press

Ober, J. 1999. *Political Dissent in Democratic Athens*. Princeton University Press

Pocock, J. G. A. 1975. *The Machiavellian Moment: Florentine Political Thought and the Atlantic Tradition*. Princeton University Press

Price, J. 2001. *Thucydides and Internal War*. Cambridge University Press

Rawls, J. 1996. *Political Liberalism*. 2nd edn., New York: Columbia University Press

  1999. *The Law of Peoples*. Cambridge, MA: Harvard University Press

Reeve, C. D. C. 1998. *Aristotle*, Politics. Indianapolis, IN: Hackett

Robinson, R. 1995. *Aristotle*, Politics, *Books III and IV*. 2nd edn., Oxford University Press

Rodin, D. 2003. *War and Self-Defense*. Oxford University Press

Rosler, A. 2005. *Political Authority and Obligation in Aristotle*. Oxford University Press

Schmitt, C. 1996. *The Concept of the Political*, trans. G. Schwab. Chicago University Press

Schütrumpf, E. 1980. *Die Analyse der Politik durch Aristoteles*. Amsterdam: Grüner

  1991–2005. *Aristoteles' Politik*. 4 vols., Berlin: Akademie Verlag

Sepúlveda, J. G. 1548. *Aristotelis de Republica Libri VIII*. Paris

Skinner, Q. 1978. *The Foundations of Modern Political Thought II: The Age of Reformation*. Cambridge University Press

  2002. *Visions of Politics II: Renaissance Virtues*. Cambridge University Press

Tuck, R. 1999. *The Rights of War and Peace*. Cambridge University Press

Vernant, J. P. 1990. *Myth and Society in Ancient Greece*, trans. J. Lloyd. New York: Zone Books

Walzer, M. 2006. *Just and Unjust Wars: A Moral Argument with Historical Illustrations*. 4th edn., New York: Basic Books

NOTES

1. Skinner 1978: 349.
2. Unless otherwise stated, in this chapter "ethical" and "moral" are taken as synonymous.
3. For the claim that politics is the continuation of ethics, see Habermas 1973: 42. For Aristotle's alleged fusion of moral and political philosophy

see Rawls 1996: 134. I am grateful to Luciano Venezia for reminding me of this last passage.

4. See e.g., Pocock 1975: 335.

5. For the pedigree of republicanism see Skinner 2002: 10–38, and for a general description of the differences between political Aristotelianism and republicanism see e.g., Geuna 2006: 67.

6. See Keyt 2007: 222, who refers to *NE* I 7, 1098a8–12.

7. Here I follow Everson 1988: 86. Otherwise I follow Reeve, except for the rare case of a translation of my own.

8. The reference to practical wisdom (*phronêsis*) might suggest that the range of this account is not as wide as I take it to be. However, Aristotle's wording ("no shred of" (*mêthen morion echonta*)) and the examples he gives (children and madmen) suggest that what he has in mind is some rather minimal intellectual activity – although I am happy to grant that many children and madmen may well be capable of remarkable levels of intellectual activity, or at the very least that some of them manage to win general elections and run very powerful corporations.

9. See Frede 2001: 83–84.

10. See Kraut 2002: 361.

11. See Kraut 2002: 366.

12. See Robinson 1995: 7.

13. See Keyt 1991: 240. See Marco Zingano, Chapter 8.

14. See Pierre Pellegrin, Chapter 4.

15. Grotius 2005: 265–66. See also Kraut 2002: 219.

16. See Kymlicka 1995: 93, 125.

17. However, for very serious doubts about the consistency of Aristotle's moral approach to citizenship in *Pol.* VII–VIII on the grounds of his recommendations on the treatment of slaves see e.g., Annas 1996: 740.

18. Emphasis added.

19. In fact, it is Rawls who may be said to be following Aristotle's approach to political justice at *Pol.* III 9–13 rather than the other way around, since Rawls also starts "from the fundamental ideas of a democratic society" (Rawls 1996: 40) and offers as justification for his theory of political justice "what is, or can be, held in common," beginning "from shared fundamental ideas implicit in the public political culture in the hope of developing from them a political conception that can gain free and reasoned agreement in judgment" (Rawls 1996: 100–1). On Aristotle and Rawls see Richard Kraut, Chapter 14.

20. This claim is the launch pad for the subsequent discussion of the summation argument in *Pol.* III 11.

21. Ostracism was the method used by the Athenian citizen body of banishing a citizen for ten years by way of writing on a fragment of pottery (*ostrakon*) the name of the citizen to be banished and counting the *ostraka* so that the citizen who attracted the largest number among at least 6,000 votes was thereby ostracized.

22. See *NE* VII 1, 1145a15–20, 1145a25 on superhuman, heroic, or divine excellence and brutishness.

23. See Keyt 1991: 275.

24. Emphasis added. On the common good see Donald Morrison, Chapter 7.

25. It is noteworthy that Aristotle refers to "acknowledgement" or "agreement" as a requirement for ostracism in the context of its monarchical use. This might be intended as a constraint upon kingly decisions: kings should proceed as though votes have been cast on who should be ostracized.

26. Emphasis added. Ostracism differed from exile or dishonour (*atimia*) in that its attendant privation of citizenship and property rights was temporary: the ostracized citizen had the right to return and resume all his rights after the term of his banishment.

27. Emphasis added.

28. My translation.

29. Aristotle actually claims that the age of incommensurable moral virtue was long gone by the time ostracism itself was put in practice. See III 15, 1286b11–13, 1286b20–22; V 10, 1313a3–8.

30. Miller 1995: 246.

31. Hobbes 1991: 147–48.

32. Let us bear in mind that ostracism is much more lenient a measure than exile and definitely more so than killing (see III 17, 1288a24) or the Roman *senatus consultum ultimum* and its attendant declaration of hostility upon those reputed to be harmful to the republic.

33. Broadie and Rowe 2002: 133. Aristotle also claims that militarism – the view that waging war is the aim of the political community – is incoherent as shown by the failure of the Spartan policy of making military virtue the entire business of politics. See II 10, 1271b2–6 and VII 14, 1334a6–9.

34. Coady 2008: 47.

35. It is noteworthy, nevertheless, that the nobility or morally admirable nature of war makes him claim that soldiers are not just necessary but are parts of the city properly speaking (see VII 4, 1326a20–21).

36. This is why there is nothing conceptually wrong with the US Strategic Air Command's motto: "Peace is our profession."

37. If I may indulge in non-conventional advertising, for Aristotle's view on self-defense against "domestic" or "internal" enslavement see Rosler 2005: 239–58, esp. 244–45. See also Antony Hatzistavrou, Chapter 11.

38. Aristotle, however, does not rule out self-imposed slavery as a result of peace and leisure for those who only cultivate military virtue: see VII 15, 1334a38–40.

39. I am grateful to Richard Kraut for bringing my attention to the need for elaborating on this first cause of justified war.

40. Walzer 2006: 52.

41. Kraut 1997: 97.

42. Rodin 2003: 127.

43. To be sure, this purely extrinsic relationship between a political community aiming at the best possible life and its territory would not be able to support a war of self-defense in the case of invaders who, although as such they do encroach upon somebody else's territory, are kind enough to offer another piece of land in its stead to make sure the same Aristotelian good life could be led elsewhere. There is no denying that whereas someone committed to the intrinsic approach to territory typical of garden-variety nationalism would be required to simply dismiss the offer entirely as senseless without even considering it, Aristotle's instrumental approach to territory would commit his best citizens to assess the pros and cons of the removal offer. Aristotle could reply nevertheless that even his own best citizens will surely end up finding the removal offer a rather costly affair and that invasions are hardly ever preceded by tempting moving-out offers anyway.

44. I follow Meister's 1915 order of presentation of Aristotle's three causes of justified war.

45. Classical republicans like Cicero made much the same point: See e.g., *Philippics*, VIII 12. Richard Kraut claims that, in spite of what the text suggests, Aristotle's wars of enslavement are not so much a matter of principle as necessary only in case "slaves captured in wars of defense might not be sufficient in number to provide for the city's needs" (Kraut 1997: 143).

46. Anscombe 1981: 52.

47. For the claim that Aristotle's best citizens will not only turn to wars of enslavement but actually forge their *polis* on the occasion of a literal colonial war of enslavement see Ober 1999: 306.

48. Schmitt 1996: 49. It is somewhat to Aristotle's credit, nevertheless, that as he puts forward his philosophical account of change in *Post. Anal.* he proves to be impartial enough to answer the questions "Why did the Persian war come upon the Athenians?" and "What is the explanation

of the Athenians' being warred upon?" by saying that "men make war on those who have first done them wrong" (94b1), and to claim that this is precisely what the Athenians did since "they attacked Sardis with the Eretrians" (Barnes 1984 I: 156). It was Grotius 2005: 396 that called my attention to this passage.

49. Covarrubias 2006: 186 (*correctio in moribus*).

50. This is one reason why the best regimes will need naval personnel, sailors, etc. See VII 6, 1327b1–15.

51. Vernant 1990: 44. Should the best *polis*, as the leader of a confederation, be entitled to make war on *poleis* accused of defaulting on their confederal duties, the latter may well fail to see any benefit in being attacked on that account (recall VII 14, 1334a1.)

52. Ober 1999: 305 rightly points out that "notably, Aristotle nowhere mentions . . . a just war fought to free those who were unjustly enslaved." The hegemonic argument has been interestingly enough read both as a plea for humanitarian intervention (Defourny 1977: 200) and *approvingly* as a justification for colonization and occupation (Meister 1915: 485). Perhaps it is no accident that the line between humanitarian intervention, on the one hand, and colonization and occupation on the other, becomes rather blurry at times.

53. For instance, Cicero did not mind calling Carthage a "just and legitimate" enemy although he surely did not approve of the reasons why she made war on Rome (see Atkins and Griffin 1991: 142). The *justus hostis* approach was to re-emerge and become typical of European warfare from the end of the sixteenth century up to the First World War (see e.g., Neff 2005: 83–214).

54. Here again Aristotle anticipates one of Rawls' favorite idioms. However, unlike Aristotle, Rawls concedes outfront there may well be many well-ordered societies (Rawls 1999).

55. Here I follow Sepúlveda's translation, which renders this *"ne alteri alteros laedant"* (1548: 84).

56. Cf. *NE* VIII 4, 1157a28. Aristotle is not prevented by his endorsement of the just war theory from entertaining an embryonic form of the modern deterrence policy at II 6, 1265a18–28. See Schütrumpf 1991: 225.

57. See *Oxford Classical Dictionary*, 3rd edn., s.v. "Alliance," 65.

58. Hanson 1989: 35. See also Vernant 1990: 29, 38.

59. See Walzer 2006: 34–37.

60. See Kraut 1997: 143.

61. See also Thucydides on Pericles' Funeral Oration (II, 41). I am grateful to Marguerite Deslauriers for this reference.

62. *De fort. Alex.* I 6 (De Alex. 329b). See Meister 1915: 484. Cf. III 15, 1285a20–22.

63. Barnes 1984: 639. Gentili 1612: 108, has called my attention to this passage.
64. Actually it may go the other way around: political hegemony as a result of having defeated the barbarians. See Schütrumpf 2005: 495.
65. See Schütrumpf 2005: 339–40 on VII 2, 1324b9–17 where Macedonia is counted as a barbarous *ethnos*.
66. I am grateful to Fred D. Miller, Jr. for reminding me of Aristotle's endogenous application of the principle.
67. Emphasis added. I cannot help associating Aristotle's proviso with the proverbial Yiddish counterfactual: "If my grandmother had testicles she would be my grandfather." Proud as I was of this Yiddish saw, Panos Dimas told me once that there is a Greek saying to much the same effect.
68. *Rep.* V, 470b. See Price 2001: 68–69.
69. As Tuck 1999: 68 reminds us, it was on the basis of Aristotle's commitment to political particularism that late medieval and early modern Aristotelians made a stand against "the idea of a world state, whether it was couched in the language of papalism or in that of humanism (the *societas* or *respublica humana*)."
70. Hegel 1991: 344.

# 7    The common good

## INTRODUCTION

Such figures as Aristotle, Cicero, Aquinas, Rousseau, and T. H. Green have all appealed to some notion of the "common good."[1] Like "liberty" and "equality" and "justice," "the common good" is a value people tend to admire, and toward which they can feel loyalty. Over time, the notion of the common good has been reinterpreted in many ways. Among its near-synonyms are "the public interest," "the common welfare," and "the general happiness." Aristotle stands at the beginning of this tradition. As we will see, Plato does have a notion of the common good.[2] But Aristotle is the first philosopher to make the common good a central organizing concept of his political theory.

The basic idea of Aristotle's notion of the common good can be explained quite simply. On Aristotle's view, political society is an association of people who live and work together for the sake of living a good life. This good life for all, which is the inherent end or goal of political society, and which good rulers strive to bring about, is the "common good." While this much is clear, the details and implications of this basic idea require interpretation.

In the second section of this chapter I shall use the notion of "common goal" as a guide to develop an interpretation of the common good as the happiness of all citizens. In the third section, I compare this interpretation with three other leading interpretations of Aristotle's notion of the common good. My aim will be to give a concise

For helpful comments on this essay, I am grateful to Steven White, Thomas Osborne, and the editors of this volume. Special thanks are due to David Riesbeck for a set of remarkably detailed and penetrating comments.

and accessible presentation of the major views. The rest of the chapter treats three special topics concerning the Aristotelian common good: the common good as the aim of the ruler; the common good and justice; and the common good and friendship.

### THE COMMON GOOD AS COMMON GOAL

Aristotle's two main expressions for "the common good" are *to koinon agathon* and *to koinêi sumpheron*. Aristotle uses them interchangeably, though they have slightly different overtones in Greek. *Koinon* means "common"; *agathon* means "good"; and *sumpheron* is a specialized word for "good" that always implies "good for something." Thus "the common good" is an exact translation of *to koinon agathon*. "The common good" is also a correct translation of *to koinêi sumpheron*, but a translation that brings out this expression's special overtones is "mutual advantage."

Aristotle's term for "community" or "association" has the word for "common" at its root: *koinon*, common; *koinônia*, community. This fact of language underwrites a very simple argument that the goal of politics is the common good. According to Aristotle, the *polis* (translated variously by "state," "city-state," and "political society") is a community, a *koinônia*. The *polis* is the most comprehensive community suited to the good life: generally speaking, other communities or associations are parts of the *polis*.[3] As Aristotle understands the notion, all communities are purposive: their members have joined together for some goal. Thus every community (*koinônia*) implies a common (*koinon*) goal. But Aristotle also holds that every goal of human action is a (real or apparent) good. Therefore every community (*koinônia*) exists for the sake of a common good (*koinon agathon*). The *polis*, as the most comprehensive and authoritative community, exists for the sake of the most comprehensive and authoritative good. The common good of the political community is thus the ultimate end of human action.

Notice that this "common good" is common to the members of the *polis* (or any other community) as their common *project*, as an aim that is common to all of them as agents.[4] But many of Aristotle's remarks concerning the common good, and even the second of his favored expressions for it (*to koinêi sumpheron*, "mutual advantage"), suggest that as he intends it, the common good is common *benefit*, that is common to the members as *beneficiaries*, and not only, or not primarily, as *agents*. (To speak playfully in the language of the grammarians, the dative "in common" (*koinêi*) in the phrase *to koinêi sumpheron* is not a dative of agency, but a dative of interest.)

To find an anchor in Aristotle's thought for the idea that the purpose of communities is the benefit of their members is not difficult. In the beginning chapters of the *Politics* Aristotle describes various ways in which the motive behind human associations is advantage or benefit. Human associations are valuable to their members both for obtaining the necessaries for continued living – mere "life" – and for living well. Both of these are types of advantage or benefit.[5] The political community is the most comprehensive community suited to the good life, and therefore has both the appropriate resources for and the natural aim of providing the most complete and comprehensive benefit to its members, namely, happiness or living well in all its aspects throughout an entire life.

This line of thought suggests that these two ways in which the common good of a political community might be common to its members, as agents and as beneficiaries, are not only compatible, but are united in Aristotle's thinking. A political community is one in which the common benefit of its members is their common goal.

### A CENTRAL TEXT

Aristotle's most important discussion of the common good comes in the introduction to his discussion of constitutions, at *Politics* III 6–7. Here is Aristotle's description of the common good as goal:

First, then, we must set down for what purpose the city-state is constituted, and how many kinds of rule deal with human beings and communal life. In our first discussions, indeed, where conclusions were reached about household management and rule by a master, it was also said that a human being is by nature a political animal. That is why, even when they do not need one another's help, people no less desire to live together (*tou suzên*), although it is also true that the common benefit (*to koinêi sumpheron*) brings them together, to the extent that it contributes some part of living well (*zên kalôs*) to each. This above all is the end (*telos*), then, of everyone, whether in common (*koinêi*) or separately. (III 6, 1278b15–24)

Aristotle assumes here three levels of "good" which the city can help provide to its members: (1) mere life or survival;[6] (2) living together; and (3) living well. The difference between the second and third type of good is quite important. Aristotle holds that humans are naturally political. Aristotle means this to imply that humans enjoy each other's company and conversation. Also included in this conception is the idea that an essential aspect of the human good is shared activity and shared values, and the social conversation (*logos*) through which these values emerge. These are all aspects of "living together." But human social life, "living together," is not the *same* as "living nobly" or "living well" or "happiness," though it does constitute part of it. "Living well," on Aristotle's view, requires not simply living together with others, but rather being virtuous and sharing with them in virtuous activity. Moreover, some virtues are or can be exercised privately; and they, too, contribute to living well, even though they are not part of living with others. On Aristotle's view, in most circumstances mere living is a good; and so is social life. But neither of these is the (ultimate) goal of either the political community or of individual self-interest. The ultimate goal is living well.

The strict universality of the city's concern for its members is emphasized in this passage twice: "contributes to *each*" and "*everyone* in common or separately." There are two reasons for this strict universality. First, each member participates in the community for the sake of the good life for himself; any member who perceives that the community takes no interest in his welfare, or who believes that he obtains no benefit in it, will have a reason to withdraw. The second reason is a matter of justice: anyone who contributes to the well-being of others through participation in the political community has a claim on the community to receive a similar benefit in return.[7]

Although Aristotle implies that the city must be concerned with and contribute to the happiness of each of its members, he does not imply that the city must succeed in making each of its members completely happy, or that they would be justified in expecting it to. What brings people together in the city is the common good, "in so far as they each obtain *some part* (*meros*) of living well." The restriction is odd, if not alarming. Does Aristotle mean to imply that the city does not need to try to make all of its citizens completely happy? Is it enough for some citizens to have a minimal *share* in the good life, so that the city can concentrate its efforts on making a privileged few completely happy? Or is Aristotle simply acknowledging the inevitable limitations of nature, which, under even the best of circumstances, will prevent any city from giving all of its citizens completely happy lives? In that case all that the city can do, and all its members can reasonably expect, is that it will provide each of them with a portion of happiness (though it will try to provide each of them with as large a portion as possible).

The *goal* of the political community is specified by the *maximal* fulfillment of the motives which animate it. For that reason, the Aristotelian common good is not the provision of a certain set of necessary conditions for happiness, such as security and prosperity and education, but rather complete happiness itself. Similarly, the *goal* of the political community is not to provide this happiness for any portion of its members, but for all of them. Thus, the Aristotelian idea that the political community comes together and persists for the sake of the good life suggests that the Aristotelian common good is (nothing less than) complete happiness for all of the members of the community. Or perhaps more accurately (since politics cannot hope to change nature) as much of the good life for every member of the community as each person's inborn character and abilities permit.[8]

### GOOD AND BAD FORMS OF RULE

When in *Politics* III 6–7 Aristotle comes to distinguish good from bad constitutions,[9] he again makes clear that the common good includes the good of everyone. According to Aristotle, a good ruler rules for the sake of the common good, whereas a bad ruler rules for the sake of himself or his group. A good ruler aims at the good of all citizens, whereas a bad ruler is "partial." Aristotle says, "Whenever the one, the few, or the many rule for the common benefit, these constitutions must be correct. But if they aim at the private benefit, whether of the one or a few or the multitude, they are deviations" (III 7, 1279a28–31).[10] The rule of a single person for the sake of the common good he calls a kingship; good rule by several people is an aristocracy; and good rule by the multitude is "polity."[11]

The good ruler aims at the common good. This implies that the good ruler should try to help all of its citizens lead excellent lives, so far as possible. But the fact that the ruler ought to be *concerned* with

making all of its citizens happy does not imply that all citizens, or
even any citizen, is justified in demanding of the city that it *make*
them happy, or even *give them all they need* to become happy. Aristotle implies that citizens have a right not to have their interests
ignored; and he even implies that they have a right to obtain *some*
benefits from the city in return for their participation. But he does
not imply, in this passage or elsewhere, that citizens have a right to
benefit equally from the city, its administration and its laws.[12] "The
aim of a good constitution is the common good": this implies that all
citizens should benefit from the city's concern for their welfare; but
it does not imply that all citizens ought to benefit *equally* from the
city's efforts. Every citizen should receive "some part" of living well,
but not necessarily an equal part. Aristotle's notion of the common
good, as such, does not imply any particular answer to distributional
questions, apart from the minimal constraint that no one should be
left out.

The underlying reason why the notion of the common good as
such does not imply an answer to most distributional questions is a
fundamental aspect of specifying ends. A specification of the "end,"
the goal to be aimed at, does not normally tell one what trade-offs
to make under conditions that obtain when the end cannot be fully
realized. Assume that the goal of politics is the maximal happiness
of everyone. But under all realistic conditions, not everyone can be
made, or be enabled to become, maximally happy. One reason for
that are people's inborn limitations, which politics can do nothing
about. But under all realistic conditions, another set of factors which
limit how happy people can become are limited resources and opportunities, and administrative attention. Politics can decide how to
allocate these resources. Therefore, political decisions can affect people's opportunities for happiness, in partial competition with other
people's opportunities. But the mere specification of the goal, "the
happiness of the citizens," may not provide a criterion for making
these allocational decisions.

The slogan, "the aim of politics is to promote the common good"
is thus in important ways quite vague. The most obvious and most
important vagueness is that what constitutes "living well" can be
interpreted in different ways by different people – and by different
regimes. A less obvious but still important vagueness is that knowing what the ultimate goal is does not necessarily give one a criterion

of choice in ordinary circumstances. Contrast this slogan with the following utilitarian one: "The criterion of right political action is to maximize the sum of the citizens' individual well-being." This utilitarian slogan is much more informative that the Aristotelian slogan. It is also *compatible* with the Aristotelian slogan. One way to aim at the common good, understood as the happiness of all the citizens, is to act so as to maximize the sum of the citizens' well-being. But as we shall see in the next section, this is not the only way.

## FOUR INTERPRETATIONS OF THE "COMMON GOOD"

When Aristotle uses the term "the common good," what exactly is he referring to? Aristotle never presents an explicit answer to this question.

One natural misunderstanding of Aristotle's notion of the common good should be cleared away at the start. Probably the most widespread *contemporary* notion of the common good is "public good." A public good, as understood by economists, is a good that is equally available to all: one person's use of the good does not make it less available to others, and no one can be effectively excluded from use of the good. Clean air is one example of a public good. The system of free public highways is also a public good. National defense is another.[13]

None of these goods belong to the political "common good" in Aristotle's sense, because they are instrumental. Aristotle distinguishes between (1) mere instrumental means or necessary conditions for the achievement of the end; and (2) the end itself and its intrinsic parts.[14] Aristotle's common good is the goal of politics, and the goal of politics is the good life. Public highways and clean air are not *part* of the good life. Instead, they are helpful or necessary conditions for the good life. They are thus means towards the common good that is the goal of politics, but not part of that common good.[15]

One plausible interpretation of the Aristotelian common good fits well with the strict universality of the common good as goal:

1.    The common good is the happiness of all citizens.[16]

The strength of this view is that it makes sense of the common good's role as both common goal and common benefit. Human beings desire to lead good lives. People band together into city-states because (according to Aristotle) that form of social organization is most suited to enable its members to lead good lives. The goal of the citizens, taken together as a group, is the happiness or welfare of those very citizens. The common goal is the common benefit.

In the opening chapters of Aristotle's *Politics* (I 1–2) this line of reasoning is present, though inexplicit. More direct evidence comes from Aristotle's discussion of political community in the *Nicomachean Ethics*:

> Now all forms of community are like the political community; for men journey together with a view to some particular advantage, and to provide something that they need for the purposes of life; and it is for the sake of advantage that the political community too seems both to have come together originally and to endure, for this is what legislators aim at, and they call just that which is to the common advantage. (VIII 9, 1160a9–14)

A significant problem with this view is that "the common good" seems not to be genuinely common. A genuinely common good is a single thing that all members of a group share in, or which is beneficial to all. The archetypal example of a genuinely common good is a child: as Aristotle says, a child is a common good for its parents (*NE* VIII 12, 1162a29). In the political context, the archetypal example of a genuinely common good is the constitution. A good constitution is a single thing that all citizens share in and benefit from.

By contrast, the common good as the happiness of all citizens is not a single thing that is beneficial to all of the citizens. Instead, it is a sort of sum or mass of many things, the happiness or welfare of each of the many citizens. Each citizen's happiness is beneficial to that citizen, but it seems false to say that the whole mass – the happiness of all of my fellow citizens – is beneficial to me.

But this problem is not so severe as it seems. The happiness of all the citizens is "common" in the sense that every citizen is related to it in the same way. It is true that the happiness of all citizens is not a "single thing" in the way that a constitution or a *polis* is. The happiness of all the citizens is a sum or mass and not an organic whole. But there is no good reason to insist that the common good must be an organic whole. The happiness of all the citizens is a (very large!) *good*, and the happiness of all the citizens stands in a *common* relationship to each citizen, namely, each citizen's happiness is a *part* of the happiness of all.

In the *Politics*, Aristotle repeatedly contrasts the common good with the good of some individual or group.[17] These passages are strong evidence for this interpretation. When Aristotle contrasts the common good with the good of, say, the ruling class, he is not contrasting two organic wholes, e.g. "the interrelated social life of the whole city" with "the interrelated social life of the ruling class." Instead he is contrasting two "masses": the welfare of the members of the ruling class vs. the welfare of all the members of the city.

A different interpretation of the common good that does view the common good as an organic whole is:

2.   The common good is the good condition of the web of shared activities that constitute social life.

What makes a group of people into a community (*koinônia*) is shared activity. As the most comprehensive community suited to the good life, the *polis* has within it many types of shared activity, ranging from friendly games of dice, to raising children, to participating in politics. Every citizen is related to a variety of other citizens through a variety of social relations. And certain shared activities relate each citizen to all of the others, such as participation in political life. Imagine all of the shared activities within a *polis*, gathered together in your mind as a single interrelated web of social life. This web satisfies the criteria we were looking for: it is a single thing, and every member of the community shares in and benefits from it. The common good as "the good condition of the interrelated web of social life" brings out strongly the *communal* aspect of the *common* good.

This interpretation of the common good faces two serious problems. First, Aristotle nowhere articulates the concept of a single thing which is all-of-social-life taken together. Second, this common good leaves out many activities that are included in the happiness of all the citizens. Many solitary activities make an important contribution to happiness. The most famous example of this in Aristotle is theoretical contemplation, such as thinking about the nature of god. On Aristotle's view this activity is the best and highest of which human beings are capable – yet it can be done by a single person alone in his study. Theoretical contemplation makes a crucial contribution to human happiness, yet solitary theoretical contemplation does not form part of social life. The goal of the individuals who come together to form political society is to lead the best lives they can, not merely to lead the best social lives they can. A good ruler works to promote the overall welfare of his subjects, and not just their social lives. Solitary theoretical contemplation is not part of human social life. But it is a component of human welfare; according to *Nicomachean Ethics* X 7, it is the *highest form* of human good. Furthermore, even a stretched interpretation of "the interrelated web of social life" which includes all good human activity, even solitary activity, within the common good remains too restrictive. The common good that is the goal of the good ruler must include more than just human activity: it includes *all* aspects of the citizens' happiness, including, e.g. their nutrition and their health and even their reputation as well.

A third view of the common good seeks to combine the advantages of the previous two. The contribution that shared activities make to the happiness of their participants is typically *essentially* shared. A good friendship is valuable to both friends, and cannot be valuable to one unless it is valuable to the other. Through social life, each person's happiness is dependent on, and in a certain sense involves, the happiness of others. Therefore, it is a mistake to view each person's happiness as a separate item that can be added together with the happiness of the others, as is required by interpretation (1). The happiness of all the citizens is a single, interrelated whole. The happiness of all the citizens includes solitary activities as well as social life. But because the happiness of each citizen is essentially intertwined with the happiness of the other citizens, "the happiness of all citizens" is not the sum of the separate happy lives of all citizens, but rather a whole in which each citizen has a share, and is thus a single thing common to all. This gives us a third view of the common good:

3.   The common good is the happiness of all citizens, understood as an interrelated, inseparable whole.[18]

A problem with this view is that Aristotle does not explicitly refer to any such entity as "the happiness of citizens, understood as an inseparable whole." The argument for this interpretation is philosophical. As John Cooper puts it:

Aristotle's theory of the *polis koinônia* [political community] proposes for its citizens a common good larger than the good each could have achieved simply by living a socially and psychologically isolated life of virtue. Each participates, as a sort of co-agent, in the good consisting of all the other citizens' virtuous activities...Each is implicated in the actions of all the others, as an approving and supportive partner, much as the interactions of a mother and father in their cooperative activities of child-rearing, or in a good conversation.[19]

However, the bond between citizens is not nearly this tight. Perhaps actions of my fellow citizens that strengthen the social fabric or improve the functioning of government do benefit me, even if I am unaware of them. But it is incorrect to say that I am a co-agent or approving partner in actions I know nothing about. And my fellow-citizens perform many virtuous activities privately that make no difference to my welfare. In a house on the other side of town, a doctor treats a dying man with kindness. The doctor acts virtuously, but his action does not benefit me.

In fact, Cooper's particular version of this interpretation restricts the common good to the virtuous activities of all the citizens. This may be the most important component of citizens' happiness. But human social life includes a great deal more than virtuous activity: for example, enjoying a sunset together, and playing checkers. So Cooper's version of this interpretation is too restrictive.[20] And an objection we've already seen applies equally here: there is a great deal more to human welfare than social life, and the common good that is the goal of the good ruler must include *all* aspects of the citizens' welfare.

A perennial area of disagreement in metaphysics and social philosophy is that between *individualism* and *holism*. *Individualism* is the view that individual human beings are fundamental, and social wholes such as families and churches and states are "nothing but" or "are reducible to" the individuals out of which they are composed. *Holism* is the view that these social wholes are "something over and above" and are "emergent" or "not reducible to" the individuals who make them up.

Individualism and holism come in many different flavors.[21] One useful distinction is between holism about *entities*: Is the city-state nothing but the citizens who make it up? – and holism about *value*: Is the goodness or well-being of the city nothing but the goodness or welfare of the individual citizens who make it up?

First, holism about entities: Is the city of Athens (or the United States) *nothing but* its individual citizens, or is it something irreducible? Second, holism about value: is the good or happiness of the city *nothing but* the good or happiness of its individual citizens, or is it something more?

Near the beginning of the *Nicomachean Ethics*, Aristotle says that the ultimate goal of human action is the good aimed at by political science (I 2, 1094a18–1094b12; I 4, 1095a14–16).[22] Just as prudence aims at the good or happiness of an individual,[23] so political science aims at the good or happiness of the city-state.

Scholars disagree about the metaphysics of the good of the city. Some say that the good of the city *just is* or *is nothing but* the good of the individual citizens. This is the "individualist" or "reductionist" interpretation. Others say that the good or happiness of the city is an irreducible property of the city as a whole. This is the "holist" interpretation. In various places, Aristotle contrasts the individual good with "the common good," with "the good of the city" and with "the happiness of the city." It is thus natural to assume that for Aristotle "the common good," "the good of the city," and "the happiness of the city" are equivalent. Therefore, the issue of individualism versus holism is often described by scholars as an issue about the common good: Is the common good nothing but the happiness of the individual citizens, or is it a holistic property of the city?[24]

The third interpretation of the common good we have considered implies a holism about value: "the happiness of the citizens" is an irreducible, interrelated whole.

A fourth interpretation of the common good involves holism of both kinds:

4.    The common good is the happiness of the city.[25]

Aristotle's treatment of the city and its happiness, especially in *Politics* VII, is holistic.[26] Aristotle says:

The happy city-state is the one that is best and acts nobly. It is impossible for those who do not do noble deeds to act nobly; and no action, whether a man's or a city-state's, is noble when separate from virtue and practical wisdom. But the courage, justice, and practical wisdom of a city-state have the same capacity and are of the same kind as those possessed by each human being who is said to be just, practically wise, and temperate. (VII 2, 1323b30–36)

Aristotle's city is not simply a collection of citizens. Aristotle famously says that the city is a structured whole, in which the constitution (*politeia*) is the form, and the individual citizens constitute the matter. On Aristotle's view, the city is not just an entity reducible to its citizens. The city is itself an agent. It performs actions that are better and worse, wise and not wise, etc.[27] The noble actions of the happy city are not a large number of actions performed by all the citizens. The city acts nobly when *it* awards honors to a deserving citizen. Similarly, the city has virtues and vices. A city may be just or unjust, courageous or cowardly. The city's virtue does not consist in some quantity of citizens having virtue. If a city has a majority of virtuous citizens, but is ruled only by a bad king, the city will be unhappy and behave badly. Aristotle says that a tyrannical city is one that rules forcibly over its neighbors (VII 2, 1324a10–11). A tyrannical city is not one in which most of its citizens are tyrants.

The happiness of the city and the happiness of the individual have the same structure. Happiness for a city, like happiness for an individual human being, is a life of activity in conformity with virtue.[28]

Of the four interpretations of the common good, I shall argue in favor of the first. Aristotle's common good is the happiness or welfare of all of the citizens. The second interpretation, that the common good is the good condition of the citizen's common social life, is inadequate because human beings aim at the best life they can manage, and limiting the goals of politics to social life leaves out too much that is valuable. The third interpretation, that the common good is the happiness of all the citizens considered as an inseparable whole, fails because the happiness of the citizens is *not* that kind of whole: in many different ways, each individual citizen's happiness is partly dependent on the happiness of other citizens, but the dependence is only partial. By contrast, Aristotle's conception of the happiness of the city is a genuinely holistic notion. On his view, the city is a structured whole, made up of citizens, which acts well or badly and has virtues or vices and has a life. But for that very reason, the fourth interpretation fails: the common good is not the happiness of the city. The common good is the individualistic notion, the individual well-being of every citizen, taken together, whereas the good or happiness of the city is a property of the city as such, namely, the well-being of the city as a structured whole.

### PLATO AND ARISTOTLE ON THE AIM OF THE RULER

In Book I of Plato's *Republic*, Thrasymachus claims that the just and true ruler will rule for the sake of his own advantage, and not for the sake of his subjects (*Rep.* I, 340d–341a). Socrates counters with an argument from the nature of crafts. The aim of each craft is to produce good things of which it is the craft. The goal of a potter, as such, is to make good pots and the goal of a furniture-maker is to produce good beds and tables. The shepherd's task is to care for the sheep, and the goal of a physician is to provide what is good for the body, i.e. health. The "ruler's art" is similar:

And so, Thrasymachus, no one in any position of rule, in so far as he is a ruler, seeks or orders what is good for himself, but only what is good for the person or thing that he rules – for whose benefit he himself exercises his craft. Everything that he says or does is said or done with this in mind, with a view toward what is good and proper for what is ruled. (*Rep.* I, 342e6–11)

Socrates argues that the good ruler will seek the advantage of those over whom he rules. Since Aristotle was Plato's student, he no doubt had this Socratic claim in mind[29] when he formulated his distinction between good and bad forms of rule. But Aristotle's distinction between good and bad rule differs from Plato's in two respects.

First, in Socrates' example the craftsman is distinct from the object of his craft.[30] Just as a potter is different from his pots, so a shepherd is distinct from his flock of sheep. The root idea of a shepherd ruling over his sheep is a *different* root idea from that of ruling for the common good. The shepherd is distinct from the flock. The shepherd does not rule for the common good of himself and the flock. Aristotle would say that there is no commonality there. A ruler ruling for the common good includes himself (and his family and friends) within the whole whose good he aims at. The good ruler seeks the common good of *all citizens*, including himself. Using his technical terminology, Aristotle suggests that good rule is *essentially* for the sake of the ruled, but *coincidentally* also for the sake of the rulers, because they, too, are citizens.[31]

A more serious difference between Plato's and Aristotle's views on the aim of the ruler is this. Plato's "welfare of the ruled" includes the welfare of all inhabitants (or, as animal rights advocates will be quick to point out, all *human* inhabitants). Aristotle's notion of "the common good of the citizens" is much more restrictive. First and most notoriously, slaves are excluded. Second, resident foreigners are not included. "The common good" sought by Aristotle's good ruler does not include the welfare of slaves or resident foreigners. From the point of view of the good rulers, the welfare of slaves and foreigners has only instrumental value. Starving, rebellious slaves and violently angry foreigners are not good for a city. So the good ruler will have grounds to look after slaves and resident foreigners to the extent that doing so will promote the common good of the citizens; not beyond that.

A third restriction flows from Aristotle's particular theory of citizenship. Not all native or indigenous inhabitants count as citizens. The definition of citizenship is a difficult problem for Aristotle. His eventual conclusion is that the best criterion of citizenship is "having a share in office" (III 1, 1275a22–33). This means, basically, sharing in important political rights like the right to vote, or serve on a jury, or be eligible for a post in government. By this criterion, in an oligarchy, where only the wealthy have political rights, the poor do not count as citizens, and therefore their good is not part of the common good.[32] Plato's good ruler seeks the welfare of everyone under his rule.[33] Aristotle's good ruler seeks the common good of the citizens – which excludes slaves, resident foreigners, and native inhabitants without political rights.

### JUSTICE IS THE COMMON GOOD

In several places Aristotle identifies the common good and justice, or anyway "a kind of justice."[34] The basic impulse behind this identification is easy to understand. On the one hand, law aims to specify and to prescribe what is just; on the other hand, law aims to promote the common good. So the single aim of legislation can be expressed either as "the just" or as "the common good," and these two expressions must therefore be equivalent.

To any modern reader of Aristotle, the claim that "justice is the common good" is immediately suspect. It is a commonplace of moral philosophy that the demands of justice and the demands of common welfare easily conflict. Sometimes the salvation of society will require harming innocents. Sometimes laws that scrupulously honor the rights of a few will cause substantial harm to the rest of society.

A charitable modern reader might be willing to grant that each of these descriptions of the proper aim of law has an intuitive appeal; it is a "reputable opinion," in Aristotle's language. But since these two descriptions of the aim of law conflict with each other, the job of a clear-headed theorist is to choose between them, and not – as Aristotle does – to pretend that they coincide.

If this commonplace of modern moral philosophy is correct (and I have no wish to dispute it), there remain several alternatives for interpreting Aristotle's doctrine that justice is the common good. Either Aristotle is falsely and confusedly asserting that two conflicting aims coincide; or else he is doing something subtler, and re-interpreting one of the aims in terms of the other. Perhaps the rhetorical force of his identification is to assert that justice is (not what people ordinarily think that it is, but rather) the common good; or else, to assert that the common good is (not what people ordinarily think that it is, but rather) whatever is just.

The crucial evidence for deciding between these alternatives is provided by Aristotle's discussion of "general justice" at the beginning of Book V of the *Nicomachean Ethics*:

Since the lawless man was seen to be unjust and the lawful person just, evidently whatever is lawful is in a way just (*panta ta nomima esti pôs dikaia*). For the provisions of legislative science are lawful, and each of these, we say, is just. Now the laws in their enactments on all subjects aim at the common good (*tou koinêi sympherontos*) of all, or of the best, or of those in control, whether their control rests on virtue or on some other such basis. So in one way we call just whatever produces and maintains happiness and its parts for a political community. (*NE* V 1, 1129b11–19)[35]

"The just is whatever produces and maintains the common good." In this phrase, which concept explicates which? Do we turn to the common good to learn what is just? Or do we turn to the concept of justice to learn what is in the common good?

This passage is most naturally interpreted as re-interpreting justice in terms of the common good. Aristotle's argument is that lawlessness is unjust and lawfulness just. Of course there are bad laws, but these are not the product of legislative science, i.e. the art of establishing good laws. The identification of the just and the lawful does not apply to bad laws, but only those which accord with legislative science. Now all laws aim at the common good – either of all, or of those in control. But, since the proper aim of law and of the legislative science is the common good of the community, justice is "whatever produces and maintains happiness and its parts for a political community" (NE V 1, 1129b18–19).

This last statement is a straightforward consequentialist, welfare-maximizing conception of justice. And like all such conceptions, it calls for re-interpreting and revising those aspects of the inherited common-sense conception of justice which conflict with it. On this conception of justice, if the happiness of the community can only be preserved by depriving a small minority of what they would otherwise deserve, then justice requires "violating the rights" (as we would say) of the few.

Aristotle says that everything lawful is "in a sense" just, and that we call "in one way" just whatever promotes the welfare of the community. Can we use these qualifications as a means to soften Aristotle's doctrine? Perhaps what Aristotle means is merely that there is one use of the term "just" according to which everything lawful is just, and all legal provisions which promote the welfare of the community are in this sense just. But there is another sense of justice in which it is just for people to get what they deserve (or in more modern language, have a right to). There are these two senses of justice, and Aristotle's remarks in this passage need not commit him to any view about how to resolve the issue when these two senses of justice conflict.

Unfortunately, Aristotle's qualification "in a way just" is not plausibly interpreted in this manner. In this stretch of text Aristotle is discussing the type of justice which he calls "complete virtue in relation to others" and is commonly called by Aristotle scholars "general justice." (Aristotle contrasts this type of justice with "particular justice," i.e. justice which is one particular virtue among others.)[36] When Aristotle says that the lawful is "in a way" just and that laws which promote the welfare of the community are "in one way" just, what he means is that they exemplify general justice, and not that they are only partially or prima facie just.

But one might object that Aristotle's distinction between general justice and particular justice does not solve the problem of conflict between the goals of welfare-maximization and individual desert, but merely relocates it. What would Aristotle say about cases in which the demands of general justice and of particular justice conflict? If general justice calls for maximizing general welfare, and particular justice for (inter alia) giving people what they deserve, then in certain cases general justice may demand that we harm the innocent while particular justice demands that we spare them.

This objection is well-founded. Aristotle simply assumes a consistency between general justice and particular justice (as he assumes a consistency between general justice and all other virtues). But given the way he characterizes general justice (it is both "the whole of virtue" and "obedience to law, which aims at the common good"), this assumption is unjustified. Aristotle's accounts of general and particular justice have no way to rule out the possibility that in some respects and on some occasions, the maintenance of general welfare might require giving to certain individuals less than they deserve.

On the other hand, the strict universality of Aristotle's conception of the common good does suggest one strong claim about distributive justice. If the promotion of the happiness of every member of the political community is the appropriate goal of politics and the law-giver's art, then either all members of the community merit a share of happiness, or else the goal of politics is patently unjust. Although Aristotle does not explicitly discuss the question in these terms, he is committed to the former option. His analysis of the various regimes shows the principle that "all members of the community deserve a share of happiness " at work: each regime excludes from political participation, and hence from "the community" in the relevant sense, all those who do not, by the lights of the regime, deserve to participate in the good life as that regime conceives it.

### CIVIC FRIENDSHIP AND THE COMMON GOOD

Aristotle brings up the identity of justice and the common good in his discussion of the relationship between justice and civic friendship:[37]

As we said at the beginning, friendship and justice would seem to have the same area of concern and to be found in the same people. For every community there seems to be some sort of justice, and some type of friendship also...All communities would seem to be parts of the political community. For people keep company for some advantage and to supply something contributing to their life. Moreover, the political community seems both to have been originally formed and to endure for advantage; for legislators also aim at advantage, and the common advantage is said to be just...All these [other] communities would seem to be subordinate to the political community, since it aims not at some present advantage, but at advantage for the whole of life. (*NE* VIII 9, 1159b25–27, 1160a8–14, 28–30)

Aristotle says that friendship and justice have the same concerns, and that they vary together according to the type of community. The political community is the comprehensive community and aims at the comprehensive good for its members, namely, happiness or living well. Political justice is therefore the comprehensive common good.

This line of reasoning is familiar from the passages already discussed. What is new in this passage is its implications for civic friendship. Since friendship is correlative with justice, and political justice aims at the common good, so also civic friendship must aim at the common good. Friends wish their friends' good for their friends' own sake. The good that civic friends wish for their friends, i.e. for all other members of the civic association, is nothing short of happiness.

The quoted passage implies that all members of the civic association, *qua* civic friends, have the same concern as the statesman or legislator, namely the happiness of their fellow citizens. This does not mean that citizens are unqualifiedly beneficent, or have the utilitarian desire to maximize the amount of happiness in their society as an ultimate and unrestricted motive. Aristotle makes it quite clear that in his view civic friendship, like the political community within which it arises, is based on reciprocity. Civic friendships, like all friendships and all human associations on Aristotle's view, have the character of an alliance.[38]

Later on, Aristotle reports (with tacit endorsement) the view that a difference between a public service ("liturgy") and an act of friendship is that in friendship the benefits are reciprocated (*NE* VIII 14, 1163a29–30). The public-spirited acts of a citizen motivated by a sense of justice and civic friendship are not purely altruistic or beneficent: they are based on (in at least the sense of "produced by motives that are causally dependent on") an expectation of reciprocal benefits. Aristotle's distinction between acts of public service and acts of friendship implicitly recognizes a category of political action which transcends the limits of justice and political friendship.

## CONCLUSION

A pervasive feature of Aristotle's philosophy is "teleology." On Aristotle's view, the characteristic behavior of all living things is purposive: living things do what they do "for the sake of an end." Aristotle's teleology extends beyond individual living things. The heavens move as they do in order to produce the seasons and a hospitable climate. The elements earth, water, air, and fire are not alive, yet Aristotle explains their motion teleologically. Aristotle's *polis* is not an individual living thing (though it is made up of living things), but it, too, is purposive. Political society is an association of people who live and work together for the sake of living a good life. The goal of political society is thus the common good, i.e. the happiness (*eudaimonia*) of all citizens.

## WORKS CITED

Allen, D. J. 1964. "Individual and state in the *Ethics and Politics*." In *Entretiens sur l'Antiquité Classique* IX, *La 'Politique' d'Aristote*. Geneva: Fondation Hardt

Cooper, J. 1991. "Political animals and civic friendship". In *Reason and Emotion*. Princeton University Press

2011. "Political community and the highest good." In *Being, Nature, and Life in Aristotle: Essays in honor of Allan Gotthelf*, eds. R. Bolton and J. Lennox. Cambridge University Press

2012. *Pursuits of Wisdom: Six Ways of Life in Ancient Philosophy from Socrates to Plotinus*. Princeton University Press

Finnis, J. 1986. *Natural Law and Natural Rights*. Oxford: Clarendon

Fortenbaugh, W. 1991. "Aristotle on prior and posterior, correct and mistaken constitutions." In *A Companion to Aristotle's Politics*, eds. D. Keyt and F. Miller. Oxford: Blackwell

Gagarin, M. 2002. *Antiphon the Athenian: Oratory, Law, and Justice in the Age of the Sophists*. Austin, TX: University of Texas Press

Harte, V. 2002. *Plato on Parts and Wholes*. Oxford: Clarendon

Herzog, R. 1974. "Gemeinwohl." In *Historisches Worterbuch der Philosophie*, ed. J. Ritter. Basel: Schwabe

Hibst, P. 1991. *Utilitas Publica – Gemeiner Nutz – Gemeinwohl*. Frankfurt: Peter Lang

Irwin, T. H. 1988. *Aristotle's First Principles*. Oxford: Clarendon

Kempshall, M. 1999. *The Common Good in Late Medieval Political Thought*. Oxford: Clarendon

Khan, C. 2005. "Aristotle, Citizenship, and the Common Advantage." *Polis* 22: 1–23

Kraut, R. 2002. *Aristotle: Political Philosophy*. Oxford University Press

Miller, F. D. 1995. *Nature, Justice and Rights in Aristotle's Polotics*. Oxford University Press

Morrison, D. 1999. "Aristotle's Definition of Citizenship: A Problem and Some Solutions." *History of Philosophy Quarterly* 16: 143–65

   2001a. "The Happiness of the City and the Happiness of the Individual in Plato's *Republic*." *Ancient Philosophy* 21: 1–23

   2001b. "Politics as a Vocation, according to Aristotle." *History of Political Thought* 22: 221–41

   forthcoming. "Aristotle on the Happiness of the City." In *Aristote et l'excellence politique*, eds. E. Bermon, V. Laurand and J. Terrel

Murphy, M. 2006. "The common good." In *Natural Law in Jurisprudence and Politics*. Cambridge University Press

Olson, M. 1965. *The Logic of Collective Action; Public Goods and the Theory of Groups*. Cambridge, MA: Harvard University Press

Osborne, C. 1994. *Eros Unveiled: Plato and the God of Love*. Oxford: Clarendon Press

Reeve, C. D. C. 1998. *Aristotle, Politics*. Indianapolis, IN: Hackett

Schütrumpf, E. 1991–2005, *Aristoteles' Politik*. 4 vols, Berlin: Akademie Verlag

White, N. 2002. *Individual and Conflict in Greek Ethics*. Oxford: Clarendon

### NOTES

1. Cicero, *On the Commonwealth* frag. 39a; Aquinas, *Summa Theologica* I–II 90; *On Kingship* I 8–15; Rousseau, *Social Contract* I 9; II 1; Green, *Prolegomena to Ethics* III–IV. For the historical development of the idea of the common good, see Herzog 1974; Hibst 1991; Kempshall 1999.

2. See below, note 11 and p. 89.

3. See I 1, especially 1252a16, and *NE* I 2, especially 1094b6–9. There are particular exceptions, such as an alliance between cities, and households and villages that exist outside of any city. Aristotle holds that sovereign states larger that the *polis*, i.e. empires, are too large to be effectively governed.

4. In this chapter I use "member" in a restrictive sense. Only citizens are "members" of the *polis*. Therefore not all *inhabitants* of the city count as *members*. Slaves and resident aliens (metics) live in the city, but they are not citizens. They live within the city's boundaries, but they are not members of political society.

5. *Pol.* I 1–2. See also VII 13, 1331b31–1332a7, and *NE* VIII 9, 1160a10–30.

6. He discusses this in the lines immediately following the quoted passage.

7. *NE* VIII 9, 1160a9; VIII 14; *Pol.* III 6, 1279a8–13.
8. *NE* IX 8, 1169a8–11; *Pol.* VII 9, 1329a21–24.
9. Starting at 1279a17. Cp. *NE* V 1, 1129b15.
10. See Fortenbaugh 1991.
11. Cf. *NE* VIII 12, 1160a31ff. Aristotle's use of the common good to distinguish between good and bad rulers is anticipated by Plato at *Republic* III, 412d and *Laws* IV, 715b2 ff. These two passages make slightly different points. The *Laws* passage contrasts caring for some people and not at all for others. The *Republic* passage is consistent with (and I would argue that it presupposes) a concern for the happiness of everyone, but raises the possibility of favoritism, i.e. unequal concern. Further relevant texts in Plato include: *Laws* 697c–d; *Statesman* 293a–e, 296d–297b. The contrast between the individual good and the common good is a commonplace in classical Greek political thinking. For the idea of the common good, see Dinarchus, *Against Demosthenes*, 99; Demosthenes, *Phillipic* 2, 12; *On the Crown*, 217, 295; Isocrates, *On the Peace* 91; *Letters* 6, 3; 7, 4; Xenophon, *Cyropaedia* I 2, 2; *Hellenika* I 4, 13; and the most famous passage of all, Pericles' funeral oration in Thucydides, 2.35–46.
12. Justice requires that a good ruler be impartial. But the ruler's impartiality does not require treating people the same or benefiting them by an equal amount. It implies instead that when the ruler treats people differently, he does so for good reasons. For a contrary interpretation, see Kraut 2002: 390.
13. For a discussion of public goods, see Olson 1965.
14. *EE* I 2; *Pol.* III 5; VII 9. The distinction implicit in Aristotle's discussions of wealth, I 8–10; III 9, 1280a33–b34.
15. On the notion of the common good as the necessary conditions for a good life, see Finnis 1986: 185 and Murphy 2006: 65–71.
16. Murphy calls this the "aggregative" conception of the common good, and defends it in Murphy 2006.
17. *Pol.* III 7 is the central text for this.
18. A classic defense of this approach is Cooper 1991. For a rich and subtle restatement, see Cooper 2011, esp. 239–48, and Cooper 2012: 123–36.
19. Cooper 2011: 247.
20. Another objection to Cooper's interpretation is that it makes civic friendship into a kind of virtue friendship, whereas Aristotle presents it as a friendship for the sake of advantage. On these issues see Irwin 1988: 402–6.
21. Miller 1995: ch. 6, provides a useful typology of individualistic vs. holistic views of the common good, as does White 2002: 124–34. For an important distinction between two kinds of holism, see Harte 2002: 158–67.

22. Morrison 2001b.

23. Book VI 5–8.

24. Miller 1995: ch. 6; Kraut 2002: 206–14.

25. This is an example of what Murphy 2006 calls a "distinctive good" conception.

26. I explain and defend this claim more fully in Morrison (forthcoming).

27. For more on this point, see Bryan, Garsten, Chapter 13.

28. Compare *NE* I 7, 1098a15–19 (on the happiness of the individual) with *Pol.* VII 2, 1323b30, quoted above.

29. Along with *Laws* IV, 715b2 ff. and *Gorgias* 514d5–505e4.

30. What Socrates says does in a way allow for the craftsman and his object to be the same. For example, a physician can heal himself. But the "ruling element" here is the physician's soul, which heals his body. So the craftsman and his object are not exactly the same after all.

31. III 6, 1278b30–1279a8.

32. On such "paradoxes of citizenship" see Cooper 1991: 364; Morrison 1999; and Khan 2005.

33. In the *Republic*, Plato does not say explicitly whether the ideal city contains slaves, and the point is disputed among scholars. But since Plato holds that there is a single art of ruling, it follows that good rule over slaves must be for the benefit of the slaves.

34. *NE* V 1, 1129b11–15; VIII 9, 1160a9–30; *Pol.* III 12, 1282b17; *Rhet.* I 6, 1362b27–28.

35. On this passage see Allan 1964: 64–72. The idea that "the just is the lawful" is an important one in Greek political thought. See Antiphon the sophist, frag. DK 44, and Gagarin 2002: 65–80.

36. *NE* V 2. For an account of these various types of justice, see Miller 1995: 68–73.

37. On civic friendship in Aristotle, see Cooper 1991.

38. See Osborne 1994: ch. 6.

# 8    Natural, ethical, and political justice

Aristotle's notion of natural justice has aroused many controversies among commentators, and it would be promising too much to attempt to settle on a single interpretation, much less a new one. I will offer an interpretation of Aristotle's idea of natural justice that tries to preserve its openness to different approaches, but at the same time states some guidelines any interpretation (I surmise) should follow in order to offer a sound reading of the text. These guidelines are three in number, stated here as T1, T2, and T3. Together the three of them establish a close connection between the *Ethics* and the *Politics*. Such a connection looks trivial at first glance, but at the end of the day proves to be very rewarding – or so I think. I will begin with some general comments on political naturalism in section I, and will then dedicate a section to each of these three theses.

I

Justice is central to Aristotle's political thought. Political theory deals with constitutions and cities; it aims at establishing the best constitution in general, as well as the constitution most appropriate to given circumstances. To do this, political theory first has to know what our living well consists in, and living well is either reducible to living justly, or at least has justice as one of its essential features. This is already evident in Aristotle's distinction between correct and deviant constitutions. The constitution is the very heart of a *polis*, for a *polis* is a community of citizens sharing a constitution, so that a change in constitution will result in an accordant change in the *polis* (III 3, 1276b1–4). Correct constitutions aim at the common benefit, whereas in the deviant ones, what is sought is only the benefit of the ruler(s). Now, common benefit is not only the prosperity (in the sense of great wealth) of most citizens; rather it is primarily living well, where that means living according to what is unqualifiedly just (*kata to haplôs dikaion*; III 6, 1279a18–19).[1]

Since justice is a basic ethical notion, ethics lies at the foundations of politics. In a general sense, a just person is a moral person, such that being just is essentially the same as being moral, except that justice is directed to one's relations towards other people, whereas moral virtue concerns one's actions towards oneself too. For to be just and to be moral are the same disposition, but they are not manifested in the same way: justice is the disposition to act virtuously towards other people; virtue is the disposition with no such qualification (*NE* V 1, 1130a12–13). Politics thus builds on ethical notions, and a student of ethics will naturally go to politics in order to bring to completion what Aristotle calls "the philosophy of human affairs" (*NE* X 9, 1181b15). The notion of justice operates as a hinge between both disciplines, and it comes as no surprise that most of the references from *Politics* to *Ethics* point to Book V, the treatise on justice.[2] And the reverse is also true: besides those passages in *Ethics* that place ethics within political science and take the latter as the architectonic science of human affairs, it is Book V that refers to, and is conceived in close connection with, the *Politics*. For instance, in V 1 mention is made of the legislator and of the different constitutions (*NE* V 1, 1129b11–19), a typical topic of the *Politics*; and in V 2, it is said that it will be investigated later whether it is the same to be a good man and to be a good citizen, a question whose answer is found in *Politics* III 4. Not only does the *Politics* build on the ethical notion of justice, but it also completes and finds solutions to problems raised previously in *NE* V. And that, I contend, is particularly true in the case of natural justice.

In order to avoid confusion, it is useful to distinguish between general politics, the common and architectonic science of human affairs, and special politics, which is a branch of the first, and deals with constitutions and cities, in contrast to ethics, which is the other branch of general politics and deals with individual happiness. Ethics is subordinated to general politics, but provides special politics with its basic concepts and notions. Both politics (and ethics as well), like other philosophical disciplines, are subject to the general Aristotelian teleological approach. This means that the end of a thing, or its *telos*, governs its constitution and development. One is to judge or explain a thing in light of its completion, where the thing presents itself in its fully developed and perfect state. Teleological explanation is not seen as incompatible with mechanical necessity; quite the contrary, it leaves a place for such necessity, but it makes mechanical necessity subservient to final ends. Most emblematic of this framework is Aristotle's statement that hands are not the cause of man's intellect, but that man has hands because of his intelligence: the mechanical causes linked to having hands are subordinated to the fact that man is an intellectual being.[3]

In Aristotle's political thought, such a teleological approach results in what one may call political naturalism.[4] The main point of political naturalism, for what concerns us here, is the reiterated Aristotelian thesis that man is by nature a political animal.[5] This thesis can have two readings, a narrow and a broad one. According to the broad reading, it means that man is a sociable animal; due to language and intelligence, man is the most gregarious among all animals that live in groups. On the strict reading, it means that human beings live in cities, which are not only more complex structures than villages or households, but, more importantly, are constituted in order that men not only survive, but live well. On this narrow reading, there is no animal other than man that can be political, for being political in this sense requires having *logos* – speech or reason – and only human beings have *logos*. Aristotle sometimes stresses the broad, sometimes the narrow reading. In Book I of *Politics*, for instance, he is eager to go from the one to the other within a few lines: after stating that man is a political animal in the sense of living in cities, he goes on to say that human beings are more of a political animal than bees or other gregarious animals are (I 2, 1253a1–18).

However, being political by nature does not mean that human beings come to live in cities as a biological upshot of their instincts. It means instead that nature endows human beings with impulses that lead them to live in groups, and that human beings have the ability to organize those groups into cities, in so far as human beings are endowed with perception of what is harmful or beneficial, and hence of what is just or unjust. A parallel passage in *Nichomachean*

*Ethics* helps us understand Aristotle's argument here. In *NE* II, Aristotle contends that, as moral virtues come about as a result of habit, none of them arises in us by nature, for nothing that exists in this sense of "nature" can form a habit contrary to it, but human beings can be virtuous or vicious (*NE* II 1, 1103a18–23). He then says that moral virtues arise in us neither by nature nor contrary to nature, but that by nature we are able to receive them and make ourselves perfect by acquiring them. Aspasius, in his commentary, notes that to describe a feature with the phrase "by nature" has several senses, and can mean that:

1.  a feature *x* is always co-present (as things that are heavy by nature are borne downwards and light things upwards);
2.  *x* is not co-present from the beginning, but after a time comes for the most part to be present, even if we do not busy ourselves about it (as with the natural growth of teeth);
3.  *x* is liable to occur to an object as contraries are said to exist by nature (as with disease and health in a body);
4.  *x* is liable to occur to an object that is more inclined to it and rather has impulses towards it (as health is by nature, in contrast with disease, which is contrary to nature).

According to Aspasius, virtue does not belong to people by nature in senses (1) and (2), "but it would be by nature in the third and above all the fourth of the senses mentioned."[6] This list may not be exhaustive, but it is enough for our purposes in the *Politics*: man is by nature a political animal in sense (3) and notably in sense (4), comprising both a passive inclination and an active impulse to live in cities.[7] The *Nicomachean* passage mentions another important point. Aristotle says that, as we become virtuous, we improve ourselves and are made perfect by habit (II 1, 1103a25–26). The same is true in the *Politics*. Anyone who is without a city (who is *apolis* not just by accident or bad fortune) is either *phaulos* or else a superhuman (I 2, 1253a3–4). A *phaulos* is not a beast, but a human being who, because of his vicious character, has debased himself beyond the pale of his own moral endowment – and Aristotle envisages the case of so ruining himself that such a person becomes incurably incapable of living with others (*NE* V 10, 1137a26–30). The superhuman is above human condition, a sort of godlike being, out of human reach. Now, the *polis* provides the conditions under which we develop ourselves as human beings possessing *logos*, the condition under which we perfect ourselves as agents that do things "according to reason or not without reason" (*NE* I 7, 1098a7–8).

Being a political animal means that perfecting themselves as agents in this way requires men to live in a *polis*. Political life is not so much a necessary condition for physical existence, as it is a requirement for the perfection of human agents interacting with others. And interacting well is equivalent to interacting justly. Now, Aristotle distinguishes between two senses of justice. A man is just in a general sense if he follows moral rules; in this sense, being just is the same as being moral, except that justice is moral virtue related to other people, whereas virtue may also concern the agent himself. The second sense of just, or special justice, is a species of this general justice: it concerns the sphere of gain and loss, either in distributive or in corrective dimensions.[8] This distinction is of far-reaching importance. For by making special justice a species of general justice, Aristotle circumscribes a new domain, the domain of justice as legal practice, as we know it nowadays (despite obviously many historical differences). But he also equates general justice with being lawful, *nomimon* (*NE* V 1, 1129b34), and this has important consequences too. For being just in the generic sense cannot be simply being law-abiding, for Aristotle recognizes that laws may be unjust, and some are indeed unjust (the laws of deviant constitutions: III 11, 1282b4–13). However, if man is made perfect regarding agency only in the *polis*, if the constitution is the form of a *polis*, being the organization of its various offices, particularly those of authority over everything, namely, government (*politeuma*), such that government is the core of constitution (III 6, 1278b10–11), it looks as if obedience to authority is built into the very idea of a man made perfect as an agent, given that being in a *polis* has been built into the very essence of man, and being just is tantamount to being lawful.

Special politics was grounded on ethics, but acting morally towards others requires being lawful, and this implies being obedient to the ruler or governing class, which belongs to special politics. There is thus a circular reference between special politics and ethics, which may look problematic to a modern mind.[9] For circularity risks creating a serious difficulty, unless a single concept turns out to ground both ethics and (special) politics. Political justice does play exactly this role as unqualified justice, for, as such, it is the same as general politics, the common ground to special politics and ethics. Political justice obtains between citizens, on the basis of some form of equality, and is permeated by law (*NE* V 6, 1134a30). "Political good is justice, and justice is the common benefit" (III 12, 1282b17–18; see *NE* VIII 9, 1160a13–14), so that political justice is in this sense unqualified justice.[10] This is why Aristotle writes that "It is evident, then, that those constitutions that look for the common benefit turn out to be correct, according to what is unqualifiedly just, whereas those which look only to the benefit of the rulers are mistaken and are deviations from the correct constitutions" (III 6, 1279a17–20). As the correct constitutions strive for common benefit, they satisfy what is unqualifiedly just. And by so doing they are politically just. The equality in question, which brings about common benefit, as we will see, is virtue, so that, in the perfect case, the best political man is also the most virtuous one. The individual has in a sense no escape from the *polis* and its constitution, for it is only under its rule that he can attain perfection as an agent. But he need not seek to escape from it either, for in a relevant sense being lawful is equivalent to being moral or just – at least in the correct constitutions. For in the correct constitutions common benefit prevails, and this is the unqualifiedly just, that is, this is political justice.[11]

## II

I would like now to introduce the first of the three theses I will explicate in the remaining sections of this chapter.

T1: Political justice is the basis for all human justice.

This is a very strong thesis and deserves careful scrutiny. First of all, human justice is contrasted here with any other sort of justice, such as divine justice. Whatever divine justice may be, if there is such a justice, it is not our concern here; our only focus is on human justice. Secondly, as we saw, Aristotle distinguishes between general justice and being moral: general justice is the same as moral virtue, only that it is other-related. But is general justice the same as political justice? I think the answer is positive, because any case of justice other than political justice will prove to be a case of justice only in so far as it is somehow related to political justice. A *polis* is a community that turns out to be the end to which the other communities are subordinated: the couple of male and female, the master-slave relation, both of these constituting the household, and the village; once several villages reach self-sufficiency, a *teleios koinônia*, a perfect community, or a *polis*, is attained. Aristotle recognizes just or unjust relations in a couple, or between master and slave, and in general in the household. He says, for instance, that the master-slave relation is based on justice when the one is naturally superior, and the other naturally inferior, so that "slavery is both just and beneficial" (I 5, 1255a3). In *EE* VII 10, 1242a19–36, it is said that, as justice concerns members of a community, and male and female already form a community, there is justice for couples too. So these are non-political forms of justice, as Aristotle explicitly acknowledges. But they are all justice of a sort, *dikaion ti*, in which *ti* brings in an *alienans* meaning: not a case of justice strictly speaking, but something similar to justice. This might be taken in a negative sense: the non-political forms of justice fall short of justice, strictly speaking. But I think Aristotle intends to make a positive claim: thanks to a certain relationship to political (general) justice, they lift themselves into justice, but only up to a point.[12] And the relation that raises them up to a certain point is *resemblance*. For Aristotle says that despotic justice, paternal justice, and household justice are not the same as political justice, but *resemble* it (*homoion: NE* V 6, 1134b9). The reason for this is that there are no just or unjust acts towards what belongs to oneself – a slave is a form of property, and children also, at least up to a certain age; and this is why justice between wife and husband resembles political justice more (*mallon; NE* V 6, 1134b15), for a wife is like property to a lesser extent than any of the others. Any case of justice other than political justice cannot but be justice *of a sort*, and thus falls short of justice strictly speaking, but is nonetheless a case of justice in so far as it *resembles* political justice (*NE* V 6, 1134a29–30; *ti dikaion kai kath' homoiotêta*).[13]

Now, *resemblance* has a technical meaning in Aristotle. Two cases are possible. If two things resemble each other, they do so either in virtue of a genuine connection between things, or in virtue of a spurious connection. For the latter, for instance, Aristotle speaks of *akrasia* by resemblance in his treatment of spirit, honor, or gain (*NE* VII 4, 1148a3; 1148b6; 1148b13; *NE* VII 5, 1149a3, VII 9, 1151b33); for, strictly speaking (*NE* VII 5, 1149a21–24), *akrasia* refers to a conflict between reason and very specific desires (those connected to the senses of touch and taste). People speak of *akrasia* of gain, honor, or spirit, but, according to Aristotle, this is because of a spurious connection based on mere resemblance, for there is actually no *akrasia* in these cases. As a matter of fact, connections of spurious resemblance and metaphor go together; one says, for instance, that animals have practical wisdom, but this is only because of a spurious resemblance to men which make us speak metaphorically (*NE* VII 6, 1149b32).[14] But sometimes resemblance reflects a genuine connection. According to the *Nicomachean* discussion of friendship, for instance, the three kinds of friendship are correctly spoken of as "friendships" due to their resemblance (*NE* VIII 4, 1156b20; *NE* VIII 5, 1157a32; *NE* VII 11, 1152b5). Resemblance mirrors a genuine connection among them – there is no metaphor here.[15]

Many things resemble one another, as Aristotle reminds us (*NE* VII 9, 1151b33); one has to see in each case whether the connection is genuine or spurious. In the case of justice, household and despotic relations are said to be just because of their resemblance to political justice; the latter is unqualifiedly justice, the former are justices of a sort. Are they genuine or spurious resemblances? I think they are genuine. In Aristotelian teleological thought, associations of individuals in couples and households do not stand on their own, but represent stages toward, or are parts of, the perfect community, the *polis*. As communities, they have justice of a kind; each just relation takes on the metaphysical status of the corresponding community, which is a part of the *polis*. As justices of a sort, they are no mere metaphor; on the contrary, their resemblance reflects their teleological dependence on political justice, in so far as the corresponding communities are parts of the *polis*. This same metaphysical basis imposes a reference point (political justice) onto the resemblance relationship, for, though resemblance as such is a symmetrical relation, so that A resembles B no more than B resembles A, in this case, as one precise item (the *polis*) is the *telos* towards which the other ones are stages, it occupies the primary position and generates a kind of justice (that is, political justice) which the other ones are supposed to resemble.

However, it is also possible to speak metaphorically about resemblance to justice, such that no genuine connection corresponds to it. This is the case when one speaks of a man being just to himself, as Plato did in the *Republic*, claiming that all justice is reducible to psychic justice, meaning by this the just relation of one part to the others within the soul.[16] Aristotle rejects without further ado the Platonic notion of psychic justice, remarking that there is no justice between a man and himself, and it is only "metaphorically and by resemblance" (*NE* V 11, 1138b5–6) that there is justice between certain parts of him. Worse, as Plato conceives of justice as reason commanding the nonrational parts of the soul, such justice would resemble despotic or household justice, rather than political justice, for the latter requires equality, but the former inequality, as is also the case for the rational part commanding the nonrational ones. So if there were psychic justice, it would be a resemblance of a resemblance, for despotic justice is already a resemblance of political justice – quite an ironic remark against Plato.

There is still another way of speaking of justice, in which one *claims to be just*, but such a claim fails to represent really just relations. Aristotle says that all constitutions are a certain form of justice, given that every constitution is a community, and all communities rest on some sort of justice (*EE* VII 9, 1241b13–14). Hence, there is justice even in the deviant ones, and one should consequently ask "what oligarchic and democratic justices are" (III 9, 1280a8–9). They are not unqualified justice, for deviant constitutions look at private benefit, not at common benefit (III 7, 1279b6–10). One might say that they are just privately (III 13, 1284b23–24, applied to ostracism). But is this really justice? All grasp "justice of a sort" (*dikaion ti*; III 9, 1280a9), such that all take it to mean equality (in which all are right), but they judge equality wrongly (*krinousin kakôs*; III 9, 1280a14) as wealth (oligarchy), or as freedom (democracy). Now, there is a *claim of justice* indeed, for no one claims to found a community based on injustice. But it is a false claim. Aristotle has no specific word to convey such a *claim of justice* as that made by oligarchs or democrats, and refers to it by the phrase *dikaion ti*, "justice of a sort," already applied to such cases as despotic justice. But here there is no justice at all, only a (false) *claim of justice*. Such a claim does not enjoy that resemblance to (political) justice that makes despotic just relations justice of a sort. A sign of this is that Aristotle says that deviant constitutions (and consequently their claims of justice) are contrary to nature (III 17, 1287b41), but never says the same of domestic or despotic justices.

### III

The central place ascribed to the *polis* and to political justice is no novelty in antiquity, although the Aristotelian teleological framework provides it with more consistent foundations. But Aristotle makes a second move, and this move is a novelty in ancient political philosophy.

T2: There are various kinds of political justice.

A classical question in ancient times was about the best regime. Aristotle tackles this problem too, but offers a new answer. In a sense, he conforms to the traditional standards: he recognizes that one of the tasks of political philosophy is to determine which is the best constitution, and proposes his candidate for such a controversial question: kingship, "the first and most divine constitution" (IV 2, 1289a40), in face of which even polity and aristocracy "fail utterly" (IV 8, 1293b25: *diêmartêkasi*). But there is an important novelty here. To come up with one *best* constitution, Aristotle has first to discuss what a *good* constitution consists in, that is, what a *correct* constitution is. And on this topic, he determines that there is not only one correct constitution, but a variety of them. Indeed, there are three: kingship, aristocracy, and polity. For they all look to the common benefit, and in so doing they all put into practice political justice. Thus, to answer a classical question – What is the best constitution? – Aristotle proposes three constitutions, which are all correct because they all search for the common benefit. And this is a new and far-reaching move.

To understand the significance of this move, one has to go back to the relation between general and special justice. Special justice is a species of general justice, the other-related moral virtue, which is its genus. Every case of special justice is a case of general justice, but not every case of general justice is a case of special justice. Special justice is justice concerned with grasping the right amount of goods, such that if a man has undue gain, he will act unjustly in this specific sense of justice. To take an Aristotelian example, a man who commits adultery to gratify his lust and happens to lose money is unjust in the sense of general justice, but not unjust in the sense of special justice, whereas the one who commits adultery for the sake of gain is not only unjust in the general sense, but also and specifically unjust in the sense of special injustice. The notion of gain (and its contrary, loss) refers not only to materially acquired goods, but includes any external good, such as honor or safety (*NE* V 2, 1130b2). The vice attached to special justice is *pleonexia*, having more; in contrast, being just in this sense amounts to having the gain one deserves, according to a proportion (*analogon ti*, *NE* V 3, 1131a29). The proportional rule makes the relation *equal*: if A made one-third of *X*, and B two-thirds of it, then A deserves one-third and B two-thirds of what is produced or whatever by X. The central notion of *special* justice is hence equality *of certain goods*, but, as a type of general justice, its key notion is *equality (to ison)* of certain goods. The proportion will be either "geometrical" or "arithmetical," to use the Aristotelian jargon: if it is distributive justice, it will be "geometrical" in the sense that it is proportionate to the merits of the persons involved; if it is corrective justice (either commercial or juridical), it will concern only the loss or gain of the objects about which the action or transaction was made, independently of other merits the agents might exhibit, in accordance with an "arithmetical" proportion. Both distributive and corrective justice will follow a rule of commensurability fitted to their natures, and will be just in so far as they preserve some equality.

Thus, in a *polis*, special justice requires some sort of equality, for it is a type of justice, and general justice is equality. All agree on this: "Justice seems to be equality, and indeed it is" (III 9, 1280a11; V 1, 1301a26–27). But equality with regard to what? There are different answers, depending on the context and the subject in question. In a commercial transaction, for instance, gains and losses are to be equalized in accordance with some proportion. But to answer this question in the most general, or abstract, but still relevant way, one has to see what the end of the *polis* is: namely, living well. And living well is acting nobly: "So political communities must be taken to exist for the sake of noble actions, and not for the sake of living together" (III 9, 1281a2–3). It remains only to name that in relation to which, in the most abstract way, everything else is to be equalized, as gains and losses in a commercial transaction: "The best life, both for individuals separately and for cities collectively, is a life of virtue sufficiently equipped with the resources needed to take part in virtuous actions" (VII 1, 1323b40–24a2). Thus, Aristotle's answer to the question of what, in its most general expression, is to be equalized, is equality of virtue. Moral virtue is the measure of justice in the correct constitutions. In order to be spread over all the *polis*, the city must provide leisure and other prerequisites for the citizens' (moral) flourishing.

However, one thing is to distribute the material preconditions for virtue as everyone is supposed to be capable to become virtuous, another thing is to cope with the citizens' variable realization of this same capacity to become virtuous. And here there is a brute fact in political life that one has to take into account: we do not all develop an equal share of virtue. Human nature could have been such that we all would develop an equal share of it, but as a matter of fact it is not. On the contrary: judging by the life people actually share, "since happiness is the highest good, and happiness is some sort of activity of virtue, that is, a perfect exercise of it, and since, as it happens, some people manage to get a share in virtue, whereas others do so only to a small degree or not at all, it is clear that this is why there are different kinds of city-states and a variety of constitutions" (VII 8, 1328a37–41).[17] From this brute fact – the fact that we are unequal with regard to the practice of virtue – flow some consequences. One consequence is the triple refraction of the best constitution in kingship, aristocracy, and polity: a multitude should be under kingship when there happens to be someone so superior in virtue that it would be unfair that he be ruled by others; the multitude is suited to aristocracy when there is a qualified group of people whose possession of virtue makes them proper rulers to other free men; and a multitude is fit for polity when there naturally arises within it a group, similar to the hoplites, which is capable of ruling and being ruled, and distributes the offices to the rich on the basis of merit (III 17, 1288a8–15).[18] Another consequence is that, as the virtue of a citizen is suited to the constitution of his *polis*, "consequently, if indeed there are several kinds of constitution, it is clear that there cannot be a single virtue that is the virtue – the perfect virtue – of a good citizen" (III 4, 1276b30–33). There are thus several justices (V 9, 1309a37–39), and education, which is so central a task for every *polis*, is to be adapted to each one (V 9, 1310a16–17).

The grip of ethics on special politics proves again to be quite strong. The three correct constitutions are ordered on the basis of how moral virtue is present in political activities. Kingship, the divine constitution, occupies the first position in so far as, in it, political and moral virtues coincide. The king is the one who surpasses everyone else in virtue, so that it would be unfair for him to be ruled instead of ruling – unfair to so high a degree that he is not even to be restrained by laws.[19] He enjoys such a privileged place because he is himself the moral law in its perfection. Second is aristocracy, in which a group of virtuous citizens hold power and authority over other free men. Polity comes third; it is a correct constitution, but it stands in the last place, for it is a multitude of men, not necessarily virtuous individually, but all having a part of virtue, such that, collectively taken, they prove to be similar to the virtuous men.

It looks as if the greater their number, the lesser their individual moral quality: one man, surpassing all others in virtue; a few virtuous men, but such that they can be surpassed by a king; a multitude having only a share in virtue, but behaving collectively as virtuous men do. Aristotle gives us no justification for this decreasing proportion of virtue. It seems to be a brute fact, something experience teaches us to reckon with; perhaps it is a remaining trace of Platonic pessimism. It is worth noting that, when Aristotle discusses polity, he assumes that virtue cannot govern directly, because it is the multitude that rules. Instead, many individuals, each of whom has only some share in virtue (even a small one), govern collectively, and distribute offices according to property qualifications – not necessarily to themselves, but to the rich. This is not exactly what one would nowadays call a democracy. In fact, it is only in the constitution "of our prayers," which is free of all factual limitations, that Aristotle envisages a regime in which all, or a majority, of the citizens take turns sharing in government, having full comprehension of human well-being and acting virtuously. But this is what we wish for, not what we see around us. When Aristotle looks at the world as it is – not at the traditional political systems, but at human nature as it proves to be – his expectations are limited. Aristocracy is the virtuous government that is most attainable,[20] but it is always liable to be either surpassed in justice by a king of high-standing moral qualities, or downgraded to a multitude of rulers and ruled, virtue being preserved collectively, but not individually.

IV

I can now state my third thesis, which is in line with the first two and will bring my argument to a close.

T3: Natural justice is part of political justice, and is to be contrasted with conventional justice.

The main passage on natural justice is *NE* V 7, 1134b18–35a5. This is a much-discussed passage. Roughly speaking, commentators have to choose between two opposing positions: (a) it is the *polis* that calls any justice into existence, including what is called "natural justice"; or (b) there is a kind of justice that men recognize, independently of the form of community to which they belong, for such a justice is grounded in the very nature of man.[21] I will side with (a), but I am more interested here, not in arguing for a position, but in trying to understand how such different positions came to be attributed to Aristotle.

To begin with, it should be noted that this passage places natural justice within the realm of political justice.[22] The contrast is not with political, but with conventional[23] justice, natural and conventional both being parts of political justice. In this sense, one should reject any interpretation that takes natural justice to be something possessed in a state of nature.[24] What is natural, as opposed to conventional, need not be ante-political – and Aristotle explicitly denies that it is. A second remark concerns conventional law. Conventional law is such that in the beginning it makes no difference whether it is enacted in this way or another, but once enacted, it does make a difference if one does things in one way or another (V 7, 1134b20–21). Now, it is sometimes supposed that such enactments concern only trivial things, such that it makes no real difference whether there is an enactment or none at all. This may be the case for some of them, but is surely not the case for all, and possibly not for most of them.[25] All constitutions have three parts: (i) deliberation about public affairs; (ii) division of offices issues; and (iii) organization of lawsuits. All three parts depend crucially on conventions. Take for instance the selection of officials: "Either all select from all by election, or all select from all by lot (and from all either by sections – by tribe, or by deme or clan, until all the citizens have been gone through – or from all on every occasion); or from some by election or from some by lot; or partly in the first way and partly in the second" (IV 14, 1300a23–27) – and there are still other alternatives regarding the selection of officials, such as selecting officials only in summertime, or not during harvests, and so on. Or take the case of ostracism:

here again conventions are decisive (V 8, 1308b4–19). Or again expo-
sure, deeply embedded in conventions (VII 16, 1335b19–25). They
are all conventional – but none is trivial. The law is often arbitrary
with respect to the manner in which some action is accomplished.
That the action should be accomplished somehow is not, however,
an arbitrary matter. The very fact of being a citizen, which is so central for a *polis*, depends on arbitrary conventions, such as having both
parents as citizens, or only one, either the father or the mother (III 2,
1275b22–24), but that a *polis* should have citizens is not an arbitrary
matter.

   That so many laws are in fact arbitrary has misled people to think
that all law is rooted in arbitrariness, assuming that if there were
a natural law, it would be unchanging, but every law is liable to
change. Now, Aristotle resists this argument, at least for human
justice,[26] for although every law is liable to change, some are natural, and some are not, according to him. But instead of explaining
how liability to change is not incompatible with being natural, he
only says that it is plain which laws are conventional, and which are
natural, given that both sorts are changeable.[27] This is disappoint-
ing, and the analogy he provides next (the right hand is superior by
nature, and yet it is possible that everyone should become ambidextrous) gives no definite clue about how to understand his claim.[28] He
adds that laws by convention are similar to units of measurement:
they are not everywhere of equal size, but are liable to change. Similarly, justice by convention[29] is not everywhere the same, granted
that neither are the constitutions; nevertheless, there is only one
constitution which is the best everywhere.[30] One knows from the
*Politics* that this constitution is kingship; but it is not clear how this
comparison explains the relation between natural and conventional
justice.

   If any clue is to be found, it lies somewhere between *NE* V and
the *Politics*, for, as we saw, these are conceived of as closely connected texts.[31] Now, there is only one constitution which is the best
everywhere (kingship); and yet, there are three correct (and natural)
constitutions. This already suggests variability of a kind. The three
constitutions search for common benefit; to attain it, they enact
laws. And enactments inevitably bring arbitrariness in. Variability
of another sort proliferates. You ought to bury your parents; but how
to do it? By covering the bodies with a thin layer of dust, putting

bodies deep in the soil, or keeping the ashes in an urn? Natural and conventional laws are irremediably entangled one with another in the correct constitutions; nonetheless, we can distinguish them. This is the clue for how to distinguish them: one best constitution, but correctness already and naturally refracted into three constitutions. Variability, but no arbitrariness, for they all look to common benefit. Arbitrariness enters when constitutions are to have a body of laws. And constitutions cannot but have a body of laws. The picture Aristotle puts forward is not one of two separate domains, governed by legal justice, on the one hand, and natural justice on the other, but of a common domain (political justice), within which natural justice is like an old tropical tree overwhelmed by numerous epiphytic plants, that is, by legal justice, but such that one can detect which law stems from which domain. If one does not make such distinctions, the ensuing blur will tend to favor conventionality, as if one were to lose sight of the tree beneath all those epiphytic plants: "Fine things, and just things, which political science investigates, involve great variation and irregularity, so that they may be thought (*dokein*) to exist by convention alone, and not by nature" (*NE* I 3, 1094b14–16).

However, commentators have looked elsewhere to find clues on how to interpret *NE* V on natural justice. Three passages in the *Rhetoric* look promising at first glance. In I 10, law is presented as either private or common; and common law is said to be "all those unwritten principles which are supposed to be acknowledged everywhere" (*Rhet.* I 10, 1368b8–9). In I 13, natural justice is said to be common to all, "as everyone to some extent divines" (*Rhet.* I 13, 1373b7).[32] Three examples are given: Sophocle's Antigone in her struggle to bury her brother Polyneices; Empedocles and his prohibition of slaughtering animals; and the condemnation of slavery, denounced by Alcidamas as contrary to nature. Finally, in I 15, Aristotle notes that Antigone appeals to the universal law as more just than written laws, and that one should assume that principles of equity are permanent and changeless, and consequently that common law does not change either, since it is the law of nature (*Rhet.* I 15, 1375a31–33). But *Rhetoric* is not of much help. The examples in I 13 are rather surprising. Empedocles' prohibition of eating animals is hardly an opinion Aristotle would hold; in *Politics* I 8, 1256b15–20 he expressly argues against it. The same can be said about

Alcidamas' opinion on slavery: slavery is, according to Aristotle, natural in a relevant sense. Moreover, in what regards Antigone, who is mentioned twice, Aristotle seems to suggest in I 15 that appealing to natural law is tantamount to appealing to a law that never changes, in open conflict with what he says in the passage on natural justice. It looks better to be wary of collecting clues from the *Rhetoric* – either on the grounds that its examples are not to be taken too seriously, or that, in I 15, Aristotle is simply illustrating how to persuade other people by means of nontechnical proofs, without committing himself to adhering to any of the content of these proofs.[33]

Nonetheless, the *Rhetoric* hints at something that is worth pursuing: a form of justice that allows individuals to make claims against enacted laws and decrees of the *polis*. This may be an appeal for equity, and thus remain within the juridical system, but it may also go beyond. Two examples, one in the *Politics*, the other in *Nichomachean Ethics*, are telling in this regard. In *Nichomachean Ethics*, Aristotle says that, as there is no friendship or justice towards inanimate things, no more is there friendship or justice towards a slave in so far as he is a slave, for a slave is an inanimate tool. And he adds: "In so far as he is a slave, then, one cannot be friends with him, but only in so far as he is a human being; for there seems to be a justice of a kind (*ti dikaion*) that obtains for any human being in relation to anyone capable of sharing in law and taking part in agreements" (*NE* VIII 11, 1161b5–7). This excludes, for instance, wantonness, or cruelty, solely on the basis of someone's being a human being, irrespective of his position in a political system. Hence it doesn't seem to fall under the cases of justice by resemblance, as was the case for despotic justice. Similarly, in the *Politics* Aristotle writes, *en passant*, that "one should not hunt human beings for a feast or sacrifice" (VII 2, 1324b39–40), which probably is meant to include any human being you may meet when hunting, in so far as they are human beings, irrespectively of any other (political) consideration. Aren't those cases quite distinct, outside the limits of the *polis* and imposing on the *polis* justice claims solely on the basis of human nature?

Those cases go beyond T1, but T1 is not incompatible with them. As a matter of fact, they have a common ground. One of the assumptions for T1 was the idea that ethics gives special politics its ground. Now, being moral, in a very basic sense, consists in accepting other people as recipients of respect and consideration. Morality's bedrock consists in treating other people as people like us, and thus implies no longer conceiving of myself in an absolute or central position, but in some sense as equal to others. This basic trait is captured by the philosophical notion of *altruism*: acknowledging other people as such, so that selfishness is tempered by recognition of others as people like us. There are several ways of recognizing other people as such, as different historical moral systems testify. Such recognition may be rather restricted, or expansive, or as thin as possible, or quite thick – one may take the other to be a rational person, independently of time and culture, or a historically determined person, living in a precise place, adopting such and such habits. In the *Politics*, this moral foundation is present as the basic idea that justice is a sort of equality – one may dispute what should be equal (oligarchs take it to be wealth; democrats, freedom; aristocrats, virtue: IV 1294a10–11), but everyone agrees that justice is equality. What Aristotle is doing when he appeals to cases such as the absolute interdiction on human hunting, I surmise, is drawing the limits of morality, setting up the boundaries of acknowledgement of other people as worthy and deserving of respect. This is a very basic position. It does not say yet whether this position is a detached, impartial view of others, or a committed and engaging communal perspective, but it already makes the balance between what is within and what is without the moral domain.[34] Making room for other people from my own vantage point – this is the demarcating line of the moral point of view. In this sense, as one draws the line between moral and immoral behavior, one simultaneously demarcates the boundaries of politics and justice. It is thus not T1, for T1 describes what is within these boundaries. But it is not incompatible with T1: indeed, it is those very boundaries that constitute the domain of ethics, which are the grounds for politics. No justice has an ante-political dimension, but all justice depends on those very limits that draw an area within which morality springs, thrives, stagnates, or fails. If this is so, the *polis* that calls any justice into existence rests precisely upon those very limits that delineate the domain of ethics, and impose acknowledgment of other people as human beings like us, at least in so far as to be a political animal is in a relevant sense to be a moral agent.

WORKS CITED

Aubenque, P. 1980. "La Loi chez Aristote." *Archives de Philosophie* XXV: 147–57

Brunschwig, J. 1996. "Rule and exception: on the Aristotelian theory of equity." In *Rationality in Greek Thought*, eds. M. Frede and G. Striker. Oxford University Press

Cooper, J. 1996. "Justice and Rights in Aristotle's Politics." *Review of Metaphysics* XLIX: 859–72

Destrée, P. 2000. "Aristote et la question du droit naturel." *Phronesis* XLV: 220–30

Irwin, T. H. 2007. *The Development of Ethics*, vol. I. Oxford University Press

Joachim, H. 1951. *Aristotle: the Nicomachean Ethics*. Oxford University Press

Keyt, D. 1987. "Three Fundamental Theorems in Aristotle's Politics." *Phronesis* XXXII: 54–79

Konstan, D., trans. 2006. *Aspasius, On Aristotle's Nichomachean Ethics 1–4, 7–8*. London: Duckworth

Kraut, R. 1996. "Are there Natural Rights in Aristotle?" *Review of Metaphysics* XLIX: 755–74

 1997. *Aristotle Politics, Books VII and VIII*. Oxford University Press

 2002. *Aristotle: Political Philosophy*. Oxford University Press

Miller F. D. 1989. "Aristotle's Political Naturalism." *Apeiron* XXII: 195–218

 1991. "Aristotle on natural law and justice." In *A Companion to Aristotle's Politics*, eds. D. Keyt and F. Miller. Oxford: Blackwell

 1995. *Nature, Justice, and Rights in Aristotle's Politics*. Oxford University Press

 1996. "Aristotle and the Origins of Natural Rights." *Review of Metaphysics* XLIX: 873–907

Newman, W. 1887. *The Politics of Aristotle*. 4 vols., Oxford University Press

Pellegrin, P., trans. 1990. *Aristote: Les Politiques*. Paris: GF Flammarion

Reeve, C. D. C. 1998. *Aristotle, Politics*. Indianapolis, IN: Hackett

Rosler, A. 2005. *Political Authority and Obligation in Aristotle*. Oxford University Press

Yack, B. 1990. "Natural Right and Aristotle's Understanding of Justice." *Political Theory* 18: 216–37

NOTES

1. "Unqualified justice" translates *to haplôs dikaion*, that is, justice taken without further qualification or specification. It is opposed to justice

under some qualification, such as "household justice," which applies to just relations obtaining between master and slave.

2. This is a common book (*NE* V = *EE* IV). Four out of six references are to Book V: II 2, 1261a31; III 9, 1280a18; and III 12, 1282b20; VII 14, 1333a8 most probably refers to V 1, 1129b30–31. The other two (IV 11, 1295a36 and VII 13, 1332a22) concern the definition of happiness, and may refer either to *NE* or to *EE*. The first reference, though (as well as another passage closely connected to it, VII 8, 1328a37–38), seems to refer to *NE* VII 13, 1153b10–11, which is a common book, and most likely belongs originally to *EE*. For the last one, it is less clear. Perhaps it refers to *NE* III 6 or IX 9, but it may also refer to *EE* VII 2, 1236b39–37a3 (or 1248b26, as Newman proposes). In general, thus, the *Politics* refers rather to *EE* than to *NE*.

3. *De part. anim.* IV 687a8–10, criticizing Anaxagoras' opinion to the contrary.

4. There has been much debate about Aristotle's political naturalism; for a recent and stimulating treatment of this topic, see Keyt 1987, which addresses criticisms of three major theses of Aristotelian political naturalism: (i) man is by nature a political animal; (ii) the *polis* is a natural entity; and (iii) the *polis* is prior in nature to the individual. Political naturalism is to be distinguished from natural justice; see section IV.

5. This is the celebrated thesis that *anthrôpos politikon zôon estin*. The phrase appears in *NE* (I 7, 1097b8–11 and IX 9, 1169b18; see also VII 12, 1162a17–19); *EE* (VII 10, 1242a22–23); *Politics* (I 2, 1253a1–4, 7–8; III 6, 1278b19); and *Historia Animalium* I 488a9.

6. Konstan 2006: 38, 27–28.

7. But there is also an important disanalogy: in ethics, there is only one way of being virtuous (*NE* II 6, 1106a28–33), whereas in politics, as we will see, there are several ways of being politically just.

8. Distributive and corrective justices are the two main divisions of special justice; "justice" in this context means fairness in arrangements and procedures. Corrective justice presupposes by its own name that there is some wrongdoing to be redressed, and it is further subdivided into voluntary and involuntary (see *NE* V 3–4).

9. For a discussion about disobedience to law, see Rosler, to whom "the fact that Aristotle equates *to dikaion* with *to nomimon*, the lawful, should not lead us to believe that the requirements of moral justice, on Aristotle's view, may not be stronger than potentially competing claims of (positive) law. When Aristotle identifies justice with the lawful, he has a general sense of law(ful) in his mind, i.e. he refers generally to moral rules, habits, conventions, and practices" (Rosler 2005: 135).

10. Private benefit is the opposite of common benefit; as it is opposed to unqualified justice (III 13, 1284b23–25), common benefit is unqualified justice. In *NE* V 6, 1134a24–26, however, it is said that "we must not forget that we are looking for what is just without qualification and political justice," and this can be taken as distinguishing one from the other (see Miller 1996). But this is not necessary, for they also may provisionally be taken as distinct for the sake of research (*to zêtoumenon*), so that they will eventually turn out (not in *NE*, but in the *Politics*) to be the same.

11. A connected issue is to determine whether the common benefit is taken collectively (the community as a whole) or distributively (each and every citizen). This is a pressing issue, but does not concern directly my point here. For a detailed discussion, see Miller 1995.

12. Aristotle says the that male-female relation has justice of a sort, *even if there is no polis* (*EE* VII 10, 1242a26–27), which shows that, in his teleological framework, there is no problem of communities existing previously to *polis* (that is, being prior in generation), so long as they exist for the sake of the *polis*, that is, so long as they attain their perfection only in *polis*. *Pre*-political communities and, hence, *pre*-political kinds of justice are compatible with a teleological approach; what is incompatible with it would be *ante*-political communities and kinds of justice, in the sense that they would exist with no regard to, and independently of, the *polis*.

13. *ROT*'s translation gives: "justice in a special sense and by analogy," which is misleading; Rowe's is much better: "just in a way and in virtue of a certain resemblance."

14. On metaphor and resemblance, see *Top.* VI 2, 140a10–11.

15. On resemblance and identity of species, see *Top.* I 7, 103a19–23 (on water flowing from the same source).

16. See e.g., *Republic* IV, 443d: "One who is just does not allow any part of himself to do the work of another part or allow the various classes within him to meddle with each other" (Grube's translation, revised by Reeve).

17. The passage says that happiness is the highest good and that it consists in some sort of activity of virtue, viz. the complete exercise of virtue, and, as it happens, some people can attain *it* (VII 8, 1328a39: *autês*), whereas others have little or none of it. *It* can refer either to *happiness* or to *virtue*. Reeve takes it to refer to *happiness* ("some people are able to share in happiness"); Kraut leaves it indeterminate in his translation ("some can share in it"), but, in his commentary, takes it to refer to *virtue* ("here Aristotle implies that there are many who have little or no capacity for virtue," Kraut 1997: 100). I take it to refer to *virtue*; some

evidence for this reading is that the phrase "complete exercise of virtue" is used to refer to justice in V 1, 1129b31, and it is the different perceptions of justice that are the cause of different constitutions. Some people have lives "inimical to virtue" (VII 8, 1328b40), such as vulgar craftsmen or tradesmen, and this fact has a huge impact on politics. Nevertheless, if one takes the pronoun to refer to *happiness*, the outcome will be the same: virtue is the proper cause of happiness and is closely connected to it (as in VII 8, 1329a22–23). One can miss a happy life because of lack of external goods, or bad fortune, but this will not brutally interfere with one's political choices; what instead has an impact on them is the presence, or absence, of virtue, the proper cause of happiness. What is important to note here is that people have different *practices* or *realizations* of virtue, although we all have the same *capacity* to become virtuous: the contrast lies between *dunamis* and *energeia*; the former is equal for all of us, but not the latter. I translated *tous men endechesthai metechein autês tous de mikron ê mêden* as "some people manage to get a share in virtue, whereas others do so only to a small degree or not at all" in order to underline this contrast.

18. The passage highlights the fact the all three cases must evolve *naturally* (*pephuke*; for kingship: 1288a8; aristocracy: a10; polity: a13), and not by external imposition.

19. Kings are a law to themselves: see III 13, 1284a13–14; III 17, 1288a3. This is likely to be reminiscent of Plato's *Statesman*.

20. Because kingship is too rare; nonetheless, aristocracies also "either fall outside the reach of most *poleis* or border on so-called polities" (IV 11, 1295a32–34).

21. Representatives of the two positions are, respectively, Newman 1887 and Joachim 1951, from whom I borrow the formulations. I examine the topic in terms of "natural justice," instead of "natural rights," which, however, sounds more palatable to modern ears. Recently, Miller (1995) strongly argued for introducing the notion of "rights" in order to correctly interpret Aristotle's political philosophy, but some doubts, to my mind, still remain. For a more cautious position, see Kraut, to whom "a modern right carves out a zone in which one is relieved from the task of having to contribute to the common good" (Kraut 1996: 763) and such an idea is absent from Aristotle's political philosophy. See also Cooper 1996.

22. In the *Magna Moralia*, on the contrary, political justice is equated with conventional justice, and opposed to natural justice (I 1195a7–8). This should make any reader wary of importing readings from the *MM* into the doctrine on natural justice present in the *Ethics*, and can also be taken as one (more) sign of *MM*'s inauthenticity.

23. Conventional justice translates *to nomikon*, also referred to as *nomôi*, *kata nomon* (in accordance with the traditional contrast between nature and convention, *phusis* and *nomos*), *sunthêkei* or *kata sunthêken* (by agreement). Most of the time, it refers to written laws, but it may also include unwritten practices and habits, but such that they have a determinate or fixed expression: *Rhet.* I 13, 1373b4–6; *Pol.* VI 5, 1319b40–20a1.

24. This corresponds to $natural_2$ in Miller's terminology. In contrast, $natural_1$ is formulated by him couched in terms of rights as: "a $natural_1$ right is *based on natural justice.*" According to him, "Aristotle has a theory of $natural_1$ – but not $natural_2$ – rights." To Miller, "modern theories of $natural_2$ rights typically treat rights as universal and inhering in human beings as such apart from any social or political relations. $Natural_1$ rights have no such implications" (Miller 1995: 88).

25. Aristotle distinguishes between two cases: (a) it is indifferent, in the beginning, for instance, whether we sacrifice two sheep or a goat to the gods, but it is not indifferent whether we sacrifice something to the gods or not at all; and (b) it is indifferent whether there is or not such enactment, as in the case of a sacrifice for Brasidas (a city would be pious even if no sacrifice is ever made for him). Case (b) is assimilated to decrees, and Aristotle refers to (b) in general as "decree-like enactments" (*NE* V 7, 1134b25). But it is not true that we would be indifferent to (a) "were it not for a prior agreement" (Yack 1990: 220): there is an intrinsic value in sacrificing to the gods, even though it is not determinate how to do it. A doctor might determine non-arbitrarily that pregnant women should exercise, but whether that exercise should be a daily walk to a designated temple or something else is an open question (VII 16, 1335b12–16).

26. For, he says, among gods there is presumably no change at all (*NE* V 6, 1134b28–29).

27. Adopting Bywater's punctuation (*NE* V 7, 1134b32: *eiper amphô kinêta homoiôs*) and not Susemihl's (*eiper amphô kinêta, homoiôs dêlon*). Bywater's text can mean that (i) both are *equally changeable* (*ROT*'s reading) or (ii) "*both sorts alike* are changeable" (Rowe's). But (i) is false, and it is this falsity that probably led Susemihl to change punctuation. Another way to avert (i) is to add a question mark (*eiper amphô kinêta homoiôs?*), a solution already proposed by Grosseteste (*si ambo mobilia similiter?*), and adopted by Joachim and Gauthier.

28. The right hand is by nature stronger than the left hand, according to Aristotle, and remains so, even though one can become ambidextrous. He is reacting to Plato, who calls it a "prejudice" to think that the right hand is naturally stronger, and consequently proposes to adapt education and training to both hands (*Laws* VII, 794d–95d).

29. The phrase is *ta mê phusika all' anthrôpina dikaia* (V 7, 1135a3–4). This is surprising: what is *not natural* is what is conventional, but why to refer to it as *what is human*? It cannot be in contrast with what is divine, for we are within political justice, including natural justice. I see two possibilities: either (i) *ta anthrôpina* refers to actual enactments, based on real experience, in contrast with idealized conditions (as in the constitution "of our prayers"); or (ii) *ta anthrôpina* highlights the fact that we are now dealing with practical matters, and no more with theoretical ones, as in the case of the right hand, mentioned in 1134b34. Option (ii) looks more plausible in context.

30. *Pantachou* means that, taking the constitutions collectively, there is always one, kingship, which is the best. Aubenque (1980) once took it in a distributive sense, meaning that, in each case, there is one constitution that is the best (such as polity, for a ruling multitude, and aristocracy, when a few rule). He later retracted this, but French literature is still influenced by the distributive reading (for instance, Pellegrin 1990: 39).

31. For a different direction, namely, a biological perspective on natural justice, see Miller 1991.

32. The verb *manteuesthai*, "to divine," can be read in two ways. In a positive sense, it would mean that everyone has some correct pre-notion of universal justice, in keeping with Aristotelian optimism according to which everyone has a share in truth (*EE* I 6, 1216b30–35). For this positive reading, see Destrée 2000: 233. On the negative reading, however, people do have some rough idea of universal justice, but this vague idea is to be altered and corrected in the direction explored by *NE* V. Yet, due to its pervasiveness, it can be quite helpful in rhetoric precisely as vaguely assumed. So the complete passage is this: "Common law is the law of nature. For there really is, as everyone to some extent divines, a natural justice and injustice that is common to all, even to those who have no association or covenant with each other" (*Rhet.* I 13, 1373b6–9) – a common belief Aristotle will correct and elucidate in his *Politics* and *Ethics*.

33. Yack 1990; Brunschwig 1996.

34. See Irwin 2007: para. 129.

# 9 Law, governance, and political obligation

One of the most significant differences between ancient political philosophy and its early modern equivalent consists in the awareness of the problem of political obligation. Whereas authors such as Hobbes, Locke, Montesquieu, and Kant pay much attention to it, we find it sparsely treated in ancient thought. A famous exception is Plato's *Crito* (50a–53a), but there are only few further examples. There seems to be some truth in the commonplace that the historical change is inspired by the Pauline saying, "Let every soul be subject unto the higher powers; for there is no power but of God" (Romans 13:1). The biblical passage is often quoted in medieval and early modern political thought in order to discuss the idea of unconditional civil obedience. Hence the historical difference is usually explained as follows: once political authority is requested by God, citizens have to be strictly loyal regardless of the moral qualities of the states or the competences of their rulers. Modern (post-) Christian political philosophy therefore has to deal with the inherited problem of how strict political obligation must be conceived.

If this explanation were correct, then the Pauline type of "political loyalism" (as we might call it) would be absent from ancient philosophy. *A fortiori* Aristotle's *Politics* would be free of such loyalism. We are used to thinking that it is based on an intellectualist version of eudaimonism and perfectionism. But surprisingly, in several passages Aristotle expresses his conviction that citizens should be strictly loyal towards the political communities they are living in. They have to obey the commands of the rulers, follow the laws given by legislators, and abide by the rules prescribed by the constitution. Moreover, Aristotle does not support the idea that one should dramatically revise a given legal order, let alone abolish an existing constitution. Furthermore, there seems to be little if any evidence that he endorses civil disobedience or a "right of resistance" in the modern sense. And finally, Aristotle is clearly opposed to any rebellion (*stasis*) as one of the major evils a state can face.

On what basis, however, might Aristotelian citizens be obliged to follow the laws and commands imposed on them by the *polis*? In the first part of this chapter, I will scrutinize the question of how Aristotle deals with legal and political change, with civil disobedience, and with suboptimal political constitutions. For Aristotle, there are only few cases of a legitimate modification of legal orders, but he permits, as we will see, two sorts of political resistance: that of the people whom he calls "free by nature" (*eleutheroi phusei*) against a tyrant and that of a civil society against a strongly suboptimal *polis*. In the second section, I will describe the background of Aristotle's loyalism in his political anthropology and his theory of education. In the final section, I will argue that Aristotle shares a position which is, in modern theory, usually called "normative individualism." As we will see, the Aristotelian version of political loyalism is not an anti-intellectualist element in his theory. I will try to show that it is compatible with his overall position and philosophically attractive.

I

In which cases does Aristotle demand unconditional loyalty? And what are the circumstances under which he allows for political reforms or civil disobedience? A passage which provides a very general answer to the question of civic loyalty is *Politics* III 4. Here, Aristotle tells us that the preservation (*sôtêria*) of the community should be the work (*ergon*) of all citizens in the same sense in which the protection of a ship has to be the shared task of the sailors, regardless of their specific functions (III 4, 1276b26–29). Unfortunately, this passage formulates only a broad idea of political obligation; it leaves more or less open which sort of loyalism Aristotle is actually defending. It even seems unclear if the sailors and the citizens have to do something extra to preserve their ship and their city, respectively, or if they simply do it by fulfilling their respective tasks. Consequently, the comparison of the *polis* with a ship may amount to nothing more than the demand that everyone maintains the existence of the *polis* by following his immediate self-interest.[1] Read in this way,

Aristotle's idea would then be that a human being living outside a *polis* is always worse off than a citizen, even under the poorest constitutional circumstances. This is certainly one of Aristotle's basic assumptions in the *Politics*.[2] But as an answer to the question of political obligation it is unsatisfying. Even if it might be true that any political order is preferable to a pre-civil state, this gives the citizens quite insufficient reason to accept political loyalism. We would object that a given constitution should be improved rather than followed uncritically on the view that a pre-civil state would be even worse. Has Aristotle something to say about this problem?

We should first have a look at the problem of insufficient laws. Are there cases in which Aristotle permits a change of the existing legal rules? Under which conditions should an established, but suboptimal law be replaced by a better one? The most informative text on this question is *Politics* II 8.[3] In this passage, Aristotle enumerates some arguments for and against a possible modification of established laws. One point in favor of a change, he claims, is that politics can be seen as a science (*epistêmê*), and that one finds considerable change in sciences over time, e.g. in medicine or gymnastics. What Aristotle has in mind is that both of these disciplines greatly benefited from their historical development. Another point which he advances is that there exist many older laws which are "simple and barbarian"; Aristotle provides some examples, such as the case of the law on homicide which had been valid in Kyme and was altered later.[4] A final point is that "generally speaking, everyone seeks not what is traditional but what is good" (*zêtousin d' holôs ou to patrion alla tagathon pantes*; II 8, 1269a3–4). Our ancestors, he adds, may have been very simple-minded people, and we shouldn't feel obliged to follow them. Finally, as he tells us, a law is something highly general which cannot account for all particular cases.

But despite these arguments, Aristotle tells us, one should nevertheless be cautious about a possible change of laws. The crucial passage is this:

(1) Even when laws have been written down, they ought not always to remain unaltered. As in other sciences, so in politics, it is impossible that all things should be precisely set down in writing; for enactments must be universal, but actions are concerned with particulars. Hence we infer that sometimes and in certain cases laws may be changed. (2) But when we look

at the matter from another point of view, great caution would seem to be required. For the habit of lightly changing the laws is an evil, and, when the advantage is small, some errors both of lawgivers and rulers had better be left; the citizen will not gain so much by making the change as he will lose by the habit of disobedience. (3) The analogy of the arts is false; a change in a law is a very different thing from a change in an art. For the law has no power to command obedience except that of habit, which can only be given by time, so that a readiness to change from old to new laws enfeebles the power of the law. (II.8, 1269a8–27; trans. following the revised Oxford edition)

As J. Brunschwig rightly indicated, our text leaves some room for changing laws.[5] Aristotle implicitly concedes that there might be circumstances under which the improvement has to be more than only small (cf. *hotan gar hê to men beltion mikron*; II 9, 1269a13–14); but a modification which is rather substantial should not be made lightly. However, the analogy between scientific progress and legal improvement is generally doubtful for Aristotle. He confines appropriate changes of existing laws to a few cases only. The most important of them is equity (*epieikeia*) (1): whenever a written law turns out to be insufficient, one needs a person who is capable of supplementing the lacking legal details. Given that a law cannot cover all the situations occurring in reality and is at least sometimes inappropriate for a case under consideration, a supplementary regulation is justified.[6] But this holds true only for smaller amendments, i.e. for cases of ad hoc adjustments which do not principally call into question the stability and persistence of a given constitution altogether.[7] In (2), Aristotle justifies his position by indicating that frequent changes are undesirable since they establish an attitude of disloyalty and disobedience among the citizens. In (3), the analogy of sciences and legal orders is rejected on the basis of an argument from habituation. Unlike a science, the legal order must be internalized by the citizens and must hence not be altered without a serious reason. The effectiveness of a law, Aristotle informs us, is immediately linked with the stable willingness of the citizens to follow it.

This final point seems to be both interesting and disturbing. On the one hand, it gives us an idea of the importance Aristotle ascribes to legal education (see below, section II). On the other hand, he appreciates political stability more than a fuller adequacy of the legal order – except in cases of great injustice (but these are rare) and in cases of *epieikeia* (but these are uninteresting for our problem). We would certainly criticize his line of argument for its negligence on manifest cases of more or less suboptimal legal prescripts.

Is this restriction of legal modification a major problem for Aristotle's political philosophy? His *Politics* usually figures, as I have already noted, as the classical reference work for political eudaimonism and perfectionism. A eudaimonist and perfectionist political philosophy considers the state as some sort of instrument, namely, as a means for the well-being of its citizens. Following such an account, the task of the political organization is to develop the relevant human capabilities, especially the rational and the moral ones, and to lead them to perfection; this process brings about their happiness. If this is an adequate view of what Aristotle claims, then the legitimacy of a state must directly depend, for him, on the amount of happiness which it yields for its citizens. According to this criterion, Aristotle should evaluate each constitution with regard to its contribution to *eudaimonia*. He should recommend that the citizens revise inappropriate or inefficient constitutions and even abolish or replace them with better ones. If there is no other means to deal with the situation, he should allow for emigration and the foundation of a new city, for civil disobedience, or even a rebellion against the rulers. In one respect at least, Aristotle delivers what we expect: he allows for new foundations of a city in order to create a better constitution. His ideal city of *Politics* VII–VIII seems to be (like Plato's Magnesia in the *Laws*) a new colony, as his considerations on the best location show.[8]

The next question we should consider is if Aristotle leaves room for civil disobedience. Here, we have to distinguish between different cases. On the one hand, we should differentiate between an individual or a small group of citizens who are resisting a government, and the case in which a complete community is opposed to a ruler. On the other hand, we should discern civil disobedience against tyranny from resistance to a legal order.

The first thing to note here is that Aristotle does not pay much attention, by and large, to the problem of civil disobedience, either in *Politics* III, where he discusses deviant constitutions such as the different versions of democracy and oligarchy, or in the case of tyranny. We can find only scarce traces of it in the *Politics*. Civil disobedience is certainly excluded in cases of a single person or a small group being opposed to a state. But Aristotle apparently allows for one exception:

the case in which a tyranny tries to enforce the obedience of excellent persons (*epieikeis*). As Aristotle understands the concept of tyranny, one must be confronted with a political order characterized by the total absence of rationality, lawfulness, and regularity. The persons to be subjected by the tyrant must belong to the small group of "men who are free by nature" (*phusei ... eleutheroi*).[9] Note that even in this case Aristotle does not formulate a genuine right to resist, but at least he contends that:

there is also a third kind of tyranny, which is the most typical form, and is the counterpart of the perfect monarchy. This tyranny is just that arbitrary power of an individual which is responsible to no one, and governs all alike, whether equals or betters, with a view to its own advantage, not to that of its subjects, and therefore against their will. No freeman willingly endures such a government. (IV 10, 1295a17–23)

In this quotation, Aristotle does not claim that free-born persons are not willing to accept the rule of a tyrant. Nor does he spell out his idea of appropriate means of resistance. All he says is that none of the free people accepts it voluntarily (*outheis gar hêkôn hupomenei tôn eleutherôn tên toiautên archên*). Furthermore he does not claim that an actually occurring resistance was justified. But I think one can nevertheless follow A. Rosler's interpretation (2005); he sees here an Aristotelian right to civil disobedience as an implication of the fact that free-born persons must not be enslaved. In fact, Aristotle says that naturally free persons should not be ruled despotically and must not be enslaved; given that a tyranny implies an enslavement in the full sense of the word, he ascribes to them the right to resist.[10]

Two further texts discussed by Rosler, however, namely *Politics* V 1, 1301a35–40 and V 2, 1302a22–29, are less helpful for an analysis of Aristotle's theory of civil disobedience. In the first passage, as I read it, Aristotle only claims that the *epieikeis* will not cooperate with tyrants. Basically, Aristotle argues that one should follow even imperfect laws. On Rosler's reading, the *epieikeis* abstain from their right to disobey and to resist since they know the value of political stability. But this is contradictory: either they are threatened with enslavement and hence ought to resist; or they are not in danger of enslavement, in which case they have no right to resist. There is, however, a further text which contains the idea of civil disobedience in a clearer form: *Politics* III 15. It discusses how many troops a king might have; Aristotle determines that a monarch must have a sufficient number of soldiers for his personal safety, but should not have enough to defend himself against the entire people:

> There is also a difficulty about the force which he is to employ; should a king have guards about him by whose aid he may be able to coerce the refractory? If not, how will he administer his kingdom? If he is the lawful sovereign who does nothing arbitrarily or contrary to law, still he must have some force wherewith to maintain the law. In the case of a limited monarchy there is not much difficulty in answering this question; the king must have such force as will be more than a match for one or more individuals, but not so great as that of the people. (III 15, 1286b27–37)

It is not exaggerated to conclude from this that Aristotle concedes to the people the option of getting rid of their monarch if necessary. To summarize: Aristotle basically accepts the idea of civil disobedience, but he restricts legitimate cases to resistance against tyrants and to cases in which the complete citizenship is involved. For Aristotle, it is not up to an individual or a small minority to oppose the majority.

Let us now turn to the problem of a possible improvement of seriously defective constitutions. Can Aristotle adequately deal with questions of authority in cases of less favorable political conditions? Modern theorists would probably follow the conceptual distinction between ideal and non-ideal theories advanced by John Rawls; to put it roughly, an ideal theory attempts to describe the normative principles for the conduct of people and the design of institutions that would be appropriate to a morally and politically perfect order with optimal compliance of the citizens, whereas non-ideal theory is concerned with the principles that would be adequate for these purposes under less perfect circumstances, and with somewhat defective compliance. Aristotle, by contrast, seems to be not that much interested in applying an abstract normative principle but in preserving the stability of a given *polis*. We can see, especially in *Politics* V–VI, that his concept of non-ideality has nothing to do with the difficulty of applying a normative principle but, rather the other way around, improving a given suboptimal order without weakening its stability. Aristotle, for example, is convinced that the laws of a *polis* have to be adapted to the constitution in which they occur; the legislator has to conform the laws to the given constitution.[11]

II

If a political philosopher emphasizes the necessity of authority and civil obedience, this might be for one of several fairly different reasons, e.g. (a) he might believe that even in a fully just and well-ordered state not all citizens will have the capacity to assent to its decrees; (b) he might assume that at least suboptimal or non-ideal political situations necessitate authority and obedience; (c) he might think that even optimal political situations imply the difference between particular and generalized uses of rationality; (d) he might believe that even a highly suboptimal political order merits obedience since it is still better than anarchy; (e) he might be a political collectivist, organicist, and anti-individualist and hence believe that the individual is not at the core of political theory; and (f) he might not trust in the rationality of political order, but favor authority. In my opinion, only (e) and (f) are completely absent in Aristotle's political thought, whereas aspects (a)–(d) play a certain part in Aristotle's views.

Let us briefly look at (e) and (f). Is it possible that Aristotle defends some sort of authoritarian collectivism? But, of course, we find no traces of collectivism or organicism in Aristotle. One anti-individualist element seems to be that Aristotle does not clearly distinguish between the moral and the political type of normativity. We tend to assume that "moral cases" of political failure provide the best reasons which legitimize civil disobedience: for example, we need only think of resistance against racist, sexist, nationalist, or fundamentalist laws or governmental actions. Now I doubt if Aristotle could cope with this phenomenon anyway, and this is for the following reason: whereas we would think of moral normativity as a phenomenon which is fundamentally different from political norms (which have rather to do with external success, economic prosperity, finding compromises, taking one's responsibility seriously, etc.), Aristotle combines the two realms and describes, as we saw, political virtue as at least convergent with an optimal moral character. We find a clear indication of this in *Nicomachean Ethics* V 3, where justice of the *iustita generalis* type is characterized as a comprehensive compliance with all sorts of laws. In our view, Aristotle neglects that morality has to do primarily with certain basic claims and entitlements, with rights and duties that should be reasonably ascribed to an individual in social life, while politics concerns not only the moral aspects of social life, but also its functional and prudential aspects; hence political theory must deal with institutions and administrations, procedures, and arrangements which serve non-moral collective purposes. The practices of paying taxes, serving in the army, participating in a jury, deliberating on questions of foreign policy, and the like are phenomena which cannot be adequately (at least not fully) subsumed under the heading of leading a morally good life. So it is precisely because of the inappropriate separation between these two issues that Aristotle doesn't leave sufficient room for civil disobedience. He simply seems to be unable to accept a possible discrepancy between moral and political aspects – or maybe he doesn't even see the problem at stake.

But on a closer look, this description turns out to be superficial. Aristotle basically knows the sort of difference which we render in terms of moral and political normativity: in suboptimal political constellations, an individual cannot become a fully rational and happy person. He even defends some sort of normative individualism in the sense that it is individual happiness – understood as practicing theoretical activities in a state of leisure (cf. VIII 3, 1338a1–5) which is the end of political institutions; the political realm does clearly have an instrumental character with regard to the *eudaimonia* of the citizens as individuals.

Does Aristotle mistrust political rationality, (e)? In fact, the crucial question about political loyalism is how much reason is involved in the obedience practiced by the citizens. What role does Aristotle attribute to individual rationality, and what function does he assign to the reason of state (*raison d'état*)? Is political obligation in a given state based on rational insight, or is it founded on unconditional obedience? I want to label the first attitude *rational political loyalism* and the second one *authoritarian political loyalism*. As we will see, Aristotle's refusal of radical political and legal change cannot be traced back to some sort of authoritarianism or anti-intellectualism (section III).

But how can we reconcile what he says about civic loyalty with his normative individualism? The answer is this: Aristotle wants to preserve a stable legal order since he believes that the constitution ultimately *coincides with* the moral life within a city. The citizens are accustomed to leading a certain life, and this life is, to a considerable extent, the effect of the existing legal order. Even if this might be a suboptimal one, it would cause more trouble to alter it than to preserve it. Aristotle believes that a legal or constitutional change always amounts to a considerable amount of disarrangement. He devotes much attention to the question of political stability, as the following quotation indicates:

> But of all the things which I have mentioned, that which most contributes to the permanence of constitutions is the adaptation of education to the form of government, and yet in our day this principle is universally neglected. The best laws, though sanctioned by every citizen of the state, will be of no avail unless the young are trained by habit and education in the spirit of the constitution [eithismenoi kai pepaideumenoi en tê politeia], if the laws are democratic, democratically, or oligarchically if the laws are oligarchical. For there may be incontinence in states as well as in individuals. (V 9, 1310a12–19)

The text describes a non-authoritarian idea of political stability: stability should be based on an avoidance of collective incontinence (akrasia). As Aristotle points out, the right education, even if "generally neglected nowadays," provides the most important contribution to a stable constitution. Hence, the aim of a well-considered political education is not to overcome non-ideal conditions, as we might expect in the case of democracies and oligarchies. On the contrary, the aim is to stabilize these constitutions by avoiding collective akrasia and by getting identified with the politeia.

What does it mean to be educated in the spirit of a democratic or oligarchic constitution? Aristotle emphasizes that his idea of education has nothing to do with simple obedience:

> Now, to have been educated in the spirit of the constitution is not to perform the actions in which oligarchs or democrats delight, but those by which the existence of an oligarchy or of a democracy is made possible. (V 9, 1310a19–22)

According to this passage, the goal of education must be to qualify citizens for good governance within the established constitution, even if it is a deviant one. Prima facie, this looks as if Aristotle simply accepted suboptimal political constitutions as inalterable. Maybe one chance to improve such poleis results from the influence of "good citizens" on them.[12] Anyway, the background of his loyalism is a psychological idea of legalism. According to Aristotle, the character of the citizens is always the product of the established laws and the *politeia*. The individuals are deeply shaped by their legal order. A good legislator should take that into consideration; since the best is the same in private and public life, he must "imprint it on the souls of men" (VII 14, 1333b37–38). People with a doubtful character, however, create constitutions in which goods other than intellectual and moral virtues are most appreciated. And their citizens become like the constitutions under which they are living. In the optimal case, the agency of people is quite similar to a behavior based on virtue, as the following quotation from the *Nicomachean Ethics* makes clear:

And the law bids us to do both the acts of a brave man (e.g. not to desert our post nor take to flight nor throw away our arms), and those of a temperate man (e.g. not to commit adultery nor to gratify one's lust), and those of a good-tempered man (e.g. not to strike another nor to speak evil), and similarly with regard to the other virtues and forms of wickedness, commanding some acts and forbidding others; and the rightly-framed law does this rightly, and the hastily conceived one less well. (*NE* V 1, 1129b19–25)

Since the legal order imposes on us a stable habit of rule-following, Aristotle attributes to the law the capability to cause at least an imitative, quasi-virtuous moral attitude. Hence the virtue of a good citizen at least approximates the virtue of a good man, and in the case of an optimal constitution the virtue of a good citizen coincides with that of a good person.

At this point, a few words should be said about Aristotle's political anthropology. In legitimizing rule and political authority, much depends on how a political thinker interprets the human ability to lead a self-determined life, i.e. the rational and the irrational aspects of human beings, their moral and immoral tendencies, their inclinations, emotions, desires, and the like. In this respect, Aristotle's standpoint is somewhat ambiguous. On the one hand, he believes that a considerable number of male adult persons (at least of Greek origin) possess a natural capacity for reasoning which is perfectible in the sense that it can be brought to a full degree of realization. These people are the *eleutheroi phusei* mentioned above. What is necessary for their perfection is an intense moral and cognitive education, since at a first stage, men are far from possessing a rational personal attitude sufficient to lead an autonomous and morally adequate life. If such human beings are educated in an appropriate way, they thereby attain perfection and good life. On the other hand, Aristotle thinks that men are in permanent danger of going astray in their lives, being determined by affections and desires. As he claims, "man is, when perfected, the best of animals, but, when separated from law and justice, he is the worst of all" (I 2, 1253a31–33). The Aristotelian *polis* therefore considers moral education as one of its basic tasks.

On the flip-side of this, the pessimistic part of Aristotelian political anthropology contains the following ideas: according to Aristotle, the rule of men over men is less desirable than the rule of law. This idea has a precise Platonic equivalent. In the myth of Plato's *Statesman* (268d–274e) as well as in the *Laws* (IX, 875b–c), we find the idea that something is basically wrong with political governance as we know it: under our political conditions, human beings are inadequately subjected to the will of other humans ruling them. Ideally speaking, taken as rational agents, human beings should be free and autonomous, acting on their own insight. Now according to this view, humans turn out to be insufficiently reasonable; hence, they must be governed by someone endowed with superior mental abilities. The best solution to this problem would be that a god guides humans like a shepherd leads his sheep, as was actually the case, according to Plato, in the past age of Kronos. In our age, however, that of Zeus, we have to rely on human rulers. Given their partly irrational nature, too, they will always be tempted to misuse their administrative power. Therefore, we should be careful to limit their competences. Moreover, they normally do not possess enough rational insight to lead a state, and so they tend to produce injustice and instability. An appropriate political order would have to cope with these aspects of the human condition, taking into account both the autonomy and rationality and the infirmity and weakness of humans. Also for Plato, the most important political task is to establish a system of physical, moral, and cognitive education which improves the personality of the citizens.

Aristotle shares the Platonic conviction that human beings are physically weak and hence too violable to live in autarchy and isolation; they need mutual support and hence their lives should be organized according to a division of labor (like that formulated in *Republic* II). Aristotle once even mentions the idea of divine rulership: a great number of citizens could only be ordered by law if they were led by the "divine power which keeps together the universe" (*Pol.* VII 4, 1326a31–33). By contrast with Plato, he puts a lesser emphasis on the value of an insight-based kingship. But similarly, he assumes that humans are morally weak and therefore inclined to all sorts of irrational behavior and dominated by irrational affections; hence they need an intense moral and cognitive education in order to become fully rational beings. This moral education must be provided by the *polis*, and it is precisely the job of the legislator (*nomothetês*) to establish a constitution which optimally serves this purpose.

The decisive consequence for political loyalism is this: any political change (*kinêsis* or *metabolê*) would radically alter, according to Aristotle, the conditions of agency for the citizens. Hence it is better to improve democracies *qua* democracies and oligarchies *qua* oligarchies than to radically transform a given constitution. Since people are brought up with the old laws and since their characters are deeply shaped by them, it is a great danger to revise established social rules. Aristotle's account of moral education has, to some extent at least, a 'behaviorist' flavor: citizens who are raised up under a certain constitution do reflect exactly the laws and rules they followed so far. Aristotle claims that the constitution is, as it were, the way of life (*bios*) of a city (IV 11, 1295a40–b1).

At this point, however, we are facing a considerable problem which might be called the "paradox of rational autonomy." In the passage from the *Nicomachean Ethics* quoted above, law enforces a behavior which only emulates the one recommended by rational autonomy. Hence in the case of legal enforcement, precisely the element of insight is lacking. So, paradoxically, the reason for being enforced to avoid bad behavior and to do good actions is not accessible to the major part of the population. The average citizen is unable to follow the sense of the decrees imposed on him – even if it might be a system of completely rational and omnilaterally advantageous laws. When we look at *Politics* VII–VIII, we find that Aristotle describes an appropriate moral education in surprisingly behaviorist terms. As we learn from *Nicomachean Ethics* II 1–2, he is in favor of a type of repetitive practical habituation, at least at the beginning of the educational process. Apart from this, Aristotle advances a quite elitist view of what it means to be a rational agent in the full sense (a *phronimos* or *spoudaios*). He reserves that for a small group of insightful people; only these lead a truly autonomous and happy life. In *Politics* III 4, for example, he explicitly declares that the ruling person should be decent, good, and insightful, whereas the citizens need not possess actual insight (III 4, 1276b14–16). They only have to believe that the constitution is rational.

### III

By the expression "normative individualism" I mean a higher-order tenet which allows us to differentiate between concrete political principles. According to this position, the individual's fundamental interests are the basic criteria of political legitimacy. It clearly suggests this direction when Aristotle claims that "the best constitution is necessarily this order in which everybody (*hostisoun*) does the best and lives happily" (VII 2, 1324a23–25).[13] But given that normative individualism is what Aristotle defends, why then does he put so much emphasis on the aspect of civic loyalty? I want to address the following questions: Does Aristotle successfully reconcile his idea of political obligation with a eudaimonist and perfectionist account of politics? And isn't it risky for normative individualism to accept political loyalism?

At first glance, political obligation seems to be incompatible with eudaimonism; for it is based on the idea that the citizens unconditionally obey and act loyally towards official authorities, regardless of their self-interest. If this picture of what political obligation means were correct, then it would fit much better into the framework of a holistic or organicist account of politics than into that of normative individualism.

The crucial problem here is to resolve the dilemma between two principles that seem to be inescapable for an Aristotelian approach: (i) in order to follow my self-interest in well-being, I must possess a full degree of rational autonomy; hence I should primarily rely on my own practical judgments and not obey, at least not unconditionally, the rules of a political order. (ii) In order to make a political order functionally efficient, the state must require authority, sometimes even unconditional obedience; hence the state has to limit the rational autonomy of its citizens.

It is the merit of Andrés Rosler's inspiring monograph *Political Authority and Obligation in Aristotle* to have shown that the dilemma in fact is escapable. Aristotelian political obligation should not be understood in a narrow sense.[14] As Rosler points out, authority in the Aristotelian *polis* need not rule out that the citizens are considered as rational, autonomous agents. What political obligation actually implies is only that authoritative orders given by the *polis under certain conditions* override one's own balance of practical reasons. These conditions include that a citizen temporarily does not possess sufficient information or full insight regarding the reasons for a certain law or a particular political decision. In such cases, he has good reasons to trust in the rationality of his obedience, provided that the ruling persons themselves have full knowledge and are oriented towards common welfare. These types of considerations advanced by the citizens are second-order reasons, and they can transitionally override their first-order reasons. As Aristotle puts it, it is enough that a citizen has correct opinion (*doxa alêthês*) on a given issue, while political rulers must have a more complete knowledge (*phronêsis*; III 4, 1277b7–17), given that the citizen can reasonably trust in the knowledge of the ruler, and in the rationality and morality of the law.

But there remains a difficulty, namely, the tension between political expertise and eudaimonic knowledge. Even if one concedes that a common citizen might have little expertise about the good of the *polis* and the ways to obtain it, this doesn't imply that he also knows little about his own happiness. It is implausible to assume that only the office holders (possibly a very small group, if not a monarch) are in full possession of both knowledge of politics and of individual happiness. In order to guarantee the happiness of the citizens, they should themselves participate in political knowledge, and they should have access to political offices. Hence, an attractive way out of this difficulty is what might be called the "republican solution": all citizens have to be highly involved in the relevant processes of political governance; political participation in the governance of the *polis* might even be an aspect of a full realization of their rational autonomy. To abide by the legal order and to follow the orders of ruling persons does not, at least not under favorable circumstances, resemble the case of an army whose soldiers have to obey unconditionally, even in this case of an opaque command. In a republican city, there exists no principled gap between one's own interests and the regulations a citizen has to comply with.

And indeed, Aristotle defends such a republican idea of politics. His position is characterized by the emphasis on the elements of political participation. In a number of passages, Aristotle postulates that a constitution needs the assent and the consensus (*homonoia*) of the citizens in order to work well.[15] Since all fully rational persons belong to those who are "free by nature," they will only follow a constitution which does not subject or subjugate them, but involves them in all procedures of governance. Aristotle describes justified political rule by contrasting it with despotic authority in *Politics* I: political rule takes into consideration that people who are free by nature must not be treated like slaves.[16] In *Politics* III 6, Aristotle points out that those political leaders who are oriented towards the common good of the *polis* are ruling over free and equal citizens and that they resemble coaches or trainers who themselves participate in the exercises they command. Everyone has to learn how to rule by learning to be ruled. Accordingly, Aristotle defines political governance as rule over equal and free people (III 4, 1277b7–17). All free citizens should participate in political offices, at least if a government of the extraordinarily competent individuals cannot be obtained (II 2, 1261a37–b6). So he repeatedly affirms a rotation principle in distributing political power (e.g. III 6, 1279a8–13). In the same vein, he advances some elements of political control (administrative periods should be limited, offices cannot be held twice by the same person, office holders are to be chosen by lot). Furthermore, he develops to some extent the idea of a publicly shared deliberative practice which has the advantage, he thinks, of combining adequate individual judgments (III 11, 1281a42–b10). Even if, for Aristotle, democracy is one of the deviant constitutions which are not sufficiently directed to the common good, it is the "most measured" or the "least evil" form of them (IV 2, 1289b4–5), and it is not too far away from the best constitution, the *politeia* (III 8).[17] At least one form of democracy, namely, that of *Politics* IV 4 (1291a31–38), is described as an ideal balance between the social classes.[18] And finally, his reflections on the best possible state in *Politics* VII show that he supports the republican solution as that of the "virtuous *polis*."

A possible objection to this solution might be that rational autonomy, at least in a strong sense of the term, seems to make political institutions generally superfluous. The perfectly developed person needs no external force in order to be directed towards what is valuable for him or her. Seen from an Aristotelian point of view, however, this objection is somewhat mistaken. Aristotle wants everybody to live under the most rational form of governance which is available – notwithstanding the question whether it is oneself or someone else who possesses the basic insight. Rational autonomy does not exclude that political leaders might practice some sort of legitimate paternalism. To be sure, a person who has adequate knowledge of what is good for him or her does not need additional support to foster his or her happiness. But even such a person has to live, according to *Politics* I 2, within the protecting framework of a *polis* given that he is neither a maverick nor someone divine. One can add that a political community and its institutions are permanently necessary, namely, for the following three reasons. First, it takes a *polis* to educate such a perfect person until he or she reaches the condition of full autonomy, and perhaps also to provide support during old age or in other states of infirmity. Second, there must be a political community which, by way of command and obedience, directs the lives of those who are unable to gain a full rational identity. This sort of paternalism is legitimate if the state provides insufficiently rational people with that degree of happiness that they are able to adopt according to their capacity of virtue and intellect (VII 1, 1323b21–23). Third, there must be political institutions which have to meet decisions efficiently and which have to organize the "division of labor" within the *polis* that is described, e.g. in *Politics* III 4. Since there are many tasks to be fulfilled in the political realm, it takes an administrative order to manage them.

Nevertheless, modern readers will find the republican solution partially unconvincing. We don't believe that someone else might have better knowledge about *my* way to happiness than I myself have – even if all citizens are involved in the administration of political offices. We would not be willing to accept the idea of legitimate paternalism in as wide a sense as Aristotle does. But Aristotle does not acknowledge the idea that there exist individual ways to happiness, let alone individual forms of happiness. He defends an antipluralism, more precisely a monistic version of perfectionism. Aristotle thinks that there is only one optimal form of human life and hence only one ideal form of political constitution.[19] Consequently, he believes that paternalism is legitimate if it is practiced by the best possible *polis* and in order to bring about an optimal personal state, that of a happy individual.[20]

What then does the multitude of actually existing constitutions mean according to Aristotle? Is the existing plurality due to the various subjective preferences of human beings, to an irreducible objective diversity in the endowments of people, or to a multitude of culturally different forms of happiness? At first glance, one might assume that Aristotle accepts the idea of legitimate diversity when he says that "different men seek after happiness in different ways and by different means, and so make for themselves different modes of life and forms of government" (VII 8, 1328a41–b2). But at a closer look, he doesn't. For Aristotle, there is only one form of happiness, i.e. the *energeia* of the best part of soul, namely, its intellectual activity. This holds true both for the *Nicomachean Ethics* and for the *Politics*.[21] The best human activity can only be practiced in a theoretical life. We find also clear indications that Aristotelian political theory finally leads to an intellectualist account of the best life for humans. The context of the short quotation is the following:

Now, whereas happiness is the highest good, being a realization and perfect practice of excellence, which some can attain, while others have little or none of it, these varieties [of men] are clearly the reason why there are various kinds of states and many forms of government; for different men seek after happiness in different ways and by different means, and so make for themselves different modes of life and forms of government. (VII 8, 1328a37–b2)

It is obvious from this passage that Aristotle does not concede a genuine diversity of forms of happiness. There is only one best life for Aristotle – that of intellectual activity under conditions of leisure. And there is only one best *polis* – that which makes the good citizens happy. For Aristotle, there are no further and more specific forms of happiness, related to the individual nature of a person. *A fortiori*, we don't find in his writings the idea of a sort of happiness based on subjective preferences. What he says in this quotation, instead, is that the various ways in which people can lag behind the full extent of happiness yield the different political constitutions. This has to do with the alleged fact that men are naturally unequal in their intellectual and moral capacities (cf. II 2, 1261a22–24). Read in this way, the plurality of political forms is nothing but a multitude of defective political states.

But this leads us back to our original problem. Given that there is only one perfect form of human life and only one single optimal constitution, why doesn't Aristotle restrict his political loyalism to this one *polis*? Every suboptimal political order, one might think, is defective in bringing about human perfection and hence more or less detrimental to its citizens. We might expect him to allow for disobedience and resistance as far as the perfect *politeia* is not established. A passage which seems to point in this direction is *Politics* IV 10. As we saw in section I, he contends that no free-born person would ever voluntarily accept a certain (especially bad) type of tyranny (IV 10, 1295a15–16). Aristotle has a clear consciousness that the citizens can resist even good laws. They can disobey good laws, and they can obey both good and bad ones:

> But we must remember that good laws, if they are not obeyed, do not constitute good government. Hence there are two parts of good government; one is the actual obedience of citizens to the laws, the other part is the goodness of the laws which they obey; they may obey bad laws as well as good. And there may be a further subdivision; they may obey either the best laws which are attainable to them, or the best absolutely. (IV 8, 1294a3–9)

As the text clearly implies, laws always depend on the compliance of the citizens of a *polis*. Its constitution is good to the degree in which good laws and civic loyalty come together. But why should one obey even if someone's *polis* is in a suboptimal condition?

Here is the place where law comes in. A *politeia* is a corpus consisting of laws which regulate both public affairs (particularly the distribution of offices) and private life (concerning the aims of the community).[22] Aristotle consequently believes that, in political communities, law is precisely identical with reason and order. In *Politics* VII 4 he declares that "law is some sort of order" (*ho de gar nomos taxis tis estin*) and that "a good legal system necessarily is a good order" (*kai tên eunomian anankaion eutaxian einai*; VII 4, 1326a29–31).[23] In his appreciation of a lawful social order Aristotle goes as far as to claim that, in the majority of cases (with the exception of an extremely competent king) it is better to have a legal system instead of ruling persons. He declares at *Politics* III 10, 1281a34–39 that "perhaps one should say that it is generally bad that a human is the ruler and not the law since a human is facing affections in his soul."

This brings us back to the "republican solution." We wondered how Aristotle could possibly reconcile his legalism with the principle of equality. The following quotation provides one of the basic political convictions of Aristotle; it shows in which way his commitment to equality is connected with institutions and procedures dominated by law:

(1) That is why it is thought to be just that among equals everyone be ruled as well as rule, and therefore that all should have their turn. We thus arrive at law; for an order of succession implies law. And the rule of the law, it is argued, is preferable to that of any individual. (2) On the same principle, even if it be better for certain individuals to govern, they should be made only guardians and ministers of the law. For magistrates there must be – this is admitted; but then men say that to give authority to any one man when all are equal is unjust. (3) There may indeed be cases which the law seems unable to determine, but such cases a man could not determine either. But the law trains officers for this express purpose, and appoints them to determine matters which are left undecided by it, to the best of their judgment. Further, it permits them to make any amendment of the existing laws which experience suggests. (III 16, 1287a16–28)

The passage deals with the question of a possible legitimacy of kingdom. Aristotle justifies the rule of law by pointing out its rationality, stability, and impartiality. In (1), he derives the necessity of a lawful order from equality. In the majority of cases, he affirms in (2), it is preferable to establish a sound legal order instead of relying on individuals with outstanding cognitive abilities. He emphasizes additionally in (3) that the law has an educational effect on the citizens, forming and improving their moral behavior. Moreover, he points out the deep formative impact of being law-abiding for someone's character:

Therefore he who bids the law rule may be deemed to bid God and Reason alone rule, but he who bids man rule adds an element of the beast; for desire is a wild beast, and passion perverts the minds of rulers, even when they are the best of men. The law is reason unaffected by desire. (III 16, 1287a28–32)

Establishing a lawful social system is a preferable choice since law does not imply all the shortcomings which are characteristic for human beings. And additionally, it is even capable of improving the behavior of the citizens. In chapter X 9 of the *Nicomachean Ethics*, we find a related statement where Aristotle describes the law-giver as a person who is able to create rules of social life which are helpful for the improvement of human beings. He claims that in order to bring about an appropriate moral education, the legislator should possess a sort of competence similar to that of a doctor (*NE* X 9, 1180b23–28). In other words, the law-giver is seen both as a theoretical expert who disposes of abstract knowledge and as a practical specialist who can apply this knowledge to a particular situation. He has a competence based on knowledge of the essentialist and perfectionist type: the *nomothetês* knows what human beings fundamentally are and what it takes to improve them efficiently. According to Aristotle, the legislator is competent in distributing different tasks to the "parts of the soul" (VII 14, 1333a37–39). The final result of a successful educational process is that the person will be completely guided by law. As Aristotle points out elsewhere, someone who has internalized what the law-giver wants him to do "has so to speak become the law for himself" (*NE* IV 8, 1128a32; cf. *Pol.* III 13, 1284a13–14).

So far, our textual evidence clearly amounts to some sort of normative individualism. For Aristotle, the yardstick by which a *polis* should be measured is the criterion to what extent its constitution and its laws are helpful for human development. The *polis* is a means to providing good living conditions for its citizens and to improving them; and hence, political loyalism is basically reasonable. One could perhaps doubt this conclusion by indicating that Aristotle sometimes claims that every part of reality should be subject to the natural order; according to him, there is no room for disorder in our world. This sounds as if he wanted to defend some sort of naturalism following the principle "If every part of the universe is well-ordered, human society must not be exempt from this." But this principle would mix up descriptive and prescriptive elements and is certainly far from being persuasive. In *Politics* I 5, for example, Aristotle claims that all entities, including social relations, are principally characterized by ruling parts and ruled ones:

For in all things which form a composite whole and which are made up of parts, whether continuous or discrete, a distinction between the ruling and the subject element comes to light. Such a duality exists in living creatures, but not in them only; it originates in the constitution of the universe; even in things which have no life there is a ruling principle, as in a musical mode. (I 5, 1254a28–33)

Aristotle emphasizes the naturalness and ubiquity of order in the universe. Clearly, this does not rule out that there are advantages for the ruled parts, a thought well-known from the case of natural slavery. So his "naturalism of order" fits his normative idea of political governance well. We can hence summarize that Aristotle justifies political governance by pointing out the importance of laws for the rationality of living conditions. Ultimately, it is for the *eudaimonia* of the citizens that a political order is established.[24]

### WORKS CITED

Brunschwig, J. 1980. "Du mouvement et de l'immobilité de la loi." *Revue internationale de philosophie* 34: 512–40

Hamburger, M. 1951. *Morals and Law: the Growth of Aristotle's Legal Theory*. New Haven, CT: Yale University Press

Heinaman, R. 2007. "Eudaimonia as an Activity in the Nicomachean Ethics I.8–12." *Oxford Studies in Ancient Philosophy* 33: 221–53

Horn, C. 2006. "Epieikeia: the competence of the perfectly just person in Aristotle." In *The Virtuous Life in Greek Ethics*, ed. B. Reis. Cambridge University Press

Kraut, R. 1984. *Socrates and the State*. Princeton University Press
  1996. "Are there Natural Rights in Aristotle?" *Review of Metaphysics* 49: 755–74
  2002. *Aristotle: Political Philosophy*. Oxford University Press

Miller F. D. 1995. *Nature, Justice, and Rights in Aristotle's Politics*. Oxford: Clarendon
  2007. "Aristotle's philosophy of law." In *A History of the Philosophy of Law from the Ancient Greeks to the Scholastics*, vol. 6, eds. F. D. Miller and C. A. Biondi. Dordrecht: Springer

Mulgan, R. G. 1977. *Aristotle's Political Theory*. Oxford University Press

Polansky, R. 1991. "Aristotle on political change." In *A Companion to Aristotle's Politics*, eds. D. Keyt and F. Miller. Oxford: Blackwell

Reeve, C. D. C. 1998. *Aristotle, Politics*. Indianapolis, IN: Hackett

Rosler, A. 2005. *Political Authority and Obligation in Aristotle*. Oxford University Press

Saunders, T. J. 1995. *Aristotle, Politics, Books I and II*. Oxford: Clarendon

Schroeder, D. N. 1981. "Aristotle on Law." *Polis* 4: 17–31

Schütrumpf, E. 1991. *Aristoteles, Politik Buch II/III*. Berlin: Akademie Verlag

2005. *Aristoteles, Politik Buch VII/VIII*. Berlin: Akademie Verlag
2006. "Erziehung durch den Staat. Beschränkung und Befreiung der Individualität in Aristoteles' bestem Staat." In *Wissen und Bildung in der antiken Philosophie*, eds. Ch. Rapp and T. Wagner. Stuttgart: Metzler
Weber, S. 2014. *Aristoteles über Herrschaft und Recht*. Berlin/New York: de Gruyter

NOTES

1. To be sure, this cannot be meant in a Hobbesian sense; Aristotle famously rejects Lycophron's prudential contractarianism in *Pol.* III 9.
2. According to *Pol.* I 13, 1253a18–29, the part (i.e. the human individual) cannot live without the whole (the *polis*) in the same sense in which a separated hand is unable to survive.
3. II 8, 1268b25–1269a28. Cf. the detailed analysis in Brunschwig 1980.
4. The law under consideration is a highly unjust one. An accusation of murder might be substantiated if the accuser were to call a sufficient number of his relatives. Only written laws, not unwritten ones, can be altered (*kinoumena*); on this, see Schütrumpf 1991: 278.
5. Brunschwig 1980.
6. In several places, Aristotle points out that a written law cannot account for all given cases. Then it takes the virtue of equity (*epieikeia*) to deal with the situation. On the question of generalism and particularism see Horn 2006.
7. On this distinction and Aristotle's background in Hippodamus' theory see Saunders 1995: 145–46.
8. See on this point Schütrumpf 2005: 73–74.
9. The famous passage I 5, 1255a1–3 contrasts those who are "free by nature" with those who are "slaves by nature."
10. Rosler 2005.
11. Cf. III 11, 1282b1–13 and IV 1, 1289a10–15.
12. Following the interpretation of Kraut 2002: ch. 10, I will not support a deviant state according to its mistaken *telos* (wealth in the case of oligarchy and freedom and equality in the case of democracy), but will try to correct it.
13. For parallel passages see e.g., I 2, 1252b27–31; III 9, 1280a31–38; III 9, 1280b29–35; and III 9, 1280b39–1281a4.
14. Rosler 2005.
15. On *homonoia* as the essential feature of political friendship see particularly *NE* VIII 1, 1155a22–26 and *NE* IX 6, 1167a22–28.
16. The fundamental character of this difference between the political rule and despotic rule is pointed out by Simon Weber 2014.

17. It does not even seem radically different from the ideal city of *Pol.* VII and VIII.

18. See on this Mulgan 1977.

19. See e.g., VII 1, 1323a17–24. Cf. Schütrumpf 2006.

20. Obviously, the best *polis* described by Aristotle in *Politics* VII and VIII is a paternalistic state. But on the other hand, as modern perfectionist philosophers point out, a certain paternalism cannot be completely absent from liberal states, as the following three points make clear: (i) No liberal state can tolerate a completely subjective or decisionist form to determine one's preferences. Every state must be able to rule out certain intolerant religious or political ideas, especially those based on racism, nationalism, sexism, and intolerance. (ii) The same holds true for cases in which we can speak of self-damaging, self-destruction, or self-humiliation. Even liberals must acknowledge that cases can occur in which the state should defend the "well-considered interests" of a person against his actual desires (take e.g. the interdiction on selling one's own kidneys). (iii) Even (and perhaps especially) liberals emphasize the ideas of self-improvement. They point out that a state should encourage as many people as possible to gain knowledge and competences and to develop their abilities. But this presupposes a substantial idea of what it means to cultivate valuable talents – valuable for the agent, his or her social context, or for the society as a whole. In contemporary political philosophy, however, one might transform the Aristotelian account into a "liberal perfectionism", as defended e.g. by Joseph Raz, Steven Wall, George Sher, and Jeffrey Stout.

21. Heinaman 2007: 221–22 lists all relevant passages in the *NE*, the *EE*, and the *Politics*.

22. III 6, 1278b8; IV 1, 1289a15–18.

23. Cf. III 16, 1287a18 and II 5, 1263a23.

24. I 2, 1252b30 and III 9, 1281a1–2.

# 10 Claims to rule: the case of the multitude

## INTRODUCTION: FRAMING THE CLAIMS TO RULE OF THE MANY, THE FEW, AND THE ONE

Aristotle's assessment in *Politics* III 10–18 of the claims to rule of those who would hold power in different regimes is most famous for its consideration of the claims of the multitude to rule. The arguments he advances for what has been dubbed the "wisdom of the multitude" have been widely acclaimed as a normative justification of the epistemic value of full-scale democratic participation involving deliberation among diverse participants.[1] I argue that this reading fails to appreciate important aspects of the context and two concomitant limitations of the argument. Its context is the broad sweep of the argument in this stretch of the *Politics*, which prescinds from the conventional method of evaluating Greek regimes at the time that considered each potential claimant as having its own distinctive claim to rule: for example, the many typically claimed to rule on the basis of freedom, whereas the few appealed either to wealth or to virtue. Instead, Aristotle's repeated strategy is a logical critique, pointing out that no such claim will necessarily secure the rule of its

The stimulus for this argument came from teaching a graduate seminar on "Knowledge and Politics" at Princeton University in Fall 2010. Earlier versions of this contribution were fruitfully discussed with the Laurence S. Rockefeller Visiting Faculty Fellows for 2010–11 at the Princeton University Center for Human Values; the participants in the 2011 Columbia University Workshop on Democracy and the Republic; and the participants in the first meeting of the Popular Sovereignty Network in 2012, funded by the Arts and Humanities Research Council of the United Kingdom. Valuable comments were likewise provided on earlier versions by Danielle Allen, Paul Cartledge, Jimmy Doyle, Antony Hatzistavrou, Kinch Hoekstra, Josh Ober, Malcolm Schofield, and the editors of this volume.

usual ideological proponents, because any such claim might instead be best fulfilled by another group instead, who can trump the usual group on the basis of their very own favored criterion. For example, if wealth is the criterion, then the wealthy few who tend to advance this as the criterion may be rightly subjected to the rule of the even wealthier (by aggregate) many (III 11, 1282a39–41), or conversely of an even wealthier single individual (III 13, 1283b17–18). As Aristotle sums up at one stage:

All this seems to make it evident, then, that none of the definitions on the basis of which people claim that they themselves deserve to rule, whereas everyone else deserves to be ruled by them, is correct. For the multitude would have an argument of some justice against those who claim that they deserve to have authority over the governing class because of their virtue, and similarly against those who base their claim on wealth. For nothing prevents the multitude from being sometimes better and richer than the few, not as individuals but collectively. (III 13, 1283b27–35)[2]

This broad strategy leads to a first significant limitation of the argument in III 11, which is that the claims of the multitude there are assessed not in relation to any and all criteria for rule, but specifically in relation to the criteria for wealth and virtue that would normally be advanced by the few – of which virtue is, of course, Aristotle's own favored normatively best criterion for rule (III 18, 1288a32–39). The result of this assessment is the second significant limitation of the III 11 argument. It concludes that the multitude can outperform the few rich or virtuous individuals on grounds of wealth or virtue only collectively, never individually, and that their doing so is (I argue) primarily a function of sheer aggregation rather than of deliberation or diversity.[3] The institutional manifestation of the multitude's proper claim is that, being able to exercise collective but not individual virtue, it should play a role in "deliberation and judgment" which is exemplified in the text in only a single way: as the participation in election and inspection of officials of the kind which Solon as Athenian legislator accorded them. *Politics* III 11 and the associated chapters do not, then, set out to defend a doctrine of the "wisdom of the multitude";[4] in context, they are rather assessments of the extent to which the multitude might trump the few on the basis of virtue or wealth, as two possible specifications of a claim to rule on which the multitude's political roles are to be both allotted and limited. We turn now to the specification of claims to rule as claims to offices, followed by the III 11 and III 15 assessments of the claims of the multitude to rule, and then the objections considered within III 11 to those claims, followed by a brief conclusion.

## INSTITUTIONAL FRAMEWORK: FROM CLAIMS TO RULE TO CLAIMS TO OFFICE

A new line of argument is initiated in III 10, where Aristotle raises a "problem (*aporian*) as to what part of the state is to have authority (*to kurion*), since surely it is either the multitude, or the rich, or decent people, or the one who is best of all, or a tyrant" (III 10, 1281a11–13). In response to this question, he will eventually distinguish two forms of authority: the authority of the laws, and the authority of the "ruler (*ton archonta*) whether one or many [who] should have authority (*einai kurious*) over only those matters on which the laws cannot pronounce with precision" (III 11, 1282b1–6). The question then becomes: who should these "rulers" be, which turns out in practice to mean, who should hold the offices in the city?

*Politics* III 11 takes up the claim of one particular group to serve as such rulers, setting out to examine "the view that the multitude rather than the few best people should be in authority (*kurion einai*)," which "while it involves a problem . . . perhaps also involves some truth" (III 11, 1281a40–42). Its central line of argument begins by positing a case in which the many "are not as individuals excellent [or 'virtuous'] men" (III 11, 1281a42–1281b1). This case poses a conundrum for Aristotle: given that his overarching framework specifies virtue as the goal of the *polis*, how could there be merit in any claim to rule by men who are not individually virtuous?[5]

In the course of answering this question, Aristotle must clarify what it means for any man or group of men to "be in authority," given that he will eventually distinguish the authority of any such human "ruler" from the overarching authority of the laws. The key to understanding III 11, I submit, is to see that the question of human rule under the authority of the laws[6] is cashed out as a question of relation to office. (We will see that Aristotle eventually distinguishes two forms of rule corresponding to two forms of relation to offices: holding office, and choosing and monitoring those who do.) This move is made in III 11 when Aristotle begins to answer his own question of what, in particular, the free multitude should "have authority over (*kurious einai*)" by saying that "it would not be safe to have them participate (*metechein*) in the most important offices,"[7] but that "to give them no share and not to allow them to participate (*metechein*) at all would be cause for alarm" (III 11, 1281b23–24, 25–26, and 28–29, respectively). Thus, the issue of the multitude's participation is framed not as an issue of their general participation in politics, but specifically as a question of their relation to the offices.

This reading is supported by the explanation which Aristotle gives of the alarm that exclusion of the multitude from "participation" would cause. This explanation addresses not any and every form of political participation, but specifically their exclusion from office: "For a state in which a large number of people are excluded from office (*atimoi*) and are poor must of necessity be full of enemies" (III 11, 1281b25–30). *Atimoi* means literally without honor, referring in context to the honor of holding political office. The problem of the multitude's participation which Aristotle is considering is not their participation in politics generally, but specifically their relation to the offices.

In this light, we can better appreciate the solution to the problem of the multitude's participation in relation to office which Aristotle gives. It is stated first as a general principle, of which only a single exemplification is given, an exemplification which I will call the "Solonic scheme"[8] (though strictly speaking, it is credited to "Solon and some other legislators"):

The remaining alternative, then, is to have them participate in deliberation and judgment (*bouleuesthai kai krinein*), which is precisely why Solon and some other legislators arrange to have them participate in election (*tas archairesias*) and inspection (*tas euthunas*) of officials (*tôn archontôn*), but prevent them from holding office (*archein*) alone. (1281b31–34)

Many readers of this passage assume that "deliberation" (*bouleuesthai*) refers generally to broad forms of democratic participation in the assembly and council (*boulê*), while "judgment" (*krinein*) refers to the people's participation in the jury courts.[9] But given that the solution is presented as a response to the concern that "it would not be safe to have the multitude participate in the most important offices," and that it is exemplified only by the

Solonic scheme, the context of the passage is better understood as restricted to the functions of such participation in relation to offices alone. That is, "deliberation and judgment" are to be understood as roles exercised in relation to office holding, not as more general political functions, and they are exemplified in the multitude's roles in electing and inspecting officials while being excluded from holding the most important offices themselves. These were roles which were carried out in the assembly, council, and courts, as I will shortly explain, but which did not exhaust the broader political functions of those institutions. While this reading does not exclude the possibility that Aristotle would have approved such broader functions for the multitude and for these institutions in political deliberation and judgment more generally, I find only their roles in relation to office holding being explicitly defended here.

How might the multitude exercise "deliberation and judgment" in relation to the holders of political office? In the Athenian democracy to which the mention of Solon refers us, we can understand "deliberation" in the council and assembly to refer to the means by which officials were elected and scrutinized in advance of taking office, and "judgment" in the council and the courts to refer to the means by which their performance was inspected and held accountable. In the fourth century BC, in which modified elements of Solon's scheme were still in place, the election of officials (*tas archairesias*) involved nomination by the council, followed by the actual election in a special meeting of the assembly called the *archairesia*.[10] And if we conceive of the process of election as including the subsequent procedure of *dokimasia* or scrutiny before being allowed to take up office (so perhaps better termed selection than simply election), we find a further role for both the council and the courts, each of which carried out some procedures of *dokimasia*.[11] Similarly, the inspection of officials (*tas euthunas*) in fourth-century Athens involved both the council and the courts. A board of ten officials called *logistai* was first chosen by lot to carry out an inspection of accounts and preside over a court hearing in which any citizen could accuse the magistrates being scrutinized of financial abuses; a second phase was carried out by a board of ten other officials called *euthunoi*, one per tribe chosen from the council, scrutinizing any other abuses and allowing accusations to be brought before a court as well.[12] We should, however, note a caution in respect of the Solonic mention. For the

tendency in the fourth century to idealize an ancient Solonic constitution means that Aristotle's analysis is not to be taken as descriptive of the actual workings of the democracy in his day. Rather, the
restriction of his analysis to election and inspection of officials only
should be considered as an intervention in shaping the ideal of a
Solonic (and so good) constitution itself.

A final note on the institutional shape given to the case for the
multitude's participation in this chapter is that the laying out of the
Solonic scheme is followed by an explanation:

For (*gar*) when they all [sc. the many] come together their perception is adequate, and, when mixed with their betters, they benefit their states, just as a
mixture of roughage and pure food-concentrate is more useful than a little of
the latter by itself. Taken individually, however, each of them is imperfect
in relation to judging (*peri to krinein*). (1281b34–38)

Aristotle's conclusion to this passage refers back to the *krinein*
which is the second half of the role of the people in "deliberation
and judgment" in relation to the offices. Even in these roles, exemplified by the Solonic scheme of electing and inspecting officials, the
people do best when they supplement the roles of the individually
virtuous. This is not, in other words, a mixed constitution with a
purely popular institution within it. Rather, the multitude need to
be aggregated with the individually virtuous even to carry out the
limited functions in relation to the most important offices – those of
"deliberation and judgment" – which they may safely be allowed.[13]

### ARGUMENTS FOR THE "WISDOM OF THE MULTITUDE" IN III 11 AND III 15

What are the arguments on the basis of which Aristotle draws
the conclusion exemplified by the Solonic scheme, that the people should participate in "deliberation and judgment" in the form of
electing and inspecting officials? We turn now to the main line of the
III 11 argument which will issue in the conclusion just considered.
The first analogy in III 11 is, famously, the so-called "democratic
feast," a passage which I cite in Reeve's translation but interpret differently from many commentators:

PASSAGE A: For the many, who are not as individuals excellent men, nevertheless can, when they have come together, be better than the few best people, not individually but collectively, just as feasts to which many contribute (*ta sumphorêta deipna*) are better than feasts provided (*chorêgêthentôn*)[14] at one person's expense (*ek mias dapanês*). (1281a42–1281b3)

Compare this to a passage in III 15, in one place modifying Reeve's translation:

PASSAGE E [we will cite three intervening passages as B, C, and D shortly]: as things stand now, people come together to hear cases, deliberate, and decide, and the decisions themselves all concern particulars. Taken individually, any one of these people is perhaps inferior to the best person. But a city-state consists of many people, just like a feast to which many contribute (*hestiasis sumphorêtos*), and is better than one that is single (*mias*) [I offer "single" as vs. Reeve's "a unity"] and simple (*haplês*). (1286a26–30)

Passage A makes clear that the contrast refers to the responsibility for bearing the expense of the meal: whatever is meant there by *ta sumphorêta deipna* must contrast with what is provided at "one person's expense." If we assume, as seems reasonable, that *sumphorêta* in A and *sumphorêtos* in E refer to the same attribute, it follows that the contrast in E must also be with a "single and simple" *bearer of expense*. We will see that this responsibility for bearing the expense may take the form of provision "in kind," not necessarily provision of money. So the contrast in both passages is between a meal the expense of which is borne collectively, and a meal the expense of which is borne by a single individual.

Is this meant to be a purely logical contrast, or might Aristotle have some specific institutional practices in mind? I suggest that the contrast is meant to be primarily a logical one rather than a specific institutional commentary. This is suggested by the use of *sumphorêtos*, which is descriptive rather than being part of any established public vocabulary for common meals. Aristotle could have referred much more specifically, for example, to Spartan common meals by using the established vocabulary of *ta phiditia* or *ta sussitia*, or to specific Athenian public feasts using their names, had he wished to do so. Instead his studied lack of specificity here may be no accident. I think it is best understood in line with the overall thesis of this chapter: that his fundamental point in III 10–18 about claims to rule is a logical analysis of rival claims rather than one which seeks to build up a particular political case.

Having said this, it is a useful exercise to consider what examples of common meals he might conceivably have had in mind in drawing the contrast to make his logical point. Consider these four alternatives.

(1) "Potluck." This is the standard and widely shared interpretation, which refers not to a specific Greek practice but to a generally conceived practice. The term "potluck" is used by Josiah Ober, Jeremy Waldron, and James Lindley Wilson, among others[15] (compare Liddell and Scott, rev. Jones' use of "picnic" in glossing these passages: s.v. *sumphorêtos*). These authors understand "potluck" in a strong sense, which I will indicate by capitalizing it as Potluck. As they explain Potluck, it means not only a meal to which each guest contributes (which is all that the Greek specifies), but also and specifically a meal to which each guest contributes by bringing a distinctive and special dish, such that it is the variety of such dishes which explains the superiority of a potluck meal over a meal cooked by one person. But as noted above, Passage A refers not to meals cooked by a single chef, but to meals provided at a single person's expense.[16] The strong Potluck reading adds the idea of the source and variety of the cooking itself to the text's focus on the source of the expense alone.

This elaboration might be warranted if we had clear evidence of such Potluck meals in the strong sense in ancient Greece. There is no such clear evidence from Athens, though Ober speculates that voluntary associations may have held such meals;[17] neither Waldron nor J. L. Wilson offer any Greek examples. Perhaps the best case for the Potluck proponents would be to appeal to a particular aspect of the way in which common meals were provided at Sparta. There, citizens were required to supply fixed amounts of grain, wine, cheese, and figs (I comment further on this requirement below), but they were also required to contribute a certain fixed amount of *opsônion*, "a catch-all heading which would include meat, fish, and side-dishes [and] would be the most variable of the items of the mess dues."[18] So in this context citizens might have sometimes contributed prepared side-dishes; and also, the dishes consumed in the "after-course" of the dinner were prepared at home and brought as voluntary contributions for that purpose.

It is conceivable that Aristotle was thinking of either or both of these aspects of Spartan practice – the occasional bringing of side-dishes, and the bringing of already prepared dishes for the "after-course."[19] But it is implausible for two reasons. First, the details do not actually fit the strong Potluck reading that well. The "after-course" is not part of the dinner proper; for its part, the *opsônion* did not *require* the bringing of a prepared dish, as it could be fulfilled instead by contributing an amount of meat or fish, and in fact it is specified in both principal sources for Spartan messes as a *financial* requirement ("a small amount of money" in Plutarch, *Lyc.* 12.3; 10 Aiginetan obols in Dikaiarkhos Fr. 23, in Athenaeus 4.141C).[20] Second, the broader institutional structure of Spartan shared meals was (apart from these two rather minor elements) not exemplary of Potluck in the strong sense at all. Apart from the *opsônion*, four out of the five requirements for citizen contributions to those meals were stated in kind, as required contributions of ingredients (measures of grain, wine, cheese, and figs). So Sparta as a general case is in fact best suited to exemplify not a strong Potluck reading, but rather a much weaker notion of in-kind contributions which constitute bearing one's share of the expense. One can call this potluck in a weak sense if one likes, as it involves individual contributions, but it lacks the elements of distinctive originality and diversity which the strong Potluck reading stresses.

This brings us to our second candidate case (2), which is precisely "Sparta" – now construed as a case of primarily in-kind mess contributions. Given the way in which four out of the five requirements for citizen contributions to the Spartan *phiditia* were specified, it is both possible and I think most plausible that if Aristotle was thinking of any specific case of "a meal to which many contribute" when composing Passages A and E, it was the Spartan mess that was in his mind. For he refers to Spartan messes repeatedly throughout the *Politics*, and their actual structure fits naturally with the description of a meal "to which many people contribute."[21] The superiority of the common mess on this reading would be in its aggregation of individual foodstuff contributions. True, the *opsônion* and the after-dinner dishes might also provide a measure of welcome diversity. But the primary way in which citizens were required to contribute individually was by piling the common stores and supplies of grain, wine, cheese, and figs higher.

Alternative reading (3) might be named "common meals as social participation." James Lindley Wilson advances a strong Potluck reading, but then adds that the common meals are also to be understood as "developing a cooperative practice that provides the city both material and social sustenance."[22] Now Aristotle certainly values the way in which common meals can serve to "make property communal," as he explains in adducing Sparta and Crete in the course of criticizing Socrates in Plato's *Republic* (1263b40–1264a1, a passage which Wilson cites). But there is no evidence in Passages A or E that this is the point he is making there. This interpretation goes well beyond the contrast drawn in the text, which in both passages focuses exclusively on the question of whether many contribute to the meal in the sense of bearing its expense (so contributing either in-kind or financially) or whether the expense is borne by only a single person.

(4) "Athens." A novel interpretation is advanced by Daniela Cammack (2013), who suggests that Aristotle had an Athenian referent in mind in drawing both halves of the contrast in each of our passages. Her point of departure is the use of the word *hestiasis* in Passage E. This word can mean simply "feast" or "meal" and is not exclusively a term used for or in Athens.[23] The Athenians did have a specific liturgical role of *hestiator*, which involved one person being chosen to provide a collective meal for his tribe at certain civic festivals.[24] But there is an obvious problem in thinking that Aristotle might have meant in writing *hestiasis* to refer to this specific Athenian liturgy. *Hestiasis* in Passage E is used to describe the *collectively provided* feasts – yet for most of the life of the democracy, and in all the definite evidence that we have, the *hestiator* acted as an *individual* (and so the reference is here on the wrong side of the divide). Cammack speculates, however, that this liturgy may in the late fourth century have begun to be exercised by groups rather than by individuals, on the model of a similar known change in the *trierarchon* liturgy, and that it was this contrast between the new-model and the old-model *hestiatores* of which Aristotle may have been thinking.[25] Cammack's proposal is ingenious. But it is speculative, and since we have solid evidence for Spartan in-kind contributions to common meals and no solid evidence for a newly collectivized Athenian practice of *hestiator*, I suggest that the former is more plausibly considered the case which Aristotle might have

had in mind, if he was indeed thinking of any specific institutional arrangement at all.

It is not possible to settle the question of which cases Aristotle's distinction is intended to cover, or whether he had any specific cases in mind at all, rather than making an intentionally general and logical point. The most important things to take away from my discussion of this analogy are two-fold: first, that it contrasts meals provided at one person's expense with those provided at the expense of many. Second, since all that is mentioned is the basis of expense, it seems that it is the sheer additive nature of the expenses (so multiplying the "value" of the dinner, understood as its costing Xn rather than merely X) which is the most natural and immediate way to construe that contrast, in the absence of any further specification or explanation by Aristotle. Indeed, it is just this additive feature which is drawn on in the application of the analogy. For example, later in III 11, Aristotle applies the analogy to justify the many, who have collectively (he assumes) a higher property assessment than the few, electing and inspecting the magistrates who have qualified to be elected as such in virtue precisely of their property holdings (1282a38–41).

I conclude the discussion of this analogy with two observations. The first is to note an irony of the fact that Sparta has emerged as the clearest plausible case for Aristotle to have had in mind, if he were indeed thinking of specific institutions at all. Speaking elsewhere in the *Politics* of the Spartan practice in which "each individual has to contribute" (literally, *pherein*, 1271a29–30, the same verb as is used to constitute *sumphorêtos*) to the common meal, he says that this is "scarcely democratic at all," as it has the effect of excluding the very poor who cannot afford to contribute (1271a34). By implication, it is the Cretan practice in which messes are "publicly supported" (*apo koinou*, 1271a28) that is more genuinely democratic. The irony is that a meal described as one to which "each individual has to contribute" is here explicitly judged by Aristotle precisely *not* to be the very model of a "democratic" feast. It is not Sparta, but Crete, which is more democratic, and it is so precisely because its common meals are provided *not* by individual contributions but by already collectivized resources (thus it provides "more communally," *koinoterôs*, 1272a16; see also *apo koinou*, 1271a28). A more truly "democratic" possible feast consists not of individual contributions (and so *a fortiori* it is not a Potluck) but is rather provided out of resources which already belong to the public. Immediate individual contributions do not, on this account, make for what is maximally "democratic" in any form.

My second conclusion, however, is to counsel caution with all of the possible institutional candidates canvassed above. For again, it is striking that Aristotle eschews any formulation that would point unmistakably to any one particular institution (he avoids the words *sussitia* and *phiditia*; and *hestiasis* appears on the wrong side of the divide to pick up the most natural and well-attested Athenian liturgical referent). Had he wanted to indicate a clear institutional referent, he could easily have done so. Instead, the contrast he draws is evidently logical while being only arguably institutional. The logic of a meal to which each individual contributes resources, whether financial or material, is that such resources will be superior to those of a meal to which only a single person contributes resources. Those resources may vary in quality as well as in quantity – as with the Spartans contributing the results of that week's hunt to their messes to meet their *opsônion* obligation, for example. But the point is that such collective contributions will furnish a greater measure of resources, measured by expense per capita, compared to those that any one person could furnish. In assembling the resources, we can distinguish the part provided by each, and it is this composite nature of the collective contribution that in Passage E is contrasted with a contribution which is "single and simple." But Aristotle says nothing in this analogy about the complexity of the whole as compared to the parts. His focus is rather on the provision of more parts which add up to make the whole better resourced, as compared to a single such part which is, logically, resourced less well.[26]

Aristotle does not spell out whether the better resourcing is quantitative only, or qualitative as well. That is not necessary for him to effect the logical argument about the bearing of expense: if two people both bear the same amount of expense (call it X) towards a meal, it follows that we will have a meal worth 2X (however we spend the X), which is twice as much as if one of them had borne the same amount (X) alone. The single payer/provider will be "single" by definition (*mias* means "single" or "one," not "unity" in an evaluative sense as Reeve's translation implies) and "simple" in providing only one single contribution in contrast to the collective composite of the other kind.

In the way that Aristotle deploys this analogy, then, he nowhere mentions the thought that collectively provided meals are better because people bring diverse and original elements to them. (It may be that among the collective provision is a greater variety of meats, say – but then again it may not.) Rather, the point is that they are better in so far as many people contribute a measure of expense, so outstripping the provision in terms of the expense borne by any one single individual. And this is precisely in line with the overall logical point that Aristotle is making about the multitude throughout III 10–18, as we observed in the first section above. Whatever basis of merit to rule may be claimed by a single person or a small group, the multitude can potentially trump them on the same basis: for the multitude have collectively more virtue, wealth, and better birth than any one individual can muster (barring the emergence of the one man of supreme virtue and practical wisdom whom Aristotle at moments of the *Politics* envisages, who would in turn trump them all).

On my reading so far, the value of the collectively funded feasts in Passages A and E should be read as aggregative and, specifically, as additive, rather than as dialectical and deliberative as Jeremy Waldron, among others, has influentially argued.[27] Yet that must confront an immediate objection. Aristotle goes on from Passage A to introduce three more analogies and examples in a continuous line of argument which I break up for convenience into three passages. Consider the first two:

PASSAGE B: For being many, each of them can have some part of virtue and practical wisdom, and when they come together, the multitude is just like a single human being, with many feet, hands, and senses, and so too for their character traits and wisdom. (1281b4–7)

PASSAGE C: That is why the many are better judges of works of music and of the poets. For one of them [judges][28] one part, another another, and all of them the whole thing. (1281b7–10)

On the face of it, Passages B and C look problematic for my reading. For they seem to refer precisely to distributed, diverse contributions made by members of the multitude, and even in C to deliberative or at least combined judgment. However, I read them differently. The many feet, hands, and senses in B are many versions of the same bodily limb or organ. That is, the multitude multiply (aggregatively) the feet and hands of a single person, making up a single gigantic human being who disposes of the *same kind* of bodily limbs and organs as an ordinary individual, but just of *more* of them.[29] Thus, B is consonant with my aggregative reading of A (the feast), in which what Aristotle is emphasizing is simply that the multitude (in A, embodied in the city's institutions) can provide *more* of whatever quality it is that the elite claim to be able to provide.

C is more difficult, both because it is so compressed, and because it seems to refer to a distribution of functions rather than a mere aggregation of parts relating to any given function. The reference is to the ten judges who were appointed by lot for each festival to judge the plays presented annually at the City Dionysia and the Lenaea. All judges voted on all the plays, but the distributed reference in Aristotle's text seems to be to the implicit parts of those plays, or perhaps to the individual plays as parts of the three-play sequences in which tragedies were judged:[30] one judge responds to one part, another judge to another, yet all vote on the plays as wholes and all their votes are aggregated.[31] Here, it may be true that different judges respond to different parts of the plays, or different plays among the three, which introduces an element of individual diversity. Yet in so doing, each judge formulates an overall judgment of the field of competition as a whole, taking each play as a whole, and it is this (similarly structured) overall judgment which is aggregated by the voting procedure into a single collective judgment. While some diversity is in view here, the logic of aggregation is still what Aristotle should be understood primarily to be emphasizing.

This interpretation is supported by the passage which follows on immediately from C:

PASSAGE D: It is in this way that excellent men differ from each of the many, just as beautiful people are said to differ from those who are not beautiful, and as things painted by craft are superior to real things: they bring together what is scattered and separate into one – although, at least if taken separately, this person's eye and some other feature of someone else will be more beautiful than the painted ones. (1281b10–15)

Here, Aristotle briefly inverts the issue at stake. He is now describing how the virtuous individual is *superior* to the many as an individual, notwithstanding the aggregative feats which the many can perform. The virtuous individual is superior because he unites and unifies virtue (which is, I take it for Aristotle as for Socrates, indeed a unity) within himself. And this unity is superior to any aggregative effort *even where* the parts to be aggregated among the many are individually superior to the elements inhering in the virtuous individual – this is the burden of the last line of D. That is, D supports the claim that Aristotle most prizes the good (or virtuous) man who is also a good (virtuous) citizen, over and above the functional collective virtues which the multitude may be able to muster up by aggregation. (This is why it is important not to over-translate *mias* in Passage E as "unity," as Reeve does: neither there nor here do the multitude have true unity on their side.) If A to C were intended by Aristotle as an argument for the deliberative superiority of the multitude, Aristotle could not in D hold the unity of a virtuous individual to be superior to the unity which the multitude could in that case also achieve. Instead, he holds the multitude to achieve aggregation but not true unity when compared to a virtuous individual.

Passages A–D together conclude Aristotle's positive arguments for the claim that the multitude should be in authority in III 11. In the remainder of the chapter, he applies these arguments to delineate just what functions they warrant the multitude in carrying out. He does so by limiting the question to that of the higher offices, and exemplifying their role in deliberation and judgment of officials in the terms of the Solonic scheme, as explained in the second section above. Having laid out his solution of the problem of the multitude's relation to the offices, Aristotle envisions and replies to three objections, to which we will shortly turn. Before doing so, it is useful to assemble here the additional analogies and arguments which will be offered for the abilities of the multitude in the context of III 15.

That chapter investigates the question of "whether it is more beneficial to be ruled by the best man or by the best laws" (III 15, 1286a8–9), concluding as in III 11 that "laws must be established" (III 15, 1286a22), but acknowledging that there will be gaps and also imperfections in the law's judgments of particulars. The question of which individuals or groups should rule is again distinguished from the overall authority of the laws: "As to what the law cannot judge (*krinein*) either at all or well, should the one best person rule (*archein*), or everyone?" (III 15, 1286a24–25). Thus, we see that the problem of this part of III 15 is once again posed in terms of office holding: serving as an *archontes* or office holder. Although the Solonic scheme is not mentioned here, the meaning of *archein* is rule once again construed in relation to the holding of offices.

Aristotle sets out to answer his question of whether it is the one best person, or everyone, who should rule, by first illustrating the case of "everyone" ruling with what he calls the current practice involving certain collective roles in relation to rule: "For as things stand now, people come together collectively to hear cases, deliberate, and decide" (*dikazousi kai bouleuontai kai krinousin*; III 15, 1286a26–27). Again, one might be tempted to read this as a general description of the people's political roles. But that would be a mistake. For the pairing of *bouleuesthai* and *krinein* signals a reference back to the III 11 discussion of the multitude's roles in relation to office holding (it is the same verb which Reeve translated there at 1281b31 as "judgment" and here at 1286a26–27 as "decide"), just as the introductory framing of the III 15 question sets up the same distinction between men ruling as office holders, and the laws having authority, that we met earlier.

Why then does Aristotle add "to hear cases," using a verb applying specifically to jurors (*dikazesthai*), to the start of the list? If *bouleuesthai* and *krinein* refer in III 15 (as they did in III 11) to functions of popular deliberation and judgment exercised specifically in relation to the holders of offices, then by prefacing them with *dikazesthai*, Aristotle is adding a specific reference to serving as a juror in the courts as a role in relation to office holders, not as a juror more broadly. This makes sense in view of the Athenian courts' role precisely in the process of inspection (in so far as the courts were the fora in which accusations on the basis of the inspections, *euthunai*, could be brought) and perhaps also in election (in so far as one might take *dokimasia* to have been an element in the process of selecting officials more broadly conceived). If so, then the addition of *dikazesthai* to the III 11 formula pairing *bouleuesthai* and *krinein* still remains squarely within the parameters of the concern with offices, rather than invoking any broader or general popular role in deliberation or judgment.

It is in this context that we should also understand Aristotle's introduction of two further analogies and arguments in III 15, which

I call Passages E and F. We have quoted and discussed E already, so I comment here only on F, but quote them both for the sake of sequential context:

PASSAGE E: as things stand now, people come together to hear cases, deliberate, and decide, and the decisions themselves all concern particulars. Taken individually, any one of these people is perhaps inferior to the best person. But a city-state consists of many people, just like a feast to which many contribute (*hestiasis sumphorêtos*), and is better than one that is single (*mias*) [modifying Reeve's translation] and simple (*haplês*). (1286a26–30)

PASSAGE F: Besides, a large quantity is more incorruptible, so the multitude, like a larger quantity of water, is more incorruptible than the few. The judgment of an individual is inevitably corrupted when he is overcome by anger or some other passion of this sort, whereas in the same situation it is a task to get all the citizens to become angry and make mistakes at the same time. (1286a31–35)

Passage F applies the now familiar logical pattern of assessing any claimed basis for rule independently of its typical ideological associations, so that it may turn out to count against rather than for its conventional proponents. In this case, the judgment of individuals who might claim to rule *qua* individuals is assessed as more vulnerable to emotion than the judgment of the multitude whose claim to rule is collective. We see the logical nature of the criterion, and its presupposition for applicability, reinforced in the lines following F, where Aristotle endorses as "clear" the thought that of "a number who were both good men and good citizens," the larger number would be more incorruptible in ruling by holding office (*archôn*) than would a single man (1286a39–b1). But notice here that Aristotle couches his point in comparative terms. Even in this hypothetical case, he does not describe the whole multitude as virtuous. Rather, he contrasts a single official with "a greater number" of those who are virtuous both as men and as citizens. So this passage too stops short of a general endorsement of democratic participation. Instead, it makes a hypothetical, comparative, and logical case: if one is able to compare a single virtuous official with a greater number who are also virtuous, the latter will be more incorruptible than the former.

One might object to this reading that the contrast between the one and the greater number seems here to be couched in relation to the possibility of either of them ruling in the form of holding office. This would then accord a new possible political function to the multitude of actually holding office, as opposed to the III 11 solution and Solonic scheme in which the multitude do not hold high office, but only participate in deliberation and judgment as exemplified by the selection and inspection of officials. And that in turn might mean that Aristotle here is envisaging a broader political role for the multitude. But a more deflationary reading is consistent with the logical analysis throughout this stretch of the text. For his talk of comparative numbers can again be read purely logically: as a contrast between one and more, rather than as a specific reference to the popular multitude. In that case, he is not necessarily defending a role for the multitude as a whole here, but rather a role for a larger group of virtuous men (which may still stop well short of the full multitude) rather than a single man.

In any case, while incorruptibility may favor the greater number over the few, it is not tantamount to the whole of virtue, which is the criterion with which Book III will conclude (in Chapter 18) that "the best (*aristên*) [of the three kinds of correct constitution] must of necessity be the one managed by the best people (*tôn aristôn*]" (III 18, 1288a33–34). That chapter still drives home the logical point that such virtuous rule may in practice be best exemplified by "one particular person or a whole family or a number of people" (III 18, 1288a35–36), rather than being a criterion which uniquely or naturally favors any one person's or group's claim to rule. Nevertheless, Aristotle concludes the chapter and the book with the reminder that "the ways and means by which a man becomes excellent are the same as those by which one might establish a city-state ruled by an aristocracy or a king" (III 18, 1288a39–41). That is, individual excellence and virtue are only ever the province of a relative few or perhaps one individual alone. The many can at best produce a collective virtue, but not enjoy individual virtue, and so the restriction of their claim to participate in ruling to the roles of selection and inspection of officials still seems to hold good.

### OBJECTIONS TO THE "WISDOM OF THE MULTITUDE" AND ARISTOTLE'S REPLIES

We return to III 11. Having offered the Solonic scheme as an exemplification of what it means for the multitude to participate in "deliberation and judgment" with respect to high offices without being eligible to hold them themselves, Aristotle turns to meet two objections to "this organization of the constitution" (III 11, 1281b39). He identifies a first *aporia* which I call Objection 1, elaborated in two parts referring, respectively, to inspection and election of officials, and a second which I call Objection 2.

Objection 1 begins with the case of inspection, offering the thought that just as the only proper judge (able to exercise *to krinai*; III 11, 1281b40) of an expert is another expert, so too the only proper inspector of an official or magistrate is someone else qualified to hold that position. The first part of the objection (1A) is summed up thus: "Therefore, just as a doctor should be subject to inspections (*tas euthunas*) by doctors, so others should also be inspected by their peers" (III 11, 1282a1–2). The idea is that people who are not qualified to hold certain offices are *a fortiori* not qualified to inspect those who do hold them. Notice that 1A is framed by applying the political term *tas euthunas* to the inspection of the doctors, thus tying it closely and unmistakably to the Solonic solution in which the many, not fellow experts or high office holders, are able to inspect the performance in office of the few.

Aristotle's reply begins by distinguishing three senses of the word "doctor," as applying variously "to the ordinary practitioner of the craft, to a master craftsman, and thirdly, to someone with a general education in the craft," the latter being a group which exists in all of what are called crafts (III 11, 1282a3–5). He remarks that in practice, we assign the function of judging (*to krinein*) to those with a general education as well as to those who know. That is, even when knowledge is a requirement, this doesn't necessarily underwrite the special claims of experts. Aristotle is appealing to everyday processes in which people judge the practitioners of the *technai* (those with a general education in rhetoric judging orators, perhaps), as support for the specifically political practice of popular participation in the inspections of officials.

Objection 1B then applies the same sort of thought specifically to the process of election (*peri tên hairesin*), now invoking the other half of the Solonic scheme: "since choosing (*to helesthai*) [a form of the verb *haireô* used in describing Solon's scheme] correctly is also a task for experts" (III 11, 1282a8–9). 1B is illustrated by the thought that it is geometers who should choose geometers and captains who should choose captains. After a further, rather opaque example,

Aristotle states the overall burden of Objection 1 in terms which once again refer unambiguously to the problematic of office holding for the multitude and the exemplary Solonic scheme: "According to this argument, then, the multitude should not be given authority (*eiê...kurion*) over the election of officials (*tôn archairesiôn*) or the inspection of officials (*tôn euthunôn*)" (III 11, 1282a12–14).

The answer to Objection 1 is offered in two thoughts. The first invokes the earlier argument (a reference back to Passages A, B, and C) that the many may be "a better or no worse [judge] when they all come together" than the individually superior judges who truly know (1282a16–17). The second is new to this section of the *Politics*: that in some *technai*, the makers or practitioners "might not be able to judge (*krineien*) either solely or best" (III 11, 1282a17–18), because those who use the products of the craft may be even better able to judge (*krinei*, 1282a21). Examples are adduced of the household manager judging a house better than its builder, the captain judging a rudder better than its carpenter, and the guest judging a feast better than its cook. So the multitude do have a role in judgment, as they will very often be the users rather than the expert makers of the products of craft. But this precisely supports the Solonic scheme and the solution it exemplifies: it underwrites a role for the multitude in judging office holders rather than in holding high office themselves.

Having solved the "problem" elaborated in Objection 1, Aristotle introduces a second related problem which I call Objection 2 (a new *aporian* is introduced at 1282a23–24, following the solution of the first one that had been presented as an *aporian* at 1281b39):

For it is held to be absurd for inferior people to have authority (*einai kurious*) over more important matters (*to meizonôn*) than decent people do. But inspections and elections of officials (*hai d'euthunai kai hai tôn archôn haireseis*) are very important things (*megiston*). (III 11, 1282a25–27)

"Important" here (repeated twice, in the comparative form of *to meizonôn* and in the absolute form of *megiston*) clearly refers back to the problem of the popular participation in relation to offices, to which the Solonic scheme was offered as an exemplary solution: for the debate there was about whether the multitude should be allowed to "participate in the most important offices (*tôn archôn tôn megistôn*)" (III 11, 1281b26). This is an important restriction arising from context. It means that Aristotle's discussion is again limited to the question of their role in relation to offices, and again specifically invokes the two institutional practices of the Solonic solution.

This restrictive context is crucial to understanding the subsequent example of "some constitutions" which Aristotle goes on to give in elaborating Objection 2:

And in some constitutions, as we said [sc. in what is done by "Solon and some other legislators" back at III 11, 1281b32], these [sc. the functions of election and inspection of officials back at III 11, 1281b32–34] are assigned to the people, since the assembly has authority over all such matters. And yet those with low property assessments and of whatever age participate in the assembly (*tês ekklêsias metechousi*), and in deliberation (*bouleuousi*) and court-judgment (*dikazousin*), whereas those with high property assessments are the treasurers and generals and hold the most important offices (*tas megistas archas*). (III 11, 1282a27–32, giving plural "assessments" at a32)

The explicit back reference to "some constitutions, as we said" makes it indisputable that Aristotle is referring again to the Solonic scheme (in fact described earlier as a scheme of Solon and some other legislators) that he had used to illustrate his solution to the role of the people in relation to the offices. So when he refers to what "the assembly has authority over," it is not anything and everything that the assembly does, but specifically "these...matters," namely, the election and inspection of officials. As we have seen, the election of officials took place in a special meeting of the assembly. The new objection is then to a particular feature of this relationship of official selection to these officials themselves: the officials, who are individually wealthy, are selected in the assembly, nominated by the council, and scrutinized and judged in the council and the courts, by a multitude including men who are individually relatively poor. (Here, with the introduction of a new phrase for assembly participation, *bouleuesthai* seems to be targeting the role of the council, with *dikazesthai* in place of *krinein* now targeting the role of the courts.) That is, Aristotle is driving home that the Solonic scheme of participation by the multitude in electing and inspecting officials is precisely the kind of case of "inferior people" having authority over their betters which Objection 2 attacks.

Despite this clear indication that Objection 2 is targeting the Solonic scheme, in responding to the objection Aristotle makes a move which risks leading us to construe his concern here as more general. This is his application of the term "ruling" (*archôn*) to the court, the council, and the *dêmos*: it is these bodies which rule, he says, as opposed to the individual juror, councilor, or assemblyman (III 11, 1282a34–36). Now in one way, his application of this point is quite consistent with the reading we have been giving: he points out that these collective bodies are wealthier than the few office holders, so that (*pace* Objection 2), this is not a case of the inferior (on the ground of wealth) having authority over the superior, because the many are collectively superior in terms of wealth to the few. But there is one important aspect of his response which nuances, while not contradicting, our reading of the solution to popular participation in rule as exemplified by the Solonic scheme.

This is his expansion here of the idea of "ruling" to include not just holding office, but also sitting in deliberation and judgment about the office holders. Whereas earlier in the chapter, he had contrasted the role of the multitude in deliberation and judgment with the role of "ruling" construed as holding office (III 11, 1281b34), here he accords the title of "ruling" also to the collective bodies themselves, precisely in virtue of their exercise of the Solonic scheme's functions. So the idea of rule expands, not to give the multitude functions other than deliberation and judgment cashed out as election and inspection of officials, but rather to include those very functions now as constituting a form of rule. We might say that having limited *archein* to office holding earlier in the chapter, Aristotle now acknowledges a new and distinct form of *archein* which includes electing and inspecting the *archontes* themselves.[32] It is not correct to read the response to Objection 2 as a general justification of popular participation in the courts, assembly, and council (since it is introduced and concluded with reference to the Solonic scheme's functions only). Yet it is true that here Aristotle accords the title of rule to the people as constituted in these institutions, who do not exercise the function of rulers *qua* the highest officials, but, in electing and inspecting those officials, nevertheless exercise a genuine form of rule.

## CONCLUSION: ARISTOTLE AS SCHUMPETERIAN?

Aristotle's argument for democratic judgment allows certain multitudes, in certain circumstances, to manifest virtue in collectively making decisions. Yet such collective functional virtue never goes so far as to make the individuals of the multitude into good men as well as good citizens, and so it cannot constitute a best regime overall. *Politics* III 11 does not set out to justify the broad collective functions of the assembly, council, and courts. Read in context of the overall argument initiated in III 10 and concluded in III 18, it is concerned only with the people's relationship to the most important offices, and invokes these institutions only in the course of demonstrating how the people might play a role in "deliberation" and "judgment" about officials rather than in holding office themselves.

These roles are strikingly close to those of a modern representative democracy, in which the people elect their officials and pass judgment on their performance in broad terms at the ballot box, though not through specific institutions of inspection. Joseph Schumpeter argued for a minimal interpretation of democracy in which the people simply elect their rulers, and by deciding whether to re-elect them, might be said also to inspect them in a minimal sense.[33] The institutional arrangements invoked by Aristotle in III 11 share the same minimal logic:[34] in relation to the authority of office holding, the people should not exercise that authority themselves by holding offices, but only elect and inspect their officials' performance. But unlike Schumpeter, Aristotle concludes that such election and inspection (as exemplary of deliberation and judgment) actually constitute a genuine form of rule. For Schumpeter, the people "do not actually rule" in electing their rulers.[35] For Aristotle, they precisely do. While the rule of officials must be distinguished from the rule of those who elect and monitor them, both are genuinely forms of rule.

### WORKS CITED

Allen, D. S. 2000. *The World of Prometheus: the Politics of Punishing in Democratic Athens.* Princeton University Press

Bookman, J. T. 1992. "The Wisdom of the Many: an Analysis of the Arguments of Books III and IV of Aristotle's *Politics.*" *History of Political Thought* 13: 1–12

Bouchard, E. 2011. "Analogies du pouvoir partagé: remarques sur Aristote, *Politique* III.11." *Phronesis* 56: 162–79

Cammack, D. 2013. "Aristotle on the Virtue of the Multitude." *Political Theory* 41(2): 175–202

Figueira, Thomas J. (1984). "Mess Contributions and Subsistence at Sparta."
    *Transactions of the American Philological Association* 114: 87–109
Frede, D. 2005. "Citizenship in Aristotle's Politics." In *Aristotle's* Politics:
    *Critical Essays*, eds. R. Kraut and S. Skultety. Lanham, MD: Rowman
    & Littlefield
Hansen, M. H. 1999. *The Athenian Democracy in the Age of Demosthenes:
    Structure, Principles, and Ideology*, trans. J. A. Crook. Norman, OK:
    University of Oklahoma Press
Kraut, R. 2002. *Aristotle: Political Philosophy*. Oxford University Press
Lane, M. 2013. "Political expertise and political office in Plato's *States-
    man*: the statesman's rule (*archein*) and the subordinate magistracies
    (*archai*)." In *Plato's* Statesman: *Proceedings of the Eighth Symposium
    Platonicum Pragense*, eds. A. Havlícek and K. Thein. Prague: OIKOY-
    MENH
MacDowell, D. M. 1975. "Law-Making at Athens in the Fourth Century
    B.C." *Journal of Hellenic Studies* 95: 62–74
Murray, O. 1990. "Sympotic History." In *SYMPOTICA: A Symposium on
    the Symposion*, ed. O. Murray. Oxford: Clarendon Press
Ober, J. 2005. "Aristotle's natural democracy." In *Aristotle's* Politics: *Crit-
    ical Essays*, eds. R. Kraut and S. Skultety. Lanham, MD: Rowman &
    Littlefield
    2008. *Democracy and Knowledge: Innovation and Learning in Classical
    Athens*. Princeton University Press
    2013. "Democracy's Wisdom: an Aristotelian Middle Way for Collective
    Judgment." *American Political Science Review* 107(1): 104–22
Reeve, C. D. C. 1998. *Aristotle*, Politics. Indianapolis, IN: Hackett
Schmitt Pantel, P. 1992. *La cité au banquet: histoire des repas publics dans
    les cités grecques*. Paris: Boccard & Ecole française de Rome
Schofield, M. 2011. Aristotle and the democratization of politics." *In Epis-
    teme etc.: Essays in Honour of Jonathan Barnes*, eds. B. Morison and K.
    Ierodiakonou. Oxford University Press
Schumpeter, J. A. 1996 [1943]. *Capitalism, Socialism and Democracy*.
    London: George Allen and Unwin
Waldron, J. 1995. "The Wisdom of the Multitude: Some Reflections on
    Book 3, Chapter 11 of Aristotle's *Politics*." *Political Theory* 23: 563–
    84. Reprinted in *Aristotle's Politics: Critical Essays*, eds. R. Kraut and
    S. Skultety. Lanham, MD: Rowman & Littlefield
Wilson, J. L. 2011. "Deliberation, Democracy, and the Rule of Reason in
    Aristotle's *Politics*." *American Political Science Review* 105: 259–74
Wilson, P. 2000. *The Athenian Institution of the Khoregia: the Chorus, the
    City and the Stage*. Cambridge University Press

NOTES

1. Waldron 1995: 569–70 argues that Aristotle is invoking the dialectical fruits of "deliberation" rather than the mere summation of diverse views. Kraut 2002: 405 also adverts to the value of discussion to explain the merits of decision by certain multitudes. Ober 2008 stresses by contrast not so much deliberation but recognition of one another's diverse forms of expertise: "What is needed is a body of decision makers capable of recognizing (through social knowledge) who really is expert, and capable of deciding (by voting) how much weight to give various domains of expertise in 'all things considered' judgments" (112).

2. Translations of the Greek are drawn from the edition and translation of the *Politics* by C.D.C. Reeve (1998), sometimes modified; the Greek is taken from the Oxford Classical Text.

3. On this point, I concur with the minority opinions expressed by Frede 2005: 181 and Schofield 2011: 295, who remarks about the idea of deliberative democracy as legitimating political decisions that "I don't think this is at all Aristotelian." But Schofield finds a broader resonance and significance to Aristotle's argument for democratic theory than I do; I note specific disagreements as they arise below.

4. Bouchard 2011 offers a reading of *Politics* III 11 which is likewise directed to challenging Waldron's claim that Aristotle offers a "doctrine" to this effect. Both she and Cammack 2013, focus primarily on Aristotle's analogies; while I discuss the analogies, in some important respects similarly, my focus is on the overall logic of the chapter within the longer stretch of argument from III 10–18. A different breakdown of six arguments about "the wisdom of the many" contained within Books III and IV as a whole is given by Bookman 1992.

5. As we saw, Aristotle will in III 13 generalize this question: those who think the criterion of political rule is wealth or birth rather than virtue still need to confront the possibility that the multitude may have a better claim to rule than the few on each of those very criteria.

6. On the shift from the rule of men to the rule of law as an anti-democratic move in both Plato and Aristotle, see Allen 2000.

7. This restriction of the magistracies to certain property classes is actually consonant with Athenian practice. Hansen observes that Solon excluded the *thêtes* from all state offices, and allowed only citizens from the top class (for the treasurers of Athena) or top two classes (for the nine archons) to serve in the most important offices; he notes some evidence that by the fourth century these restrictions seem to have fallen into abeyance, but also countervailing evidence in which property class continued to matter in various ways (Hansen 1999: 30, 45).

8. In fact, the election of the generals (*stratêgoi*) was not Solonic, but Cleisthenic, and seems to have been open to the top three classes from the beginning; while the treasurers of Athena were from the time of Solon to that of Aristotle chosen by lot, but from the highest property class only (note, however, the seemingly paradoxical statement of fourth-century practice in the *Ath. Pol.*, 47 1: "there are ten Treasurers of Athena, one picked by lot from each tribe; in accordance with Solon's law (which is still in force) they must be *pentacosiomedimni*, but the man picked by lot holds office even if he is very poor," trans. Moore). Aristotle's point in naming only these two offices, one chosen by lot and the other by election, may be to highlight that the selectivity of Athenian magistracies comes from the varying property restrictions which apply to them.

9. One example is Kraut 2002: 405, who takes "deliberation and judgment" at 1281b31 to signal that Aristotle "is thinking of the familiar legal apparatus of assemblies . . . and courts," although at 406–7 he notes rightly that Aristotle is also thinking of the institutions of *euthuna* and *archairesia*. Another is Schofield 2011:299, translating *meizonôn* at 1282a38 as "the bigger things" and construing these as the big issues controlled by the council, assembly, and courts. But I suggest that *meizonôn* there is "the greater [officials]": it picks up "the most important offices" (*tas megistas archas*) being held by those "with high property assessments" (*apo megalôn*) at 1282a31–32, and makes these comparative in contrast with *plêthos*.

10. Hansen 1999: 159–60, 233–35.

11. Hansen 1999: 218–20.

12. Hansen 1999: 222–24. There was also a distinct board of ten selected from the council, also called *logistai*, who "prytany by prytany, inspected the administration of public funds by the magistrates": Hansen 1999: 360–61.

13. Reeve 1998 offers the useful parallel of *Generation of Animals* 728a26–30, where menstrual fluid is said to be "not pure" sperm and so to need to be acted upon by the latter to produce a baby, and a parallel is drawn with ripening fruit, which possesses nourishment that needs to be acted upon to be made more pure.

14. While this verb could refer to the specific Athenian individual liturgy of organizing a chorus which could involve a sacrificial meal if victorious (Wilson 2000: 102), I follow the standard Greek dictionary (Liddell and Scott, rev. Jones) in giving the verb in this incidence a more general and metaphorical meaning of "supply, furnish" (*chorêgeô*, q.v., where this passage is listed).

15. Ober 2005: 238 and Ober 2013: 110; Waldron 1995: 567; Wilson 2011: 264.

16. Cammack 2013 which was shared with me after a full version of this contribution had been submitted to the editors of the volume, offers a challenge to the "potluck" reading similar to mine here, though we differ in our views of the institutional referents that may be intended and the extent to which a specific institutional referent may be intended at all, as will be explained in what follows.

17. Ober 2013.

18. Figueira 1984: 90.

19. Cammack 2013 dismisses the relevance of Spartan common meals on the grounds that Aristotle elsewhere compares them unfavorably to the Cretan version. But that is no reason to dismiss the relevance of the Spartan case to Aristotle's distinction: he would be using it to make a logical point, not endorsing its value.

20. Figueira 1984: 89–90, who notes that the fact that these later sources state the amount of the *opsônion* in money is not necessarily surprising, since in the fifth and fourth centuries at least Spartans are known to have kept stores of gold and silver, and to have habitually calculated in foreign currencies when serving abroad (*pace* Ober 2013, who suggests that since Plutarch tells us more generally that Spartans did not use gold or silver money, they could not have reckoned their mess contributions in financial terms). I am indebted to Josh Ober for constructive challenges that prompted me to rethink my argument in this section of the chapter, and for sharing with me his own views and work.

21. I discuss these references and Aristotle's criticism of aspects of the Spartan practice below.

22. Wilson 2011: 264.

23. Compare *Pol.* VI 7, 1321a35–39, where Aristotle discusses *hestiasis* in a well-ordered oligarchy. I owe this reference to Kinch Hoekstra.

24. Schmitt Pantel 1992: 121–31; Wilson 2000: 24.

25. Against Hansen 1999: 114, she rereads a speech of Demosthenes (39.7–8) to suggest that this is not ruled out, since there both *hestiator* and *trierarchon* are referred to in the singular when the change in personnel for the latter liturgy to a plural group had already taken place. See Cammack 2013.

26. Strict logic would actually allow that it is possible for one person to be so rich that he or she can contribute more than everyone else combined. But Aristotle does not seem to have held that to be a practical political possibility anywhere in the argument of Book III. So in calling his argument "logical," I do not mean that it is logically watertight on this point, but that it is an argument which is independent of any particular case for a certain political outcome.

27. Waldron 1995: 569.

28. Cammack 2013 rightly observes that there is no verb in this sentence, and suggests reasons to infer that it could be meant to be something like "supply," in order to read "part" (*morion*) as "part of virtue" in both analogies, so meaning here that each member of the judging group supplies a part of virtue. But I follow most translators and commentators in assuming that it is most likely in Greek, where no verb is given, to supply the relevant verb from the previous sentence (in this case "judge," *krinein*), so meaning "judge part of the tragedy."
29. Wilson 2011: 264–65.
30. Comedies in contrast were judged as individual plays.
31. An alternative reading is developed by Cammack 2013, who like me stresses the aggregative logic in these examples generally. Schofield 2011: n.18, takes "all judge all" to be something like "communal reflection on each others' contributions."
32. Lane 2013 discusses the relation between *archein* (rule) and *hai archai* (offices) in Plato's *Statesman*.
33. Schumpeter 1996 [1943]: 232–83.
34. Bouchard 2011: 172 likewise points out (in French) the "minimal" nature of the participation of the multitude constituted by their role in the *euthuna* or inspections of officials.
35. Schumpeter 1996 [1943]: 247.

# 11 Faction

In the fifth book of the *Politics* Aristotle discusses the issue of change in political constitutions.[1] He focuses primarily (though not exclusively) on constitutional changes which are brought about by faction (*stasis*).[2] In this chapter I examine Aristotle's account of faction. I support two main theses:

1. Aristotle distinguishes different types of faction based on the diverse motives of agents of faction. Those who start faction may be motivated by a wide variety of considerations ranging from ideological concerns to personal vengeance.

2. Aristotle studies the phenomenon of faction from two related but distinct perspectives. On the one hand, he tries to explain the phenomenon of faction by reference to factors which influence the psychology of those who start faction. On the other, he offers a sociological account of the origins of faction in terms of ideological conflict and the injustice of the constitution.

The chapter is divided into three sections. In the first section I try to substantiate the first thesis. In particular I argue that Aristotle distinguishes two different types of faction: politically motivated faction and faction due to personal rivalry. I draw a further distinction within the first type of faction. On the one hand, those who desire

Earlier drafts of this chapter were presented at a workshop of the Yorkshire Network for Ancient Philosophy at the University of Hull and at a seminar at Queen's College, Oxford. I have benefited from comments received on both occasions. For written comments I am particularly grateful to the editors of this volume and to Melissa Lane, Stephen Priest, Esther Rogan, and Andrés Rosler.

greater political power may believe that their current constitution deprives them of their fair share of political power. I call this subtype of politically motivated faction "injustice-induced faction." On the other, the desire for greater political power may be triggered by an unjust desire to have more. I call the second subtype of politically motivated faction "greed-induced faction." These diversely motivated factions have common political consequences. The generated political dissent threatens the existence of the constitution.

In the remaining two sections I focus on the second thesis. In the second section I explore Aristotle's psychological account of politically motivated faction. I argue that Aristotle draws a distinction between three different factors which influence the psychology of agents of faction. First, he identifies a nexus of beliefs and desires that inclines the agents to start faction but does not always suffice to propel them to act. Second, he identifies the ends that those who start faction pursue. Third, he identifies what I call "motivational enablers" which are reasons that strengthen the resolve of those who are already inclined to start faction.

In the third section I focus on Aristotle's sociological account which explores how political structures and ideologies effect political changes. He locates the origin of faction in the injustice of the constitution which is conceived as a political structure, namely, an organization of political offices. He relates the injustice of the constitution to the ideology of the ruling class.

## TYPOLOGY OF FACTION

The general theme of the fifth book of the *Politics* is constitutional change. The first type of constitutional change Aristotle distinguishes is change *of* constitutions, for example, change from democracy to oligarchy (V 1, 1301b6–10). But constitutional change is not always a change of constitutions. Sometimes the constitution remains the same but simply changes hands (V 1, 1301b10–13). Sometimes constitutional change is a matter of degree. For example, a certain city-state may become more or less democratic (V 1, 1301b13–17). Finally, sometimes one part (primarily a governing institution) and not the whole of the constitution changes (V 1, 1301b17–26).

These types of constitutional change share a common feature. The manner (*tropon*) in which constitutional change occurs involves the use of force or deception (V 4, 1304b5–17). In this respect the constitutional changes which are the object of Book V differ significantly from legitimate transfers of power within a constitution (for example, through elections or rules of succession).

Aristotle identifies faction as a major vehicle of constitutional change. I translate with "faction" the Greek word *stasis*. Finley calls *stasis* a "portmanteau-word."[3] It covers a wide spectrum of conflicts ranging from personal rows to political dissent. In the context of Book V of the *Politics, stasis* denotes a specific type of private or political conflict that threatens the constitution.[4] The translation of *stasis* as "revolution" is not altogether successful, because "revolution" has implications which do not accord with uses of *stasis* in the *Politics*. For example, Aristotle uses *stasis* to describe conflicts between oligarchs which result in constitutional change. These could hardly be characterized as "revolutions." "Faction" is preferable as a translation of *stasis* since it both captures the idea that the relevant conflict threatens the constitution and names types of political dissent not captured by "revolution." "Faction" has an additional advantage as a translation of *stasis* as it successfully conveys the dual meaning of *stasis*, which may denote not only the conflict people engage in but also a group of people who engage in the conflict.[5]

The motives of those who start faction are a major focus of Aristotle's study of faction in Book V. He illustrates those motives by adducing an array of historical examples, from which we can reconstruct an interesting typology of faction.[6] I call the first type of faction Aristotle distinguishes "politically motivated faction". At V 2, 1302a31–34 (a passage which I discuss in detail in the section on the psychology of faction) Aristotle claims that some of those who start faction aim at getting more political honors (and the wealth which accrues from them) than they possess under the current constitution.[7] These agents of faction are clearly motivated by political considerations. He also remarks that the desire for increased political power is sometimes just and sometimes unjust (V 2, 1302a28–29), which introduces a further distinction between two subtypes of politically motivated faction.

First, those who start political faction may be motivated by a sense of political injustice; namely, they may believe that the constitution deprives them of their due share of political power. Aristotle mentions relevant cases in the first chapter of Book V. He discusses factions started by the rich in democracies and the people (i.e. the poor) in oligarchies.[8] In both cases those who start faction believe that they hold less political power than they deserve. This belief is partly justified, as both the oligarchic and the democratic principles of distribution of political power contain some justice (*dikaion ti*; V 1, 1301a25–36). I will call this subtype of politically motivated faction "injustice-induced faction."

Factions motivated by a sense of political injustice are not restricted to factions started by the rich in democracies or the people in oligarchies. They may also be started by rich people who are discriminated against within the context of a specific form of oligarchy (for relevant cases see V 6, 1305b2–16). The discrimination may arise from specific qualifications of the oligarchic principle of distribution of political power (for example, in certain oligarchies relatives may be precluded from holding office simultaneously).

Aristotle identifies another motivating factor which operates in the political realm. It primarily consists in a desire to have more (*pleonektein*). This desire is a predominant motivating force of actions of the notables rather than the people: "the majority of citizens ... are quite content with an equal share; whereas if the rich are granted superiority by the constitution, they act arrogantly and try to get even more for themselves (*hubrizein zêtousin kai pleonektein*)" (V 7, 1307a18–20). Aristotle explicitly assumes that the actions of the notables in oligarchies and aristocracies are determined by this desire to have more: "Because all aristocratic constitutions are oligarchic in character the notables in them tend to get more" (V 7, 1307a34–35).

In these passages the aims of the notables are political. In accordance with his account of the aims of those who start faction at V 2, 1302a31–34, we should understand that these notables do not simply want to get any type of honor or profit. Rather, they desire to attain political honors and the profit which accrues from the possession of political power. So when Aristotle speaks of the notables' desire to have more, he does not have in mind some general acquisitiveness but rather a specific and excessive desire for political power.

Aristotle understands this motivating factor to be different from a sense of political injustice. First, the association of the desire to have more with arrogance (*hubrizein*) suggests that in this context this desire is intrinsically unjust.[9] By contrast, as we have seen, he allows that the sense of political injustice which motivates the rich in democracies or the people in oligarchies to start faction is just to an extent. Second, considerations of political injustice motivate people when they are not in power. But once they are in power, considerations of political injustice become immaterial to them. As Aristotle remarks, "equality and justice are always sought after by the weaker party; the strong (*oi kratountes*) pay no heed to them" (VI 3, 1318b4–5).

Some cases of politically motivated faction Aristotle mentions are best understood as having been caused by this excessive desire for political power rather than by a sense of political injustice. These cases include politically motivated factions which are caused by the rivalry of oligarchs who seek popular leadership (*dêmagôgountôn*) (V 6, 1305b22–39). These ambitious oligarchs try to gain more political power than they already possess by currying favor with either the people or other oligarchs. As Newman observes, they act "with a view to their own aggrandizement."[10] We may understand in a similar fashion the predominant motive of two further kinds of agent of faction: the tyrants who started as popular leaders (V 10, 1310b14–31) and the notables in aristocracies who try to become monarchs (V 7, 1307a2–5).[11]

We may thus identify a second subtype of politically motivated faction.[12] It is actuated by an unjust desire to get more political power. For convenience I will summarily call it "greed-induced faction."

Apart from politically motivated faction, Aristotle identifies a second general type of faction. At the beginning of Chapter 4 of Book V Aristotle gives six examples of faction in which neither the primary motivation of those who initiate factional conflict nor the ends of their actions are political. In all these examples, factions arise from what he calls "small" (*smikrôn*) issues (V 4, 1303b18). The first is an example of a rivalry between two young members of the ruling class in an oligarchy concerning a matter of love (V 4, 1303b20–26). The second concerns a quarrel between two brothers over an inheritance (V 4, 1303b32–37). The remaining four examples concern fights between notables concerning issues of marriage to heiresses in which one of the rival parties felt insulted (V 4, 1303b37–1304a17). In the first example a faction was initiated by a rivalry between two notables or two families and then divided all members of the ruling class (V 4, 1303b25–26). In the other examples the whole city joined in the faction (V 4, 1303b31–32).

It is plausible to assume that in these examples those who initiate a factional conflict are moved by anger (see the use of *chalepênas*: V 4, 1303b24) and seek revenge. They are subjects of arrogant treatment (*hubristhentes*; V 4, 1304a2), and, as Aristotle observes, "[p]eople are particularly apt to be led by their angry spirit on account of arrogant treatment" (V 10, 1312b29–30). He also remarks that "most angry people act out of revenge not ambition" (V 10, 1311a34–36). Furthermore, those who initiate a factional conflict are all members of the ruling class and there is no suggestion that their political rights are in any sense restricted. In this respect they differ significantly from, on the one hand, the poor in oligarchies or the rich in democracies and, on the other, some rich people who are excluded from political power in oligarchies. So, their anger neither stems from nor is coupled with political discontent. We can thus say that they are not motivated by political considerations and their actions do not have a clear political end.

Aristotle indicates that he wants to differentiate factions due to personal rivalry from factions that have a clear political end. In Chapter 6 (1306a31–b1), he singles out the kind of faction he mentions in the examples at the beginning of Chapter 4 (which, as we have seen, are motivated by a desire for revenge) as an independent cause of the destruction of oligarchies. This cause of the destruction of oligarchies is differentiated from other causes which involve factions motivated by political considerations, like a desire to share in political power by those excluded by the oligarchic constitution (V 6, 1305a37–b22), or by an unjust desire for more political power (V 6, 1305b22–39).

Though factions due to personal rivalry do not have direct political ends, they may have important political consequences. Like politically motivated factions which aim directly at constitutional change, they also pose a threat to the constitution. This is why Aristotle claims that the factions arising from small issues (like personal disputes about a love affair or an insult) are about important issues

(V 4, 1303b17–18).[13] So, what unifies factions is not that they are initiated by people who have direct political ends or motives but rather
that they have important political consequences, namely, that they
put the existing constitution at risk.[14]

Nevertheless, politically motivated faction, and in particular
injustice-induced faction, is more central to Aristotle's explanatory
account of faction than faction due to personal rivalry. First, in his
psychological account of the origins of faction in Chapter 2 (which I
discuss in the following section) Aristotle refers exclusively to politically motivated faction. Second, in his sociological account of faction (which I discuss in the section on the sociology of faction) he
focuses exclusively on injustice-induced faction. We have, thus, reason to think that he treats politically motivated faction and in particular injustice-induced faction as the paradigmatic type of faction.

### PSYCHOLOGY OF FACTION

The fact that Aristotle offers a typology of faction based on the
motives of agents of faction indicates that political psychology forms
a significant part of his study of faction. The importance he ascribes
to political psychology is further evinced in his account of the general causes of faction in Chapter 2 of Book V, which focuses on politically motivated faction.[15] Aristotle identifies three different general
causes of politically motivated faction. The first relates to the mental
states of those who start faction, primarily their dominant motivating beliefs and desires (V 2, 1302a20–31). The second concerns the
aims of agents of faction (V 2, 1302a31–34). Aristotle takes the third
cause to be concerned with "origins" (archai) and "causes" (aitiai)
of faction which are connected with the mental states and aims of
agents of faction (V 2, 1302a34–35) (though the precise nature of this
connection is not straightforwardly clear). Thus, Aristotle traces the
causes of faction to elements of the psychology of agents of faction.

How should we understand each one of these causes and how are
they related to each other? Aristotle gives the following account of
the first cause:

Those who desire equality start faction when they believe that they are getting less, even though they are the equals of those who are getting more;
whereas those who desire inequality (that is to say, superiority) do so when

they believe that though they are unequal, they are not getting more but the same or less. (Sometimes these desires are just, sometimes unjust.) For inferiors start factions in order to be equal, and equals do so in order to be superior. So much for the condition of those who start faction. (V 2, 1302b24–31)

The mental states Aristotle refers to are a nexus of beliefs and desires. The agents of faction believe that the constitution treats them unfairly. This belief is conditioned by their views about the extent of political power they deserve (which in the following section I identify with their political ideology). Those who start faction desire to implement their preferred principle of distribution of political power. This account of the mental states of agents of faction fits nicely the condition of the rich in democracy and of the people in oligarchy, cases which Aristotle mentions in Chapter 1.[16] In democracy the rich believe that they deserve more political power than they actually hold and desire to establish a political order which guarantees that they get more. In oligarchy the people believe that they are getting less political power than they deserve and desire to change the constitution so that they actually achieve equal political power.

Aristotle's elliptical remark that sometimes the desire to implement a new constitution may be unjust indicates that he intends the first cause to account for the condition of agents of greed-induced faction, as well as agents of injustice-induced faction. The cause of this subtype of politically motivated faction would again be a nexus of beliefs and desires of agents of faction, primarily, their unjust desire to have more coupled with the belief that the distribution of political power under the current constitution does not satisfy their political ambitions.

The second cause of faction concerns the ends for the sake of which people start faction. According to Aristotle, these ends are either the attainment of political honors and the material profits which accrue to one or one's friends from the possession of political power,[17] or the avoidance of political dishonor and fines (V 2, 1302b31–33). Aristotle shifts from the beliefs and desires of agents to the ends the agents aim at achieving by starting faction. This account of the ends of agents of faction further elucidates their mind-set.

Aristotle provides the following account of the third cause:

The cause and origins of the changes, in the sense of the factors that dispose people to feel the way we described [that is, in the account of the first cause of faction in Chapter 2] about the issues we mentioned [that is, about the ends of faction as described in the account of the second cause of faction in Chapter 2], are from one point of view seven in number and from another more. Two are the same as those just mentioned, but not in their manner of operation. For people are also stirred up by profit and honor and not simply in order to get them for themselves, which is what we said before, but because they see others, whether justly or unjustly, getting more. Other causes are: arrogance, fear, superiority, contempt, and disproportionate growth. Still other ones, although operating in another way, are electioneering, carelessness, gradual alteration, and dissimilarity. (V 2, 1302a34–b5)

I would like to make two initial remarks about this passage. First, it is not clear why Aristotle thinks that electioneering, carelessness, gradual alteration, and dissimilarity operate in a different way from the other factors which fall under the rubric of the third cause. One possible explanation is that in contrast to those factors they do not always causally contribute to the occurrence of factional conflict.[18] Electioneering, carelessness, and gradual alteration may sometimes cause constitutional change without causing faction (V 3, 1303a13–25). Dissimilarity (or, more precisely, the political empowerment of dissimilar groups)[19] may cause faction only in societies that have not yet learned how to properly integrate dissimilar groups (V 3, 1303a25–26).

Second, honor and profit are mentioned in both the second and the third cause, but their manner of operation is different. In his account of the second cause Aristotle refers to the attainment of honor and profit (or the avoidance of dishonor and fines) by the agent and his friends. Furthermore, honor and profit are the ends of faction. By contrast, in his account of the third cause Aristotle refers to the perception that people other than the agent (or his friends) are achieving honor or profit. This perception functions as a motivational enabler of political factions in a sense which I explain shortly.

What is the relation between the third cause and the other two causes Aristotle identifies in Chapter 2? It has been suggested that the causal factors which come under the heading of the third cause are temporally prior to the other two causes and in fact cause the agents of faction to realize that they are worse off under the constitution and to desire its change.[20] The idea is that, for example, an occasion of extreme arrogance by the rich in an oligarchy may make the poor realize that they are treated unfairly, create in them a desire for equal political power, and lead them to actions which aim at the attainment of political honor and profit.

This interpretation, however, does not square with the level of entrenchment of the relevant mental states and aims of either the oligarchs or the democrats which motivate them to start faction.[21] The unwillingness of the rich (as well as of anyone who has abundance of external goods) to be ruled (coupled with lack of knowledge of what is involved in obeying someone else) is "a characteristic they acquire right from the start at home while they are still children; for because of their luxurious lifestyle they are not accustomed to be being ruled even in school)" (IV 11, 1295b15–18). It is presumably similar early habituation to a life of subservience and lack of resources which makes the poor accustomed to being ruled like slaves (IV 11, 1295b19–20), fills them with envy for the rich (IV 11, 1295b21), and makes them desirous of their wealth (IV 11, 1295b31–32). So, the relevant mental states and aims of either the oligarchs or the democrats which come under the rubric of the first two causes grow out of deeply rooted character traits of agents of faction fostered by early habituation to particular lifestyles.

I suggest an alternative interpretation of the relation between the third cause and the other two causes Aristotle identifies in Chapter 2. On this interpretation the nexus of beliefs, desires, and ends of agents of faction captured by Aristotle's account of the first two causes is considered an entrenched feature of their psychology. This entrenched feature inclines them towards starting faction. But it may not suffice to propel them to act. The agents may consider certain conflicting reasons which may disincline them from starting faction and prevail in their practical deliberations. These reasons involve negative assessments of the prospects of the success of a revolt. As Aristotle observes, when the people acquire great power the rich may be unwilling to engage in faction, and vice versa. Similar considerations prevent the truly virtuous from starting faction (V 4, 1304b2–5).

Sometimes, however, these inhibitions are overcome. I suggest that this is because additional reasons strengthen the underlying beliefs and desires of the agents which incline them to factionalize or weaken the strength of the averting reasons. The causes of political faction which come under the rubric of the third cause in Chapter 2 are additional reasons of this kind. For example, the arrogance or the acquisitiveness of the rulers in an oligarchy may lead the people to overcome their doubts about the prospect of a revolt and to resolve to start faction. Similarly, the fear of some notables that the people may be plotting against them (see e.g., the case mentioned at V 3, 1302b22–24) may weaken any reservations which kept their inclination to factionalize in check and lead them to action. In the same manner the practical deliberations of agents of faction may be influenced by their perception of others getting honors or themselves being dishonored (V 2, 1302b10–14); their gaining superior power (V 3, 1302b15–21); their contempt towards the political order established by the constitution (V 3, 1302b25–33); the disproportionate growth of their class (V 3, 1302b33–1303a25); or the political empowerment of an ethnically different tribe (V 3, 1303a25–1303b3).[22]

These reasons function as "motivational enablers," in the sense that they enable the entrenched beliefs and desires of the agents that incline them to start faction to propel the agents to action. They defeat any countervailing considerations which restrained the beliefs and desires in favor of faction. In the absence of such motivational enablers, although the agents may feel discontented with the existing constitution and be inclined to start faction, they may never start faction.

Motivational enablers depend in an important sense on the entrenched beliefs and desires of the agents. As we have already seen, Aristotle indicates that the factors that come under the heading of the third cause relate to the operations of the first cause. Arrogance, for example, does not by itself *directly* cause faction. It causes faction by strengthening the motivational clout of the sense of injustice which already permeates the hearts of agents of faction or by defeating countervailing considerations. Thus, arrogance operates differently in politically motivated factions which are the subject of Chapter 2 than in factions due to personal rivalry. There, the arrogance of a notable generates in the heart of his victim a desire for revenge which becomes the starting point of faction. In that case, the arrogance of the notable is not a consideration which is to be added to pre-existing reasons in favor of faction or defeats some averting reasons but creates *ab initio* a reason for faction.

Motivational enablers operate both in cases in which one has a partly justified sense of not having received one's due in political terms and in cases in which one harbors unjust political ambitions due to greed. For though one's unjust ambitions may incline one to start faction, they may be outweighed by averting considerations relating, for example, to the negative prospect of realizing one's ambition. But some additional considerations may change one's perception of the balance of reasons. For example, political superiority may strengthen one's resolve to pursue political ambitions and help one to overcome previous inhibitions.

What kind of entities count as causes on Aristotle's three-fold account of the causes of faction? As we have seen, the first cause comprises mental states, namely, beliefs and desires, and the second cause comprises ends of actions. The third cause is not unified. Some motivational enablers are mental states of the agents of faction: envy for the honors others receive, fear of punishment or unfair treatment, contempt for the constitution and its officers. Others, however, are the objects of mental states of agents of faction rather than the corresponding mental states themselves. For example, Aristotle identifies the arrogance of officials, that is, their acquisitive behavior, as a cause of faction rather than the poor's perception of the acquisitive behavior of officials. In a similar manner Aristotle speaks of the superiority of an individual, that is, his actual possession of superior power or wealth, as the cause of faction, and not of the sense of superiority he may enjoy. And it is the actual disproportionate growth of one class and the actual political empowerment of dissimilar groups, rather than the perceived growth and the perceived political empowerment, respectively, which count for Aristotle as causes of faction.

The identification of certain causes with objects of mental states, rather than the corresponding mental states themselves, accords with relevant ordinary uses of "cause." For example, when I say that the perpetrator's arrogance caused the victim's outburst I mean to identify the arrogant behavior of the perpetrator and not the victim's perception of it as the relevant cause. Though it is true that if the victim were unaware of the perpetrator's arrogant behavior she might be able to control the disposition to initiate faction, the point I want to make is that it is the perpetrator's behavior that makes the victim unable to control herself. If someone interpreted my statement as meaning that the victim's perception of the perpetrator's arrogant behavior caused her outburst I would respond that she has missed the point of my statement. In a similar manner, Aristotle should be understood as conveying the idea that the actual arrogant behavior of oligarchs – and not the poor's perception of that behavior – causes the poor to start faction (by making them overcome their inhibitions and fostering their desire for equal political power).

It is clear then that in Chapter 2 Aristotle tries to elucidate the psychology of politically motivated faction. He identifies the main mental states which incline the agents to start faction and the aims of agents of faction. He also singles out reasons (some of which are mental states of the agents and some of which are objects of relevant mental states) which enable the agents to overcome their inhibitions and start faction.

### SOCIOLOGY OF POLITICAL FACTION

Aristotle does not try to explain the origins of faction only by reference to elements of human psychology. He also offers what I call a "sociological" account of faction which focuses on class ideology and the constitution understood as a political structure, namely, an organization of political offices. On this account what causes faction is an aspect of the constitution, namely, its injustice. The injustice of the constitution consists in a mistaken principle of distribution of political offices. For example, the injustice of democracies and oligarchies consists in their failure to combine proportionate and numerical equality in the distribution of political offices, while the injustice of so-called aristocracies and polities consists in the wrong mixture of democracy and oligarchy. What counts as the cause of faction from Aristotle's sociological perspective is the injustice of the constitution per se and not the mental states of agents of faction, such as their perception of the injustice of the constitution or their sense of being treated unfairly in political terms. An unjust constitution comes about once the ideology of the ruling class is implemented.

Aristotle's interest in the sociology of faction becomes clear in the first chapter of Book V. There, Aristotle links the causes of political factions to one of the two main factors that explain the diversity of constitutions.[23] The first factor relates to the actual class stratification of a city-state.[24] By "class stratification" I understand the stratification of the three traditional Greek classes: the well-born, the rich, and the free men. Aristotle alludes to this factor in Chapter 1 when he remarks that given that wealth and freedom are more widespread than good birth and virtue, two constitutions primarily arise: oligarchy and democracy (V 1, 1301b39–1302a2). Aristotle's remark relates to his more general thesis that different people are suited for different constitutions, a claim he elaborates at III 17, 1288a6–29. Aristotle explains that different multitudes may be naturally suited for aristocracy, polity, or kingship. Thus, the actual class stratification of an existing city-state may explain the diversity not only of deviant but also of correct constitutions.[25]

The second factor is more complex. Aristotle describes it as follows:

Many constitutions have come into existence because, though everyone agrees about justice (that is to say, proportional equality), they are mistaken about it...For democracy arose from those who are equal in some respect thinking themselves to be unqualifiedly equal; for because they are equally free, they think they are unqualifiedly equal. Oligarchy, on the other hand, arose from those who are unequal in some respect taking themselves to be wholly unequal; for being unequal in property they take themselves to be unqualifiedly unequal. The result is that the former claim to merit an equal share of everything, on the grounds that they are all equal, whereas the latter, being unequal, seek to get more (for a bigger share is an unequal one). (V 1, 1301a26–36)

The principle of distribution of political power is unqualifiedly just when it accords with the general principle of proportionate equality of benefits. The principle of proportionate equality states that the distributed benefits should be proportionate to the merit of their recipients (see *Nicomachean Ethics* V 3). Given that the distribution of *political* power is concerned, the relevant merit of individuals must be determined on the basis of their contribution to the political life of the city-state.[26] At *Politics* III 12, 1283a14–22, Aristotle states two criteria according to which the contribution of individuals to the political life of the city-state is assessed. The first criterion concerns the contribution of individuals to the existence of the city-state. On this criterion all three traditional Greek classes, the well-born, the wealthy, and the free-born, have some legitimate claim to political offices and power. The second criterion relates to how well individuals would manage the city-state if they were given political power. As Aristotle clarifies, to satisfy the second criterion the possession of neither freedom nor wealth nor good birth suffices. Rather one must possess political virtue (III 9, 1281a1–8).

Thus, Aristotle relates the diversity of constitutions to mistaken views about the principle of distribution of political power. Each of the traditional Greek classes overstates the value of its contribution to the existence of the city-state and its management. The overstatement is gross. Each class believes that its own mark of status (good birth, wealth, or freedom) is the sole standard for the assessment of one's contribution to the existence of a city-state and its management. We may understand the content of these beliefs as comprising the political "ideology" of each class.

The content of the ideological beliefs of each class differs from the content of those beliefs which are treated as causes of faction according to Aristotle's account of the first cause in Chapter 2. The former beliefs are about the correct principle of distribution of political power; that is, they are about the amount of political power each class *deserves*. The latter beliefs are about how well each class *fares* in the current constitution. The relevant measure is the ideology of each class, that is, the views of each class about how much power each class deserves. Obviously, the former beliefs condition the latter; that is, democratic ideology furnishes the people in oligarchies with a framework of concepts and ideas that enables them to understand that they are treated unfairly as members of a political group (and not simply as private persons) and that the solution to their predicament is political (i.e. constitutional change).

The first factor of the diversity of constitutions allows us to explain the diversity of all constitutions, while the second factor allows us to explain the diversity only of deviant and some *mixed* constitutions.[27] As we have seen, Aristotle takes the oligarchic and democratic principles of the distribution of political power to misrepresent the unqualified principle of the distribution of political power and to be ideological constructs. By contrast, correct constitutions get it right about what is unqualifiedly just (III 6, 1279a17–19). So, we may formulate Aristotle's account of the diversity of constitutions in the first chapter of Book V as follows:

*Diversity of constitutions.* (a) Constitutions differ because of the different class stratification in different city-states; and (b) deviant and some mixed constitutions in particular also differ because of the different political ideologies of the traditional Greek classes.

Aristotle relates the cause of faction to (b) (V 1, 1301a25–26). He claims:

> All these constitutions [that is, oligarchies and democracies] possess justice of a sort (ti dikaion), then, although unqualifiedly speaking they are mistaken. And this is why (dia tautên tên aitian), when one or another of them does not participate in the constitution in accordance with their assumption [about the principle of distribution of political power], they start faction. (V 2, 1301a35–39)

In this passage Aristotle refers to injustice-induced faction. He traces its origin to the prevailing political ideology in a city-state. When the ideology of either the rich or the people prevails in a city-state, a distribution of political power is established which is deficient with respect to the unqualified standard of political justice. As a result, the classes which do not share in political power are treated unjustly in political terms.

It is important to stress that, according to Aristotle, those who are - excluded from political office in deviant constitutions do not simply think of themselves as being unjustly treated in political terms. Aristotle believes that they actually suffer some injustice; their political ideology rests on an overstated perception of their status and not on a complete misrepresentation of its value. As Aristotle puts it, oligarchy and democracy possess "justice of a sort" (dikaion ti; V 2, 1301a25–36). In normal circumstances all classes have some legitimate claim to political power.[28] At the very least they all contribute to the existence of the city.[29] So, when the political ideology of one class prevails in a city, the classes that are excluded from political power are in fact discriminated against.

We can ascribe to Aristotle the following explanatory schema of the occurrence of (injustice-induced) faction: political ideologies generate political injustice (understood as unjust distribution of political power) and political injustice in turn causes faction. On this schema, the proximate cause of faction is the political injustice which is incorporated in the principles of the constitution. The relevant political injustice results from the implementation of the political ideology of the ruling class.

At the beginning of Chapter 1 Aristotle focuses on the political ideology of oligarchy and democracy considered in general. His explanatory schema, however, applies equally to specific forms of oligarchy or democracy. For example, instead of speaking of the general oligarchic ideology, one might speak of the correctness of specific oligarchic principles of distribution of political power. According to these principles, there might be restrictions on the amount of wealth one would need to possess in order to hold political office. On the assumption that these principles depart from the principle of unqualified political justice, they will lead to systemic political injustice. In this case, it will not only be the poor who are treated unfairly but also possibly some rather wealthy individuals. Consequently it may not only be the poor who will start faction in oligarchies, but also those wealthy individuals who are politically discriminated against. This allows us to explain why Aristotle believes that oligarchies are threatened by two kinds of faction: the first is started by the people, while the second is started by some of the rich, namely, those who are politically discriminated against (V 1, 1302a9–11).[30]

As we have seen, the principle of distribution of political power must accord with the principle of unqualified proportionate equality. Unqualified political injustice amounts to unqualified political inequality. Furthermore, the debate between the opposing political ideologies of different classes may be described as a disagreement not only about what is unqualifiedly (politically) just but equivalently about what is unqualifiedly equal. This allows Aristotle to speak of inequality as the cause of factions (V 1, 1301b26–27).

Let us reflect on Aristotle's account of the cause of faction in Chapter 1. First, on this account only the deviant and some mixed constitutions become unstable due to faction. This accords with Aristotle's general thesis that the correct constitutions are devoid of faction (see III 15, 1286b1–3 and IV 11, 1296a7–9). Second, Aristotle focuses on two deviant constitutions, oligarchy and democracy, and their ideologies. This choice of focus makes good sense within the overall context of Aristotle's theory of constitutions. On the one hand, as Aristotle explicitly states in Chapter 1, most cities are governed either by oligarchs or by the people. On the other, the majority of the other constitutions, i.e. the so-called aristocracies and polities, are mixtures of oligarchy and democracy. As we will see, he clarifies that their principal source of demise is to be located in their failure to achieve a good mixture of oligarchy and democracy (V 7, 1307a6–11).

Third, political injustice or inequality is analyzed by Aristotle in structural terms, as an aspect of the constitution. Aristotle defines the constitution as a political structure, namely, an organization (*taxis*) of political offices (IV 3, 1290a7–13). A constitution is unjust if its organization of political offices departs from the principle of unqualified proportionate equality. More specifically, political injustice or inequality consists in incorrect adherence to a single principle of distribution of political offices or incorrect mixture of different principles of distribution of political offices. For example, in Chapter 1 Aristotle implies that democrats treat political equality essentially as numerical equality, while oligarchs use proportionate equality for the distribution of all offices.[31] Consequently, in democracies all political power is distributed on what amounts to the principle of numerical equality (that is, offices of equal value are distributed to free men) while in oligarchies on the principle of proportionate equality (that is, higher offices are distributed to the wealthier). (Presumably Aristotle thinks that unqualified proportionate equality entails that *some* offices may be distributed on what amounts to the principle of numerical equality: some offices of equal value may be distributed to free men.) This is where the mistake in these constitutions lies:

It is a bad thing for a constitution to be organized unqualifiedly and entirely in accord with either sort of equality. This is evident from what actually happens, since no constitution of this kind is stable. The reason (*aition*) is that when one begins from an erroneous beginning (*archê*), something bad inevitably results in the end. Hence numerical equality should be used in some cases, and equality according to merit in others. (V 1, 1302a2–8)

In Chapter 7, Aristotle traces the political injustice of (so-called) aristocracies and polities to their incorrect mixture of the oligarchic and democratic principles of distribution of political offices:

Polities and aristocracies are principally overthrown... because of a deviation from justice within the constitution itself.[32] For what begins the process (*archê*) in a polity is failing to get a good mixture of democracy and oligarchy, and in aristocracy, failing to get a good mixture of these and virtue as well, but particularly the two. I mean by the two democracy and oligarchy, since these are what polities and most so-called aristocracies try to mix. (V 7, 1307a5–12)

Fourth, it is clear from the last two cited passages that political injustice or inequality understood in structural terms is identified as a cause of faction. These two passages tell against an interpretation which credits Aristotle with what I call a "psychologically reductionist" account of the causes of political factions, according to which only the mental state of those who start factions, namely, their perception of political injustice or inequality, counts as a cause of faction.[33]

On the one hand, the incorrect adherence to a single principle and the incorrect mixture of different principles of distribution of political power, which are identified by Aristotle as causes of faction, are clearly not equivalent with or reducible to perceptions of injustice or inequality. On the other, as we have already seen in the section on the psychology of faction, Aristotle allows that objects of mental states and not the corresponding mental states themselves may be validly considered causes of faction. For example, for Aristotle it is the acquisitive behavior of the oligarchs which causes the revolt of the people and not the latter's perception of it. In a similar manner we may understand him as saying, for example, that it is the incorrect mixture of democracy and oligarchy which causes faction in polities and not the perception of incorrect mixture by the citizens. This way of identifying the cause of faction is in perfect harmony with ordinary ways of explaining social events. For example, one may explain social violence in the post-Reconstruction South by reference to the Jim Crow system (and its mistaken combination of segregation and equality), or one may treat apartheid as the cause of the revolt of black people in South Africa.

Thus, I believe that Aristotle offers a more complex explanation of the occurrence of injustice-induced faction than the reductionist interpretation allows for. Aristotle explains faction from two different perspectives, a sociological and a psychological perspective.[34] On the one hand, he traces the origin of faction to political injustice or inequality understood as an aspect of a political structure, namely, the constitution. Aristotle introduces this sociological account of the causes of faction in the first chapter of Book V of the *Politics*. On the other, he offers a psychological account of the causes of faction. He focuses on the motives of agents of faction and their aims. On this psychological account, a sense of political injustice counts as a cause of faction. It is the mental state which inclines people to start faction, directs their minds towards the attainment of political ends, and, in the presence of appropriate motivational enablers, propels them to act.

What is the relation between these two accounts of the causes of faction? The key to understanding their relation is found in a remark Aristotle makes in his presentation of the first cause of faction, namely, the entrenched beliefs and desires of agents of faction, in Chapter 2. He claims: "The principal general cause of people being in some way disposed to change their constitution [i.e. of people having the nexus of beliefs and desires which inclines them to start faction] is the one we have in fact already mentioned [i.e. in Chapter 1]" (V 2, 1302a22–24). Aristotle claims that the disposition of agents of faction, namely, the nexus of beliefs and desires which inclines them to start faction, is itself the outcome of the workings of the causal factors he discussed in Chapter 1, namely, the political injustice of the constitution and the ideology of each class. This means that, for example, the people in an oligarchy come to believe that they are treated unjustly in political terms and develop a desire for redistribution of political power because (a) they live in a city in which all political power is in the hands of oligarchs; and (b) they believe that they deserve equal political power.

We may understand the causal influence of political injustice and ideology on the nexus of beliefs and desires which inclines agents to start faction as follows. The distribution of political power within an institution shapes people's social lives by affecting their political options. Those who are deprived of political power are bound to feel resentment and envy and to desire to change their condition. Political resentment and envy feed on the entrenched psychological features of the rich and the poor which I have already mentioned, such as the unwillingness of the rich to be ruled, or the envy of the poor for the wealth of the rich. The political ideology of the oppressed furnishes them with a particular conceptual framework that enables them to account for their predicament, and with a set of normative ideals that enables them to shape their political ends. As a result they understand themselves as victims of political injustice; that is, they realize that they are discriminated against as members of a class.

They also understand that the remedy to their political predicament is constitutional change (and not, say, personal revenge). Consequently, they become inclined to take political action and start faction.

Thus, political injustice understood in structural terms relates in two ways to the mental states that motivate agents of faction. On the one hand, it is the object of those mental states: Agents of faction believe that the constitution wrongs them and desire to remedy its injustice. On the other, in conjunction with political ideology it is the cause of those mental states: it generates and shapes them. The injustice of the constitution generates in the people a sense that they are treated unfairly in political terms and a desire to change the constitution.

### CONCLUSION

Aristotle offers a comprehensive account of the nature of faction and its causes. He studies faction from two distinct perspectives. On the one hand, Book V may be read as an intriguing essay on the political psychology of faction. Aristotle explains faction by reference to elements of the psychology of agents of faction and presents a rich taxonomy of faction based on the diversity of their motives. On the other, he studies faction from a sociological perspective. From this perspective, the primary focus is not the agents of factions and their motives. Rather Aristotle focuses on the constitution of a city-state which is understood in structural terms as an organization of political offices. He traces the origin of faction to the injustice of the organization of political offices which results from the implementation of the ruling class's ideology.

### WORKS CITED

Barker, E. 1946. *The Politics of Aristotle*. Oxford University Press

De Ste Croix, G. E. M. 1981. *The Class Struggle in the Ancient World*. London: Duckworth

Finley, M. 1983. *Politics in the Ancient World*. Cambridge University Press

Kalimitzis, K. 2000. *Aristotle on Political Enmity and Disease*. Albany: SUNY Press

Keyt, D. 1999. *Aristotle Politics Books V and VI*. Oxford: Clarendon Press

Lukes, S. 1968. "Methodological Individualism Reconsidered." *British Journal of Sociology* 19: 119–29

Miller, F. D. 1995. *Nature, Justice and Rights in Aristotle's Politics*. Oxford: Clarendon Press

Mulgan, R. G. 1977. *Aristotle's Political Theory*. Oxford: Clarendon Press

Newman, W. L. 1887–1902. *The Politics of Aristotle*. 4 vols, Oxford University Press

Ober, J. 1991. "Aristotle's political sociology: class, status and order in Aristotle's *Politics*." In *Essays on the Foundation of Aristotelian Political Science*, eds. C. Lord and D. O'Connor. Berkeley, CA: University of California Press

Polansky, R. 1991. "Aristotle on Political Change." In *A Companion to Aristotle's Politics*, eds. D. Keyt and F. D. Miller. Oxford: Blackwell

Reeve, C. D. C. 1998. *Aristotle*, Politics. Indianapolis, IN: Hackett

Skultety, S. C. 2009. "Delimiting Aristotle's Conception of *Stasis* in the *Politics*." *Phronesis* 54: 346–70

Weed, R. 2007. *Aristotle on Stasis*. Berlin: Peter Lang

Wheeler, M. 1977. "Aristotle's analysis of the nature of political struggle." In *Articles on Aristotle*, vol. II, eds. J. Barnes, M. Schofield, and R. Sorabji. London: Duckworth

Yack, B. 1993. *The Problems of a Political Animal*. Berkeley, CA: University of California Press

NOTES

1. For discussions of the fifth book of the *Politics* see Newman 1887–1902; Mulgan 1977: 116–38; Wheeler 1977; Polansky 1991; Yack 1993: 209–41; Miller 1995: 276–308; Keyt 1999; Kalimitzis 2000; Weed 2007; and Skultety 2009. Throughout the chapter I use Reeve's (1998) translation.

2. Electioneering, carelessness in the selection of officials, or unnoticed small constitutional alterations may sometimes cause constitutional change without the occurrence of faction (*Pol.* V 3, 1303a13–25); see p. 283.

3. Finley 1983: 105.

4. For example, for Aristotle the private rivalry between two young notables counts as stasis (see *stasiasantôn*; V 4, 1303b21–22) even before other notables join in (i.e. before the rivalry acquires a political character) (V 4, 1303b25–26).

5. See Keyt 1999: 63–65.

6. I thus disagree with Skultety (2009: 349–51), who takes stasis to have a narrow scope and denote only a specific type of faction which is roughly equivalent to what I call "injustice-induced faction."

7. I agree with Wheeler (1977: 162) that when in Chapter 2 Aristotle mentions profit as one of the aims of those who start factions he has in mind material goods which result directly from possession of political power. Of course, Aristotle does not think that according to the principle of unqualified justice one should profit from one's possession of political office. He claims that "the most important thing in every constitution is for it to have the laws and the managements of other matters organized in such a way that it is impossible to make profit from holding office" (V 8, 1308b30–33).

8. Normally Aristotle equates the people (*dêmos*) with the poor when he refers to democracy. In the main text I use "the people" and "the poor" interchangeably.

9. Not all instances of having more and all desires to have more are unjust. Aristotle allows that sometimes the relevant desires are just (V 2, 1302b24–29) or more accurately just to an extent (in view of V 1, 1301a35–36). For example, the desire of the rich in democracies to have more political power is just to an extent. My point is that when the desire to have more is coupled with arrogance, as is the case in V 7, 1307a18–20, Aristotle takes it to be intrinsically unjust.

10. Newman 1887–1902, vol. 4: 352.

11. Aristotle mentions another case of political faction. He claims that in general those in power start faction when, after a superior achievement, they do not want to share power (V 4, 1304a37–38). This kind of faction can be reduced to the two subtypes of politically motivated faction I distinguished. If those rulers believe that they deserve as a matter of political justice a greater share of power, then they are moved out of a sense of injustice. If they are just greedy, they should be considered to start faction out of an intrinsically unjust desire to have more.

12. Recognition of the second species of political factions brings Aristotle's thought close to Thucydides', which recognizes the motivating power of political ambitions as a main cause of factions (*History* 3.82.6).

13. Cf. Keyt 1999: 94–95.

14. It is probably true that factions due to personal rivalry are not a threat to the constitution unless people who are motivated by political considerations join in. But this does not speak against distinguishing between important (i.e. political) and small (i.e. non-political) issues which are the starting-points of faction as Aristotle does. Another concern may be that issues of marriage in particular had important implications for the political and legal status of people. But Aristotle does not seem to have in mind the political and legal significance of marriages at the beginning of Chapter 4; otherwise he would not have considered factions over them to be about "small" issues.

There is a further complication concerning Aristotle's typology of faction. He mentions as a cause of the destruction of tyrannies and kingships attacks (*epitheseis*) against the *person* of the ruler (V 10, 1311a31–32). These attacks are contrasted to attacks against the *office* of the ruler (V 10, 1311a32) which have a clear political motive, i.e. a sense of political injustice (V 10, 1311a22–28). The attacks against the person of the ruler are motivated by a wide range of non-political, personal motives: inter alia, revenge (V 10, 1311a33–1311b6), disgust at sexual relations (V 10, 1311b7–23), and love of fame (the fame reached for killing a tyrant) (V 10, 1312a21–39). Though some of these attacks involve conspiracies or plots (V 10, 1311a39) and thus the collaboration of numerous people, Aristotle does not call these attacks "factions" (*staseis*). It is unclear why they do not count as factions arising from small issues which have nevertheless significant political consequences like factions due to personal rivalry. In this context Aristotle applies the label "faction" only to the revolts which start with those who participate in a tyranny (V 10, 1312b9–17) or a kingship (V 10, 1312b40–1313a1) (which I take to be greed-induced factions).

15. I will not examine how Aristotle's doctrine of four causes connects to his account of the causes of faction (for relevant discussion, see Polansky 1991 and Keyt 1999: 75–79). I am somewhat skeptical about the viability of the connection. First, as Keyt (1999: 75–76) admits "the explanatory framework of the four causes is scarcely visible in the *Politics*". Second, Aristotle draws a distinction between the ends of action and the psychological disposition of agents in the *Nicomachean Ethics* (VII 3, 1146b14–18) and in *Rhetoric* (I 10, 1368b27, 12, 1372a4–5) which maps the distinction between the first two causes in *Politics* V 2. But neither in the *Nicomachean Ethics* nor in *Rhetoric* does he relate this distinction to his doctrine of the four causes. Cf. Skultety 2009: 349 n. 5.

16. See his reference to the first chapter of Book V at *Politics* V 2, 1202a22–24; cf. the discussion at p. 293.

17. See above note 7.

18. This explanation has been suggested by Newman (1887–1902, vol. 4: 296); cf. Barker (1946: 206–8).

19. See below note 22.

20. See Skultety 2009: 350 ff.

21. Furthermore, the main textual evidence in its support is at best ambivalent. The relevant text reads: *ai d' aitiai kai archai tôn kinêseôn, othen autoi te diatithentai ton eirêmenon tropon kai peri tôn lechthentôn* (V 2, 1302b34–35). We need not, with Skultety, take this text to show that the factors which come under the rubric of the third cause *generate*

the relevant mental states and aims of agents of faction described in Aristotle's account of the first and the second cause. *Diatithentai* may signify something like "becoming in the grip of" the desire for political power. In this case, the third cause may be understood, not to generate a desire towards getting political power, but to turn this desire into the dominant motivation of the agent.

22. I assume that Aristotle ascribes causal significance not to the mere presence of an ethnically different group but to its political empowerment (say, its acquisition of citizenship rights). This becomes clear from the fact that Aristotle speaks of members of ethnically different groups as co-founders and late-settlers. I believe that Aristotle assumes that agents of faction have entrenched racist attitudes which are fostered by the political empowerment of an ethnically different group. Aristotle's remark that "every difference seems to result in factional division" (V 3, 1303b14) suggests that those entrenched racist attitudes are simply an aspect of one group's entrenched hostile attitudes towards any other different group. Aristotle gives another example of intra-group entrenched hostile attitudes: he claims that groups living in different locations of a city-state may end up in factional division (V 3, 1303b7–14). Again his point seems to be that the political empowerment of these groups, functioning as a motivational enabler, fosters the resolve of members of these groups to start faction. The political empowerment of dissimilar groups does not lead to faction in all societies but only in those in which groups have not learned yet how to cooperate (V 3, 1303a25–26).

23. Cf. the discussion of the diversity of constitutions in *Pol.* IV 3–4.

24. I use "class" rather loosely and not in its specific Marxist sense (cf. Finley 1983: 10). I cannot discuss here de Ste Croix's challenging Marxist interpretation of Aristotle's account of class conflict (1981: 69–80). For a criticism see Yack 1993: 209–18. For a contrast between Marxist and Weberian accounts of Aristotle's political sociology see Ober 1991.

25. Correct constitutions include kingship, aristocracy, and polity. Deviant constitutions include tyranny, oligarchy, and democracy. Apart from these six constitutions Aristotle mentions certain mixtures of democracy and oligarchy, the so-called aristocracies and polities. Newman (1887–1902, vol. 4: xii–xxi) and Miller (1995: 252 ff.) take so-called aristocracies and polities to be correct constitutions. As we will see, Aristotle allows that some aristocracies and polities (presumably the so-called aristocracies and polities) may be prone to faction because of a departure from justice within their constitution (V 7, 1307a5–7). This creates some doubt about whether so-called aristocracies and polities may count as correct constitutions.

26. This explains why Aristotle takes the aims of injustice-induced faction to be political honors and wealth which accrues from them (V 2, 1302a20–34) (see above note 7).

27. The so-called aristocracies and polities; cf. above note 25. Tyranny is also considered a mixture of ultimate oligarchy and ultimate democracy (V 10, 1310b3–4).

28. That is, excluding cases in which a supremely virtuous individual who exceedingly surpasses all other members of the city in virtue lives in a city (III 17, 1288a15–29). In these cases Aristotle believes that justice requires that this supremely virtuous individual be given absolute power and everyone else be subordinated to his authority.

29. It is possible that on the basis of his celebrated argument for the authority of the multitude (*Pol.* III 11) Aristotle believes that at least in some cases (III 11, 1281b15–17) the collective judgment of each class may be valuable to the management of the city.

30. Given that Aristotle has not introduced in Chapter 1 the unjust desire to have more as a political motive, I do not think that he refers to greed-induced faction at V 1, 1302a9–11. Furthermore, according to the logic of Aristotle's explanatory schema of the occurrence of faction, different forms of democracy may systemically discriminate against some of the poor free-men. However, as a matter of historical reality this is not so. Aristotle observes that in democracies, no serious factions arise among the people (V 1, 1302a11–13).

31. Given Aristotle's initial claim that both oligarchs and democrats agree that justice is proportionate equality (V 1, 1301a26–28), I take Aristotle to mean that the democrats' conception of proportionate equality amounts to numerical equality (see Newman 1887–1902, vol. 4: 291; cf. Keyt 1999: 73–74).

32. The relevant vehicle of the demise of so-called aristocracies and policies is faction. This becomes clear from the example of Thurii, which Aristotle uses to illustrate the change from a so-called aristocracy to democracy (V 7, 1307a27–33).

33. See e.g., Yack 1993: 218–24; Miller 1995: 277; Skultety 2009.

34. I am convinced by Lukes 1968 that nothing crucial hangs on the debate between methodological individualism and holism. For this reason I see no point in trying to ascertain in which of those opposing camps Aristotle can most plausibly be considered to belong.

# 12 Education, leisure, and politics

Aristotle's *Politics* ends with a whole book dedicated to the education of youth he judges appropriate for his ideal city. In scholarship on the *Politics*, not much literature has been devoted to this part, as if it represented no more than a sort of appendix or additional thoughts on a minor subject. But from Aristotle's point of view (and, perhaps, contrary to ours) this theme is absolutely central to his project.

In *Politics* III 9, Aristotle claims that true politics, and therefore true "political science," should aim at living well, and not just at barely living, and he therefore vigorously argues against the (in fact very Hobbesian and modern) minimalist view according to which politics is first of all a matter of making alliances in order to avoid war and conflict, with security as its main aim. For according to such a view, "law becomes an agreement, 'a guarantor of just behaviour towards one another,' as the sophist Lycophron said, but not such as to make the citizens good and just" (III 9, 1280b10–12). And since living well, or "happiness" (*eudaimonia*, that is, a human life that is truly worth living), consists in some activities according to some "excellences" (*aretai*, that is, both "moral virtues" and intellectual excellences) which require an appropriate education, one of the tasks of true politics, if it is to aim at living well, must therefore consist in providing citizens with an appropriate education. It is even the main task of politicians or legislators: "it is through habituation that legislators make the citizens good; this is what every legislator aims

I am grateful to the Assos audience for their criticisms and suggestions which helped me revise and (hopefully) improve my interpretation, and to Marguerite Deslauriers and Marco Zingano for their very helpful written comments on a penultimate draft of my chapter.

301

at, and if they fail to do it well, they miss their mark: precisely this distinguishes a good political constitution from a bad one" (*NE* II 1, 1103b2–6).[1]

In this chapter, I will first try to reconstruct how Aristotle defends this central claim. I will then review how he implements it.

## EDUCATION AND POLITICS

Before assessing why Aristotle attributed to politicians the task of education as their main concern, let us quickly review the main reasons why he took education to be absolutely crucial. As he says (in agreement with Plato) at the beginning of his *Nicomachean Ethics*, every human being can be defined as a being desiring happiness. In the foundational (yet famously disputed) so-called "function argument" at *NE* I 7, 1097b21–98a20, Aristotle seems to advocate a biological, or at least a biologically based, conception of what this desire amounts to: since human beings can be characterized in contrast to other animals as living beings endowed with *logos*, that is both language and reasoning, a typically human life should be characterized in the same way, and a good or happy human life should thus be defined as such a life lived according to some goods, or virtues. Many moderns have accused Aristotle of the naturalistic fallacy, implicitly passing from biological description to obviously normative content. But if Aristotle does take that main difference between human species and other animals as a biological given, he doesn't use it here as a biologically based argument. It is by an implicit and common agreement that we consider *logos* as the *conditio sina qua non* of human life in a normative sense, and the goods or virtues as the way this *logos* must be implemented in order to assess what a happy human life should amount to. A human life with no *logos* would amount to the life of a horse or an ox, which none of us would agree to live, and a human life deprived of all goods and virtues wouldn't be considered to be happy. As Aristotle declares in his *Politics*, not without humor, "no one would call a person blessedly happy who had no shred of courage, temperance, justice, or intelligence, and is afraid of the flies buzzing around him, stops at nothing to gratify his appetites for food or drink, betrays his dearest friends for a pittance, and has a mind as foolish and prone to error as a child's or a madman's" (VII 1, 1323a26–33). Moral virtues as well as intellectual excellences are goods without which nobody would be considered a happy man. But, of course, as Aristotle never tires of repeating (perhaps in part against some old aristocratic views), such excellences are never natural; they must be learned in one way or another. In such a perfectionist and eudaimonist view of human life, education is nothing marginal or simply negative (e.g. teaching the appropriate ways to behave in society), but absolutely central. We do need education in order to be able to become good, or virtuous, which is a prerequisite for living a happy life. Education is the first and main condition for fulfilling our natural desire for happiness.

Now, why should education be entrusted to the city, that is, more precisely, to legislators? I suggest that we consider the famous passage from the *Politics* in which Aristotle states that "man is a political animal" as providing us a first answer to this question:

A complete community, constituted out of several villages, once it reaches the limit of total self-sufficiency, practically speaking, is a city-state. It comes to be for the sake of living, but it remains in existence for the sake of living well. That is why every city-state exists by nature, since the first communities do. For the city-state is their end, and nature is an end; for we say that each thing's nature – for example, that of a human being, a horse, or a household – is the character it has when its coming-into-being has been completed. Moreover, that for the sake of which something is, that is to say, its end, is best, and self-sufficiency is both end and best. (I 2, 1252b27–53a1)

As many scholars have complained, the passage is highly compressed and convoluted, and the reader is left wondering what exactly Aristotle means by nature, and what the obviously central concept of self-sufficiency is intended to express. Without expanding on the elaborate controversies this passage has given rise to, it seems that the first thing we need to observe is that Aristotle is evidently using two different concepts of nature. On the one hand, he clearly enough affirms that human beings are political animals like other gregarious animals by nature, that is, by mere nature, or by what we would call instinct: like those other animals, we are naturally inclined to live with other members of our species. The family is in this sense a natural entity, and so is the city, since a city is an aggregate of villages (this is the traditional translation of the Greek *kômos*, but a better rendering of the word in this context would be "clan"), which is in turn an aggregate of families. But men are not only political animals in this naturalistic sense; they are also political animals in the sense that a city is what constitutes an end or perfection, and correlatively this justifies Aristotle's claim that the city is natural in this sense too. Here again, one may accuse Aristotle of the naturalistic fallacy, as he seems to shift from the first to the second sense of "nature" in an unjustified manner, as if because men were naturally inclined towards their fellow humans, they would necessarily find their end, or their happiness, in a city. But one should read Aristotle the other way around to see why he can so easily mix both senses in this passage: since, according to Aristotle, "nature does nothing in vain," it is precisely because a city is an end that makes possible our happiness, that we are naturally inclined to it. But why should a city constitute our end and enable our happiness?

The main concept here seems to be self-sufficiency (*autarkeia*), which is the concept Aristotle uses to describe his notion of the city as an end or a good. What does this concept mean? At first sight, one might think that the word must have a purely biological or economic sense: a city is self-sufficient in so far as it manages to be independent from outside as to its subsistence, and can therefore make its inhabitants self-sufficient too. And indeed, in his reconstruction of the birth of a city from families and clans, Aristotle asserts that men aggregate themselves because of their needs, for they couldn't survive alone. In this sense, as he says, "cities have formed for the sake of living," and he adds a little further on that, since human beings cannot be self-sufficient by themselves, "an impulse toward this sort of community exists by nature in everyone" (I 2, 1253a29–30). But clearly enough, this can't be all Aristotle wants to say in our passage. For the most important point is not only to live, but to live *well*. He explicitly declares that when it is self-sufficient, a city allows for such living well: the self-sufficiency that people seek as the central good of a city is thus self-sufficiency for living well. So the question is, again, what sort of good does a city provide its inhabitants in order to offer them self-sufficiency in their living well? I suggest that this is the question Aristotle intends to answer in this excerpt, which follows the previous one:

It is evident from these considerations, then, that a city-state is among the things that exist by nature, that a human being is by nature a political animal, and that anyone who is without a city-state, not by luck but by nature,

is either a poor specimen or else superhuman. Like the one Homer con-
demns, he is also "clanless, lawless, and homeless." For someone with such
a nature is at the same time eager for war, like an isolated piece in a board
game. And this is why a human being is more of a political animal than a
bee or any other gregarious animal. Nature makes nothing pointlessly, as we
say, and no animal has rational speech (*logos*) except a human being. A voice
is a signifier of what is pleasant or painful, which is why it is also possessed
by the other animals (for their nature goes this far: they not only perceive
what is pleasant or painful but signify them to each other). But speech is for
making clear what is advantageous or harmful, and hence also what is just
or unjust. For it is peculiar to human beings, in comparison to the other animals, that they alone have perception of what is good or bad, just or unjust,
and the rest. And it is community in these that makes a household and a
city-state." (I 2, 1253a1–18)

The text, I propose, offers two types of goods the city is supposed to
provide. The first part of this quotation can be interpreted as referring to the common activities people may share when living in a city.
As the Homer quotation makes clear, a "lawless and homeless" man
would favour an "internecine war" (as Homer says right after the passage Aristotle quotes), that is, he would refuse any collaborative war
against the common Trojan enemy; or he would stand like an "isolated piece" in a board game, not participating in the common game.
And, indeed, this is what Aristotle explicitly says in a parallel passage from his *History of Animals*: "Political animals are those whose
function (*ergon*) becomes one common thing, which not all the gregarious animals do. Such are the human being, the bee, the wasp,
the ant, and the crane" (I 1, 448a7–10). He strongly insists there that
what makes an animal a political animal (with the term "political"
obviously being very broad here, amounting to "social") is his ability
to engage in some shared and common activity (like making honey
in the case of bees, etc.). It seems, then, that the first good that the
city offers is the possibility of sharing activities.

   Moreover, if men have in common with some animals a predis-
position to sharing activities with their same-species fellows, Aristotle adds a crucial comparison: men are "more political than any of
these gregarious animals," and this is because – nature doing things
well – they have *logos*, rational speech, allowing them to express
their "sense of the good and bad" which is something "proper" to
them. The comparative "more political" sounds odd here, especially

since animals obviously do not share any type of city which would be at stake here. But what Aristotle probably wants to say by this is, first, that only humans, because they have *logos*, can share in activities that are typical of a city, and that they are thus political beings in a more genuine sense; and, second, because they are beings seeking to live well thanks to these activities (and not only living as in the case of animals), human beings are even more in need of a shared life than any other gregarious animal. Without such a life, indeed, as Aristotle repeats after Homer, you would be like a cyclops, which for the Greeks represented the wild, pre-human life,[2] as in the case of Philoctetes, who no longer partook in human life and no longer had an existence worth living.[3] Thus, since a flourishing or happy life consists in certain activities, our natural desire for happiness is necessarily linked to our natural propensity or desire for the shared life that make possible such activities. Aristotle himself summarizes this in Book III: "In our first discussions, indeed, where conclusions were reached about household-management and rule by a master, it was also said that a human being is by nature a political animal. That is why, even when they do not need one another's help, people no less desire to live together. Although it is also true that common advantage brings them together, to the extent that it contributes some share of noble living to each" (III 6, 1278b17–21).

So, to get back to our original question, as to why education is a political concern, we have here a general, yet strong, answer: it is because we are "political animals," that is animals who need to live in a city in order to fulfill their desire for happiness by sharing in some values and in activities that express those values, that the way to be prepared for such a life must be provided by the city we live in.

One might wonder, though, why it is the city that must see to such an education, and not the family (as was the case in Aristotle's time), which is also referred to as a community of values (see I 2, 1253a1–18, quoted earlier). And indeed, this is precisely one of the main reasons why Aristotle so vehemently defends the institution of the family against Plato's proposal to dismantle it. It is thanks to natural affection, Aristotle argues against Plato, that a family educates its members to care for one another and cultivate the concord that is a central good in a city. And also, and even more importantly, it is through the family that we, when young, first access the values and virtuous activities that should lead towards happiness. As Aristotle says: "For the things a father says, and the habits he imposes, have the same force in a household as legal provisions and customs in a city; or even more force, because of the bonds of kinship and beneficence; for offspring are naturally predisposed to feel affection for and to be obedient to fathers" (*NE* X 9, 1180b3–7). This clearly recognizes the importance of embedding an education towards values within a family circle.[4] And Aristotle even flatly admits that in cases where a city fails to foster the virtue of its citizens, families can and, in fact, should play this role (*NE* X 9, 1180a30–32).

However, in principle, education is better implemented by the *polis* for at least two sets of reasons.[5] First, since living virtuously is no easy or pleasant thing for most people, especially when they are young, they need authority and sometimes harsh castigation, which an individual loving father may not be willing to provide enough of. And Aristotle also remarks that most of us need such a constraint all our lives. But the argument is not only about force or degree of authority; he also adds, very interestingly, that "people become hostile to an individual human being who opposes their impulses, even if he is correct in opposing them, whereas a law's prescription of what is decent is not burdensome" (*NE* X 9, 1180a22–24). In other words, if the father plays the role the law should play, he will weaken the strong community of his own family, which consequently will also undermine his children's propensity to share common values. (Perhaps Aristotle might also be thinking of the role model fathers enjoy; by opposing his children's impulses directly, fathers may undermine the effect of being such a role model for them.) The second set of arguments is about the nature of the knowledge one should have in order to be qualified to provide an education properly. Contrary to what one might think in defending the family and what we call private education, providing a genuine education requires a specific knowledge, which not every family is capable of. Aristotle compares this knowledge to that of doctors and musicians. In both cases, experience is needed, and Aristotle insists that having learned a list of prescriptions is not at all enough to make a good doctor. But if Aristotle recognizes the need for experience, it is in the sense that experience provides a basis for distinguishing and judging (the verb *krinein* means both) a good treatment from a bad one. Similarly, a good legislator is one who has a certain universal knowledge, a reliable and firm knowledge of what youth should be taught. Aristotle here opposes both the Sophists who (at least according to him) deny that we can attain scientific knowledge that will allow the legislator to discriminate between good and bad educational laws (*NE* X 9, 1181a11–19), and the democratic conception of the matter, which he quite ironically compares to that of the Cyclops, under which every father chooses whatever he pleases for his children (*NE* X 9, 1180a26–29). Given its crucial importance, it would be foolish to leave education to sheer luck or fancy. If one is to attain real happiness owing to a genuine education, or more precisely, if one is to be able to help one's fellow citizens to obtain it, one would be well advised to acquire the right science of legislation thanks to Aristotle's lessons.

### HAPPINESS AND LEISURE

Since a constitution is basically a system of values, the education it gives its citizens will consist in educating them in those values. For example, taking wealth as the central value in the happiness, or human flourishing, of its citizens, an oligarchical city will promote the value of wealth and the activities providing wealth. But Aristotle is looking for the education that will best promote genuine happiness which he therefore locates at the core of his description of the best possible city. Thus, in making his proposal as to the best possible education, his first concern is to reflect on what exactly happiness consists in. What are the sorts of values and activities the best *polis* must teach and promote in order to enable its citizens to live a happy life? This is what Aristotle, relying on his ethics, reviews at the beginning of Book VII 1–3, and again in Chapters 13–14.

He advocates two fundamental criteria in discriminating these values and activities. The first criterion is finality: a good is that much better when it is desired for its own sake and does not serve as a means to another good. Thus, money is undoubtedly a certain good, but is only a good in that it is desired because it permits us to acquire other goods we desire for their own sakes. And that is why Aristotle so often insists on the fact that a constitution and hence an education that promises wealth as its central good could not be genuinely satisfying: it promises a good which cannot really be central to human happiness. And that is also why Aristotle, even if he praises Sparta for having instituted public education aimed at all its citizens, reiterates his critique of their central value: victory in war. Victory is certainly a good, but it is a "good" because of its further aim: victory is a means to peace. Along with his critique of oligarchies considering wealth as the core value of happiness, this critique of Sparta, which is repeated like a litany in Book 7 of the *Politics*, has a positive counterpart: Aristotle's insistence on the concept of "leisure," which works as the fundamental principle of his best city or constitution. It is in fact the condition for the possibility of the exercise of those activities which implement the goods that are desired for their own sake and a condition Aristotle recognizes as natural to us:

Nature itself aims not only at the correct use of work but also at the capacity for noble leisured activity. Since this is the starting point for everything else, I propose to discuss it once again. If both are required, but leisured activity is more choiceworthy than work and is its end, we should try to discover what people should do for leisured activity. For surely they should not be amusing themselves, otherwise amusement would have to be our end in life. But if that is impossible, and if amusements are more to be used while one is at work (for someone who exerts himself needs relaxation, relaxation is the end of amusement, and work is accompanied by toil and strain), then we should, for this reason, permit amusement, but we should be careful to use it at the right time, dispensing it as a medicine for the ills of work. For this sort of motion of the soul is relaxing and restful because of the pleasure it involves. Leisured activity is itself held to involve pleasure, happiness and living blessedly. This is not available to those who are working, however, but only to those who are engaged in leisured activity. For someone who is working is doing so for the sake of some end he does not possess, whereas happiness is an end that everyone thinks is accompanied not by pain but by pleasure. (VIII 3, 1337b30–1338a5)

Now, we might consider this insistence on leisure as the pure and simple ideological position of an aristocrat, who denies all value to work and commerce, and hence refuses to consider workers and merchants as citizens of this perfect city.[6] There is no question of denying that Aristotle shared that common aristocratic prejudice of his time. But this should not obscure the core of his argument (which may still sound valid today),[7] that leisure is not only what everyone seeks as the end of one's work, but also what ensures the possibility of actions existing for their own sakes.

Yet this first criterion does not tell us what these activities are which we must exercise for their own sake. For we might, for example, work with the sole goal of amassing money in mind, considering that activity as desirable in itself. Certainly, according to the first criterion, we might say that such a man is wrong in confusing a simple means with an end. But we might also say, to cite the famous example, that a man might choose to spend his life cutting grass with a sickle just for the sake of it, and in that case, there would be no confusion between means and ends. That is why Aristotle adds a second criterion to the first, that of hierarchizing goods constituting happiness. At the beginning of Book VII of the *Politics*, he borrows the well-known Platonic division between external goods, goods of the body, and goods of the soul, assuming universal agreement that no one would ever rationally say that he could be perfectly happy without all three of them. But if it is true that one is easily tempted into thinking that pursuing wealth, power, or reputation *ad infinitum* must lead to happiness, no one would thence admit that having such things without sufficient goods of the soul, like virtues and intelligence, would really do. And without the latter, external goods might just prove fragile and subject to chance. Thus, on reflection, everyone will accept that perfect happiness will mostly depend on virtues and intelligence. The goods of the soul are therefore more worthy, and its activities are then more valuable, and given the first criterion, Aristotle concludes:

So since the soul is unconditionally more valuable, and also more valuable to us, than possessions or the body, its best states must be proportionally better than theirs. Besides, it is for the sake of the soul that these things are naturally choiceworthy, and every sensible person should choose them for its sake, not the soul for their's. We may take it as agreed, then, that each person has just as much happiness as he has virtue and intelligence, and the activities that express them. (VII 1, 1323b19–25)

Thus, the best constitution will specify "that organization in which anyone might do best and live a blessedly happy life," or more precisely, where anyone might perform the best activities that constitute the blessedly happy life (VII 2, 1324a24–25), by first giving the appropriate education that will enable anyone (by this, Aristotle means only citizens in fact) to perform those activities.

But now, what are these activities? In order to get a clear and full view of this, one needs to grapple with one of the most central, and yet famously puzzling, features of Aristotle's practical philosophy, that is, the status of what has been traditionally called "contemplation," a term coined from the Latin translation of the Greek *theôria*. As every reader of the *Nicomachean Ethics* since Antiquity has noticed, after reviewing the virtues of character in minute detail as well as all features (responsibility, choice, practical wisdom) that go along with them, Aristotle suddenly goes on to demonstrate that contrary to what his readers might have expected, the exercise of philosophizing, which he there defines as the contemplation of the eternal entities that compose our world, constitutes our supreme happiness, while the virtuous activities performed according to our moral character and practical wisdom only amount to a "secondary happiness" (*NE* X 8, 1178a9). This is deeply puzzling for two related reasons. First, this implies that the value of the secondary happiness in fact depends on the value of the perfect happiness, because, according to the typical hierarchical ladder of ends and means, the latter must be seen, as Aristotle repeatedly stresses, as the supreme end supervening over the former, and the former therefore as a means toward the latter. According to a famous analogy, practical wisdom can be compared to a doctor's job: like the doctor who prescribes for the sake of health, practical wisdom must prescribe for the sake of theoretical wisdom or contemplation (*NE* VI 13, 1145a6–9). Or as the Aristotelian author of the *Magna Moralia* would later put it: practical wisdom should play the "servant" of theoretical wisdom, "ministering to it leisure" (*MM* I 34, 1198b17–19). And, secondly, instead of presenting that perfect happiness as something that would be the evident end for any of the readers of a treatise that is called "political," he presents it as a way or form of life that is clearly different from the "political life" these readers are supposed to lead and that can hardly be said to be reachable by everyone.

These are the two central questions that I will attempt to answer: How can we make sense of the secondary happiness depending for its value on the perfect one? And how are we to understand that this perfect happiness should ultimately correspond to everyone's desire for happiness?

To be sure, this traditional distinction between the "political life" and the "philosophical life" has been, so to speak, internalized by

Aristotle, who speaks of a bi-partition of the rational soul (the *logos*), *phronêsis* being the virtue of its practical part (which he calls the *logos praktikos*), whereas *sophia* is the virtue corresponding to the theoretical part (or *logos theoretikos*; VII 14, 1333a25). We might therefore suppose that in so far as everyone possesses these two parts, everyone, at least in principle, has the possibility of exercising his theoretical logos as well, and it is worth noticing that Aristotle also uses the quantifier *qua* to differentiate these activities, or "lives": even for the man who may aim at exercising his theoretical faculty, perhaps as long and often as he can (which amounts to "doing what the immortal gods do," *athanatizein*; NE X 7, 1177b33),[8] it remains true that "in so far as he is a human being, and lives together with a number of other human beings, he must choose to perform the actions that accord with virtues...in order to live his human life (*to anthrôpeuesthai*)" (NE X 7, 1178b7). And in the same way, in *Politics* VII, he uses the quantifier of time, saying that work (*ascholia*, or literally "non-leisure") and leisure (*scholê*), which there correspond to the political and theoretical lives (more on this in a moment) are two different "moments" (*chronoi*) in one and the same life (*Pol.* VII 15, 1334a22–25). But this repeated usage of that quantifier only puzzles us further. For if these two sets of activities, the ones that correspond to the "political life," and those that correspond to the "philosophical life," coincide with two different moments of a human life which are correlative to the two different parts of each human being's soul, why restrict philosophy to only a few people? Would nature have made us *not* for the sake of the best, of *our* best? And most importantly for a reader of these two last books of the *Politics*, how could we possibly harmonize this with the repeated claim made here that each and every citizen should obtain perfect happiness thanks to access to full leisure? As one interpreter rightly puts it, "an ideal state in which some citizens would be unable to participate in the definitive good of the political community to which they belong would be very odd."[9]

The vast majority of scholars have tried to sort this out and to clear Aristotle of such oddities by focusing on the brilliant passages from the *Nicomachean Ethics* X 7–9, while taking our seemingly less philosophically attractive passages from *Politics* VII and VIII as inconclusive.[10] I propose to read the latter as in fact providing a more consistent way of solving these puzzles, as if Aristotle had tried to accommodate what he said in his *Nichomachean Ethics* to his description of his best city where, as he repeatedly says, each and every citizen should obtain perfect happiness thanks to leisure.[11]

In the beginning of Book VII, Aristotle returns to this "genres of lives" discussion. His discussion consists here in rejecting two extreme views and in finding a middle ground between the people – let's call them apolitical philosophers – who entirely reject any involvement in political affairs, and those who accuse philosophers of being completely inactive, and thus worthless as regards their city. The apolitical philosophers reject any involvement in politics mainly because they hold that politics consists in ruling despotically over others, like masters over their slaves. But true politics, Aristotle replies, consists in alternately ruling and being ruled. And so, political activities are worth doing and are part of a happy life. And indeed, fully in line with what he said in Book I, where he defined man as a political animal, Aristotle takes it for granted that a true philosopher who necessarily lives in a city could thence not possibly be some "alien cut off from the political community," but must "take part in politics with other people and participate in (his) city-state" (VII 2, 1324a15–17). Aristotle could not be clearer: political activity must be part of the happy life of every citizen of his best city, even philosophers. And if his description of the bi-partition of the *logos*-part of one's soul is to be taken seriously, one of its implications is that not exercising *phronêsis*, that is, ethical and political wisdom, would be a deficiency in practising one's own *logos*, and thus, a lack in exercising complete happiness.

And yet on the other hand, it would be mistaken to take this political activity as the only possible activity expressing happiness. Against people who take philosophers to be inactive because they allegedly wouldn't want to commit themselves to political matters, Aristotle insists that activity does not necessarily "involve relations with other people" (VII 3, 1325b20), and that the thoughts involved therein can be active even without any practical consequences. Don't we say, Aristotle asks, that an architect is acting in an important way in the building of a house even though he in fact is not materially involved in the actual building itself? Moreover, no one would ever say that the gods are unhappy (they are on the contrary taken to be paradigmatically happy), yet they perform no action that involves external objects (and more than that: for Aristotle, the gods are not even moral beings, they never exercise moral or political activities). To be sure, happiness (which can also be named *eupraxia*, that is, literally, "successful action") must be a certain activity, or a set of activities, but they must not be what we usually call practical activities, like moral or political ones aimed at a certain end. On the contrary, on the basis of the example of the architect and the gods, Aristotle claims that activities of the highest sort are precisely not practical either in the restricted sense or in the moral sense; they are, as Aristotle puts it, "autotelic" (*autoteleis*), "for their own sake," with no view to results or consequences. But by saying this, Aristotle implies (even though he won't say any more on this here) that theoretical activities are the best ones, or even, that only they are truly for their own sake, which the other activities (i.e. the ethical and political) are not. And indeed, as I have already suggested, Aristotle seems in fact to be wavering between two seemingly contradictory statements: he sometimes says very clearly and authoritatively that leisure is the *conditio sine qua non* of each and every excellence or excellent activity, ethical and political included, and it is for that very reason that laborers and merchants lacking all leisure should not be allowed to be citizens; but he also repeats – and very strongly too – that activities performed in true leisure (or, to put it another way, constituting leisure time)[12] are these autotelic activities, i.e. *theoria*. It is certainly true, as one scholar has aptly noticed,[13] that Aristotle uses two different meanings of leisure here: in the first case, it commonly means the free time we have when we don't need to work; in the second, it is a specifically Aristotelian usage, corresponding to autotelic activities which are never for the sake of something else. But this ambiguity might also, I suggest, testify to the ambiguous status of the ethical and political activities: these are both ends which are to be sought for themselves, and nevertheless means to higher ends. Thus, the *Politics*, in these passages devoted to that central question of happiness, urges us readers to answer the first of the two central questions I posed: Since even philosophers must devote part of their time to politics because they are citizens, and thus these political activities are part of their happiness, how can these activities obtain their value from the highest, purely autotelic activities, which are theoretical?

Let us try to answer this question by returning once again to the *Nicomachean Ethics*. It seems to me that the best way of understanding what Aristotle wants to say about the problem of the value of the moral virtues is to take the example of courage, which clearly serves as an explanatory paradigm for the ethical virtues, and which he also takes up again in the case of music for education in these virtues (so-called "Dorian music," intended to pave the way to courage, being itself paradigmatic of this type of ethical music). In Book III, Aristotle famously argues that courage on the battlefield is a particularly noble thing, repeatedly using the expression "for the sake of the noble" (*tou kalou heneka*) for this. As we may infer from other passages, Aristotle wants to oppose this to the concept of the useful, and therefore to indicate that courageous acts are fine things that are chosen per se, that is, things that are chosen as ends, and not as means to a further thing. As Aristotle says, these sorts of actions would be chosen even if no consequences, or even bad consequences, were to follow. It is thus tempting to conclude that as noble actions they are ends in themselves and precisely show, or are the expression of, a fine character which is a value per se and part of a valuable human life. If Aristotle doesn't disagree with the idea of courage being part of a valuable human life, he clearly does disagree with the idea, defended by the Spartans, that courage (or any other moral or political virtue, for that matter) is a value we should seek purely for its own sake. But then where does its value come from?

Without entering into the details here of this much-discussed expression and its resonance with other closely related expressions, I suggest we take "for the sake of the noble" (*tou kalou heneka*) quite literally, that is, as referring to the noble as its end, or as we would say, as its value, the "noble life" (*to kalôs zên*) being defined in Books VII–VIII of the *Politics* as the fully leisured life. And indeed, there are several indications of this in that *NE* passage. First, courage is typically the virtue that permits the soldier (that is, every citizen who defends his city) to face the "biggest and noblest dangers" (*en megistôi kai kallistôi kindunôi*) (*NE* III 6, 1115a31–32). And why is that so? Not because, as we might naturally say, life is at stake, but because, in a Greek context, a city that loses a battle might be reduced to slavery, which automatically implies the loss of citizenship and leisure, which are the very conditions for the activities that constitute our happiness.

If this is correct, we can clearly see why Aristotle can hold that such a virtue is both an end and a means towards an end. It is a means in the sense that courage assures him and his fellow citizens of the needed peace, and therefore of leisure for his leisured activities. It is also a means in the sense that these "autotelic" activities give them their value: as Aristotle points out, using the counter-example of Sparta, being courageous without such leisured activities in mind would not really be worth choosing. And yet, at the same time, being courageous with them in view makes them choiceworthy for themselves as they show the soldiers' commitment to them. And this is so even if they lose the battle: at least they will have shown their commitment to the activities that constitute their perfect happiness.[14]

### MUSICAL EDUCATION

Now, let us finally turn to the second question we posed a little earlier: How can citizens who are not philosophers (or who don't possess such highly demanding philosophical capabilities) nevertheless share in these (completely autotelic) highest activities?

How are we to make sense of the fact that perfect happiness should be within the reach of not only a happy few, but all citizens, as Aristotle promises must be the case in the best city? I suggest that reviewing Aristotle's educational programme should enable us to answer this question, which is absolutely crucial for the coherence of his presentation of his ideal city and also, perhaps, for the coherence of his entire ethical and political project.

To stick to the most important features of this program, let's focus on music, which takes up the lion's share of this description. It is not the case that music is intended to play a unique role, or perhaps even the main role, in this program, but it is paradigmatic for what Aristotle has in view.[15] And what he has in view is completely in line with his conception of a happy life in the best possible city. Music, he says there, has two main usages or domains, which are co-extensive with the distinction between the two types of lives or activities: on the one hand, it serves as a tool towards morality (this is music for education, *paideia*) and, on the other, it constitutes one way of spending leisure time (this is music for *diagôgê*). For (as Plato had already recognized) by evoking emotions intensively and providing great pleasure, some appropriate music (mainly, if not exclusively,

Dorian music), aimed at youth, is intended to foster their commitment to the moral virtues. And this is because, as Aristotle thinks is
evident, music is "imitative" of characters. It is not completely clear
exactly how Aristotle envisages this working, but one guess is that
music may represent the emotional part of certain virtues.[16] Think,
for instance, of martial music, which by being "imitative" of people
going into battle courageously, can evoke that emotion in the soul of
its audience (or should the music accompany a song like a patriotic
hymn, it can reinforce the emotional resonance of the words). And
the driving engine here is pleasure: "Since music happens to be one
of the pleasures, and virtue is a matter of enjoying, loving and hating
in the right way, it is clear that nothing is more important than that
one should learn to judge correctly and get into the habit of enjoying
decent characters and noble actions" (VIII 5, 1340a14–17).

But this domain of music is by no means the only or the most
valuable one. Even though this has sometimes been denied,[17] many
passages in Book VIII insist that music "for the sake of leisure" constitutes the best usage of music, and this is the one that legislators
must see to primarily. For this use of music is not aimed at something else, as in the previous case of educational music; here, music
is enjoyed just for itself, without being a means to something else.
A youth should learn to play some musical instrument up to a certain stage in order to become a good *kritikos*, that is, a good judge of
music: "Since one should take part in performances in order to judge,
for this reason they should engage in performance while they are
young and stop performing when they are older, but be able to judge
which melodies are noble and enjoy them in the right way, because
of what they learned while they were young" (VIII 6, 1340b35–39).[18]

Now, what exactly does this leisure music consist in and how
might this be related to philosophy? It is very unfortunate that Aristotle does not pose these central questions explicitly. However, I
think we can reconstruct what he would have answered with some
reasonable probability. First of all, it should be noticed that Aristotle
does not use a particular term for describing the kind of music that
would be suitable for such leisure. Relying on "people working philosophically on music" (perhaps his own pupil Aristoxenos), Aristotle
names three different kinds of music that correspond to the three
usages of music besides leisure: "ethical songs," i.e. Dorian music
for moral education; "enthusiastic songs" for the sake of *katharsis*

(which is supposed to cure people from excessive propensities to certain emotions); and "lively songs" for entertaining music intended to relax us after hard work.[19] Nevertheless, I suggest that we may infer from some passages, notably the two just cited above, that Aristotle considered the calm and temperate music that suits moral education to be the one suited for leisure too. This should not be interpreted, though, as if Aristotle had intended to interchange leisure and the ethical realm (which is here repeatedly described as unleisured). For, if the music is factually the same, the way it is enjoyed is quite different: in the case of music for education, Aristotle supposes children to be playing it, while these same songs or bare melodies and rhythms for leisure are addressed to adult listeners (see VIII 6, 1340b35–39 quoted above). And the adult citizen's enjoyment consists not only in emotionally enjoying it, as in the case of educational music, but also, and perhaps primarily, in enjoying the understanding of its structures, according to the education of their judgment they have received. As Aristotle says, this way of considering music is "for the sake of leisure and intelligence" (VIII 5, 1339a25–26), where "intelligence" (the word used here is *phronêsis*) most probably refers to critical judgment about the beauty of music.[20] In this sense, then, music for leisure is a *theôria* both in the sense of a spectacle where the citizens enjoy listening to people playing for them, and in the sense of an intellectual exercise that we would call an aesthetic judgment. Thus, we have here a possible answer to our question as to how this relates to *theôria* in the sense of philosophy. In both cases, we have a similar exercising of an intellectual faculty, and the emotional correlative to this is undoubtedly admiration before beauty, while their objects are different: works of art in the one case, and divine entities in the other.

But can't we say more about the relationship between these two sorts of *theôria*? Two alternative solutions have been proposed. According to one interpreter, the aesthetic sort of *theôria* should serve as a kind of exercise toward the philosophical one: understanding the forms and structure of music may prepare our minds for comprehending those of the universe.[21] But this solution sounds odd since the aesthetical *theôria* would then be reduced to a simple means to a further end, and we would then be forced to admit that in fact the perfect use of leisure engaged in completely "autotelic" activities must remain inaccessible for most citizens. As Richard

Kraut has suggested, and rightly so in my opinion, this aesthetic *theôria* accessible to every citizen of the best city should rather be considered to be an *approximation* of the philosophical one[22] – in an analogous way, I am adding to Kraut's suggestion, to human philosophical contemplation, which is explicitly said to be an approximation of divine contemplation (*NE* X 8, 1178b25–28). Beyond a doubt, for Aristotle (as well as for every other ancient philosopher), philosophy is absolutely the best activity, mainly because its objects are the most excellent and perfect ones; but still, each and every citizen must have the possibility of having his part in perfect happiness, at least in the best possible city. As Aristotle states, "The task of an excellent legislator, then, is to study how a city-state, a race of men, or any other community can come to have a share in a good life and in the happiness that it is possible for them" (VII 2, 1325a7–10).

CODA

Finally, there is a last and more general question that every reader would have liked Aristotle to have asked too: What sort of utility might such a description of the conditions for the best possible city, and especially of this best possible sort of education that should make us all perfectly happy as citizens, have for the readers of the *Politics*? For it is a repeated and central claim of Aristotle's that practical (ethical as well as political) philosophy must be for the sake of action, and not, or not only, for the sake of understanding. If, to our modern sensibilities, Aristotle may appear to be a very traditional thinker on some points (with very puritanical aesthetic taste in music as well), it would be a complete mistake to take him for the kind of philosopher who, according to Marx's famous motto, is only committed to interpreting the world instead of being willing to change it. On the contrary, Aristotle never tires of repeating that the legislator should try to improve actual constitutions. It is therefore only reasonable to think that his description of the conditions for the best possible city, which corresponds to his conception of human flourishing or happiness, should prove useful reading for his audience. To remain within the theme of education, one interpreter has suggested that if Aristotle might not have been very confident as to the eventual possibility of improving any existing constitution, at least the reader of this treatise may have been induced to improve the way of educating his own children (education being a private affair at Aristotle's time).[23] I would like to propose that we extend this suggestion further: listening to how to improve the education of their own children, which undoubtedly must have interested them, Aristotle's putative legislators must have been at least well disposed and ready to try to make the constitution they lived under more akin to the right conception of happiness they had been provided with. Comparing the constitution they actually lived under to a perfect one, ideally corresponding to their own desire for happiness, should certainly have made them profoundly dissatisfied with their present condition.[24] But reflecting on education, i.e. on a possibly better future for their own children, should have positively boosted their motivation to change whatever they possibly could change in their own, in one way or another defective, cities.

### WORKS CITED

Belfiore, E. 2001. "Family Friendship in Aristotle's Ethics." *Ancient Philosophy* 21: 113–32

Bénatouïl, T. 2011. "'Choisir le labeur en vue du loisir': une analyse de *Politiques*, VII, 14." In *Politique d'Aristote: Famille, régimes, éducation*, eds. E. Bermon, V. Laurand, and J. Terrel. Pessac: Presses Universitaires de Bordeaux

Broadie, S. 2007. *Aristotle and Beyond: Essays on Metaphysics and Ethics*. Cambridge University Press

Curren, R. 2000. *Aristotle on the Necessity of Public Education*. Lanham, MD: Rowman and Littlefield

Demont, P. 1993. "Le loisir dans la *Politique* d'Aristote." In *Aristote politique. Etudes sur la Politique d'Aristote*, eds. P. Aubenque and A. Tordesillas. Paris: PUF

Depew, D. J. 1991. "Politics, music, and contemplation in Aristotle's Ideal State." In *A Companion to Aristotle's Politics*, eds. D. Keyt and F. Miller. Oxford: Blackwell

Ford, A. 2002. *The Origins of Criticism: Literary Culture and Poetic Theory in Classical Greece*. Princeton University Press

Kraut, R. 2002. *Aristotle: Political Philosophy*. Oxford University Press

Lear, G. R. 2004. *Happy Lives and the Highest Good: An Essay on Aristotle's Nicomachean Ethics*. Princeton University Press

Lord, C. 1982. *Education and Culture in the Political Thought of Aristotle.* Ithaca, NY: Cornell University Press

Nightingale, A. 1996. "Aristotle on the 'Liberal' and 'Illiberal' Arts." *Proceedings of the Boston Area Colloquium in Ancient Philosophy* 12: 29–58

Reeve, C. D. C. 1998a. "Aristotelian Education." In *Philosophers on Education*, ed. A. O. Rorty. London: Routledge

  1998b. *Aristotle*, Politics. Indianapolis, IN: Hackett

Roochnik, D. 2008. "Aristotle's Defense of the Theoretical Life: Comments on *Politics* VII." *Review of Metaphysics* 61: 711–35

Solmsen, F. 1964. "Leisure and Play in Aristotle's Ideal State." *Rheinisches Museum für Philologie* 107: 193–220

Stalley, Richard 2009. "Education and the state." In *A Companion to Aristotle*, ed. G. Anagnostopoulos. Malden, MA and Oxford: Wiley-Blackwell

Tuozzo, T. M. 1992. "Contemplation, the Noble, and the Mean: the Standard of Moral Virtue in Aristotle's Ethics." *Apeiron* 24(4): 129–54

Woerther, F. 2008. "Music and Education of the Soul in Plato and Aristotle: Homeopathy and the Formation of Character." *Classical Quarterly* 58: 89–103

NOTES

1. Throughout this chapter, I quote Rowe's translation of the *Nichomachean Ethics*, sometimes with slight changes or adaptations.
2. See *Odyssey* IX 187–92, where Odysseus describes Polyphemos' cave: "There a giant spent the night, one that grazed his herds far off, alone, and keeping clear of others, lived in lawless solitude. He was born a monster and a wonder, not like any ordinary bread-eating human, but like some wooded peak of the high mountains, that stands there isolated from the others" (trans. Kline, slightly modified).
3. See Sophocles, where Philotectes describes himself as "without any relative and friend, alone, without *polis*, like someone dead among the living people" (*Philoctetes*, v. 1018), and even says: "I am nothing, I've been dead for you for a long time" (v. 1030).
4. On this, see especially Belfiore 2001.
5. I only report here Aristotle's arguments from *NE* X 9. On these, see also Dorothea Frede, Chapter 1. For other reasons reconstructed from the *Politics*, see Curren 2000: ch. 5.
6. On this, see especially Nightingale 1996.
7. On this, see Sarah Broadie's suggestive remarks in her inaugural lecture at the University of St. Andrews, "Taking Stock of Leisure" (Broadie 2007: ch. 12).

8. The exact meaning of this verb has been disputed among interpreters. I think the rendering, "doing what the immortal gods do," i.e. contemplating and exercising one's intellect, is more likely in this context than the traditional, religious-sounding "immortalizing oneself."

9. Depew 1991: 350–51.

10. The main exception to this trend is Depew 1991. See also Roochnik 2008 who defends the consistency of *Pol.* VII, but draws a quite different conclusion from mine.

11. By this, I don't mean that *Politics* VII–VIII were necessarily written after *NE* X. It is the case, though, or so I contend, that the way Aristotle presents his case in the *Politics* seems to answer some of the difficulties he has left unanswered in the *Nicomachean Ethics*.

12. In fact, Aristotle uses the term *scholê* (leisure time) and *diagôgê* (leisure life) almost interchangeably.

13. Solmsen 1964. On this theme, see also Demont 1993.

14. Here I am greatly indebted to Gabriel Richardson Lear's interpretation (Lear 2004: ch. 7), although I strongly disagree with her repeated claim that a soldier may be perfectly unaware of the reason why his courage is valuable. Being really virtuous for Aristotle implies that the agent knows why he is acting in such and such a way, and in our particular case of courage, he also strongly holds that being courageous for specific reasons such as seeking honor or monetary rewards (as in the case of mercenaries) would not count as true courage. On the value of moral virtues as deriving from *theôria*, see also Tuozzo 1992.

15. It is highly probable that Aristotle held somewhat similar views on the other arts. See his remark on painting at VIII 3, 1338a40–b2. As to the role of poetry, which is curiously absent from the *Politics*, see the programmatic remarks by David Reeve in Reeve 1998a.

16. On imitation in music, see Woerther 2008.

17. See especially Lord 1982. Carnes Lord's strong moralistic interpretation of music and his dismissal of its purely leisurely use has been rightly criticized by Andrea Nightingale (Nightingale 1996).

18. One may also note that Aristotle does insist on the fact that young citizens must not themselves become virtuosi or professionals since that would preclude them from enjoying music in a purely leisurely manner. (This of course sounds odd to our modern ears: while presenting art as part of the perfect, "theoretical," life, Aristotle somehow paradoxically dismisses the value of the artist himself, who is reduced to being the servant of the citizens' consuming art.)

19. These songs called *praktika* are usually called "practical" in translation, thus giving the impression that they might be related to *praxis* or human moral action. But that is a false impression, to be sure, since

if one accepted it, one would no longer be able to see the difference between them and the ethical songs. I suggest understanding *praktikos* here as referring to movement, whether it be movement of the soul or dance. (What I am suggesting relies in part on my reading of *praktika* at 1342b15, following Ross's text, instead of *kathartika* which, I think, does not make sense here.)

20. Most translaters, including Reeve and Kraut, understand *phronêsis* here as referring to the practical wisdom Aristotle describes in his *Nicomachean Ethics*. But that would contradict Aristotle's constant opposition between the unleisured political sphere and the domain of leisured *theôria*. On this, see also Ford 2002: 286–93.

21. Depew 1991.

22. Kraut 2002: 200.

23. Stalley 2009: 574–75.

24. Kraut 2002: 471–72.

# 13   Deliberating and acting together

Are there any political acts that can rightfully be attributed to the political community as a whole? Or do the actions that we casually attribute to a country or a city really belong to the political leaders who act on the community's behalf? When a country takes on a debt, for example, is it the country that acts, or only the leadership?

Aristotle raises this question at the beginning of Book III of the *Politics* and suggests that his inquiry into the essential nature of a *polis* will help to shed light on it:

When investigating constitutions, and what each is and is like, pretty well the first subject of investigation concerns a city-state, to see what the city-state is. For as things stand now, there are disputes about this. Some people say, for example, that a city-state performed a certain action, whereas others say that it was not the city-state that performed the action, but rather the oligarchy or the tyrant did. (III 1, 1274b30–35)

Later in the text Aristotle returns to the same sort of problem:

For some people raise a problem about how to determine whether a city-state has or has not performed an action, for example, when an oligarchy or a tyranny is replaced by a democracy. At these times, some do not want to honor treaties, since it was not the city-state but its tyrant who entered into them, nor to do many other things of the same sort. (III 3, 1276a8–12)

Aristotle seems to have a particular kind of practical dispute, and perhaps even a particular historical case, in mind. Newman, in his commentary on the *Politics* from the late nineteenth century, follows others in suggesting that he may have been referring to an incident in Athens that was mentioned by Isocrates and Demosthenes and, judging from the way they discussed it, was commonly known:

a group of oligarchs known as The Ten had gained power for a time during a struggle against Thrasybulus' democratic faction, and while in power they had borrowed money from Sparta on behalf of Athens. After The Ten were removed from power and the democracy was restored, the question of whether Athens had to repay the money to Sparta was brought up in the popular assembly. Some Athenians seem to have argued against repaying the loan, saying that the debt had been incurred not by Athens but by tyrants or oligarchs pursuing their own interests.[1] In spite of these arguments the Athenians, under democratic leadership, did repay the debt. Looking back on this incident later, orators pointed to this repayment as evidence of Athenian magnanimity. Isocrates referred to it as proof of the people's fairness, and Demosthenes offered it as an example that later generations should try to imitate.[2] Aristotle, in his *Constitution of Athens*, interprets the episode as an effort by the ruling democrats to put factional divisions and war behind them, and he admires the fact that unlike other popular leaders in similar situations, the democrats did not insist that the oligarchs repay the debt from their own estates, nor did they insist upon raising the money by raiding the oligarchs' property. He offers unusually direct praise for the democracy's actions in this case: "The Athenians appear to have handled their affairs, both private and public, as well and with as much statesmanship as any people have ever shown in a similar situation" (*Constitution of Athens* 40; cf. 38).

In the *Politics* Aristotle is concerned not with the details of the episode but with the philosophical question that practical disputes of this kind raise: Which actions belong to a city-state as a whole? When, if ever, can the city-state reasonably be viewed as an agent capable of acting and being held responsible for its actions? And when can actions that leaders may want to attribute to the whole city be pinned instead on them and them alone?

Stated in that form, the questions arise in other ancient political writings as well. For example, in the Mytilenian debate in Thucydides' *History of the Peloponnesian War*, the issue was whether all the Mytilenians should be held responsible for the city's having rebelled against Athenian rule, or only the leaders. First the Athenians decided to punish the whole city, killing all the men and sending the women and children into slavery, but they soon reversed their decision.[3] Plato mentions a similar topic in Book V of the

*Republic,* where he argues that when a city's guardians punish rival cities they should not act so "that in any city all are their enemies – men, women, and children – but [instead they should hold] that there are always a few enemies who are to blame for the differences" (*Rep.* V, 471a–b). More generally, the issue arises any time an author such as Thucydides states that "the Athenians" took such and such an action. Did "the Athenians" decide to sail to Sicily, or did the decision to set sail belong above all to Alcibiades who had urged the action and perhaps to Nicias who led it?[4] Translators have even wondered whether they should change Thucydides' sentences to make the subject clearer, for example saying that "the Athenian government" performed an action when the text simply reads "the Athenians."[5] In practice, of course, political leaders often attributed their actions to the whole people or to the city. Sometimes this language should be dismissed as merely rhetorical. Josiah Ober suggests that language attributing actions to "Athens" or "the Athenians" is generally "ideological" and that speaking this way hid the fact that "in reality" decisions were made and carried out by elites.[6] But is such language always deceptive, or are there any circumstances in which one can legitimately say that the city acted? The question of which actions belong to the city-state and which to its rulers is the question that Aristotle raises in the first lines of Book III.

The thesis of this chapter is that Aristotle's account of civic deliberation is an effort to describe the conditions under which actions belong to a city as a whole. One way to reach this conclusion, we will see, is to insist upon an analogy between his account of an individual's deliberation in the *Nicomachean Ethics* and his understanding of political deliberation. An individual decides how to act by deliberating, and the movements that result from deliberation are *actions* in the fullest sense of the word; they manifest human agency more than other movements a person might make. Similarly, I will suggest, a city decides to act by deliberating, and the actions that result from its deliberation are the ones that most fully reflect its political agency.

One difficulty that arises in exploring this topic is that Aristotle is not as clear as we might wish on the basic question of what political deliberation looks like. This is not because he regards deliberation as unimportant. On the contrary, he calls the deliberative element in the city the most authoritative part of it and he defines citizenship as eligibility to share in the deliberative and judging offices (IV 14, 1299a1; III 1, 1275b19). He also describes what sorts of decisions the deliberative element of the city is responsible for making: the deliberative part has authority for decisions about war and peace, alliances, laws, punishment, and the selection and auditing of officials (IV 14, 1298a3–5). He also reviews various possible modes of selecting the people who should be involved in deliberation (IV 14, 1298a9–1299a1). In spite of this emphasis on deliberation, however, he never directly addresses the question of precisely what political deliberation *is*. Our reconstruction of its function in his argument must therefore be based on the few characteristics of deliberation that he does make explicit. In particular, we will see, deliberation describes a certain kind of ruling – political ruling – that must be present for a community to count as a city or *polis* in the true sense of the word.

In recent political theory, the notion of deliberation plays a different role. Theories of deliberative democracy from the past twenty years speak less openly about the practices of ruling and being ruled than Aristotle does. Deliberation is not linked to a mode of rule in these theories; instead it is often presented as a means of avoiding the need for some citizens to rule over others. Deliberation in today's political philosophy often functions as a way of reconciling individual citizens to the basic laws in a way that makes it plausible for them to regard those laws as the indirect outcome of their own rationalized wills. If Aristotle suggests that deliberation allows a political community to produce actions of its own, contemporary political theorists tend to understand deliberation as a way for each *individual* in a community to regard the community's actions as his or her own. The difference between a *city* being responsible for political actions and *individual citizens* each being responsible for them is important to any comparison between Aristotle's account of deliberation and more recent theories of deliberative democracy.

To bring the distinctiveness of Aristotle's view into focus, I will emphasize this contrast with contemporary theories of deliberative democracy. Elsewhere I have suggested that Aristotle's comments on persuasive argument, political friendship, and the political emotions have a lot to offer contemporary theorists of deliberation, and other authors have offered similar suggestions about the usefulness of Aristotle's account for our thinking.[7] In this chapter, in contrast, I offer a reminder that our recent accounts of deliberation arise within the bounds of a democratic individualism that Aristotle simply did not share.

## DELIBERATION AND DEMOCRATIC INDIVIDUALISM

By "democratic individualism" I mean the governing assumption that we are free and equal individuals who deserve to be governed according to laws that we have, or could have, consented to, so that in obeying those laws each of us is not being ruled by any other person's will. Theories of the social contract, as found in Rousseau or John Rawls for example, offer a classic way of reconciling this individual freedom from being ruled with the obedience to law. They explain that law is legitimately binding on each of us because we have, or could have, agreed to it or to the procedures that produce it; the law reflects our own wills, at least indirectly. If Rousseau's solutions do not dominate the contemporary discussion of social contract theory, his statement of the problem in the *Social Contract* still sets its agenda: "To find a form of association that will defend and protect the person and goods of each associate with the full common force, and by means of which *each, uniting with all, nevertheless obeys only himself and remains as free as before.*"[8]

This understanding of the problem seems to make democratic legitimacy depend upon unanimity among the citizens. If the fundamental law of a city is meant to reflect the will of each one of us, and there is one fundamental law, then it would seem that our wills must overlap, or at least that they must unanimously agree about the law. To many thinkers, the requirement for unanimity seems impracticable and also potentially tyrannical. It was partly in response to this difficulty that theorists such as Jürgen Habermas, Joshua Cohen, and Bernard Manin introduced the topic of deliberation to democratic theory. Democratic legitimacy, they suggested, can emerge not only from a consensus of already-formed wills, but also from a process of deliberative decision-making that embodies democratic norms of equal access, respect, and reciprocity.[9] In place of the "univocal" agreement presumed by Rousseau's general will or Rawls' original position in *A Theory of Justice*, these writers highlighted the legitimating work that could be done by a "dialogical" deliberative process, a process that acknowledged the fact that people generally do not arrive on the political scene with fully-determined wills. If the process of determining their individual wills is a public one in which all citizens can participate, and if that same process is the one by which the fundamental law is determined, then a form of legitimacy acceptable to democratic individualism seems to be preserved even without a pre-existing unanimity among the citizens. Individual citizens would not regard a law emerging from open deliberation as an alien or arbitrary act of will ruling them from the outside, but instead as an act that they participated in initiating. Further, it was suggested, they would regard such a law as reasonable, because it emerged from a process of public discussion and justification. It is true that the problem of unanimity did not disappear once deliberation entered the theory in this way, since questions immediately arose about whether the norms guiding deliberation were themselves a matter of consensus and about whether the deliberative process should aim at achieving consensus. Still, the change from looking for a coincidence of already-formed wills to forming wills through argument allowed theorists the hope that democratic legitimacy could be achieved over longer periods of time and through a greater variety of informal social processes than standard social contract theory had envisioned.

The fundamental understanding of legitimacy, however, was only slightly changed by the deliberative turn. Adding deliberation to social contract theory highlighted the fact that our individual wills could be formed through a process of discussion with others. Legitimacy still required, however, that individuals not be governed by a will other than their own. What does it mean for self-directed individuals of this kind to act *together*? It seems that they would act together by acting *similarly*, alongside one another but with equal autonomy. Deliberation, from this perspective, appears to be a way for individual citizens to coordinate their autonomous actions.

In Aristotle's political thought, there is no assumption that each individual must be obeying himself when he obeys the law. The key issue is therefore not whether each individual citizen can regard the city's actions as his own, but whether the city as a whole can ever perform actions of *its* own. Deliberation, on Aristotle's account, is not an activity that helps individuals coordinate their similar, independent, and autonomous self-direction. Instead, deliberation is an activity that brings individuals' different, complementary, and mutually dependent acts into relation with one another in a manner that yields actions attributable to the whole of which each of them is a part. In what follows I look first at the link between deliberation and political agency, and then at the functional differentiation among citizens within the activity of deliberation. Finally, I suggest that the functional differentiation between ruler and ruled in Aristotle's thought may be part of what he thinks makes it possible for citizens in a city to act together as one agent.

## DELIBERATION AND POLITICAL AGENCY

The link between deliberation and agency is clearer in Aristotle's treatment of an individual's internal deliberation than it is in his treatment of political deliberation. In the *Nicomachean Ethics*, Aristotle raises the topic of deliberation in the course of trying to explain which actions an individual actually chooses to do. He has already argued that actions arising from passionate desire or anger should be considered voluntary, since the origin (*archê*) of the action lies within the person acting.[10] Not all actions that should be considered voluntary, however, are ones that we *choose* in the full sense of the word. According to Aristotle, there is a subset of voluntary actions that belong especially fully to the person doing them, and that are especially closely linked to his or her character and more expressive of it. These are actions performed neither in haste nor out of momentary passion, but after a process of decision-making (*prohairesis*). Animals can act voluntarily (the origin of motions lies inside them) but they cannot make choices of this kind. The ability to choose how to act is part of what distinguishes humans from other creatures (*NE* III 2, 1111b7, b15). The term deliberation (*bouleusis*) appears in the text as an explanation of this particularly human sort of decision-making. If we ask what distinguishes merely "voluntary" actions from actions that are truly "chosen," Aristotle's answer is that chosen actions are the result of deliberation (*NE* III 2, 1112a15).

What exactly does Aristotle mean by "deliberation" in this context? Deliberating about how to act begins with a desire for something that is thought to be good for the agent (*NE* III 4, 1113a15).[11] Initially, the object of desire may be something quite abstract or ill-defined. Deliberation is the process by which this original desire produces a related desire for something more specific and attainable.[12]

Sometimes this will involve considering the best means of achieving an end, but means-end thinking may not adequately describe all the sorts of practical reasoning that Aristotle has in mind. Once deliberation has led a person to settle on an object of desire that is within his or her grasp, no separate act of will is required to motivate the person to actually carry out the action; the motivation to act has been present throughout the deliberation in the form of the desire (*NE* III 3, 1113a10–15). When deliberation settles upon a specific and concrete object of desire, the action will begin as soon as the object is perceived (*NE* VII 3, 1147a28–32). There has been some debate in the scholarly literature about whether Aristotle considers this final act of perception to be a part of the deliberation itself or a separate stage, but this detail need not concern us here.[13] The main point is that deliberation is an intellectual process that produces not merely a reasoned outcome or justified norm, but a specific desire capable of motivating action. All animal action, Aristotle tells us in *De Anima*, has its origin in desire (*orexis*), but often the intellect (*nous*) seems to be involved too (*DA* III 10). Deliberation is one way that the intellect influences human desires and thus human actions. Aristotle calls the desires that emerge from this process of reflection *deliberated desires* (*NE* III 3, 1113a12), and we might call the actions that result from them deliberate actions. Whereas animals and children can perform movements that are voluntary, only fully developed humans can perform deliberate actions; only they can move in response to deliberated desires (*NE* III 2–3, 1112a15–1113a14; VI 2, 1139a20–b5; *De Mot. Animal.* 701a9 ff.). In the *Ethics*, this understanding of deliberation as a reflective refining of desire serves to explain what constitutes a distinctively human form of agency.[14]

To see the parallel to this account of individual deliberation in the political context, we can turn to the question with which Aristotle begins Book III – whether any actions can be said to belong to a city rather than to its rulers – and trace his response through the ensuing text. He begins by pointing out that a city is nothing other than a group of citizens. Immediately, then, the question of whether a city can act is reframed as one about whether a group of citizens can act together. This is already, as Malcolm Schofield has argued, quite a striking move, since it seems to incorporate a fundamentally democratic and Athenian understanding of the centrality of citizenship to the nature of cities.[15] Simply pointing out that the city is composed of citizens does not suffice as an understanding of the city's identity, however, for at least two reasons. First, emphasizing citizenship does not answer questions about which individuals should be counted as citizens. Aristotle eschews the usual definitions of citizenship based on bloodline and geography and famously argues that a citizen is "someone who is eligible to participate in deliberative and judicial office" (*archai bouleutikai kai kritikai*; III 1, 1275b18). He recognizes that the word "offices" (*archai*) usually refers to positions with limited tenure, as when someone serves as supervisor over grain for a certain length of time. He acknowledges that in some democratic regimes many citizens will not be in those sorts of offices at all, but instead will participate in the jury and the assembly. Being a juryman or a member of the assembly is not serving in an "office" in the usual sense, since there is no set term of office or definite and delimited function. Nevertheless, Aristotle wants his definition of citizenship to apply to individuals serving in these capacities. He therefore suggests that the positions of jurymen and assembly members be described as "indefinite offices" (III 1, 1275a32). Of course, not all cities have such roles; some, such as Sparta and Carthage, assign the tasks of deliberating and judging not to open juries or assemblies but to certain magistracies that are rotated among citizens. Aristotle's final definition of a citizen is therefore written in a way that applies to both democratic cities with indefinite offices and undemocratic cities without them: eligibility for any office that involves deliberation and judgment is what defines a citizen (III 1, 1275b16–20). A city acts when citizens (individuals eligible to participate in offices of deliberation and judgment) act together.

The second question about the city's identity that is left unanswered by the turn to citizenship is how the citizens must be organized. Aristotle does not mean that *any* action performed by people eligible for deliberative offices should count as an action of the city as a whole. He means instead that actions performed by those people *acting in their capacity as citizens* should count. Their capacity as citizens is not simply to occupy the offices mentioned, but to perform the function of each office. Aristotle treats citizenship less as a status than as an activity. His willingness to lump indefinite and definite offices together to arrive at a definition of citizenship shows that he regards what unifies them as most significant for determining citizenship, and what unifies them on his account is the fundamental activity of deliberating and judging.[16] Not all citizens, however, perform precisely the same activity. As we will see in more depth soon, different offices have different functions in the larger organization, and the activity of citizens in each office will therefore differ. For now, however, the point to emphasize is that an action belongs to the city as a whole when it emerges from citizens engaging in the activities of deliberating and judging called for by their (indefinite and definite) offices. This is the sense in which deliberation is central to political agency.

It is true that when Aristotle returns explicitly to the question of which actions belong to a city he does not directly cite deliberation as the key criterion. Instead, he remarks, "some do not want to honor treaties, since it was not the city-state but its tyrant who entered into them, nor to do many other things of the same sort, *on the grounds that some constitutions exist by force and not for the common benefit (koine sumpheron)*" (III 3, 1276a10–13, emphasis added). The key determinant of whether actions belong to a city in this passage seems to be whether constitutions aim at the common good. Taken by itself, out of context, this argument should seem odd. Why should a city's ability to act, or its responsibility for its actions, depend on whether the regime aims at the common good? We might think that a notion of the common good should guide a city in determining *how* to act, and also that it should guide citizens in judging whether a city acts well or badly. In the argument Aristotle gives here, however, it seems that aiming at the common good is a precondition for the city's being able to act, or have agency, at all. Why should this be?

It seems to me that deliberation may be playing a role in this argument even though it is not mentioned in this sentence explicitly. We saw in the *Ethics* that individual deliberation concerns a goal that seems to be good for the agent (*NE* III 5, 1114b1 ff.; *DA* 433b13 ff.). Since the agent in this case is the city, any deliberation would, by definition, have to concern the city's apparent good. Aristotle consistently assumes that the common good is what political deliberations are about (VII 9, 1329a4–5; *Rhet.* I 5, 1362a18–20). Thus, actions arise from deliberation, and deliberation, by definition, aims at the apparent good of the deliberating agent. Of course, rulers and citizens deliberating about the common good may be wrong about the common good, just as individuals may be wrong about their own good even after deliberating. Aristotle's account does not make correctness a necessary condition of action. It suggests only that citizens cannot be said to be deliberating on behalf of the city if they are not considering its good, and therefore that a city cannot be said to be acting if the citizens making decisions are not considering its good.

The criterion invoked here – aiming at what is thought to be the common good – is the same one that Aristotle uses to distinguish correct from deviant regimes; deviant regimes aim at the rulers' good rather than the common good (*koine sumpheron*) (III 6, 1279a16–20; IV 2, 1289a26–30). Seeing the link between deliberation about the common good and the possibility of action therefore suggests a particular understanding of the way in which deviant regimes are deviant: a deviant regime does not allow its city to act as a distinct agent. Correct regimes – organizations of office that allow and encourage consideration of a common good – are the ones that enable a city to perform actions of its own.

## DELIBERATION AND DEMOCRACY

The reconstruction of Aristotle's argument that I have just given has several surprising implications. First, it suggests that most actual regimes do not constitute cities with the ability to produce actions of their own. Most actual regimes are democracies or oligarchies or some mix of the two, according to Aristotle, and his classification labels both democracy and oligarchy as deviant forms of regimes. The second implication is that a monarch who deliberates about what he perceives to be the good of the city would seem to produce actions that belong to the city as a whole, even though no public sharing of reasons among citizens is present. Both of these implications point to the fact that deliberation has a weaker relationship to democracy in Aristotle than it does in recent political theory.

In fact, it is striking that in the passage we have examined about the relevance of the common good to a city's agency (III 3, 1276a10–13), Aristotle declines to take advantage of a familiar democratic argument about when actions belong to a city. The familiar argument is that a city cannot be held responsible for the actions of a tyrant because a tyranny is not democratic; its actions do not reflect the wishes of the people, and the people is the city. As we have seen, Aristotle instead points to the tyrant's failure to pursue the common good as the reason not to take his actions as belonging to the city. This allows him to point out, in the sentence immediately after the ones quoted above, that democracies too can be ruled "in that way," meaning tyrannically (III 3, 1276a8–15). Presumably he has in mind the cases that he mentions elsewhere in which democracy means the rule of the majority in its own interest, rather than in the interest of the whole community. He remarks upon the threat posed by a poor majority seizing and dividing up the property of the rich (III 10 1281a15–25; VI 3, 1318a25). Recall too that he specifically praises Athens for not resorting to this tactic when paying back the money its oligarchic rulers had borrowed from Sparta. A majority acting for its own sake is not the same as a majority acting for the sake of the common good, in his eyes, and is therefore not equivalent to a city acting as a single agent.

One could dismiss Aristotle's concerns about majority rule as mere anti-democratic bias. But lying beneath his warnings about poor majorities is a philosophical point important to his understanding of deliberation. The view that "the poor [should] have more authority than the rich" because they are the majority is based upon an account of equality that grants each individual the same importance (VI 2, 1317a40–1317b15). Equality is understood as equivalence. Aristotle does not regard this understanding of equal citizenship as a satisfactory one for understanding the nature of a city. His objection is clearest when he distinguishes the nature of a city from that of other associations, such as nations and military alliances. Those sorts of associations, he notes, are composed of units that are all of one kind. But, he argues, "a city-state consists not only of a number of people, but of people of different kinds, since a city-state does not come from people who are alike" (II 2, 1261a23–1261b6). He recommends his own discussion of reciprocal justice in the *Ethics*, which advocates a proportional type of equality that recognizes people's differences and knits them together into one community (*NE* V 3, 1132b32–1134a30; IX 1 1163b32–1164a2). The complementary relationships that characterize a city are not adequately captured, he suggests, by simply giving each member of a community one vote and letting the majority speak for the whole.

It is true, as we have already noted, that Aristotle begins Book III by speaking of citizens as the essence of cities and that this in itself is in some ways a strikingly democratic point of view,

seeming to point towards the modern democratic-individualist practice of regarding similar individuals as the essential material of
political communities.[17] By Chapter 9 of that book, however, he
is describing a true city as a "community of families and villages,"
granting importance to the sociological entities of family and village
that social contract theories implicitly de-emphasize in their vision
of a contract among individuals (III 9, 1280b39–40). Aristotle also
gives weight in his analysis to the different economic and political
functions that people perform in the community. When he analyzes
the variety of regimes, he classifies them by the way that each sort
combines the essential jobs found in any city – the farmers, artisans,
warriors, deliberators, and so on. Here the city is not treated primarily as a homogenized mixture of similar individuals, but instead as
a complex whole fitted together from groups playing different and
complementary functions (IV 4, 1290b24–1291a9).

Simply acknowledging social differentiation in this way does not
make Aristotle's approach undemocratic. But he does seem to accept
the political relevance of this differentiation in a manner at odds
with our sense of what democratic theory would require. This is
most obvious, perhaps, in his treatment of manual workers, whom
he thinks should be barred from citizenship whenever possible due
to the fact that their daily labors leave them no way of acquiring
the virtues needed for citizenship (III 4–5). Citizens who share a
city together need to concern themselves with one another's character as people sharing alliances do not (III 9, 1280b1). Presumably
this is because they are meant to deliberate together and deliberation requires certain character traits (III 11, 1281b15–20). Aristotle
thus notices that making deliberation central to citizenship provides
grounds for excluding certain sorts of people from citizenship: those
deemed unable to deliberate well. In today's theoretical debates,
the point that deliberation excludes certain people is usually raised
as a complaint against making deliberation central to our understanding of politics; we usually place democratic inclusion ahead
of deliberation.[18] In Aristotle, the ordering is the reverse, and the
exclusion of manual workers is accepted as a reasonable implication
of making deliberation central to politics.

An even more striking difference between Aristotle's account of
deliberation and recent democratic theories is the political differentiation that he preserves *within* the class of citizens doing the

deliberating. Although Aristotle treats citizens as equals, he also preserves a distinction between citizens who are ruling and those who are being ruled. He stipulates that all citizens can participate in deliberating and judging, but he also insists that, "all cannot rule at the same time" (II 2, 1261a31–32). Moreover, he directly discusses the fact that free citizens are often in the circumstance of being ruled (III 4, 1277a21, 25 ff.).[19] These statements seem to indicate that participating in the citizenly activities of judging and deliberating does *not* amount to ruling. Perhaps this is why he is willing to say that juries and assemblies open to all citizens can be spoken of as some kind of indefinite office but not simply as an office (*archē*) (III 1, 1275a31).

Some of the central questions about civic virtue that Aristotle raises in Chapters 2 and 3 of Book III only make sense if one puts due emphasis on the fact that at any particular moment some citizens rule while others do not. Given the heterogeneity in what it is to be a citizen, Aristotle asks, can we still say that there is one excellence of citizenship? If there are distinct kinds of civic virtue associated with the different roles that citizens play, does this not mean that civic virtue is different from human virtue, since there is just one account of human virtue? If every citizen in a city could always participate in ruling, Aristotle suggests, there might not be a disjunction between the virtues of citizenship and those of ordinary human excellence. He notes that in rulers the two sorts of virtue converge, since rulers need practical wisdom (*phronêsis*) just as an excellent human being does. But citizens who are not ruling, he points out, do not need to exercise practical wisdom (III 4, 1277a15, 1277b25–30; cf. I 13, 1260a16–17). Their excellence as citizens is different in kind from their excellence as human beings, partly because it involves sometimes being ruled by others rather than deciding for themselves how to act.

If we put together several of the thoughts collected above we find that citizens (a) cannot all rule at once; (b) do not need, in their capacity as citizens, to exercise practical wisdom when they are not ruling; and (c) can participate in deliberating and judging even when not ruling. The implication is that individual citizens, while they are taking their turn being ruled, can do a good job of participating in deliberation in institutions such as the Assembly without exercising practical wisdom.

Jeffrey Greene has recently argued that the role of a citizen-who-is-being-ruled should be of special interest for us because it is one that our political theory tends not to acknowledge and yet one that is common in our politics.[20] What precisely does such a citizen do? What are his or her excellences? In the much-discussed Chapter 11 of Book III, Aristotle emphasizes the fact that the many "are not as individuals excellent men," and opines that their weakness in practical wisdom makes it "not safe" to put them into the most important offices (III 11, 1281a42; 1281b25–27). When the people are all together, in institutions such as the assembly or the courts, they do as a group have a certain wisdom that allows decent judgments, just as the *demos* can judge dramas well.[21] Even then it is not entirely clear that Aristotle gives the wise multitude the intellectual virtue of practical wisdom (*phronêsis*). Instead, he uses a more general word for intellectual virtue (*dianoia*) (III 11, 1281b6). His terminology is consistent with the notion that deliberating and judging well do not require, nor even give an opportunity for the exercise of, the precise virtue of practical wisdom. The reason might be that *phronêsis* concerns possible actions that you yourself will take, not actions that another entity (the city or the rulers) will take.

This is not to say that the citizens deliberating and judging require no intellectual virtues. On the contrary, Aristotle stipulates that only some people will have the necessary excellences, and we have already seen that the requirements are demanding enough to disqualify manual workers (III 11, 1281b15–20, 1282a15; cf. *Rhet.* I 2, 1356b). The intellectual excellence that the deliberating but ruled citizens must have is described in the *Politics* as "true opinion" (*doxa alethes*) (III 4, 1277b27). In the *Ethics*, there is a brief discussion of an intellectual virtue that seems especially relevant, named "comprehension" in Irwin's translation (*sunesis*). Comprehension is about the same questions as practical wisdom – about the things that can be done in action – but its function is to judge rather than to choose how to act: "Comprehension (*sunesis*) consists in the application of belief to judge (*krinein*) someone else's remarks on a question that concerns practical wisdom (*phronesis*)" (*NE* VI 10, 1143a13–15). Judging well what others are saying about deliberative questions seems a fair rendering of what most citizens sitting in the Assembly need to do. The deliberation occurring in these institutions

is the sort in which a few speakers address a large audience of listeners and judges. The specific task that the listeners have is the one
that Lysias assigned to them in the last line of his speech *Against
Eratosthenes*: "You have listened, you have seen, you have suffered,
you have [the facts]. You be the judge."[22] Aristotle recommends
a very similar formula to end a speech in the final words of his
*Rhetoric*, ending also on the single word command to the audience:
"judge" (*krinate*). The intellectual virtue that is required of citizens
when they are deliberating but not ruling seems to be the ability
to judge well the arguments that are made in the Assembly about
what the city should do. Aristotle's discussion of the difference
between the virtues of a good citizen and those of a good person highlights the fact that judging well what the city should do is different
from judging well what you yourself should do, especially when you
are not ruling the city.

Aristotle's praise of systems in which the people take on the
task of judging but do not occupy the highest offices has helped to
cement his reputation as a critic of democracy.[23] But it is worth noting, as Schofield does, that the argument emphasizing the people's
excellence in listening and judging was not one put forward only
by aristocrats or oligarchs. Thucydides recounts a speech by a Sicil-
ian democratic leader named Athenagoras, who defends democracy
against its critics by arguing, "if the best guardians of property are
the rich, and the best counselors the wise, none can hear and decide
(*krinai*) so well as the many."[24] To modern democratic ears, Aristotle's approach remains appealing in some ways. Most significantly,
it invites all citizens to participate in deliberating in settings where
their deliberations will "have authority over the more important
matters" (III 11, 1282a37). On the other hand, Aristotle preserves
a hierarchy between ruler and ruled that is foreign to most theories arising in the context of democratic individualism. Rousseau's
demand – that we find a way of organizing ourselves in which we
each obey only ourselves and remain as free as before – is not met
in Aristotle's account of citizenship and political deliberation. In
recent theories deliberation is what makes a polity truly democratic,
whereas for Aristotle deliberation is what makes a democracy, or any
regime, truly *political* – a place of political rule rather than despotic
mastery.

### ACTING TOGETHER

It might be tempting for modern deliberative democrats to try to take on board Aristotle's prioritization of deliberation while leaving behind his emphasis on the distinction between ruler and ruled among citizens. Instead of giving the assembly and the juries the halfway-house status of "indefinite offices," why not grant them the full title of "offices" (*archai*) and thereby promote the ordinary citizens serving in them to the category of rulers? Why not free those citizens from the subordinate status of citizens-being-ruled and thus democratize Aristotle's understanding of citizenship more completely than he does?

The problem, from Aristotle's perspective, is that the political complementarity involved in the ruler-ruled distinction seems to be part of what allows a multitude of citizens to act together as one *polis*. The best way to understand the importance of the ruler-ruled distinction may be to place it alongside other sorts of differences that Aristotle values. As commentators have recently highlighted, Aristotle sees the benefit that diversity among the citizens' knowledge, experience, and backgrounds brings to deliberation.[25] Thus he advises using a mixture of fines and stipends, elections and lotteries, to insure that the group of citizens involved in deliberating has balanced participation from the poor and the nobles, "for they will deliberate better if they all deliberate together, the people with the notables, and the latter with the multitude" (IV 14, 1298b12–25). In the chapter on the wisdom of the multitude he remarks that the *demos*, "when mixed with their betters … benefit their states, just as a mixture of roughage and pure food-concentrate is more useful than a little of the latter by itself" (III 11, 1281b35). And he famously argues against Plato that aiming for too much unity and thereby eliminating plurality is destructive to the nature of a city (II 2).

The most common recent invocations of this argument about the benefits of plurality tend to under-emphasize the purely political kind of pluralism that we have encountered in Aristotle's thought – the pluralism that encompasses both rulers and ruled. In modern political and social theory we are comfortable discussing functional differentiation in the economic realm, as when remarking upon the division of labor. (Emile Durkheim used a line from Aristotle's

*Politics* as an epigraph to his famous treatise on that topic: "A city-state consists not only of a number of people, but of people of different kinds, since a city-state does not come from people who are alike" (II 2, 1261a23–24).[26] We are more suspicious, however, of discussing functional differentiation in the political realm, where it threatens to introduce too much inequality among citizens. Aristotle, however, insists on preserving the political difference between ruler and ruled as much as the other sorts of difference mentioned above. As we have seen, he states unequivocally that free and equal citizens "cannot all rule at the same time" (II 2, 1260a31; cf. 1276b36–1277a11), which is to say that the distinction between ruler and ruled cannot be eliminated from the city. To illustrate his remark that a city consists "of dissimilar elements" he adduces a list of examples of other complex wholes: animals, which consist of souls and bodies; souls, which consist of reason and desire; and households, which consist of men, women, and slaves (III 4, 1277a4–11). As Reeve points out in a footnote to his translation of this passage, these examples all appear in his earlier discussion of natural rulers and natural subjects in Chapter 13 of Book I, where he treats the subject of ruling and being ruled in relation to slavery and to the city.

Ruling and being ruled are necessarily present in the city because the city is an example of what Aristotle calls a "composite whole" existing by nature, and Aristotle remarks that such wholes always have ruling and ruled parts: "For whenever a number of constituents, whether continuous with one another or discontinuous, are combined into one common thing, a ruling element and a subject element appear. These are present in living things, because this is how nature as a whole works" (I 5, 1254a28–33). Composite wholes have structures; they are organized in a particular manner. Aristotle points to a musical scale as an example of a naturally existing whole, composed of parts (notes) playing different functions, in which one ruling component (the tonic note) provides the principle of organization (I 2, 1254a28–33). Analogously, Aristotle argues that the identity of a city lies not in the identity of the people in a certain location, but instead in the way that they are organized, the particular arrangement of ruling offices outlined by the constitution (*politeia*) (III 3, 1276b1–10). The arrangement of offices is just the determination, however, of who rules. The word *archê* can mean "office," "rule," and "origin" or "first principle" – and perhaps the meanings are not always separable. The *archê* is the ruling principle according to which the offices of the city are organized and political power is distributed.

The originality of Aristotle's account of the *polis* consists partly in his contention that it is built around a distinctive kind of rule. In particular, he argues that the relations of rule in a city are different from the sort of ruling that one finds between a master and a slave. That sort of ruling, he remarks, is analogous to the rule of the soul over the body. The soul commands and the body cannot do otherwise than act; it does not listen to reasons and desires and judge them, but only obeys. Indeed, according to Aristotle, a person's relationship to a slave is basically similar to his relationship to his own body, except that the slave's body is physically separable from him in a way that his own body is not (I 4, 1254a16; I 6, 1255b10). Aristotle's contention early in the *Politics* is that a *polis* is built around a different sort of rule – rule that is "political" rather than mastering. In a fascinating passage he remarks that the possibility of a different sort of rule first comes to light when we notice that the soul itself has different parts and that the relationship between the higher and lower parts is not a relation of mastery but something different: "It is, as I say, in an animal that we can first observe both rule of a master and rule of a statesman. For the soul rules the body with the rule of a master, whereas understanding (*nous*) rules desire (*orexis*) with the rule of a statesman or with the rule of a king" (I 5, 1254b2–15; cf. I 13, 1260a1–7). If people were as different from one another as body is from soul, relations of mastery would be appropriate between them (I 5, 1254b16). In most political communities this is not the case, however; citizens are to be taken as "similar in birth and free" (III 4, 1277b7–10). The relation between parts of the soul is therefore a better model for relations between citizens than the relation between soul and body is (I 13, 1260a4 ff.).

How, then, can we characterize the distinctive character of the "political" sort of rule that comes to light when examining the relations between different parts of the soul? The centrality of deliberation to Aristotle's account of the *polis* seems to help illuminate this issue. Deliberation describes the process in which desires listen to reason and are partly constituted by reasoning; the ruling that exists within the soul is based not on force but on a kind of deliberative persuasion. We now see that this sort of ruling influence is the one that suggests to Aristotle the form of rule appropriate to a *polis*. The account of deliberation in the *Ethics* takes place within an individual, but our power of articulating reasons to others through speech (*logos*) allows us also to influence others. In this way deliberation, an activity through which *nous* and *orexis* are brought into a "political" relationship with one another, can become more than an activity between the parts of an individual's soul; it can escape the boundaries of one soul and become an activity among citizens that brings them together into a whole capable of acting.

One setting in which we see the political relation between parts of the soul escape the bounds of an individual, according to Aristotle, is the influence that a husband wields on his wife, which he describes as political rather than despotic in character, meaning that the wife is reasoned with rather than forced (I 12, 1259a40–b10). Aristotle's justification for the superiority of men in that relationship is that while practical wisdom may be present in both men and women, it is more "authoritative" in men. He assumes that this superiority is "permanent." In politics, however, there is usually no permanent superiority and so the ruling position is rotated. Ruling and being ruled in turn, for Aristotle, is analogous to taking turns being the husband and the wife (III 4, 1277b17–20; I 13, 1260a19–23).[27] In a family as in a single soul, however, the presence of ruling and ruled elements is what allows the different parts to be brought together into a coherent entity able to act as one agent.

The soul and the family are not the only metaphors that Aristotle uses to express the city's nature as a composite whole made of different but complementary parts. He also mentions the crew of a ship, with its distinctions between oarsmen, lookouts, and the captain in terms of what they are meant to do, and therefore in terms of what constitutes excellence for each (III 4, 1276b20–27). Aristotle's point that citizens cannot all rule at the same time would appear in this picture as the simple question: If everyone is captain, who will pull the oars? Notice that asking this is different from asking, If we are all captains, who will have final authority? The concern here is not about anarchy or the need for sovereignty. It is rather that the tasks other than captaining are necessary and that they can be completed better if someone else is doing the captaining. From an oarsman's point of view, the need for a captain lies partly in the need to be free from the work of captaining, which would interfere with his own work. Of course this does not imply that an oarsman would not rather be a captain. It does imply that if he were a captain he would need oarsmen (who were not captains) and they would need him.

The analogue in Aristotle's account of politics is the thought that the work of citizens who are being ruled is work that needs to be done, and that it can be completed better if it is not necessary to rule at the same time. The political work of citizens who are being ruled, as we have seen, is the work of deliberating and judging. I have already suggested that this work needs to be done if any actions are to belong to the city. The question remaining is whether the work of deliberating and judging would better be completed if it were not necessary to rule at the same time.

Here is an argument that it would: deliberating myself about what I will do involves beginning with a desire for something that seems good and then making the goal more specific and achievable so that I can act to pursue it. For individuals who are in offices of rule, deciding what the city should do is also deciding what they, as its leaders, should do. Deciding both at once (using the common virtue of practical wisdom), it may sometimes be difficult for them to tell whether the good they are pursuing is their own or the city's. Individuals who are not in office, on the other hand, approach deliberations about what the city should do from a slightly different perspective. They are not deciding what they as individuals should do, at least not as directly and immediately as the rulers, so it may be easier for them to keep in mind that they are engaged in a deliberation on behalf of something outside themselves – the city. Since deliberation based on the good of the city is a prerequisite to the city's being able to produce its own actions, the deliberation of citizens who can keep the common good in view as a good distinct from (though closely tied to) their own is necessary. Again, this does not imply that citizens being ruled would not prefer to rule. It implies only that when they do rule, they will need other citizens to participate in deliberation and that those citizens will, in turn, participate more effectively if they are not ruling at the same time.

The key difference between Aristotle's understanding of deliberation and ours, then, is that he views deliberation as a model for how some can rule over others in a political manner, while we tend to view deliberation as a model for how we can each rule over ourselves even while in a political community. Aristotle accepts the rule of some citizens over others. Some citizens speak while others listen. Some citizens exercise their practical wisdom as leaders while others judge the speech and actions of the leaders critically. Some citizens view political decisions as answers to the question, "What should I do?" while others view them as answers to the question, "What should the leaders of our city do?" The activities of rulers and ruled are different and complementary to one another. They may fit together into a larger complex of activity that we can describe as itself a single civic activity of a people – but that activity is one that no individual can fully engage in, since individuals play particular roles within it. Just as internal individual deliberations presume the existence of reasoning and desiring parts of the soul, political deliberations presume the existence of different parts of the citizenry, some ruling and others being ruled.

None of these arguments directly answers the practical question of whether democratic Athens was right to repay the money its oligarchic leaders had borrowed from Sparta. Aristotle admits that he has not directly answered this query (III 3, 1276b15). He is content to outline an approach to the more general question of when actions belong to a city. His answer in Book III, I think, is that they do when a city's ruling offices are organized in a way that encourages citizens to deliberate about how to pursue what is beneficial for the city as a whole – which will often require that they take turns being freed from the duties that come with holding ruling office in the city. In Aristotle's thought, citizens can act together in a robust sense, as a single *polis*, partly because they can accept and even prize the fact that they will often find themselves in the position of being ruled by their fellow citizens.

WORKS CITED

Abizadeh, A. 2002. "The Passions of the Wise: Phronesis, Rhetoric, and Aristotle's Passionate Practical Deliberation." *Review of Metaphysics* 56: 267–97

Chambers, S. 2009. "Rhetoric and the Public Sphere: Has Deliberative Democracy Abandoned Mass Democracy?" *Political Theory* 34: 417–38

Cohen, J. 1997. "Deliberation and democratic legitimacy." In *Deliberative Democracy: Essays on Reason and Politics*, eds. J. Bohman and W. Rehg. Cambridge, MA: MIT Press

2010. *Rousseau: A Free Community of Equals*. Oxford: Oxford University Press

Cooper, J. M. 1975. *Reason and Human Good in Aristotle*. Cambridge, MA: Harvard University Press

Crawley, Richard, trans. 1982. *Thucydides, The Peloponnesian War*. New York: Modern Library

De Tocqueville, Alexis, 2000. *Democracy in America*, trans. H. Mansfield and D. Winthrop. Chicago University Press

Dryzek, J. S. 2010. "Rhetoric in Democracy: a Systemic Appreciation." *Political Theory* 38: 319–39

Durkheim, E. and Halls, W. D. 1997. *The Division of Labor in Society*. New York: Free Press

Fish, S. 1999. "Mutual respect as a device of exclusion." In *Deliberative Politics: Essays on Democracy and Disagreement*, ed. S. Macedo. New York: Oxford University Press

Frank, J. 2005. *A Democracy of Distinction: Aristotle and the Work of Politics*. University of Chicago Press

Furley, D. J. 1980. "Self-movers." In *Essays on Aristotle's Ethics*, ed. A. O. Rorty. Berkeley, CA: University of California Press

Garsten, B. 2006. *Saving Persuasion: A Defense of Rhetoric and Judgment*. Cambridge, MA: Harvard University Press

2011. "The Rhetoric Revival in Political Theory." *Annual Review of Political Science* 14: 159–80

Green, J. E. 2010. *The Eyes of the People: Democracy in an Age of Spectatorship*. New York: Oxford University Press

Habermas, J. 1996. *Between Facts and Norms: Contributions to a Discourse Theory of Law and Democracy*. Cambridge, MA: MIT Press

Irwin, T. H. 1980. "Reason and responsibility in Aristotle." In *Essays on Aristotle's Ethics*, ed. A. O. Rorty. Berkeley, CA: University of California Press

Lear, J. 1988. *Aristotle: The Desire to Understand*. Cambridge University Press

Manin, B. 1987. "On Legitimacy and Political Deliberation." *Political Theory* 15: 338–68

Meyer, S. S. 2011. *Aristotle on Moral Responsibility: Character and Cause*. Oxford University Press

Miller, F. D. 1984. "Aristotle on Rationality in Action." *Review of Metaphysics* 37: 499–520

Newman, W. L. 1887–1902. *The Politics of Aristotle*. 4 vols, Oxford University Press

Nichols, M. P. 1992. *Citizens and Statesmen: A Study of Aristotle's Politics*. Lanham, MD: Rowman & Littlefield

Nieuwenberg, P. 2004. "Learning to Deliberate: Aristotle on Truthfulness and Public Deliberation." *Political Theory* 32: 449–67

Ober, J. 2002. *Political Dissent in Democratic Athens: Intellectual Critics of Popular Rule.* Princeton University Press

O'Neill, J. 2002. "The Rhetoric of Deliberation: Some Problems in Kantian Theories of Deliberative Democracy." *Res Publica* 8: 249–68

Pope, M. 1988. "Thucydides and Democracy." *Historia: Zeitschrift für Alte Geschichte* 37: 276–96

Rawls, J. 1971. *A Theory of Justice.* Cambridge, MA: Belknap Press

Reeve, C. D. C. 1998. *Aristotle*, Politics. Indianapolis, IN: Hackett

Rousseau, J.-J. 1997. *The Social Contract*, ed. V. Gourevitch. Cambridge University Press

Sanders, L. M. 1997. "Against Deliberation." *Political Theory* 25: 347–76

Schofield, M. 2011. "Aristotle and the democratization of politics." In *Episteme etc.: Essays in Honour of Jonathan Barnes*, eds. K. Ierodiakonou and B. Morison. Oxford University Press

Waldron, J. 1995. "The Wisdom of the Multitude: Some Reflections on Book 3, Chapter 11 of Aristotle's Politics." *Political Theory* 23: 563–84. Reprinted in *Aristotle's Politics: Critical Essays*, eds. R. Kraut and S. Skultety. Lanham, MD: Rowman & Littlefield

Wiggins, D. 1980. "Deliberation and practical reason." In *Essays on Aristotle's Ethics*, ed. A. O. Rorty. Berkeley, CA: University of California Press

Winthrop, D. 1978. "Aristotle and Theories of Justice." *American Political Science Review* 72: 1201–16

Yack, B. 2006. "Rhetoric and Public Reasoning." *Political Theory* 34: 417–38

NOTES

1. Newman 1887, vol. 1: 231–32. See Isocrates, *Aereopagiticus* 68; Lysias, *Against Eratosthenes* 59; Demosthenes, *Against Leptines* 11; and Aristotle, *Constitution of Athens* 38, 40.

2. Isocrates, *Aereopagiticus* 68: "But the best and strongest proof of the fairness of the people is that, although those who had remained in the city had borrowed a hundred talents from the Lacedaemonians with which to prosecute the siege of those who occupied the Piraeus, yet later when an assembly of the people was held to consider the payment of the debt, and when many insisted that it was only fair that the claims of the Lacedaemonians should be settled, not by those who had suffered the siege, but by those who had borrowed the money, nevertheless the

people voted to pay the debt out of the public treasury." Demosthenes, *Against Leptines* 10–11.

3. Crawley 1982: 171 (3.36).

4. Crawley 1982: 358 (6.1). "The same winter the Athenians resolved to sail again to Sicily..."

5. Pope 1988: 277–78.

6. Ober 2002: 69. "When an Athenian said that 'the Athenians' made an alliance with another state, or when a public decree proclaimed that 'the demos of the Athenians' decided to sail against the enemies of Athens, the ideological underpinning was an assumption of communal action for the common, unitary, national good. In reality, of course, the decision was made and carried out by a much smaller group; the actual participants in making the decision or carrying out the action represent only a fraction of the total population implied by the language of the announcement."

7. Yack 2006; Nieuwenberg 2004; O'Neill 2002; Dryzek 2010; Chambers 2009; Garsten 2006; Garsten 2011.

8. Rousseau 1997, I.6.4; Cohen 2010: 2 (emphasis added); Rawls 1971: xviii, 10.

9. Manin 1987, 352; Cohen 1997; Habermas 1996.

10. It is true, according to Aristotle's physics, that nothing but the god can be a self-mover. For a good effort to understand how this position is compatible with the understanding of humans as self-movers, see Furley 1980.

11. Reasoning about how to satisfy a mere appetite does not yield a deliberated choice, in the full sense. See *NE* VI 9, 1142b18–20 and Irwin 1980: 128–29.

12. Wiggins describes deliberation as a search for the "best specification" of what would satisfy a desire, while Lear describes it as "the transmission of desire" from one object to another. Lear 1988: 143–51; Wiggins 1980: 228.

13. For this issue see Cooper 1975: 39–41; Miller 1984; and Abizadeh 2002: 281–82.

14. It should be noted that the issue of moral and legal responsibility is raised by Aristotle but is not held to be identical to the question of which actions are deliberated. People can be punished for actions that are voluntary but not deliberated, as when they act out of passion, anger, insensitivity or even drunkenness: Meyer 2011.

15. Schofield 2001.

16. Similarly, an emphasis on citizenly activity can be seen in Aristotle's response to the claim that people who become citizens after a revolution, such as those added to the lists by Cleisthenes, are not "really"

citizens because they do not deserve to have that status. Aristotle responds by pointing out that if they are permitted to hold the offices mentioned earlier, and thus can participate in deliberating and judging, they are in fact citizens. *Pol.* III 2, 1275b34–1276a6. On citizenship as activity, see Frank 2005 and Winthrop 1978.

17. Schofield 2011.
18. Fish 1999; Sanders 1997.
19. For more on the significance of being-ruled in Aristotle, see Green 2010.
20. Green 2010.
21. Waldron 1995: 575.
22. Lysias, *Against Eratosthenes* 12.100.
23. Ober 2002: 319–23.
24. Crawley 1982: 383 (VI 39). I owe the reference to Schofield 2011.
25. Waldron 1995; Nichols 1992: 66. "It is precisely because the members of the multitude have different contributions to make that they have a just claim to rule." Frank 2005.
26. Durkheim and Halls 1997. Thanks to Philippe Urfalino for pointing out this reference to me.
27. Compare de Tocqueville 2000: 2.3.12.

# 14 Aristotle and Rawls on the common good

## ARISTOTLE ON THE COMMON ADVANTAGE

Can Aristotle's conception of the good play a useful role in contemporary political philosophy? The answer I will give to this question is a qualified "yes." To defend my answer, I will compare his treatment of this subject with that of the most important political philosopher of the last century, John Rawls. Like Aristotle, Rawls puts the public good at the heart of his moral and political system, and so a comparative study of their differences should be fruitful. If I am right, Aristotle's theory of the good is not only defensible (when suitably adjusted), but provides a sounder basis for liberal democracy than does that of Rawls. I will begin with Aristotle, turn to Rawls, and then return to Aristotle in order to show the merits of his way of thinking.

It is clear from the familiar opening lines of the *Nicomachean Ethics* and the *Politics* that Aristotle locates the good at the center of practical thought. Every craft, inquiry, action, and decision, he says in the *Ethics*, aims at some good; the *polis*, he observes in the *Politics*, like every community, is established for the sake of some good. He urges the audience of the *Ethics* to ask: What is the good for the sake of which the political community is organized? The right answer, he argues, is that it is excellent activity of the rational soul, supported by external resources, over the course of a lifetime (*NE* I 10, 1101a14–16). This is the conception of the good that he thinks it would be best for all citizens to affirm and enact in their cooperative

I am grateful to Marguerite Deslauriers and Dorothea Frede for their helpful comments on an earlier draft.

undertakings. The ideal city he depicts in Books VII and VIII of the *Politics* is organized around it, and that is why he restates (in *Politics* VII 1–3) some of its main tenets before he proceeds to the details of his design of this best of all cities. But it would be very odd to read the *Politics* in a way that made the good relevant to Aristotle's thinking *only* in Books VII and VIII. It is implicitly in the background throughout this work, just as it remains in the background throughout his ethical treatises.[1]

In several passages, Aristotle uses the more specific term, *sumpheron* ("advantageous" or "beneficial"), rather than the broader word *agathon* ("good") to name the focal point of politics. For example, in Book VIII of the *Ethics*, he writes: "The political community seems to have come together from the beginning and to abide for the sake of advantage. For it is at this that the lawgivers aim, and justice, they say, is the common advantage. So the other communities aim at some portion of what is advantageous . . . but the political community does not aim at the present advantage but at the whole of life" (*NE* VIII 9, 1160a11–23). Similarly, the notion of advantage figures in the way he distinguishes correct from incorrect constitutions: those that look to the common advantage, and only those, are correct (III 7, 1279a17–20).

The proper role of the political community, according to his way of thinking, is to seek what is advantageous or beneficial to each of the citizens. Its goal is not to promote what is good (period) but good for no one. It is not to make the universe a better place, by increasing the amount of value in it. That notion of absolute goodness – what is good, but not advantageous – can be found in some of the leading moral philosophers of the twentieth century (G. E. Moore and W. D. Ross, for example), and it is still present in much recent thinking about intrinsic value.[2] But for Aristotle the political community must look to what is good *for* each of its members. I will speak interchangeably of what is "good for" someone and what is "advantageous" or "beneficial," and I will assume that when Aristotle asserts that all decisions aim at some good, he is moving toward the conclusion that all actions should seek what is advantageous.

Aristotle is not a pioneer in holding that we must study what is advantageous, if we are to deliberate well about the conduct of our lives and about political matters. For an inquiry into what is truly advantageous also lies at the heart of Plato's *Republic*. One of the most important conceptual points that Plato makes in this work is that there is such a thing as something's being advantageous on its own and apart from its consequences. That is what he aims to show about justice: that it would be good for someone to have justice in his soul, even if that virtue were not an effective means to achieving such further benefits as good repute or other-worldly rewards. Being good for someone, in other words, does not consist in or require being a good means to a further end; a benefit can be a non-instrumental benefit. We can safely assume that Aristotle accepts Plato's point. Accordingly, when he argues that the good consists in virtuous activity of the rational soul, adequately supplied with external goods, over the course of a lifetime, he should be taken to mean that the highest non-instrumental advantage one can acquire is to live such a life.

## RAWLS ON GOODNESS AS RATIONALITY

Such words as "advantage," "benefit," and "interest" permeate Rawls' first book, *A Theory of Justice*. He writes that justice "does not allow that the sacrifices imposed on a few are outweighed by the larger sum of *advantages* enjoyed by many" (p. 3).[3] "Although a society is a cooperative venture for mutual *advantage*, it is typically marked by a conflict as well as an identity of *interests*...Persons are not indifferent as to how the greater *benefits* produced by their collaboration are distributed" (p. 4). The theory of the good that he advances in Chapter 7 of this work – which he calls "goodness as rationality" – is a theory about what is good *for* individuals. It is, in other words, a theory about what makes something non-instrumentally advantageous or beneficial. When he says that "the two main concepts of ethics are those of the right and the good" (p. 21), he should be taken to mean that one of the two main concepts of ethics is that of being good *for* someone. So, he accepts at least this much of Aristotle's framework: one of the chief tasks of political philosophy, he believes, is to determine which things are non-instrumentally advantageous.

His conception of what is good for someone can be expressed in very simple terms, and is taken over from some twentieth century formulations of utilitarianism: the good is "the satisfaction of rational desire" (pp. 23, 27), or the achievement of a "rational plan of life" (pp. 358–59). To understand these phrases properly, one must see how Rawls uses the term "rational." One's rational goals are not necessarily the ones that one actually has; rather, as Rawls defines them, they are the aims one would have, were one to plan one's life with great care, after ascertaining all the relevant facts. As he puts it: "Our good is determined by the plan of life that we would adopt with full deliberative rationality if the future were accurately foreseen and adequately realized in the imagination" (p. 370).

This theory is developed with great subtlety and care in Chapter VII, but we need not attend to its details. For present purposes, it is important to realize that the standard he proposes to assess whether someone's goals are rational is not difficult for most people to achieve, and it provides no basis for saying that some goals are inherently more worthwhile than others. To make this point, he imagines someone whose only pleasure in life is to count blades of grass (pp. 379–80). If that plan is the one he would choose after careful deliberation, then his way of life, Rawls admits, is good for him. His conception of the good provides no basis for saying that other people have better lives than this – lives that are good for them to a higher degree than the grass-counter's life is good for him.

Once Rawls' conception of goodness as rationality is in place, he is in a position to claim that there are certain goods that have a special role to play in the design and governance of a modern liberal democracy. These are the items that he designates "primary social goods." They consist in the various political rights, liberties, opportunities, and powers that liberal democracies constitutionally guarantee all citizens; also included are the income and wealth that accrue to them by the regulation of economic institutions; and the "bases of self-respect" – that is, those social conditions that lead citizens to affirm their plans of life as worth achieving. The importance of these advantages, he thinks, is shown by the fact that individuals who do not know the content of their plans of life will, out of self-interest, want to secure more rather than fewer of them. Required to collectively choose principles of justice behind a "veil of ignorance" in an "original position" that deprives them of any knowledge of their rational goals, they will elect to govern themselves by principles and through institutions that protect their ability to lead a life of their choosing, whatever that life is. They will, for example, choose to affirm a principle of religious liberty even though, behind the veil, they do not know whether their plan of life has a secular or religious orientation. Similarly, behind the veil, they will not be indifferent to their economic well-being, even though their plan of life, beyond the veil, may be that of an ascetic. Even if abundant material resources are not needed for the fulfillment of their rational plans, they have, in the original position, reason to be concerned about their economic well-being; not knowing what their plans will be, they must protect themselves in case achieving their major goals requires significant economic resources.

One of the many remarkable features of Rawls' political theory is that it treats almost any way of life as valuable, none more so than any other, and yet it yields the result that certain advantages – the primary social goods – are ones that the political community must guarantee. Notice how different Aristotle's way of thinking is. He holds that political theory must discover which of the many ways in which people live are genuinely worthwhile, and that civic institutions should be designed to promote only these truly beneficial modes of existence. Since virtuous activity is the only correct choice as an ultimate end, a *polis* is well governed only if its laws produce good human beings who engage in excellent activities, or come as close to that goal as circumstances permit. Rawls has an expansive and minimally demanding conception of the good; Aristotle's is narrow and makes the good difficult to achieve.

## POLITICAL LIBERALISM AND PROFOUND
## SOCIAL DIVISION

Rawls' conception of the good is controversial, but before I point out what some of its difficulties are, I must turn to a further aspect of his thinking, which emerges most fully in his second major work, *Political Liberalism*.[4] A reader of *A Theory of Justice* who had not read the later work could be forgiven for taking Rawls to be saying that there is one true account of what is good for human beings – goodness as rationality. But *Political Liberalism* repeatedly points out that this is not the position he wishes to defend. Here, goodness as rationality is not put forward as a conception of the good that is unrestrictedly superior to any other. On the contrary, goodness as rationality must not be construed as a competitor with any of the controversial "comprehensive" conceptions of the good that are found in the major religions and systems of moral philosophy. Instead, Rawls upholds it as the most reasonable conception of those goods that are appropriately pursued or safeguarded in politics (pp. 176–77). It is a theory about what a liberal and democratic citizen needs, not a more general theory about what is good for all human beings whatsoever, at any time or place.

In effect, then, Rawls assumes that each citizen in a just society will have a bipartite conception of the good, one part (goodness as rationality) applying to the political realm, and the other (his partisan comprehensive view) regulating all the other spheres of his life (p. 38). The two parts exist side by side, as it were, in that neither is encompassed by the other.[5]

An important change in Rawls' thinking has occurred: he has moved from a utopian vision of a pluralistic yet harmonious democratic society to a far more pessimistic picture. The shift is signaled by the question he seeks to answer in *Political Liberalism*: "How is it possible that there may exist over time a stable and just society of free and equal citizens profoundly divided by reasonable though incompatible religious, philosophical, and moral doctrines?" (p. xx). *Political Liberalism* takes its starting point from "the fact of reasonable pluralism." By this, Rawls does not simply mean that comprehensive moral and religious doctrines *differ*; more disturbingly, many of their views, including their conceptions of what is good, *contradict* each other. One religion or philosophy says that it is good for people to engage in practice X; another says that practice X does no good at all, or perhaps is even harmful. They cannot both be right, and that is deeply regrettable.

The Rawls of *A Theory of Justice* is more sanguine. He notes in this work that in a just society the content of citizens' rational plans will almost certainly differ, but those differences are to be welcomed, not regretted. He says: "it is, in general, a good thing that individuals' conceptions of their good should differ in significant ways" (p. 393). He then adds: "Human beings have various talents and abilities the totality of which is unrealizable by any one person or group of persons. Thus we not only benefit from the complementary nature of our developed inclinations but we take pleasure in one another's activities. It is as if others were bringing forth a part of ourselves that we have not been able to cultivate" (pp. 393–94). According to this picture, each citizen is glad to cooperate with other citizens and contribute to their success in achieving their rational plans, even though those plans are unlike his own. For each citizen, guided by his conception of goodness as rationality as the sole theory of the good, takes himself to be helping all other citizens achieve what is genuinely good for them. *Political Liberalism* depicts a far less pretty social nexus: it expects a just society to be one in which citizens are convinced that the comprehensive conceptions of the good and right that guide many of their fellow citizens are deeply mistaken. Justice nonetheless demands that they contribute to civic institutions that allow those misguided ways of life to flourish.

It is in itself no objection to *Political Liberalism* that it assumes that free and democratic societies will tend to be divided in this way. But we should ask whether the whole Rawlsian framework for thinking about politics can hold together while it undergoes this shift in its thinking. In *A Theory of Justice*, all of the parties in the original position are right to assume that, although they do not know what their plan of life is, it is a plan worth carrying out, simply because it is rational. Their knowledge that they have a worthwhile plan is what motivates them to find principles of justice and civic institutions that will contribute to their success, once the veil of ignorance is lifted. But in *Political Liberalism*, no party behind the veil can tell whether the comprehensive conception of the good that he has is correct – whether, in other words, what he will value beyond the veil really is valuable. Each knows that individuals can be deeply divided about such matters. Not all of them can have a true philosophical or religious understanding of the right and the good, and there is no reason for any to suppose about himself that he has a true comprehensive theory. In fact, the parties cannot assume that *any* of their plans of life is worthwhile, when judged by the standard of a true comprehensive conception of the good. What reason do they have, then, to choose ethical principles or political institutions, when they realize that the conceptions of the good that guide them all might be mistaken?

Another problem is whether it is coherent for a person to have a bipartite conception of the good, one part (goodness as rationality) of which is used for public discourse, the other (a comprehensive conception) for all other spheres of life. Is the idea that goodness as rationality is not to be thought of as a *true* account of what is advantageous, but rather as a way of talking that we are obliged to use for constitutional matters? Is it only in our non-political deliberations that we succeed in thinking about what is really good for people? In that case, public dialogue becomes a strange form of pretense, and it is doubtful that people who think of themselves as addressing each other in this way can take civic life seriously. Another alternative is to say that whereas goodness as rationality is true-in-the-political-realm, one's comprehensive conception of the good alone is true-in-the-non-political-realm. But this form of relativism is as difficult to make sense of as the more familiar kind according to which what you say is true-for-you and what I say is true-for-me. It is part of our commonsense ethical framework that a particular action is either good (to some extent) for someone or not good (to any extent) for that person, and that in politics, just as in other spheres of life, we have to learn how to tell the difference. That, of course, is just how Aristotle (following Plato) thinks about the matter.

### GOODNESS AND PLANS

These thoughts lead me to the conclusion that when we assess Rawls' conception of goodness as rationality, we should set aside the complications that arise in his political theory after he wrote *A Theory of Justice.*[6] We should ask, in other words: How plausible a theory of advantageousness is the theory presented in Chapter VII of that work, when it is considered on its merits as a comprehensive conception? That would remain a worthwhile question, whether or not the problems that I have been raising about the later developments in his thinking have satisfactory solutions.

Recall one of the basic ideas of goodness as rationality: "Our good is determined by the plan of life that we would adopt with full deliberative rationality if the future were accurately foreseen and adequately realized in the imagination" (p. 370). Now, of course, few of us, if any, can accurately foresee the future. Most of us have limited imaginations. So, the actual plans we come to have are not in fact adopted "with full deliberative rationality." But that does not undermine Rawls' theory; it does not show that in most cases there is no fact of the matter about whether something we do or something that happens to us is good for us. That is because Rawls is not saying that our good is determined by the plan of life that we *have* adopted in ideal epistemic conditions. Nor does he mean that our good is determined by the plan of life that we *should* adopt in those conditions. His formulation specifies that it is the plan that we *would* adopt. We might object: How much confidence about what is good for us can we ever be entitled to, if Rawls' theory is correct? That is indeed worrisome, but there is, I think, a deeper and more revealing objection: even when we are justifiably confident about what plan someone would adopt in ideal epistemic conditions, our conviction that this is so rests on our conviction that he *should* adopt that plan for his own good.

To illustrate, suppose my nephew is trying to decide whether to attend university A or university B, and he asks for my advice, because I know him and these schools quite well. He has no precise career plans, but wants the best education for someone like him. I see, let's suppose, that A is a better match for his talents, interests, and temperament than B; he would mature and develop more fully at A than B, and would be happier there. I could say to my nephew: "Were you to think about your choices with full deliberative rationality, you would choose A over B." But my basis for this statement would be that this is the choice he should make, because A is better for him than B.

In this example, the order of my thinking is: "This would be best for you, and that is why you ought to make this plan." That is the normal way in which planning is related to advantageousness: we choose one plan over another because of its greater advantages. we assume that facts about what is good for us were already in place before we made our plans, and we try to ascertain those facts in order to construct our plans prudently. That is why we exercise care and imagination when we make major plans: we assume that we are discovering what is good for us, not creating what is good for us by virtue of deliberating in a careful way. Care is needed in making decisions because carelessness would lead us to overlook facts about ourselves and our situations that make it the case that some things are better for us than others. The problem for Rawls' theory of goodness as rationality is that it makes a certain kind of careful deliberative procedure *constitutive* of goodness. But there is no reason to set aside our commonsense assumption that our careful deliberative procedures are needed because there are already facts about what is good for us, waiting to be uncovered.

## THE ARISTOTELIAN PRINCIPLE AND PERFECTIONISM

Before we move away from Rawls, let's take note of two ways in which he situates himself in relation to Aristotle. First, in *A Theory of Justice* he proposes an empirical generalization that he dubs "the Aristotelian principle," which holds that "other things equal, human beings enjoy the exercise of their realized capacities (their innate or trained abilities), and this enjoyment increases the more the capacity is realized, or the greater the complexity" (p. 374). Rawls is careful to say (p. 374 n. 20) that Aristotle does not himself explicitly formulate this idea, but he holds that it is implicit in several of his doctrines regarding pleasure and the exercise of our natural powers. That is why he calls it the *Aristotelian* principle. Although it is not a normative or evaluative thesis, it nonetheless plays a significant role in his attempt to convince his readers that the just society he depicts will be stable because all citizens will freely embrace and take pride in its institutions. They will construct and sustain complex religious, cultural, and athletic organizations that hold their interest throughout their lives. They will have a strong tendency to find their lives psychologically rewarding, and this tendency will reinforce their moral commitment to the political institutions that give them the freedom to live their lives as they choose.

Here again we see Rawls painting a rather sunny picture of a just society. He invokes the Aristotelian principle to justify his optimism. *Political Liberalism* is darker in its presupposition that there are also likely to be profound divisions in a free society. It is stressful to have to interact with people whose moral, religious, and philosophical orientation is so different from yours that what you take to be good or right they take to be bad or wrong. That tension in human relations and the political struggles to which they lead is acknowledged in *A Theory of Justice*, but not emphasized; the focus of that early work is elsewhere.

A second point of contact Rawls establishes between himself and Aristotle lies in his taxonomy of moral theories, for he speaks of Aristotle and several other philosophers as "perfectionists," and he contrasts his own approach to moral theory with the one he attributes to that alternative tradition. Perfectionism, as he defines it in *A Theory of Justice*, holds that right actions maximize the good, and that the good consists in "the realization of human excellence in the various forms of culture" (p. 22). He takes Nietzsche to be a perfectionist in this sense, citing (p. 286 n. 50) the passage in *Untimely Meditations* in which Nietzsche writes: "Mankind must work continually to produce individual great human beings – this and nothing else is the task." To Aristotle he attributes a "more moderate doctrine" according to which "a principle of perfection is accepted as but one standard among several" (p. 286). As Rawls reads the *Nicomachean Ethics*, there are a plurality of goods – one of which is "the realization of human excellence in the various forms of culture," and this bundle of goods is to be maximized. He distances himself from Aristotle, so read, in two respects: the good, he holds, is the achievement of a rational plan of life; and the good is not to be maximized, because our pursuit of it must always be constrained by principles of moral rightness.

It is doubtful, however, that Aristotle should be taken to mean that the goal of politics is to produce the greatest amount of good, however it is distributed. As I pointed out from the start, the guiding principle of his political philosophy is the *common* good of all citizens. Implicit in that notion is the idea that it would be unjust to demand that some citizens suffer a loss of well-being merely in order to increase the total amount of well-being in their city. Aristotle designs civic institutions so that all will fare well (in favorable circumstances), not so that the total amount of faring well is as high as possible. Even in his discussion of slavery, he does not argue that some should be made to suffer so that the total amount of good can be realized. Rather, his defense of slavery depends on his assertion that it is beneficial for *both* master and slave.[7] It is anachronistic to read into him the idea, which came to the fore among the classical utilitarians, that the supreme criterion of right action is the simple aggregation of well-being across persons.

So, Rawls ought to have acknowledged in his discussion of perfectionism that it can take a non-maximizing form, according to which one important kind of good is the "realization of human excellence." That is the kind of perfectionist Aristotle is. We can also go beyond Rawls' discussion of perfectionism by distinguishing one variety that counts human excellence as a good thing (period), and another that counts excellence as good *for* one or more individuals. As I noted earlier, Aristotle's ethical and political theories are accounts of what is advantageous – what is good *for* people. But there are other philosophers who can be reasonably categorized as perfectionists who cast their moral and political theories in terms of what is good *absolutely* rather than what is good *for* someone. One example is G. E. Moore, who argues in Chapter VI of *Principia Ethica* that one of the principal criteria of social progress is the extent to which a society enjoys objects of beauty – a thesis that implies that aesthetic education and support of the arts is one of the principal aims of the state.[8] For Moore, absolute goodness is to be maximized, and the enjoyment of aesthetic excellence is one of the chief things that is absolutely good. For Aristotle, the *polis* is to seek the common advantage, and the chief advantages are the exercise of intellectual and ethical excellence.

Rawls rejects these and all other forms of perfectionism, because he regards the promotion of human excellence as no less objectionable than the promotion of a state religion. As he says in *Political Liberalism*: "The government can no more act...to advance human excellence, or the values of perfection...than it can to advance Catholicism or Protestantism, or any other religion. None of these views of the meaning, value, and purpose of human life...is affirmed by citizens generally, and so the pursuit of any one of them through basic institutions gives political society a sectarian character" (pp. 179–80). Perhaps what lies behind this objection is the assumption that perfectionism is inherently exclusionary. Rawls may be assuming that perfectionism divides society into an elite of connoisseurs or cultural sophisticates who can appreciate or acquire "excellence in the various forms of culture," and others who are not capable of, or not drawn to, these cultural achievements. Just as a Catholic might hold that the God he worships is the only divine being and that all other faiths are defective, so perfectionism, as Rawls treats it, allocates greater social resources to those who excel, and so other citizens inevitably occupy an inferior political status. That may be what he means by the "sectarian character" of any political society governed by a perfectionist conception of the good.

But if this is Rawls' objection, the perfectionist can reply that it is the responsibility of the state to allocate equal resources to citizens, so that all have the same opportunities to acquire the most valuable excellences they can achieve. This is precisely what Aristotle has in mind in Book VIII of the *Politics*. He argues that there must be a single publicly supported education provided to all children (VIII 1), and he includes musical training as an important part of the curriculum, in part because he thinks that the leisure of adults should be devoted to the appreciation of the harmony and rhythm that accompany poetry and drama (VIII 3, 6–7). Greek drama was not reserved or accessible to only a small elite, any more than television and video games are in our age. It should not be assumed in advance that by its very nature only a few people can be excellent or can value excellence.[9]

It is likely, however, that Rawls has a different objection to perfectionism in mind. Suppose that a Catholic were to say that there is nothing inherently exclusionary about his religion: everyone can become a member of the faith, and in fact this is precisely the reason why he wants to establish Catholicism as the state religion. The response Rawls would make to such a Catholic is that in order to be a good citizen of a liberal democratic society one need only be a reasonable person, that is, a person willing to live cooperatively with others on the basis of principles acceptable to all. It would be unfair to require that one also be a Catholic, or to give Catholics a prior claim to social resources. Similarly, he would say, good citizenship does not require that one achieve or value "excellence in the various forms of culture." To be a morally upstanding member of the political community, one need not value knowledge for its own sake, or beauty, or music, or science, or any of the other goods that perfectionists favor. Therefore, the institutions of the state should not themselves inculcate these cultural values. They should leave that kind of education to families or other non-political and non-coercive organizations.

This way of objecting to perfectionism embodies a minimalism about what the proper business of the state should be. It assumes that the education that the state should guarantee to children consists solely in their acquisition of skills that they will later need to participate in the economy and discharge their civic responsibilities. Public education in the arts, the humanities, mathematics, and the sciences cannot be justified by Rawls on the grounds that they enrich our lives, because enrichment through the love of these subjects for their own sake is a perfectionist value that can no more be invoked by the state than can religious values.

One way to see the problem created by Rawls' opposition to perfectionism is to imagine a society in which there is unequal access to outstanding cultural artifacts (music, theater, film, literary works, museums of natural history) or to natural beauty (parks, forests, mountains, wilderness). Suppose there were no public museums or libraries, no areas of great beauty open to the public, no public schools that expose students to the sciences and the humanities. As a result, the children of the poor, unlike their wealthy counterparts, develop no interest in feats of the imagination, or works of beauty, or exemplary products of the human mind. There would be something deeply wrong with such a society, even if the poor could fully achieve their limited aims. It would be an unjust society, but its defectiveness, so evident to us, is not a matter that would be of concern to the hypothetical contracting parties posited by Rawls' theory. They are not described as individuals who have a sense of beauty; they are not eager to ensure that they have access to beauty, once the veil of ignorance is lifted. For Rawls, justice has to do, primarily or exclusively, with only certain goods: political liberties and rights, and fair access to economic opportunities and wealth. For these goods are the means by which citizens can safeguard their capacity to achieve their ends, whatever those ends are. They are therefore the only goods that the contracting parties are allowed to care about. The complaint made by perfectionists is that these contracting parties are for this reason ill suited to design a good and just society.

### ARISTOTLE REVIVED: FLOURISHING AND HUMAN DEVELOPMENT

I said in my opening paragraph that Aristotle's conception of the good can still play a useful role in contemporary political philosophy – but also that my defense of it will be qualified. It is time to make good on these claims.

He holds that everything we do should be undertaken for the sake of one ultimate end: excellent activity of the rational part of the soul. He thinks that the most excellent of these activities is one in which theoretical reason reflects on the truths of philosophy and science. He assumes that some properties of human beings are essential to them, and this assumption plays an important role in his moral philosophy. All of these features of his philosophy are open to serious doubt.[10] Nonetheless, there is an extremely fruitful idea that underlies his conception of what is good for human beings. Rawls himself puts his finger on it in a footnote to his discussion of the Aristotelian principle: as he notes, according to Aristotle, "the exercise of our natural powers is a leading human good" (p. 374 n. 20). I will now try to elaborate on this key insight, and will argue that it provides a suitable guide to the design of political institutions and the conduct of citizens.[11]

The central idea is that for something to be good for any living being (and therefore for a human being) is for it to be a component of or means to its flourishing. The things that are good for human beings are the ones that play a role in our living flourishing lives – lives that go well for us in a way that is comparable to the way the lives of other sorts of creatures go well for them. For any living thing, flourishing consists in the full development of its natural powers, and since human beings have psychological and not only physical powers, a flourishing person is someone who possesses, develops, and enjoys the exercise of cognitive, affective, sensory, and social powers, as well as physical powers.

I suggest that many of the basic institutions of liberal democracy – the rights, powers, and opportunities (freedom of conscience, private property, free association) that Rawls guarantees in his first principle of justice (p. 53) – are best seen as structures that make room for and enhance the development of the powers whose enjoyable exercise constitutes a flourishing life. To take one example: Why should there be freedom of artistic and creative expression and more generally freedom of thought? My answer: the human mind more fully flowers in the rich intellectual environment that liberties of thought and expression promote. Again: Why should there be a system of private property – a network of rights that allow people to have substantial control over things of their own? Not only because doing so is a necessary condition of wealth-production (for that should never be a self-sufficient goal of the political community), but also because the independent habits of thought and action that arise when property rights are secure are in themselves good. Knowing that some portion of the world will continue to be our own to care for and enjoy, we are more energetically engaged in our social and physical environment, and so our social and cognitive powers are more fully activated.[12] Another question: Why should there be religious liberty? That is an especially interesting aspect of liberal societies, and I will turn to it in a moment.

Much more must be said about whether the notion of flourishing and the deployment of our basic powers can do as much work as I would like. It could be claimed that flourishing is almost an empty notion, and is merely a verbal equivalent for such abstract terms as "well-being" or "doing well." I believe, on the contrary, that human flourishing is a "thick concept" – a rich combination of descriptive and evaluative elements. Nearly every adult human being already possesses and tacitly uses countless assumptions about how children should develop, and in doing so they employ a conception of human flourishing that is concrete enough to guide their actions. These descriptive and evaluative assumptions are among those in which we are most confident, and so they are precisely the ones on which a normative theory should be built.

Several aspects of human flourishing make it a particularly useful notion for understanding the basis of liberal political institutions. First, although it has definite content, it cannot on its own specify in full detail how someone should live, because the broad similarities in the way we properly develop from childhood to adulthood leave room for countless individual differences. For example, among the powers that we should develop are those of the senses, and part of the value of musical and pictorial education is the way in which we learn to enjoy the exercise of our powers of sight and hearing. But differences in temperament, talent, and opportunities will lead different people to enjoy different styles of music, or to develop their talents of visual representation more than their musical skills. The same holds true of our physical powers: athletics and dance are ways in which these capacities pleasurably grow, but different skills and temperaments must be considered when we choose the direction in which they are developed. The bare notion that one's powers should mature and be pleasurably exercised does not by itself determine whether to take up this sport or that, or devote oneself to a musical instrument, or to singing, or dancing, and so on. To make those decisions intelligently, one must be free to try many alternatives, and one must arrive at some understanding of one's limitations, strengths, and proclivities. Those decisions are best left to individuals to make in consultation with those who know them intimately. They cannot be made by the remote institutions that modern governments must be.

The notion of flourishing can provide a grounding for liberal institutions in a second way: part of what it is for our cognitive powers to grow is for us to acquire the ability to make decisions on our own. If we are too limited in our ability to engage in mature forms of practical reasoning, and cannot attain any independent standpoint from which to assess the advice of others, we remain in a childlike condition, and are worse off for being underdeveloped in this way. A vigorous and free political culture is one of the social conditions that help foster the development of these cognitive skills. Healthy democracies, in which citizens are actively engaged in political deliberation, are more likely to foster the growth of the mind than are regimes in which subjects are at best the passive recipients of benefits not of their own choosing.

In a third way, goodness as flourishing is a theory of well-being appropriate to democratic culture, because nearly every normal human child has a full set of the powers whose enjoyable exercise, in their mature form, constitutes a flourishing life. Furthermore, the concepts used by developmentalism (as I call this theory of the good) are already familiar to and important in every human culture. It does not invoke ideas so abstract and complex that only an intellectual elite could apply them, and it does not appeal to authorities who, by virtue of their unique experiences or historical lineage, could claim to know the good better than others. So it is fit to be part of the public charter that citizens use when they reason collectively in the public sphere. That does not show that developmentalism is more fit to do so than is Rawls' conception of goodness as rationality. But if, as I have argued, goodness as rationality is fundamentally flawed and some other public understanding of good is needed, goodness as flourishing is well suited to play that role, partly because of its democratic credentials, but also because it passes the philosophical tests to which any conception of the good should be subjected.

To see how a conception of flourishing might underwrite the institutional arrangements of a liberal democracy, consider a state in which significant powers are given to several ministries whose goal it is to promote the various components of flourishing that I have identified. There is a Ministry of Arts, a Ministry of Knowledge, a Ministry of Sport, a Ministry of Mental Health, and so on. They are empowered to promote the well-being of citizens by the creation of schools, gymnasia, concert venues, parks, museums, health clinics, and the like. They encourage citizens to look favorably on such activities and make it possible for them to engage in them. These various ministries are fixed features of the state's constitution, which can be altered only with great difficulty. The public charter that citizens absorb from their education as members of a democratic culture justifies these ministries and their activities by grounding them in the notion of human flourishing.

The ministries I imagine as constitutionally protected in a flourishing democratic regime are not in the business of promoting high culture alone, or any elite activities that give privileges to the few at the expense of the many. The well-being of all citizens is to be the equal concern of civic institutions. The flourishing of each of them is equally important, and it is to be expected that all of them will avail themselves to the same degree of the opportunities made available to them.

Now, let's turn, very briefly, to religious liberty and ask: If it is proper for the design of civic institutions to be founded on the value of flourishing, might it not also be the case that the state ought to value religion? On my view, if there is to be an established church, or if religious ways of life are to receive more of the resources at the disposal of the state than nonreligious ways of life, then the argument for such an arrangement would have to be based on the premise that human flourishing includes a religious component. Such an argument might take one of two forms.

First, it might be said that just as a flourishing human being has cognitive, affective, social, and physical powers that are good for him to develop, so too there is a spiritual dimension to human existence, and our powers of religiosity must be nurtured and given political support. Second, a defender of a religiously oriented state might claim that our cognitive, affective, and social capacities will be seriously underdeveloped unless religious institutions prevail, and that they can prosper only with state support. The first strategy makes a religious life an independent component of flourishing, one to which religious people give far greater weight than the development of nonreligious capacities. The second makes religious practices essential *instruments* by which flourishing, as conceived in secular ways, is achieved.

The first strategy is one that I do not see how to develop. The basic problem with it is that it is not clear what it means to say that all normal human children have spiritual powers, just as they have the capacity to grow cognitively, affectively, socially, and physically. To say that certain powers are inherent in human nature is to embrace an empirical hypothesis, and so the first strategy has a formidable scientific task before it. We should not dogmatically dismiss this line of thought, because it is possible – in fact, likely – that we now have too limited a conception of the powers human beings have. At the moment, however, it seems that the second strategy is the one that is easier to deploy successfully. After all, it is empirically possible that the members of this or that political community might be unable to develop the normal powers of a human being unless their efforts to do so are sustained by religious institutions, and that without the support of the state such institutions will flounder. If those circumstances obtain, then I believe that state support of religion would be justified.

When Aristotle and Rawls face the question of how politics should come to terms with those who believe in a divine reality, they of course confront utterly different historical circumstances. *Political Liberalism* at one point poses the problem to which he seeks a solution in these terms: "How is it possible for those affirming a religious doctrine that is based on religious authority, for example the Church or the Bible, also to hold a reasonable political conception that supports a just democratic regime?" (p. xxxix). The primary allegiance of "citizens of faith" (as Rawls also calls them, p. xl) is a God who is to be loved and obeyed above all other loves and authorities. How can such people enter into just cooperative relations with secularists? His answer is that all citizens must, in their highest level public deliberations, shed their religious or nonreligious conceptual framework – their "comprehensive conceptions" of the good and the right – and interact with each by using a restricted set of terms (such as "democratic," "liberal," "reasonable," "fair") that have shared meanings.

Aristotle faces no comparable problem. Greek religion had no transcendental pretensions that posed a threat to the values of civic life comparable to the threat posed to democratic-liberal culture by an established church or a sacred scripture claiming to be the highest and most authoritative source of morality. It is remarkable that Rawls finds this project of reconciliation so difficult that its solution requires rejecting the simple idea that the state should foster the flourishing of its citizens.

## HAPPINESS

Let's round out our discussion of Aristotle and Rawls by asking what role the notion of happiness, as that concept is often understood nowadays, plays in their political philosophies. It is used by nearly all contemporary translations of Aristotle's writings as the equivalent of his word for the ultimate good, *eudaimonia*, but it is widely recognized that there are important differences between the two. "Happiness" often refers to something that can be felt; it can be attributed to people entirely on the basis of their attitudes and emotions. If someone is genuinely satisfied, on balance, with the way his life is going, then that settles the matter: he is happy with it, even if we think he might have a much better life were he to pursue different ends. By contrast, all the Greek philosophers would agree with Aristotle's remark that being *eudaimon* and living well are the same thing (*NE* I 4, 1095a19–20). It would make no sense to ask, "is it good for someone to be *eudaimon*?" because a positive evaluation of a person's life is made in ascribing *eudaimonia* to him. To describe someone as happy, however, is merely to report on his attitudes and feelings, without yet making a judgment about the value of those states of mind.

The classical utilitarian authors (Bentham, Mill, and Sidgwick) use "happiness" and "pleasure" interchangeably to designate any agreeable state of consciousness, just as they apply "pain" and "unhappiness" to any kind of disagreeable feeling. They maintain that happiness, so understood, is not only of some value, but that it encompasses all that is valuable. That doctrine, often called "hedonism," is rejected both by Aristotle and by Rawls in *A Theory of Justice*, although in *Political Liberalism* he rejects hedonism only as the conception of the good that citizens are to use in their highest-order political deliberations. In several passages of *A Theory of Justice*, he talks about the good in terms of happiness – meaning the happiness that is achieved when we attain our ends (pp. 79, 482). He is evidently assuming in that work that what is good is the achievement of rational ends provided we recognize that they have been or will be achieved and are pleased that this is so. For both Aristotle and the early Rawls, there must be pleasure in a good life, but pleasure is not the good.

Rawls notes in *Political Liberalism* that "fair shares of primary goods are clearly not intended as a measure of citizens' expected overall psychological well-being" (pp. 187–88). His point is that it should not matter, for purposes of democratic constitutional design, whether people are generally made happy or unhappy by having the rights, opportunities, and other items that are publicly designated as primary goods. Our political discourse is not to look at the psychological effects of having basic liberties, income, and so on. The "pursuit of happiness" mentioned in the Declaration of Independence is a goal that has often been invoked in democratic discourse, and might be included among the "blessings of liberty" referred to in the US Constitution.[13] But in *Political Liberalism*, Rawls is committed to saying that the thesis that happiness is a good thing – that it is one important good among many – is part of a comprehensive moral doctrine and therefore must play no role in matters of basic justice and constitutional design. He requires, in other words, that there be a division of labor in our efforts to achieve what is good for us: psychological well-being is something that each individual should be responsible for, if he so chooses, and so no one can rightly complain to the political community that he is unhappy. It is the just allocation of the primary goods that is the responsibility of society, and it must not be asked to do more than that.

Recently, several leading economists and psychologists have placed the empirical study of happiness at the center of their research.[14] Researchers ask subjects to reflect on their lives as a whole and to say how happy they are (on a scale from one number to another), or whether they are very satisfied, somewhat satisfied, neutral, somewhat dissatisfied, or very dissatisfied. One might wonder whether most people who are asked this question already had some overall attitude toward their life, or whether instead the question induces them to reflect on that vague question for the first time. Other surveys divide the lives of their subjects into various domains (one's job, finances, marriage, leisure, and so on) and ask how satisfied they are with each. A different research tool, called "experience sampling," involves asking subjects to report on how they feel about what they are doing at that very moment (cooking, shopping, watching TV, working, commuting) by rating their enjoyment of that activity on a scale between two numerical limits. Aggregating this data, social scientists can study the economic, social, and political conditions that are correlated with high or low degrees of happiness. They can, for example, compare the happiness of the rich and the poor, or that of religious people and secularists. They can ask whether the citizens of a state or canton in which plebiscites are frequent tend to report greater happiness than those that have little or no direct democracy. The implicit premise of such studies is that political institutions and economic structures should be sensitive to their effect on happiness, and that a proper goal of the state is the felt satisfaction of its citizens.

For Rawls, the assumption that happiness is good for people is part of a comprehensive moral doctrine and therefore it is impermissible for the results of such research to be brought to bear on constitutional issues. From an Aristotelian perspective as well, these empirical studies have only limited value. If being happy about something is felt satisfaction with it, it might on balance be a bad thing for someone to experience, because it is possible to be satisfied with the conditions of one's life even when they severely constrict the development of one's natural powers. The utilitarian tradition urges us to pay careful study to these empirical surveys. Aristotle and Rawls, however, are united in believing that their political significance is limited. Levels of public satisfaction, they would admit, are not totally irrelevant to public policy, for both of them weave pleasure into their conception of the good. But, they would insist, how pleased people are with their lives can never be the sole or dominant criterion for the adoption of laws and policies or for the design of constitutions.

An approach to political philosophy that de-emphasizes the role of subjective levels of satisfaction, but instead draws some of its inspiration from an Aristotelian conception of flourishing, has for several decades been proposed by Martha Nussbaum and Amartya Sen, each in different ways.[15] They endorse what they call a "capabilities approach" to social policy: the most telling way to measure the success of a society, they argue, is not simply by the quantity of what Rawls calls "primary social goods," nor simply the amount of felt satisfaction detected by empirical surveys, but what they call the central "capabilities" of members of that society. Nussbaum speaks of such capabilities as bodily health, sensation, imagination, emotional development, and practical reasoning – categories that are not distant from Aristotle's conception of the human soul as a series of potentialities for engaging in perception, feeling, and rational thought. A "capability approach" to distributive justice requires states to ensure that all citizens attain some minimal level of development in these spheres. A form of Aristotelianism thus continues to play an important role in contemporary debates about the construction and maintenance of a good and just society.

## WORKS CITED

Ackermann, B. 1980. *Social Justice in the Liberal State*. New Haven, CT: Yale University Press

Bok D. 2010. *The Politics of Happiness: What Government Can Learn from the New Research on Well-Being*. Princeton University Press

Dworkin, R. 1985. "Liberalism," in *A Matter of Principle*. Cambridge, MA: Harvard University Press

Kraut, R. 2002. *Aristotle: Political Philosophy*. Oxford University Press
2007. *What is Good and Why*. Cambridge, MA: Harvard University Press
2011. *Against Absolute Goodness*. New York: Oxford University Press

McMahon, D. M. 2006. *Happiness: A History*. New York: Atlantic Monthly Press

Moore, G. E. 1993 [1903]. *Principia Ethica*. Revised edn. Cambridge University Press

Nussbaum M. C. 2000. *Women and Human Development: the Capabilities Approach*. Cambridge University Press
2011. *Creating Capabilities: the Human Development Approach*. Cambridge, MA: Belknap Press

Rawls, J. 1996. *Political Liberalism*. New York: Columbia University Press
1999. *A Theory of Justice*. Revised edn., Cambridge, MA: Belknap Press

Reeve, C. D. C. 1998. *Aristotle*, Politics. Indianapolis, IN: Hackett

Ross, W. D. 1930. *The Right and the Good*. Oxford University Press

Sen, A. 2009. *The Idea of Justice*. Cambridge, MA: Belknap Press

White, N. P. 2006. *A Brief History of Happiness*. Oxford: Blackwell

NOTES

1. This is my own way of reading the relation between the *Nicomachean Ethics* and the *Politics*, and it is not held by all scholars. Some think

that large portions of the *Politics* are value-free empirical inquiries into political stability. I defend my view in Kraut 2002; esp. p. 183.

2. Moore 1993; see e.g., section 60, p. 153. Likewise, when Ross theorizes about goodness, he is talking about the property something has when it is, as he says, good "sans phrase." See Ross 1930: 102. For my doubts about whether there is such a property, see Kraut 2011.

3. All citations are from Rawls 1999 (the revised edition of *A Theory of Justice*). Emphases are added.

4. Rawls 1996.

5. In one sense of "neutral," Rawls' idea is that the state must be neutral between competing comprehensive conceptions. As he puts it, "the state is not to do anything intended to favor or promote any particular comprehensive doctrine rather than another, or to give greater assistance to those who pursue it" (p. 193). This sort of neutrality is now sometimes regarded as a defining feature of liberalism. Among its most prominent contemporary advocates are Ronald Dworkin, (Dworkin 1985: ch. 8); and Bruce Ackermann (1980). But older forms of liberalism (that of John Stuart Mill, for example) are certainly not neutral in this sense.

6. I do not mean that we should dismiss *Political Liberalism*. Like *A Theory of Justice*, it is a great work, and no interpretation of Rawls can ignore it. My point, rather, is that assessing the theory of the good proposed in Chapter VII of *A Theory of Justice* requires asking the same question we pose about any comprehensive conception of the good: Is it true? That question must not be evaded. In saying this, I depart from Rawls, since, in *Political Liberalism*, he urges us to withdraw that question.

7. The *goal* of slavery, Aristotle holds, is not to benefit the slave. (See Kraut 2002: 299.) But that is consistent with his thesis that a natural slave does benefit from this institution (if a slaveholder acts properly). My claim is that he takes this thesis (slaves benefit from slavery) to be indispensable to his defense of slavery. Since a *polis* is a community of *free* human beings (not slaves), its goal *is* to benefit all equally. Were its goal to benefit only some portion of the community (the rich, the poor, the few best, the middle class), it would not be correctly constituted. See Kraut 2002: 388–91.

8. Moore 1993: 237–38.

9. Aristotle says at *NE* I 9, 1099b17–19 that full ethical excellence is accessible to many people, since it is acquired through learning and practice. But he also implies here that some groups are naturally handicapped; he is of course thinking of natural slaves and women. That biased hypothesis has been refuted by all that we have learned from history and

empirical investigation. He also holds that many manual crafts and commercial activities are morally corrupting, just as personal riches often distort ethical thinking. I discuss these topics in Kraut 2002: 214–20, 277–306, 463–65, 475.

10. I do not mean that all these tenets are obviously false. I myself believe that the distinction between accidental and essential features is viable. But the other components of Aristotle's framework that I mentioned do strike me as unlikely to survive examination.

11. Some of these ideas are more fully presented in Kraut 2007.

12. Significant ownership rights, I am suggesting, are a necessary condition for the ongoing exercise of valuable human powers, but I do not mean that they are sufficient.

13. For discussion of the sense that this phrase bore at the time, see McMahon 2006: 314–31. For a different sort of historical survey, see White 2006.

14. There is a large literature on this topic. See e.g., Bok 2010.

15. See Sen 2009: chs. 11–13; Nussbaum 2000; and Nussbaum 2011.

## FURTHER READING

This is a list of scholarly works on Aristotle's *Politics*, organized by category and topic, following the traditional order of the books. Established by Thornton Lockwood, it has been shortened and adapted for this volume by the editors.

### TEXTUAL EDITIONS, TRANSLATIONS, AND COMMENTARIES

*Textual editions*

Dreizehnter, A. 1970. *Aristoteles' Politik*. Munich: Wilhelm Fink
Ross, W. D. 1957. *Aristotelis Politica*. Oxford: Clarendon

*Translations and commentaries*

Aubonnet, J. 1960–1989. *Aristote: Politique*. 3 vols, Paris: Les Belles Lettres
Keyt, D. 1995. *Aristotle Politics Books V and VI*. Oxford: Clarendon
Kraut, R. 1998. *Politics Books VII and VIII*. Oxford: Clarendon
Lord, C. 1984. *Aristotle, The Politics*. University of Chicago Press
Newman, W. L. 1887–1902. *The Politics of Aristotle*. 4 vols, Oxford University Press
Pellegrin, P. 1990. *Les Politiques*. 2nd edn., Paris: GF-Flammarion
Reeve, C. D. C. 1998. *Aristotle* Politics. Indianapolis, IN: Hackett
Robinson, R. 1995. *Aristotle's* Politics *Books III and IV*. Oxford: Clarendon
Saunders, T. J. 1996. *Politics, Books I and II*. Oxford: Clarendon
Schütrumpf, E. 1991–2005. *Aristoteles Politik*. 4 vols, Berlin: Akademie Verlag

Simpson, P. 1997. *The Politics of Aristotle*. Chapel Hill, NC: University of North Carolina Press
  1998. *A Philosophical Commentary on Aristotle's Politics*. Chapel Hill, NC: University of North Carolina Press
Susemihl, F. and Hicks, R. D. 1976 [1894]. *The Politics of Aristotle*. New York: Arno Press


## Book-length monographs

Barker, E. 1959. *The Political Thought of Plato and Aristotle*. New York: Dover
Bates, C. A. 2003. *Aristotle's Best Regime: Kingship, Democracy, and the Rule of Law*. Baton Rouge: Louisiana State University Press
Bien, G. 1985. *Die Grundlagen der Politische Philosophie bei Aristoteles*. 3rd edn., Munich: Alber
Bodéüs, R. 1982. *Le philosophie et la cité*. Paris: Les Belles Lettres. Translated as 1993. *The Political Dimensions of Aristotle's Ethics*, J. E. Garrett trans. State University of New York Press
Cherry, K. M. 2012. *Plato, Aristotle and the Purpose of Politics*. Cambridge University Press
Collins, Susan. 2006. *Aristotle and the Rediscovery of Citizenship*. Cambridge University Press
Curren, Randall R. 2000. *Aristotle on the Necessity of Public Education*. Lanham, MD: Rowman and Littlefield
Defourny, M. 1932. *Études sur la Politique d'Aristote*. Paris: Beauchesne
Frank, J. 2005. *A Democracy of Distinction: Aristotle and the Work of Politics*. University of Chicago Press
Garver, E. 2012. *Aristotle's Politics: Living Well and Living Together*. University of Chicago Press
Hamburger, M. 1951. *Morals and Law: The Growth of Aristotle's Legal Theory*. New Haven, CT: Yale University Press
Kalimtzis, K. 2000. *Aristotle on Political Enmity and Disease: An Inquiry into Stasis*. Albany, NY: State University of New York Press
Kamp, A. 1985. *Die politische Philosophie des Aristoteles und ihre metaphysischen Grundlagen*. Freiburg-München: Alber
  1990. *Aristoteles' Theorie der Polis: Voraussezungen und Zentralthemen*. Berne: Peter Lang
Kraut, R. 2002. *Aristotle: Political Philosophy*. Oxford University Press
Lord, C. 1982. *Education and Culture in the Political Thought of Aristotle*. Ithaca, NY: Cornell University Press

Mayhew, R. A. 1997. *Aristotle's Criticism of Plato's Republic*. Lanham, MD: Rowman and Littlefield

Meikle, S. 1995. *Aristotle's Economic Thought*. Oxford University Press

Miller, F. D. 1995. *Nature, Justice and Rights in Aristotle's Politics*. Oxford University Press

Mulgan, R. 1977. *Aristotle's Political Theory*. Oxford University Press

Nagle, D. B. 2006. *The Household as the Foundation of Aristotle's Polis*. Cambridge University Press

Nichols, M. P. 1992. *Citizens and Statesmen: A Study of Aristotle's Politics*. Lanham, MD: Rowman and Littlefield

Ritter, J. 1969. *Metaphysik und Politik. Studien zu Aristoteles und Hegel*. Frankfurt: Suhrkamp

Rosler, A. 2005. *Political Authority and Obligation in Aristotle*. Oxford: Clarendon

Salkever, S. G. 1990. *Finding the Mean: Theory and Practice in Aristotelian Political Philosophy*. Princeton University Press

Schütrumpf, E. 1980. *Die Analyse der Polis durch Aristoteles*. Amsterdam: Grüner

Swanson, J. A. 1992. *The Public and the Private in Aristotle's Political Philosophy*. Ithaca, NY: Cornell University Press

Trude, P. 1955. *Der Begriff der Gerechtigkeit in der aristotelischen Rechts und Staatsphilosophie*. Berlin: de Gruyter

Vergnières, S. 1995. *Ethique et Politique chez Aristote*. Paris: Presses Universitaires de France

Wolff, F. 1991. *Aristote et la politique*. Paris: Presses Universitaires de France

Yack, B. 1993. *The Problems of a Political Animal: Community, Justice and Conflict in Aristotelian Political Thought*. Berkeley, CA: University of California Press

Young, M. A. 2005. *Negotiating the Good Life: Aristotle and the Civil Society*. Aldershot: Ashgate Publishing

## Collections and anthologies

Aubenque, P. and Tordesillas, A., eds. 1993. *Aristote Politique. Études sur la Politique d'Aristote*. Paris: Presses Universitaires de France

Balot, R. K., ed. 2009. *A Companion to Greek and Roman Political Thought*. Maden, MA/Oxford: Wiley-Blackwell

Barnes, J., Schofield, M. and Sorabji, R., eds. 1977. *Articles on Aristotle 2: Ethics and Politics*. London: Duckworth

Bartlett, R. C. and Collins, S. D., eds. 1999. *Action and Contemplation: Studies in the Moral and Political Thought of Aristotle*. Albany, NY: State University of New York Press

Bermon, E., Laurand, V. and Terrel, J., eds. 2011. *Politique d'Aristote: famille, régimes, éducation.* Pessac: Presses Universitaires de Bordeaux

Boudouris, K. I., ed. 1995. *Aristotelian Political Philosophy.* 2 vols., Athens: International Center for Greek Philosophy and Culture

Fondation Hardt. 1964. *Entretiens sur l'Antiquité Classique IX, La "Politique" d'Aristote.* Geneva: Vandoeuvres

Goodman, L. E. and Talisse, R. B., eds. 2007. *Aristotle's Politics Today.* Albany, NY: State University of New York Press

Hager, F., ed. 1972. *Ethik und Politik des Aristotles.* Darmstadt: Wissenshaftliche Buchgesellschaft

Höffe, O., ed. 2001. *Aristoteles Politik.* Berlin: Akademie Verlag

Horn, Ch. and Neschke-Hentschke, A., eds. 2008. *Politischer Aristotelismus. Die Rezeption der aristotelischen "Politik" von der Antike bis zum 19. Jahrhundert.* Stuttgart: Metzler

Keyt, D. and Miller, F., eds. 1991. *Companion to Aristotle's Politics.* Oxford: Blackwell

Koutras, D., ed. 1999. *Aristotle's Political Philosophy and its Influences.* Athens: The Lyceum

Kraut, R. and Skultety, S., eds. 2005. *Aristotle's Politics: Critical Essays.* Lanham, MD: Rowman and Littlefield

Lord, C. and O'Connor, D. K., eds. 1991. *Essays on the Foundations of Aristotelian Political Science.* Berkeley, CA: University of California Press

Patzig, G., ed. 1990. *Aristoteles: Politik. Akten des XI Symposium Aristotelicum.* Göttingen: Vandenhoeck and Ruprecht

Rowe, C. and Schofield, M., eds. 2000. *The Cambridge History of Greek and Roman Political Thought.* Cambridge University Press

Steel, C., ed. 1999. *The Legacy of Aristotle's Political Thought.* Brussels: Royal Academy

Steinmetz, P., ed. 1973. *Schriften zu den Politika des Aristoteles.* New York: Georg Olms

Tessitore, A., ed. 2002. *Aristotle and Modern Politics: the Persistence of Political Philosophy.* University of Notre Dame Press

## General introductions to Aristotle's Politics

Balot, R. 2006. "Aristotle's political thought." In *Greek Political Thought.* Malden, MA and Oxford: Blackwell

Chappell, T. 2009. "'Naturalism' in Aristotle's political philosophy." In Balot 2009

Depew, D. 2009. "The ethics of Aristotle's *Politics.*" In Balot 2009

Keyt, D. 2006. "Aristotle's political philosophy." In *A Companion to Ancient Philosophy*, ed. M. L. Gill and P. Pellegrin. Malden, MA/Oxford: Wiley-Blackwell

Lord, C. 1987. "Aristotle." In *History of Political Philosophy*, eds. L. Strauss and J. Cropsey. 3rd edn., University of Chicago Press

Miller, F. D. 2003. "Aristotle: ethics and politics." In *Blackwell Guide to Ancient Philosophy*, ed. C. Shields. Malden, MA/Oxford: Blackwell

Schofield, M. 2000. "Aristotle: an introduction." In Rowe and Schofield 2000

Sinclair, T. A. 1967. "Aristotle." In *A History of Greek Political Thought*. New York: Meridian

Taylor, C. C. W. 1995. "Politics." In *Cambridge Companion to Aristotle*, ed. J. Barnes. Cambridge University Press

## TOPICS CONCERNING THE WHOLE OF ARISTOTLE'S 'POLITICS'

### Historical context

Cartledge, P. 2000. "Greek political thought: the historical context." In Rowe and Schofield 2000

Hansen, M. H. 2006. *POLIS: An Introduction to the Ancient Greek City-State*. Oxford University Press

### Place of the Politics *within Aristotle's corpus and the development of the text*

Adkins, A. W. H. 1991 [1984]. "The connexion between Aristotle's *Ethics* and *Politics*." In Keyt and Miller 1991

Aubenque, P. 1980. "Politique et éthique chez Aristote." *Ktema* 5: 211–21

Barker, E. 1931. "The Life of Aristotle and the Composition and Stucture of the *Politics*." *Classical Review* 45: 162–72

Fritz, K. V. and Kapp, E. 1977. "The development of Aristotle's political philosophy and the concept of nature." In Barnes, Schofield, and Sorabji 1977

Gerson, L. P. 1994. "Why Ethics is Political Science for Aristotle." *American Catholic Philosophical Quarterly* 68 Supp: 93–107

Lord, C. 1981. "The Character and Composition of Aristotle's *Politics*." *Political Theory* 9: 459–78

1986. "On the Early History of the Aristotelian Corpus." *American Journal of Philology* 107: 137–61

Mesk, J. 1973 [1916]. "Die Buchfolge in der aristotelischen Politik." In Steinmetz 1973

Pellegrin, P. 1987. "La *Politique* d'Aristote: unité et fractures. Eloge de la lecture sommaire." *Revue Philosophique de la France et de l'Etranger* 177: 129–59. Reprinted in Aubenque and Tordesillas 1993

1996. "On the 'Platonic' part of Aristotle's *Politics*." In *Aristotle's Philosophical Development*, ed. W. Wians. Lanham, MD: Rowman and Littlefield

Peonids, F. 2001. "The Relation between the *Nicomachean Ethics* and the *Politics* Revisited." *History of Political Thought* 22: 1–12

Santas, G. 1995. "The relation between Aristotle's *Ethics* and *Politics*." In Boudouris 1995

Schütrumpf, E. 2006. "Ernest Barker on the Composition and Structure of Aristotle's *Politics*." *Polis* 23: 286–301

Stark, R. 1964. "Der Gesamtaufbau der aristotelischen Politik." In Fondation Hardt 1964

Stocks, J. L. 1937. "The Composition of Aristotle's *Politics*." *Classical Quarterly* 31: 177–87

Theiler, W. 1972 [1952]. "Bau und Zeit der Aristotelischen Politik." In Hager 1972

Vander Waerdt, P. A. 1985. "The Political Intentions of Aristotle's Moral Philosophy." *Ancient Philosophy* 5: 77–89

1991. "The Plan and the Intention of Aristotle's Ethical and Political Writings." *Illinois Classical Studies* 16: 231–51

Willers, D. 1973 [1933]. "Aufbau der Aristotelischen Politik." In Steinmetz 1973

## General topics

Allan, D. J. 1964. "Individual and State in the *Ethics* and *Politics*." In Fondation Hardt 1964

Aubenque, P. 1964. "Théorie et practique politiques chez Aristote." In Fondation Hardt 1964

Berti, E. 1988. "La notion de société politique chez Aristote." In *Antike Rechts- und Socialphilosophie*, eds. O. Gigon and M. Fischer. Frankfurt: Peter Lang

Bodéüs, R. 1993. "De quelques prémisses de la *Politique*." In Aubenque and Tordesillas 1993

Bradley, A. C. 1991 [1880]. "Aristotle's conception of the state." In Keyt and Miller 1991

Brandt, R. 1974. "Untersuchungen zur politischen Philosophie des Aristoteles." *Hermes* 102: 191–200

Coby, P. 1986. "Aristotle's Four Conceptions of Politics." *Western Political Quarterly* 39: 480–503

Evrigenis, I. 1999. "The Doctrine of the Mean in Aristotle's Ethical and Political Theory." *History of Political Theory* 20: 393–416

Gerson, L. P. 1987. "Aristotle's Polis: A Community of the Virtuous." *Proceedings of the Boston Area Colloquium in Ancient Philosophy* 3: 203–25

Irwin, T. H. 1985. "Moral Science and Political Theory in Aristotle." *History of Political Thought* 6: 150–68

Kahn, C. 1990. "The normative structure of Aristotle's 'Politics.'" In Patzig 1990

Keyt, D. 1995. "The four causes in Aristotle's *Politics*." In Boudouris 1995

McCullough, B. 2004. "Human Nature and Reason in Aristotle's *Politics*: Rationalism in the Greek Tradition?" *Skepsis* 15: 546–66

McKeon, R. 1941. "Aristotle's Conception of Moral and Political Philosophy." *Ethics* 51: 253–90

Morrison, D. 2001b. "Politics as a Vocation, According to Aristotle." *History of Political Thought* 22: 221–41

Ober, J. 1998. "Political animals, actual citizens, and the best possible *polis*: Aristotle's *Politics*." In *Political Dissent in Democratic Athens: Intellectual Critics of Popular Rule*. Princeton University Press

Pangle, T. 2011. "The Rhetorical Strategy Governing Aristotle's Political Teaching." *Journal of Politics* 73: 84–96

Polansky, R. 1979. "The Dominance of 'Polis' for Aristotle." *Dialogos* 14: 43–56

Roochnik, D. 2010. "Substantial City: Reflections on Aristotle's *Politics*." *Polis* 27: 275–91

Rowe, C. J. 1991 [1977]. "Aims and methods in Aristotle's *Politics*." In Keyt and Miller 1991

Saxonhouse. A. W. 1992. "Aristotle: diversity and the birth of political science." In *Fear of Diversity: the Birth of Political Science in Ancient Greek Thought*. University of Chicago Press

Strauss, L. 1978. "On Aristotle's *Politics*." In *The City and Man*. University of Chicago Press

Swazo, N. K. 1991. "The Authentic Tele of *Politics*: a Reading of Aristotle." *History of Political Thought* 12: 405–20

### Anthropology and psychology

Berns, L. 1984. "Spiritedness in Ethics and Politics: a Study in Aristotelian Psychology." *Intrerpretation* 12: 335–48

Höffe, O. 2001. "Aristoteles' politische anthropologie." In Höffe 2001
Lefebvre, D. 2011. "La puissance du thumos en *Politiques*, VII, 7." In Bermon, Laurand and Terrel 2011
Lord, Carnes. 1991. "Aristotle's anthropology." In Lord and O'Connor 1991

## SCHOLARLY ARTICLES ORGANIZED ACCORDING TO THE SEQUENCE OF BOOKS WITHIN THE POLITICS

*Book I*

Booth, W. J. 1981. "Politics and the Household: a Commentary on Aristotle's *Politics* Book One." *History of Political Thought* 2: 203–26
Deslauriers, M. 2006. "The Argument of Aristotle's *Politics* I." *Phoenix* 60: 48–69
Natali, C. 1979/80. "La struttura unitaria del libro I della 'Politica' di Aristotele." *Polis* 3: 2–18

### NATURALNESS OF THE POLIS/HUMANS AS POLITICAL ANIMALS

Ambler, W. H. 1985. "Aristotle's Understanding of the Naturalness of the City." *Review of Politics* 47: 390–410
Annas, J. 1996. "Aristotle on Human Nature and Political Virtue." *Review of Metaphysics* 99: 731–54
Arnhart, L. 1990. "Aristotle, Chimpanzees, and Other Political Animals." *Social Science Information* 29: 477–551
    1994. "The Darwinian Biology of Aristotle's Political Animals." *American Journal of Political Science* 38: 464–85
Chan, J. 1992. "Does Aristotle's Political Theory Rest on a 'Blunder'?" *History of Political Thought* 13: 189–202
Cherry, K. and E. A. Goerner. 2006. "Does Aristotle's Polis Exist 'By Nature'?" *History of Political Thought* 27: 563–85
Depew, D. J. 1995. "Humans and Other Political Animals in Aristotle's *History of Animals*." *Phronesis* 40: 156–81
Everson, S. 1988. "Aristotle on the Foundation of the State." *Political Studies* 36: 89–101
Ferguson, J. 1985. "Teleology in Aristotle's *Politics*." In *Aristotle on Nature and Living Things*, ed A. Gotthelf. University of Pittsburgh Press
Keyt, D. 1987. "Three Fundamental Theorems in Aristotle's Politics." *Phronesis* 32: 54–79. Reprinted in Keyt and Miller 1991
Kraut, R. 2007. "Nature in Aristotle's *Ethics* and *Politics*." *Social Philosophy and Policy* 24: 153–75

Kullman, W. 1991 [1980]. "Man as a political animal in Aristotle." In Keyt and Miller 1991

Labarrière, J. 1988. "Zoôn politikon et zôa politika: d'une prétendue métaphore chez Aristote." In *La Condition animale. Etudes sur Aristote et les Stoïciens*. Louvain-la-Neuve: Peeters

Lloyd, G. E. R. 1996. "The idea of nature in the *Politics*." In *Aristotelian Explorations*. Cambridge University Press

Mann, C. 2010. "Politische Partizipation und die Vorstellung des Menschen als *zoon politikon*." In *Démocratie athénienne–Democratie moderne: tradition et influences. Entretiens sur l'antiquité classique*. Geneva: Fondation Hardt

Mayhew, R. A. 1997. "Part and Whole in Aristotle's Political Philosophy." *Journal of Ethics* 1: 325–40

Miller, F. D. 2000. "Naturalism." In Rowe and Schofield 2000

Mulgan, R. 1974. "Aristotle's Doctrine that Man is a Political Animal." *Hermes* 102: 438–45

Nederman, C. J. 1994. "The Puzzle of the Political Animal: Nature and Artifice in Aristotle's Political Theory." *Review of Politics* 56: 283–304

Pellegrin, P. 1990. "Naturalité, excellence, diversité: Politique et biologie chez Aristote." In Patzig 1990

Reeve, C. D. C. 2009. "The naturalness of the polis in Aristotle." In *A Companion to Aristotle*, ed. G. Anagnostopoulos. Malden, MA/Oxford: Wiley-Blackwell

Roberts, J. 1989. "Political Animals in the *Nicomachean Ethics*." *Phronesis* 34: 185–202

Trott, A. 2010. "*Logos* and the Political Nature of *Anthropos* in Aristotle's *Politics*." *Polis* 27: 292–307

Ward, J. K. 2005. "Aristotle on Physis: Human Nature in the *Ethics* and *Politics*." *Polis* 22: 287–308

Yu, J. 2005. "Confucius Relational Self and Aristotle's Political Animal." *History of Philosophy Quarterly* 22: 281–300

POLITICAL COMMUNITY AND FRIENDSHIP BETWEEN CITIZENS

Annas, J. 1990. "Comments on J. Cooper." In Patzig 1990

Cooper, J. M. 1990. "Political animals and civic friendship." In Patzig 1990

2010. "Political community and the highest good." In *Being, Nature and Life: Essays in Honor of Allan Gotthelf*. Cambridge University Press

Herrmann, F.-G. 2000. "Aristotle on the role of friendship in society." In *Political Equality and Justice in Aristotle, and the Problems of Contemporary Society*, ed. K. I. Boudouris. Athens: The Lyceum

Jenkins, J. 1999. "The Advantages of Civic Friendship." *Journal of Philosophical Research* 24: 459–71

Klonoski, R. 1996. "Homonoia in Aristotle's *Ethics* and *Politics*." *History of Political Thought* 17: 313–25

Kronman, A. 1979. "Aristotle's Idea of Political Fraternity." *American Journal of Jurisprudence* 24: 114–38

La Plante, H. 1962. "Justice and Friendship in Aristotle's Social Philosophy." *Proceedings of the American Catholic Philosophical Association* 36: 119–27

Pakaluk, M. 1994. "Political friendship." In *The Changing Face of Friendship*, ed. L. Rouner. University of Notre Dame Press

Price, A. W. 1999. "Friendship and Politics." *Tijdschrift voor Filosofie* 61: 525–45

Schall, J. 1996. "Friendship and Political Philosophy." *Review of Metaphysics* 50: 121–41

Schofield, M. 1999 [1998]. "Political friendship and the ideal of reciprocity." In *Saving the City: Philosopher-Kings and Other Classical Paradigms*. London: Routledge

Schwartzenbach, S. 1996. "On Civic Friendship." *Ethics* 107: 97–128

## ANALYSIS OF THE HOUSEHOLD

Blits, J. H. 1985. "Privacy and Public Moral Education: Aristotle's Critique of the Family." *Educational Theory* 35: 225–38

Curzer, H. J. 2010. "An Aristotelian Critique of the Traditional Family." *American Philosophical Quarterly* 47: 135–47

Veloso, C. W. 2011. "La relation entre les liens familiaux et les constitutions politiques." In Bermon, Laurand, and Terrel 2011

Wilgaux, J. 2011. "De la naturalité des relations de parenté : inceste et échange matrimonial dans les Politiques d'Aristote." In Bermon, Laurand, and Terrel 2011

## ECONOMY

Ambler, W. H. 1984. "Aristotle on Acquisition." *Canadian Journal of Political Science* 17: 487–502

Baeck, L. 1987. "Aristotle as Mediterranean Economist." *Diogenes* 138: 81–104

Brown, W. 1982. "Aristotle's Art of Acquisition and the Conquest of Nature." *Interpretation* 10: 159–96

Crespo, R. 2008. "'The Economic' According to Aristotle: Ethical, Political and Epistemological Implications." *Foundations of Science* 13: 281–94

Finley, M. I. 1977. "Aristotle and economic analysis." In Barnes, Schofield, and Sorabji, 1977

Inamura, K. 2011. "The Role of Reciprocity in Aristotle's Theory of Political Economy." *History of Political Thought* 32: 565–87

Judson, L. 1997. "Aristotle on Fair Exchange." *Oxford Studies in Ancient Philosophy* 13: 147–75

Lowry, T. S. 1974. "Aristotle's 'Natural Limit' and the Economics of Price Regulation." *Greek, Roman, and Byzantine Studies* 15: 57–63

Machan, T. R. 2004. "Aristotle and the Moral Status of Business." *Journal of Value Inquiry* 38: 217–33

McNeill, D. 1990. "Alternative Interpretations of Aristotle on Exchange and Reciprocity." *Public Affairs Quarterly* 4: 55–68

Mei, T. 2009. "The Preeminence of Use: Reevaluating the Relation between Use and Exchange in Aristotle's Economic Thought." *Journal of the History of Philosophy* 47: 523–48

Meikle, S. 1979. "Aristotle and the Political Economy of the Polis." *Journal of Hellenic Studies* 99: 57–73

   1991. "Aristotle and exchange value." In Keyt and Miller 1991

   1994. "Aristotle on Money." *Phronesis* 39: 26–44

Miller, F. D. 1998. "Was Aristotle the First Economist?" *Apeiron* 31: 387–98

Natali, C. 1990. "Aristote et la chrémastique." In Patzig 1990

Pack, S. J. 2008. "Aristotle's Difficult Relationship with Modern Economic Theory." *Foundations of Science* 13: 265–80

Picard, O. 1980. "Aristote et la monnaie." *Ktema* 5: 267–76

Polanyi, K. 1957. "Aristotle discovers the economy." In *Trade and Markets in Early Economies*, eds. K. Polanyi, C. M. Arensberg, and H. W. Pearson. Glencoe, IL: Free Press

Shulsky, A. N. 1991. "The 'infrastructure' of Aristotle's *Politics*: Aristotle on economy and politics." In Lord and O'Connor 1991

### SLAVERY

Ambler, W. H. 1987. "Aristotle on Nature and Politics: the Case of Slavery." *Political Theory* 15: 390–410

Baruzzi, A. 1970. "Der Freie und der Sklave in Ethik und Politik des Aristoteles." *Philos. Jahrbuch* 77: 15–28

Brunschwig, J. 1979. "L'esclavage chez Aristote." *Cahiers philosophiques* 1: 20–31

Brunt, P. A. 1993. "Aristotle and slavery." In *Studies in Greek History and Thought*. Oxford University Press

Burns, T. 2003. "The Tragedy of Slavery: Aristotle's *Rhetoric* and the History of the Concept of Natural Law." *History of Political Thought* 24: 16–36

Cambiano, G. 1987. "Aristotle and the anonymous opponents of slavery." In *Classical Slavery*, ed. M. I. Finley. London: Routledge

Clark, S. 1985. "Slaves and Citizens." *Philosophy* 60: 27–46
2003. "Slaves, Servility, and Noble Deeds." *Philosophical Inquiry* 25: 165–76

Deslauriers, M. 2003. "Aristotle on the Virtues of Slaves and Women." *Oxford Studies in Ancient Philosophy* 25: 213–31

Dobbs, D. 1994. "Natural Right and the Problem of Aristotle's Defense of Natural Slavery." *Journal of Politics* 56: 69–94

Faes, H. 1995. "L'esclave, le travail et l'action: Aristote et Hegel." *Archives de Philosophie* 58: 97–121

Fortenbaugh, W. W. 1977. "Aristotle on slaves and women." In Barnes, Schofield, and Sorabji 1977

Frank, J. 2004. "Citizens, Slaves, and Foreigners: Aristotle on Human Nature." *American Political Science Review* 98: 91–104

Gallagher, R. L. 2011. "Aristotle on *Eidei Diapherontoi*." *British Journal for the History of Philosophy* 19: 363–84

Garver, E. 1994. "Aristotle's Natural Slaves: Incomplete *Praxeis* and Incomplete Human Beings." *Journal of the History of Philosophy* 32: 173–96

Gigon, O. 1964. "Die Sklaverei bei Aristoteles." In Fondation Hardt 1964

Goldschmidt, V. 1973. "La Théorie aristotélienne de l'esclavage et sa méthode." In *Zetesis: Mélanges E. de Strycker*. Antwerp/Utrecht: De Nederlandsche Boekhandel

Goodley, C. F. 1999. "Politics, Nature and Necessity: Were Aristotle's Slaves Feeble Minded?" *Political Theory* 27: 203–24

Harvey, M. 2001. "Deliberation and Natural Slavery." *Social Theory and Practice* 27: 41–64

Heath, M. 2008. "Aristotle on Natural Slavery." *Phronesis* 53: 243–70

Just, R. 1985. "Freedom, Slavery and the Female Psyche." *History of Political Thought* 6: 169–88

Lévy, E. 1989. "La théorie aristotélicienne de l'esclavage et ses contradictions." In *Mélanges Pierre Lévêque III*, eds. M.-M. Mactoux and E. Gény. Paris: Les Belles Lettres

Lockwood, T. 2007. "Is Natural Slavery Beneficial?" *Journal of the History of Philosophy* 45: 207–21

Millett, P. 2007. "Aristotle and Slavery in Athens." *Greece and Rome* 54: 178–209

Nichols, M. P. 1983. "The Good Life, Slavery, and Acquisition: Aristotle's Introduction to Politics." *Interpretation* 11: 171–83

O'Neil, C. 1953. "Aristotle's Natural Slave Re-examined." *New Scholasticism* 27: 247–79

Papados, D. 2000. "Das Problem des 'Sklaven von natur' bei Aristoteles." *Philosophical Inquiry* 22: 39–63

Pellegrin, P. 1982. "La théorie aristotélicienne de l'eslavage: tendances actuelles de l'interprétation." *Revue Philosophique de la France et de l'Etranger* 172: 345–57

Preus, A. 1993. "Aristotle on Slavery: Recent Reactions." *Philosophical Inquiry* 15: 33–47

Saunders, T. J. 1984. "The controversy about slavery reported in Aristotle, *Politics* 1255a sqq." In *Maistor: Studies for R. Browning*, ed. A. Moffatt. Canberra: Byzantina Austaliensia Publications

Schlaifer, R. O. 1936. "Greek Theories of Slavery from Homer to Aristotle." *Harvard Studies in Classical Philology* 47: 165–204

Schofield, M. 1999 [1990]. "Ideology and philosophy in Aristotle's theory of slavery." In *Saving the City: Philosopher-Kings and Other Classical Paradigms*. New York: Routledge

Schütrumpf, E. 1993. "Aristotle's Theory of Slavery: A Platonic Dilemma." *Ancient Philosophy* 13: 111–24

Simpson, P. 2006. "Aristotle's Defensible Defense of Slavery." *Polis* 23: 95–115

Smith, N. 1991 [1983]. "Aristotle's theory of natural slavery." In Keyt and Miller 1991

Weil, E. 1982. "Deux notes sur Aristote et l'esclavage." *Revue Philosophique de la France et de l'Etranger* 172: 339–44

West, J. L. A. 1994. "Distorted Souls: the Role of Banausics in Aristotle's *Politics*." *Polis* 13: 77–95

INEQUALITY OF MEN AND WOMEN

Bradshaw, L. 1991. "Political Rule, Prudence, and the 'Woman Question' in Aristotle." *Canadian Journal of Political Science* 24: 557–73

Clark, S. 1982. "Aristotle's Woman." *History of Political Thought* 3: 177–91

Cole, E. B. 1994. "Women, slaves, and 'love of toil' in Aristotle's moral psychology." In *Engendering Origins: Critical Feminist Readings in Plato and Aristotle*, ed. B.-A. Bar On. Albany, NY: SUNY Press

Deslauriers, M. 2009. "Sexual Difference in Aristotle's *Politics* and his Biology." *Classical World* 102: 215–31

Dobbs, D. 1996. "Family Matters: Aristotle's Appreciation of Women and the Plural Structure of Society." *American Political Science Review* 90: 74–89

Drury, S. 1987. "Aristotle on the Inferiority of Women." *Women and Politics* 7: 51–65

Fememias, M. L. 1994. "Women and Natural Hierarchy in Aristotle." *Hypathia* 9: 164–72

Green, J. 1992. "Aristotle on Necessary Verticality, Body Heat, and Gendered Proper Places in the Polis: a Feminist Critique." *Hypatia* 7: 70–96

Koziak, B. 1998. "Tragedy, feminism, and strangers: the configuration of Aristotelian political emotion." In *Feminist Interpretations of Aristotle*, ed. C. Freeland. University Park, PA: Pennsylvania University Press

Levy, H. L. 1990. "Does Aristotle Exclude Women from Politics?" *Review of Politics* 52: 397–416

Lindsay, T. K. 1994. "Was Aristotle Racist, Sexist, and Anti-Democratic? A Review Essay." *Review of Politics* 56: 127–51

Modrak, D. K. 1994. "Aristotle: women, deliberation, and nature." In *Engendering Origins: Critical Feminist Readings in Plato and Aristotle*, ed. B.-A. Bar On. Albany, NY: SUNY Press
    2006. "Aristotle on Gender, Class and Political Hierarchies." *Philosophical Inquiry* 28: 135–58

Mulgan, R. 1994. "Aristotle and the Political Role of Women." *History of Political Thought* 15: 179–202

Sakezles, P. K. 1999. "Feminism and Aristotle." *Apeiron* 32: 67–74

Salkever, S. G. 1991. "Women, soldiers, citizens: Plato and Aristotle on the politics of virility." In Lord and O'Connor 1991

Saxonhouse. A. W. 1985. "Aristotle: defective males, hierarchy, and the limits of politics." In *Women in the History of Political Thought: Ancient Greece to Machiavelli*. New York: Praeger

Schott, R. 1982. "Aristotle on Women." *Kinesis* 11: 9–84

Senack, C. M. 1994. "Aristotle on the woman's soul." In *Engendering Origins: Critical Feminist Readings in Plato and Aristotle*, ed. B.-A. Bar On. Albany, NY: SUNY Press

Smith, N. 1982. "Plato and Aristotle on the Nature of Women." *Journal of the History of Philosophy* 21: 202–19

Sparshott, F. 1985. "Aristotle on Women." *Philosophical Inquiry* 7: 177–200

Spelman, E. V. 1983. "Aristotle and the politicization of the soul." In *Discovering Reality: Feminist Perspectives on Epistemology, Metaphysics, Methodology, and Philosophy of Science*, eds. S. Harding and M. B. Hintikka. Dordrecht: D. Reidel

Stauffer, D. J. 2008. "Aristotle's Account of the Subjection of Women." *Journal of Politics* 70: 929–41

Swanson, J. A. 1999. "Aristotle on nature, human nature, and justice: a consideration of the natural functions of men and women in the city." In Bartlett and Collins 1999

## Book II

Kraut, R. 2001. "Aristotle's Critique of False Utopias (*Pol.* II.1–12)." In Höffe 2001

CRITICISMS OF PLATO

Canto-Sperber, M. 1993. "L'unité de l'Etat et les conditions du bonheur public (Platon, *Republique*, V; Aristote, *Politique*, II)." In Aubenque and Tordesillas 1993

Dobbs, D. 1985. "Aristotle's Anticommunism." *American Journal of Political Science* 29: 29–46

Evangeliou, Ch. 1996. "Even Friends Cannot have All Things in Common: Aristotle's Critique of Plato's *Republic*." *Philosophia* 25–26: 200–12

Frank, J. 2002. "Integrating public good and private right: the virtue of property." In Tessitore 2002

Gallagher, R. 2011. "Aristotle's 'Peirastic' Treatment of the 'Republic.'" *Archiv für Geschichte der Philosophie* 93: 1–23

Irwin, T. H. 1987. "Generosity and Prosperity in Aristotle's *Politics*." *Social Philosophy and Policy* 4: 37–54

   1991. "Aristotle's defence of private property." In Keyt and Miller 1991

Mathie, W. 1979. "Property in the political science of Aristotle." In *Theories of Property: Aristotle to the Present*, eds. A. Parcel and T. Flanagan. Waterloo: Wilfrid Laurier University Press

Mayhew, R. A. 1993a. "Aristotle on the Extent of Communism in Plato's *Republic*." *Ancient Philosophy* 12: 323–40

   1993b. "Aristotle on Property." *Review of Metaphysics* 46: 803–31

   1993c. "Aristotle on the Self-Sufficiency of the City." *History of Political Thought* 16: 488–502

   1996. "Aristotle's Criticism of Plato's Communism of Women and Children." *Apeiron* 29: 231–48

Miller, F. D. 1991. "Aristotle on property rights." In *Essays in Ancient Greek Philosophy, vol. IV: Aristotle's Ethics*, eds. J. P. Anton and A. Preus. Albany, NY: State University of New York Press

Nussbaum. M. C. 1980. "Shame, separateness, and political unity: Aristotle's criticisms of Plato." In *Essays on Aristotle's Ethics*, ed. A. O. Rorty. Berkeley, CA: University of California Press

Romeyer-Dherbey, G. 2005. "L'un et l'autre dans la cité d'Aristote." *Revue Philosophique de la France et de l'Etranger* 195: 191–202

Rubin, L. 1989. "Aristotle's criticism of Socratic political unity in Plato's *Republic*." In *Politikos*, ed. K. Moors. Pittsburgh, PA: Duquesne University Press

Saxonhouse. A. W. 1982. "Family, Polity, and Unity: Aristotle on Socrates' Community of Wives." *Polity* 15: 202–19

Scott, J. T. 1997. "Aristotle and the 'city of sows': doing justice to Plato." In *Politikos*, vol. 3, *Justice v. Law in Greek Political Thought*, ed. L. G. Rubin. Lanham, MD: Rowman and Littlefield

Simpson, P. 1991. "Aristotle's Criticism of Socrates' Communism of Wives and Children." *Apeiron* 24: 99–114

Stalley, R. F. 1991a. "Aristotle's criticisms of Plato's *Republic*." In Keyt and Miller 1991

  1991b. "The Unity of the State: Plato, Aristotle, and Proclus." *Polis* 14: 129–49

### CRITICISMS OF OTHER THEORISTS

Balot, R. 2001. "Aristotle's Critique of Phaleas: Justice, Equality, and Pleonexia." *Hermes* 120: 32–44

Boyer, A. 2008. "Du nouveau chez les Anciens: Remarques à partir d'Hippodamos." *Revue Philosophique de la France et de l'Etranger* 198: 407–22

Cloché, P. 1973 [1942]. "Aristote et les institutions de Sparta." In Steinmetz 1973

David, E. 1982. "Aristotle and Sparta." *Ancient Society* 13/14: 67–103

De Laix, R. 1974. "Aristotle's Conception of the Spartan Constitution." *Journal of the History of Philosophy* 12: 21–30

Gorman, V. B. 1995. "Aristotle's Hippodamos." *Historia* 44: 385–95

Huxley, G. 1971. "Crete in Aristotle's *Politics*." *Greek, Roman and Byzantine Studies* 12: 505–15

Jouanna, J. 1980. "Médecine et politique dans la *Politique* d'Aristote (II, 1268b25–1269a28)." *Ktema* 5: 257–66

Keaney, J. J. 1981. "Aristotle's *Politics*, II, 12, 1274a22–b28." *American Journal of Ancient History* 6: 97–100

Rodrigo, P. 1989/90. "Aristote urbaniste: l'esprit de la géométrie et la Politeia." *Philosophia* 19/20: 278–97

Schütrumpf, E. 1994. "Aristotle on Sparta." In *The Shadow of Sparta*, eds. A. Powell and S. Hodkinson. London: Routledge

Spryridakis, S. V. 1979. "Aristotle on Cretan Polyteknia." *Historia* 28: 380–84

Villatte, S. 1984. "Aristote et les Arcadiens; ethnos et polis dans la *Politique*." *Dialogues d'histoire ancienne* 10: 179–202

## *Book III*

Kahlenberg, K. 1973 [1934]. "Zur Interpretation von Buch III der Politik." In Steinmetz 1973

Lendle, O. 1973. "Die Einleitung von Buch III der Politik." In Steinmetz 1973

Quinn, Timothy. 1986. "Parts and Wholes in Aristotle's *Politics*, Book III." *Southern Journal of Philosophy* 24: 577–88

Wolff, F. 1993. "L'unité structurelle du livre III." In Aubenque and Tordesillas 1993


DEFINITION AND VIRTUE OF A CITIZEN

Buckler, S. 1991. "Moral Weakness and Citizenship in Aristotle." *Polis* 10: 65–94

Bullen, P. 1997. "Lawmakers and ordinary people in Aristotle." In *Politikos*, vol. 3, *Justice v. Law in Greek Political Thought*, ed. L. G. Rubin. Lanham, MD: Rowman and Littlefield

Caujolle-Zaslawsky, F. 1993. "Citoyens à six mines." In Aubenque and Tordesillas 1993

Devlin, R. 1973. "The Good Man and the Good Citizen in Aristotle's *Politics*." *Phronesis* 18: 71–79

Frede, D. 2005. "Citizenship in Aristotle's *Politics*." In Kraut and Skultety 2005

Hansen, M. H. 1996. "Aristotle's two complementary views of the Greek polis." In *Transitions to Empire*, eds. R. Wallace and E. Harris. Norman, OK: University of Oklahoma Press

Hedrick, C. W. 1994. "The zero degree of society: Aristotle and the Athenian citizen." In *Athenian Political Thought and the Reconstruction of American Democracy*, eds. J. P. Euben, J. Wallach, and J. Ober. Ithaca, NY: Cornell University Press

Johnson, C. 1984. "Who is Aristotle's citizen?" *Phronesis* 29: 73–90

Keyt, D. 2007. "The Good Man and the Upright Citizen in Aristotle's *Ethics* and *Politics*." *Social Philosophy and Policy* 24: 153–75

Khan, C-A. 2005. "Aristotle, Citizenship, and the Common Advantage." *Polis* 22: 1–23

Lévy, E. 1980. "Cité et citoyen dans la *Politique* d'Aristote." *Ktema* 5: 223–48

Morrison, D. 1999. "Aristotle's Definition of Citizenship: a Problem and Some Solutions." *History of Philosophy Quarterly* 16: 143–65

Mossé, C. 1967. "La conception du citoyen dans la *Politique* d'Aristote." *Eirene* 6: 17–21

Roberts, J. 2009. "Excellences of the citizen and of the individual." In *A Companion to Aristotle*, ed. G. Anagnostopoulos. Malden, MA/Oxford: Wiley-Blackwell

Saunders, T. J. 1980. "Arete and Ergon in Aristotle, *Politics* III.4." *Mnemosyne* 33: 353–55

## POLITICAL ACTIVITY, DELIBERATION, AND POLITICAL LIBERTY

Barnes, J. 1990. "Aristotle and political liberty." In Patzig 1990. Reprinted in Kraut and Skultety 2005

Duvall, T. and Dotson, R. 1998. "Political Participation and Eudaimonia in Aristotle's *Politics*." *History of Political Thought* 19: 21–34

Irwin, T. H. 1990. "The Good of Political Activity." In Patzig 1990

Long, R. T. 1996. "Aristotle's Conception of Freedom." *Review of Metaphysics* 49: 775–802

Mulgan, R. 1990. "Aristotle and the Value of Political Participation." *Political Theory* 18: 195–215

  1999. "Debate: Aristotle, Ethical Diversity and Political Argument." *Journal of Political Philosophy* 7: 191–207

Muller, R. 1993. "La logique de la liberté dans *la Politique*." In Aubenque and Tordesillas 1993

Walsh, M. 1998. "Aristotle's Conception of Freedom." *Journal of the History of Philosophy* 35: 495–507


## TAXONOMY OF REGIMES

Braun, E. 1973 [1966]. "Die Ursache der Pluralität von Verfassungsformen nach Aristoteles." In Steinmetz 1973

De Romilly, J. 1959. "Le classement des constitutions d'Hérodote à Aristote." *Revue des Etudes Grecques* 72: 81–99

Ewbank, M. 2005. "*Politeia* as Focal Reference in Aristotle's Taxonomy of Regimes." *Review of Metaphysics* 58: 815–41

Hansen, M. H. 1993. "Aristotle's alternative to the sixfold model of constitutions." In *Aristote et Athènes*, ed. M. Piérart. Freibourg: St. Canisius

Leandri, A. 1993. "L'aporie de la souveraineté." In Aubenque and Tordesillas 1993

Mulgan, R. 1970. "Aristotle's Sovereign." *Political Studies* 18: 518–22

  2001. "Constitutions and purpose of the state (*Pol.* III.6–9)." In Höffe 2001

Murray, O. 1993. "Polis and politieia in Aristotle." In *The Ancient Greek City-State*, ed. M. H. Hansen. Copenhagen: Royal Danish Academy of Sciences and Letters

Newman, W. L. 1892. "Aristotle's Classification of Forms of Government." *Classical Review* 6: 289–93

Rowe, C. J. 2000. "Aristotelian constitutions." In Rowe and Schofield 2000

Samad, J. 2011. "The Fundamental Political Fact: Aristotle's Path to Establishing the Importance of a City's Regime in 'Politics' III/1–9." *Acta Philosophica* 20: 335–56

Saunders, T. J. 1979. "Some Constitutional Exactitudes in Aristotle." *Liverpool Classical Monthly* 4: 93–99

Schütrumpf, E. 1976. "Probleme der aristotelischen Verfassungstheorie in *Politik* G." *Hermes* 104: 308–31

Sidgwick, H. 1892. "Aristotle's Classifications of Forms of Government." *Classical Review* 6: 141–4


THE COMMON GOOD AND THE CORRECT/DEVIANT REGIME

DISTINCTION

Ambler, W. H. 1999. "Aristotle and Thrasymachus on the common good." In Bartlett and Collins 1999

Fortenbaugh, W. W. 1991. "Aristotle on prior and posterior, correct and mistaken constitutions." In Keyt and Miller 1991

Kahn, C. 1981. "The Origins of Social Contract Theory." *Hermes* 44: 92–108

Mulgan, R. 1979. "Lycophron and Social Contract Ideas." *Journal of the History of Ideas* 40: 121–28

Scott, D. 2000. "Aristotle and Thrasymachus." *Oxford Studies in Ancient Philosophy* 19: 225–52

Smith, Th. W. 1999. "Aristotle on the Conditions for and Limits of the Common Good." *American Political Science Review* 93: 625–36


THE PROBLEM OF DISTRIBUTIVE JUSTICE/PARTICIPATION

Bien, G. 1995. "Gerechtigkeit bei Aristoteles." In *Aristoteles. Nikomachische Ethik*, ed. O. Höffe. Berlin: Akademie Verlag

Bouchard, E. 2011. "Analogies du pouvoir partagé: remarques sur Aristote, *Politique* III.11." *Phronesis* 56: 162–79

Frank, J. 1998. "Democracy and Distribution: Aristotle on Just Desert." *Political Theory* 26: 784–802

Garver, E. 1998. "The Justice of *Politics* iii and the Incompleteness of the Normative." *Ancient Philosophy* 18: 381–416

Hantz, H. 1975. "Justice and Equality in Aristotle's *Nicomachean Ethics* and *Politics*." *Diotima* 3: 83–94

Höffe, O. 1975. "Politische Gerechtigkeit – Grundzuge einer naturrechtlichen Theorie." *Studia Philsophica* 38: 107–33

Keyt, D. 1991. "Aristotle's theory of distributive justice." In Keyt and Miller 1991

Kullman, W. 1984. "Equality in Aristotle's Political Thought." *Commentationes Humanarum Litterarum* 75: 31–44

Kussmaul, P. 2008. "Aristotle's Doctrine of Justice and the Law of Athens: a Lecture." *Dionysius* 27: 29–46

Lefevre, Ch. 1980. "Approches aristotéliciennes de l'égalité entre les citoyens." *Revue Internationale de Philosophie* 34: 541–65

Mathie, W. 1987. "Political and Distributive Justice in the Political Science of Aristotle." *Review of Politics* 49: 59–84

Mayhew, R. 2009. "Rulers and ruled." In *A Companion to Aristotle*, ed. G. Anagnostopoulos. Malden, MA/Oxford: Wiley-Blackwell

Resnick, D. 1979. "Justice, Compromise, and Constitutional Rules in Aristotle's *Politics*." *Nomos* 21: 69–86

Roberts, J. 2000. "Justice and the polis." In Rowe and Schofield 2000

Rosen, F. 1975. "The Political Context of Aristotle's Categories of Justice." *Phronesis* 20: 228–40

Schofield, M. 1999a [1996]. "Sharing in the constitution." In his *Saving the City: Philosopher-Kings and Other Classical Paradigms*. New York: Routledge

   1999b. "Equality and hierarchy in Aristotle's political thought." In *Saving the City: Philosopher-Kings and Other Classical Paradigms*. New York: Routledge

Springborg, P. 1984. "Aristotle and the Problem of Needs." *History of Political Thought* 5: 393–424

Tzioka-Evangelou, P. 2009. "The Concept of Ideology in the Political Philosophy of Aristotle." *Philosophical Inquiry* 31: 121–29

Winthrop, D. 1978. "Aristotle and Theories of Justice." *American Political Science Review* 72: 1201–16

Wolff, F. 1988. "Justice et Pouvoir (Aristote, *Politique* III, 9–13)." *Phronesis* 33: 273–96

NATURE OF PUBLIC DELIBERATION

Bookman, J. T. 1992. "The Wisdom of the Many: an Analysis of the Arguments of Books III and IV of Aristotle's *Politics*." *History of Political Thought* 13: 1–12

Braun, E. 1959. "Die Summierungstheorie des Aristoteles." *Jahreshefte des Österr. Arch. Instituts* 43–44: 157–84

Nieuwenburg, P. 2004. "Learning to Deliberate: Aristotle on Truthfulness and Public Deliberation." *Political Theory* 32: 449–67

Risse, M. 2001. "The Virtuous Group: Foundations for the Argument from the Wisdom of the Multitude." *Canadian Journal of Philosophy* 31: 53–84

Waldron, J. 1995. "The Wisdom of the Multitude: Some Reflections on Book 3, Chapter 11 of Aristotle's Politics." *Political Theory* 23: 563–84. Reprinted in Kraut and Skultety 2005

Yack, B. 2006. "Rhetoric and Public Reasoning: an Aristotelian Understanding of Political Deliberation." *Political Theory* 34: 417–38

## ANALYSIS OF MONARCHY AND ABSOLUTE KINGSHIP

Braun, E. 1973. "Königtum und Aristokratie im III. Buch der aristotelischen Politik." *Jahreshefte d. Österr. Arch. Instituts* 49: 1–19
Carlier, P. 1993. "La notion de pambasileia dans la pensée politique d'Aristote." In *Aristote et Athènes*, ed. M. Piérart. Freibourg: St. Canisius
Dietz, M. 2012. "Between Polis and Empire: Aristotle's *Politics*." *American Political Science Review* 106: 275–93
Kelsen, H. 1977 [1937/38]. "Aristotle and Hellenic-Macedonian policy." In Barnes, Schofield, and Sorabji 1977
Laurand, V. 2011. "Nature de la royauté dans les *Politiques* d'Aristote." In Bermon, Laurand, and Terrel 2011
Merlan, P. 1954. "Isocrates, Aristotle, and Alexander the Great." *Historia* 3: 60–81
Miller, J. 1998. "Aristotle's Paradox of Monarchy and the Biographical Tradition." *History of Political Thought* 19: 501–16
Mulgan, R. 1974a. "A Note on Aristotle's Absolute Ruler." *Phronesis* 19: 66–69
  1974b. "Aristotle and Absolute Rule." *Antichthon* 8: 21–28
Nagle, D. B. 2000. "Alexander and Aristotle's Pambasileus." *L'Antiquité Classique* 69: 117–32
Newell, W. R. 1991. "Superlative virtue: the problem of Monarchy in Aristotle's *Politics*." In Lord and O'Connor 1991
Vander Waerdt, P. A. 1985. "Kingship and Philosophy in Aristotle's Best Regime." *Phronesis* 30: 249–73

## RULE OF LAW VERSUS THE RULE OF MEN

Bates, C. A. 1997. "The Rule of Law of Pambasileia: competing claims for rule in Aristotle's Politics." In *Politikos, vol. 3, Justice v. Law in Greek Political Thought*, ed. L. G. Rubin. Lanham, MD: Rowman and Littlefield
Cohen, J. 1996. "Rex aut Lex." *Apeiron* 29: 145–61
Goerner, E. A. 1983. "Letter and Spirit: the Political Ethics of the Rule of Law Versus the Political Ethics of the Rule of the Virtuous." *Review of Politics* 45: 553–75
Lindsay, T. K. 1991. "The 'God-Like Man' versus the 'Best Laws': Politics and Religion in Aristotle's *Politics*." *Review of Politics* 53: 488–509

Quinn, M. 1990. "Aristotle on Justice, Equality, and the Rule of Law." *Polis* 9: 170–86

Robinson D. N. 1999. "Fitness for the Rule of Law." *Review of Metaphysics* 52: 539–52

Wexler, S. and Irvine, A. 2006. "Aristotle on the Rule of Law." *Polis* 23: 116–38

LAW

Aubenque, P. 1980. "La Loi selon Aristote." *Archives de Philosophie du Droit* 25: 147–57

Bodéüs, R. 1991. "Law and regime in Aristotle." In Lord and O'Connor 1991

De Romilly, J. 1971. *La Loi dans la pensée grecque des origines à Aristote.* Paris: Les Belles Lettres

Leyden, W. 1967. "Aristotle and the Concept of Law." *Philosophy* 43: 1–19

Lisi, F. 2000. "The Concept of Law in Aristotle's *Politics.*" *Proceedings of the Boston Area Colloqium on Ancient Philosophy* 16: 29–53

Miller, F. D. 2007. "Aristotle's philosophy of law." In *A History of the Philosophy of Law from the Ancient Greeks to the Scholastics*, eds. F. D. Miller and C.-A. Biondi. Dordrecht: Springer

Morel, P.-M. 2011. "Le meilleur et le convenable. Loi et constitution dans les *Politiques* d'Aristote." In Bermon, Laurand, and Terrel 2011

Schroeder, D. 1981. "Aristotle on Law." *Polis* 4: 17–31

## Books IV–VI

PROGRAM OF POLITICAL SCIENCE

Anton, J. P. 1995. "Timely observations on Aristotle's Architectonic of Politike Techne." In Boudouris 1995

Berti, E. 1993. "Phronesis et science politique." In Aubenque and Tordesillas 1993

Bodéüs, R. 1990. "Savoir politique et savoir philosophique." In Patzig 1990

Fritz, K. v. 1957. "Aristotle's Contribution to the Practice and Theory of Historiography." *University of California Publications in Philosophy* 28: 112–38

Gerson, L. P. 1995. "On the scientific character of Aristotle's Politics." In Boudouris 1995

Kuhn, H. 1965. "Aristoteles und die Methode der Politischen Wissenschaft." *Zeitschrift für Politik* 2: 101–20

Moraux, P. 1964. "Quelques apories de la politique et leur arrière-plan historique." In Fondation Hardt 1964

Murphy, J. B. 2002. "Nature, Custom and Reason as the Explanatory and Practical Principles of Aristotelian Political Science." *Review of Politics* 64: 469–95

Ober, J. 1991. "Aristotle's political sociology: class, status, and order in the Politics." In Lord and O'Connor 1991

Rowe, C. J. 1989. "Reality and Utopia." *Elenchos* 10: 317–36

Salkever, S. G. 1991. "Aristotle's social science." In Lord and O'Connor 1991

Schütrumpf, E. 1989. "Platonic Methodology in the Program of Aristotle's Political Philosophy." *Transations and Proceedings of the American Philosophical Association* 119: 211–20

Smith, N. and Mayhew, R. 1995. "Aristotle on what the political scientist needs to know." In Boudouris 1995

Zuckert, C. 1992. "Aristotle's practical political science." In *Politikos*, vol. 2, ed. K. Moors. Pittsburgh, PA: Duquesne University Press

## POLITY, THE MIDDLE REGIME, AND THE MIXED REGIME

Aalders, G. J. D. 1964. "Die Mischverfassung und ihre historische Dokumentation in den Politika des Aristoteles." In Fondation Hardt 1964

Biondi, C-A. 2007. "Aristotle on the Mixed Constitution and its Relevance for American Political Thought." *Social Philosophy and Policy* 24: 176–98

Bluhm, W. 1962. "The Place of 'Polity' in Aristotle's Theory of the Ideal State." *Journal of Politics* 24: 743–53

Braun, E. 1967. "Die Theorie der Mischverfassung bei Aristoteles." *Wiener Studien* 85: 79–89

Cherry, K. 2009. "The Problem of Polity: Political Participation in Aristotle's Best Regime." *Journal of Politics* 71: 1406–21

Creed, J. L. 1989. "Aristotle's Middle Constitution." *Polis* 8: 2–27

Irrera, E. 2010. "Being a Good Ruler in a Deviant Community: Aristotle's Account of the Polity." *Polis* 27: 58–79

Johnson, C. 1988. "Aristotle's Polity: Mixed or Middle Constitution?" *History of Political Thought* 9: 189–204

Lockwood, T. 2006. "Polity, Political Justice and Political Mixing." *History of Political Thought* 27: 207–22

## DEMOCRACY AND OLIGARCHY

Aubenque, P. 1993. "Aristote et la démocratie." In Aubenque and Tordesillas 1993

Chambers, M. 1961. "Aristotle's 'Forms of Democracy.'" *Transactions and Proceedings of the American Philosophical Association* 92: 20–36

Creed, J. L. 1990. "Aristotle and democracy." In *Polis and Politics. Essays in Greek Moral and Political Philosophy*, eds. A. Loizou and H. Lesser. Brookfield, VT: Avebury

Eucken, C. 1990. "Der aristotelische Demokratiebegriff und sein historisches Unfeld." In Patzig 1990

Frank, D. H. 1983. "Aristotle on Freedom in the *Politics*." *Prudentia* 15: 108–16

Geiger, R. 2001. "Die Einrichtung von Demokratien und Oligarchien (*Pol.* VI 108)." In Höffe 2001

Hansen, M. H. 2010. "Democratic Freedom and the Concept of Freedom in Plato and Aristotle." *Greek, Roman, and Byzantine Studies* 50: 1–27

Lindsay, T. K. 1992a. "Aristotle's Qualified Defense of Democracy through 'Political Mixing.'" *Journal of Politics* 54: 101–19

    1992b. "Liberty, Equality, Power: Aristotle's Critique of the Democratic 'Presupposition.'" *American Journal of Political Science* 36: 743–61

Lintott, A. 1992. "Aristotle and Democracy." *Classical Quarterly* 42: 114–28

Mara, G. 2002. "The culture of democracy: Aristotle's *Athenaion Politeia* as political theory." In Tessitore 2002

Mulgan, R. 1970. "Aristotle and the democratic conception of freedom." In *Auckland Classical Studies Presented to E. M. Blaiklock*, ed. B. F. Harris. Auckland University Press

    1991. "Aristotle's analysis of Oligarchy and Democracy." In Keyt and Miller 1991

Narcy, M. 1993. "Aristote devant les objections de Socrate à la démocratie (*Politique*, III, 4 et 11)." In Aubenque and Tordesillas 1993

Ober, J. 1999. "Political animals, acutal citizens, and the best possible polis: Aristotle's Politics." In *Political Dissent in Democratic Athens: Intellectual Critics of Popular Rule*. Princeton University Press

    2005. "Aristotle's natural democracy." In Kraut and Skultety 2005

Papageorgion, C. I. 1990. "Four or Five Types of Democracy in Aristotle?" *History of Political Thought* 11: 1–8

Salkever, S. G. 2002. "The deliberative model of democracy and Aristotle's ethics of natural questions." In Tessitore 2002

Schollmeier, P. 1988. "The Democracy Most in accordance with Equality." *History of Political Thought* 9: 205–10

Simpson, P. 2011. "A corruption of oligarchs." In *On Oligarchy: Ancient Lessons for Modern Politics*, eds. D. Tabachnik and T. Koivukoski. University of Toronto Press

Strauss, B. S. 1991. "On Aristotle's critique of Athenian Democracy." In Lord and O'Connor 1991

Talisse, R. 2007. "Why democrats need the virtues." In Goodman and Talisse 2007

Taylor, Q. 2002. "Public Deliberation and Popular Government in Aristotle's *Politics*." *Interpretation* 29: 241–60

Verbeke, G. 1988. "Zur Rezeption der aristotelischen Demokratietheorie." In *Antike Rechts- und Socialphilosophie*, eds. O. Gigon and M. Fischer. Frankfurt: Peter Lang

Wilson, J. L. 2011. "Deliberation, Democracy, and the Rule of Reason in Aristotle's *Politics*." *American Political Science Review* 105: 259–74

Winthrop, D. 1978. "Aristotle on Participatory Democracy." *Polity* 11: 151–71

Wolff, F. 1988. "Aristote démocrate." *Philosophie* 18: 57–87


TYRANNY

Bodéüs, R. 1999. "L'attitude paradoxale d'Aristote envers la tyrannie." *Tijdschrift voor Filosofie* 61: 547–62

Boesche, R. 1993. "Aristotle's Science of Tyranny." *History of Political Thought* 14: 1–25

Kamp, A. 1985. "Die aristotelische Theorie der Tyrannis." *Philos. Jahrbuch* 92: 17–34

Petit, A. 1993. "L'analyse aristotélicienne de la tyrannie." In Aubenque and Tordesillas 1993

Pons, A. 1968. "Tyrannie, politique, et philosophie." *Les Etudes Philosophique* 2: 169–84

Richter, M. 1990. "Aristotle and the Classical Greek Concept of Despotism." *History of European Ideas* 12: 175–87


STASIS AND PRESERVATION OF REGIMES

Brumbaugh, R. S. 1978. "Revolution, Propaganda and Education: Aristotle's Causes in Politics." *Paideia* 2: 172–81

Coby, P. 1988. "Aristotle's Three Cities and the Problem of Faction." *Journal of Politics* 50: 896–919

Davis, M. 1986. "Aristotle's Reflections on Revolution." *Graduate Faculty Philosophy Journal* 11: 49–63

De Romilly, J. 1977. *The Rise and Fall of States According to Greek Authors.* Ann Arbor: University of Michigan Press

Garver, E. 2005. "Factions and the Paradox of Aristotelian Practical Science." *Polis* 22: 181–205

2007. "The revolt of the just." In Goodman and Talisse 2007

Gehrke, H. J. 2001. "Verfassungswandel (*Pol.* V 1–12)." In Höffe 2001

Polansky, R. 1991. "Aristotle on political change." In Keyt and Miller 1991

Shuster, A. 2011. "The Problem of the 'Partheniae' in Aristotle's Political Thought." *Polis* 28: 279–308

Skultety, S. 2008. "Aristotle's Theory of Partisanship." *Polis* 25: 208–32

2009a. "Competition in the Best of Cities: Agonism and Aristotle's *Politics*." *Political Theory* 37: 44–68

2009b. "Delimiting Aristotle's Conception of *Stasis* in the *Politics*." *Phronesis* 54: 346–70

Swanson, J. 1997. "Aristotle on how to preserve a regime: maintaining precedent, privacy, and peace through the Rule of Law." In *Politikos, vol. 3, Justice v. Law in Greek Political Thought*, ed. L. G. Rubin. Lanham, MD: Rowman and Littlefield

Weed, R. 2007. "Aristotle on Stasis: a Moral Psychology of Political Conflict." *Polis* 24: 382–4

Wheeler, M. 1977. "Aristotle's analysis of the nature of political struggle." In Barnes, Schofield, and Sorabji 1977

## Books VII–VIII

BEST REGIME(S)

Alexander, L. 2000. "The Best Regimes of Aristotle's *Politics*." *History of Political Theory* 21: 189–216

Bartlett, R. C. 1994a. "Aristotle's Science of the Best Regime." *American Political Science Review* 88: 143–55

1994b. "The Realism of 'Classical' Political Science: an Introduction to Aristotle's Best Regime." *American Journal of Political Science* 38: 381–402

1995. "Controversy: Aristotle's Science of the Best Regime." *American Political Science Review* 89: 152–60

Braun, E. 1969. "Aristokratie und aristokratische Verfassungsform in der aristotelischen Politik." *Palingenesia* 4: 148–80

Garver, E. 2009. "Living Well and Living Together: *Politics* VII 1–3 and the Discovery of the Common Life." *Proceedings of the Boston Area Colloquium on Ancient Philosophy* 25: 43–63

Huxley, G. 1985. "On Aristotle's Best State." *History of Political Thought* 6: 139–49

Keyt, D. 1993. "Aristotle and Anarchism." *Reason Papers* 18: 133–52. Reprinted in Kraut and Skultety 2005

Lockwood, T. 2006. "The Best Regime of Aristotle's *Nicomachean Ethics*." *Ancient Philosophy* 26: 355–70

Lord, C. 1978. "Politics and Philosophy in Aristotle's *Politics*." *Hermes* 106: 336–59

Mara, G. 1987. "The Role of Philosophy in Aristotle's Political Philosophy." *Polity* 19: 375–401

Miller, F. D. 2009. "Aristotle on the Ideal Constitution." In *A Companion to Aristotle*, ed. G. Anagnostopoulos. Malden, MA/Oxford: Wiley-Blackwell

Neschke-Hentschke, A. 2001. "Die uneingeschränkt beste Polisordnung (*Pol.* VII–VIII)." In Höffe 2001

Rodrigo, P. 1987. "D'une excellente constitution. Notes sur la Politeia chez Aristote." *Revue de Philosophie Ancienne* 5: 71–93

Roochnik, D. 2008. "Aristotle's Defense of the Theoretical Life: Comments on *Politics* 7." *Review of Metaphysics* 61: 711–35

Salkever, S. 2007. "Whose Prayer? The Best Regime of Book 7 and the Lessons of Aristotle's *Politics*." *Political Theory* 35: 29–46

Samaras, T. 2007. "Aristotle's *Politics*: the City of Book Seven and the Question of Ideology." *Classical Quarterly* 57: 77–89

Thomason, W. 1994. "Aristotle: Philosophy and Politics, Theory and Practice." *American Catholic Philosophical Quarterly* 68 Supp: 109–24

WAR, PEACE, AND IMPERIALISM

Arnopoulos, P. 1998. "Plato and Aristotle on War and Peace." *Philosophia* 27–28: 142–52

Charles-Saget, A. 1993. "Guerre et nature. Etude sur le sens du *Pólemos* chez Aristote." In Aubenque and Tordesillas 1993

Gerson, L. 2007. "The morality of nations: an Aristotelian approach." In Goodman and Talisse 2007

Miller, F. D. 2007. "Aristotelian statecraft and modern politics." In Goodman and Talisse 2007

PRECONDITIONS OF THE BEST REGIME

Egerton, F. 1975. "Aristotle's Population Biology." *Arethusa* 8: 307–31

Golding, M. P. and Golding, N. H. 1975. "Population Policy in Plato and Aristotle: Some Value Issues." *Arethusa* 8: 359–72

Janssens, D. 2010. "Easily, at a Glance: Aristotle's Political Optics." *Review of Politics* 72: 385–408

Oppenheimer, J. 1975. "When Sense and Life Begin: Background for a Remark in Aristotle's *Politics* (1335b24)." *Arethusa* 8: 331–44

Romeyer-Dherbey, G. 1993. "Aristote et la poliorcétique (*Politique*, VII, 11, 1330b32–1331a18)." In Aubenque and Tordesillas

EDUCATION AND MUSIC IN THE BEST REGIME

Ardito, L. 2005. "*Mousike* and *Politikos Bios* in the Athenian Polis." *Skepsis* 16: 25–35

Bénatouïl, T. 2011. "'Choisir le labeur en vue du loisir': une analyse de *Politiques*, VII, 14." In Bermon, Laurand, and Terrel 2011

Christodoulidi-Mazaraki, A. 1999. "State and Education in Aristotle." *Philosophia* 29: 45–52

Demont, P. 1993. "Le loisir dans la *Politique* d'Aristote." In Aubenque and Tordesillas

Depew, D. J. 1991. "Politics, music, and contemplation in Aristotle's ideal state." In Keyt and Miller 1991

Drefcinski, S. 2011. "What Kind of Cause is Music's Influence on Moral Character?" *American Catholic Philosophical Quarterly* 85: 287–96

Homiak, M. 1990. "Politics as Soul Making: Aristotle on Becoming Good." *Philosophia* 20: 167–93

Koeplin, A. 2009. "The *Telos* of Citizen Life: Music and Philosophy in Aristotle's Ideal Polis." *Polis* 26: 116–32

Lord, C. 1990. "Politics and Education in Aristotle's 'Politics.'" In Patzig 1990

Nightingale, A. 1996. "Aristotle on the 'Liberal' and 'Illiberal' Arts." *Proceedings of the Boston Area Colloquium in Ancient Philosophy* 12: 29–58

Reeve, C. D. C. 1998. "Aristotelian education." In *Philosophers on Education*, ed. A. O. Rorty. London: Routledge

Solmsen, F. 1964. "Leisure and Play in Aristotle's Ideal State." *Rheinisches Museum für Philologie* 107: 193–220

Stalley, R. 2009. "Education and the state." In *A Companion to Aristotle*, ed. G. Anagnostopoulos. Oxford: Wiley-Blackwell

Woerther, F. 2008. "Music and Education of the Soul in Plato and Aristotle: Homeopathy and the Formation of Character." *Classical Quarterly* 58: 89–103

## RECEPTION OF THE *POLITICS*

### *Historical reception*

Annas, J. 1995. "Aristotelian political theory in the Hellenistic Period." In *Justice and Generosity: Studies in Hellenistic Social and Political Philosophy*, ed. A. Laks and M. Schofield. Cambridge University Press

Bien, G. 1990. "Die Wirkungegeschichte der aristotelische *Politik*." In Patzig 1990

Brieskorn, N. 2008. "Spanische Spätscholastik: Francisco de Vitoria." In Horn and Neschke-Hentschke 2008

Dauber, N. 2008. "Deutsche reformation: Philipp Melanchthon." In Horn and Neschke-Hentschke 2008

Gregorio, F. 2008. "Frankreich im 14. Jahrhundert: Nicole Oresme." In Horn and Neschke-Hentschke 2008

Hartung, G. 2008. "Deutschland im 19. Jahrhundert: Trendelenburgs Naturrechtskonzeption und ihre Wirkungsgeschichte." In Horn and Neschke-Hentschke 2008

Horn, Ch. 2008. "Hellenismus und frühe Kaiserzeit: Der Peripatos." In Horn and Neschke-Hentschke 2008

Kauffmann, C. 2008. "England im 17. Jahrhundert: Thomas Hobbes." In Horn and Neschke-Hentschke 2008

Laird, J. 1942/43. "Hobbes on Aristotle's *Politics*." *Proceedings of the Aristotelian Society* 43: 1–20

Mansfield, H. C. 1980. "Marx on Aristotle: Freedom, Money, and Politics." *Review of Metaphysics* 37: 352–67

McKeon, R. 1979. "The Hellenistic and Roman Foundations of the Tradition of Aristotle in the West." *Review of Metaphysics* 32: 677–715

Miethke, J. 2008. "Spätmittelalter: Thomas von Aquin, Aegidius Romanus, Marsilius von Padua." In Horn and Neschke-Hentschke 2008

Neschke-Hentschke, A. 2008a. "Frankreich im Zeitalter der Religionskriege: Jean Bodin." In Horn and Neschke-Hentschke 2008

2008b. "Niederländischer Protestantismus: Hugo Grotius." In Horn and Neschke-Hentschke 2008

O'Meara, D. J. 2008. "Spätantike und Byzanz: Neuplatonische Rezeption – Michael von Ephesos." In Horn and Neschke-Hentschke 2008

Ottmann, H. 2008. "Protestantische Schulphilosophie in Deutschland: Arnisaeus und Conring." In Horn and Neschke-Hentschke 2008

Pines, S. 1975. "Aristotle's *Politics* in Arabic Philosphy." *Israel Oriental Studies* 5: 150–60

Quillet, J. 1984. "Présence d'Aristote dans la philosophie politique médiévale." *Revue de Philosophie Ancienne* 2: 93–102

Rowe, C. J. 2000. "The Peripatos after Aristotle." In Rowe and Schofield 2000

Schmidt, J. 1986. "A Raven with a Halo: the Translations of Aristotle's *Politics*." *History of Political Thought* 7: 295–319

Siep, L. 2008. "Deutscher Idealismus: Hegel." In Horn and Neschke-Hentschke 2008

Söder, J. R. 2008. "Hochmittelalter: Die Wiedergewinnung des Politischen." In Horn and Neschke-Hentschke 2008

Williams, J. M. 1987. "The Peripatetic School and Demetrius of Phalerum's Reforms in Athens." *The Ancient World* 15: 87–98


## Aristotle within the framework of liberalism

Galston, M. 2002. "The Middle Way: what contemporary liberal legal theorists can learn from Aristotle." In Tessitore 2002

Goodman, L. 2007. "Aristotle's polity today." In Goodman and Talisse 2007

Halper, E. 2007. "Aristotle and the liberal state." In Goodman and Talisse 2007

Höffe, O. 2001. "Aristotles' Politik: Vorgriff auf eine liberale Demokratie." In Höffe 2001

Holmes, S. T. 1979. "Aristippus in and out of Athens." *American Political Science Review* 73: 113–28. Reprinted in Kraut and Skultety 2005

Kullman, W. 1983. "Aristoteles' Staatslehre aus heutiger Sicht." *Gymnasium* 90: 456–77

Ober, J. 1993. "The polis as a society: Aristotle, John Rawls, and the Athenian social contract." In *The Ancient Greek City-State*, ed. M. H. Hansen. Copenhagen: Royal Danish Academy of Sciences and Letters

Simpson, P. 2007. "Aristotle's regime of the Americans." In Goodman and Talisse 2007

Wallach, J. R. 1992. "Contemporary Aristotelianism." *Political Theory* 29: 613–41


## Social democrat interpretation of Aristotle (Nussbaum)

Antony, L. 2000. "Nature and Norms." *Ethics* 111: 8–26

Arneson, R. 2000. "Perfectionism and Politics." *Ethics* 111: 37–63

Charles, D. 1988. "Moral Perfectionism: Reply to Nussbaum." *Oxford Studies in Ancient Philosophy* Supp.: 184–206

Charlesworth, H. 2000. "M. Nussbaum's Feminist Internationalism." *Ethics* 111: 64–78

Crocker, D. 1992. "Functioning and Capability: the Foundations of Sen's and Nussbaum's Developmental Ethic." *Political Theory* 20: 584–612

Mulgan, R. 2000. "Was Aristotle an 'Aristotelian Social Democrat'?" *Ethics* 111: 79–101

Nussbaum. M. C. 1988. "Nature, Function and Capability: Aristotle on Political Distribution." *Oxford Studies in Ancient Philosophy* Supp.: 145–84

1990. "Aristotelian social democracy." In *Liberalism and the Good*, eds.
R. G. Douglass, R. G. Mara, and H. Richardson. London: Routledge

1992. "Human Functioning and Social Justice: In Defense of Aristotle's
Essentialism." *Political Theory* 20: 202–46

1995. "Aristotle on human nature and the foundations of ethics."
In *World, Mind, and Ethics: Essays on the Ethical Philosophy of
Bernard Williams*, ed. J. Altham and R. Harrison. Cambridge University
Press

1998. "Aristotle, feminism, and needs for functioning." In *Feminist Interpretations of Aristotle*, ed. C. Freeland. University Park, PA: Pennsylvania University Press

2000. "Aristotle, Politics, and Human Capabilities: a Response to Antony,
Arneson, Charlesworth, and Mulgan." *Ethics* 111: 102–40

### Libertarian/rights interpretation of Aristotle (Miller)

Annas, J. 1996. "Aristotle on Human Nature and Political Virtue." *Review
of Metaphysics* 49: 731–54

Brown, V. 2001. "'Rights' in Aristotle's *Politics* and *Nicomachean Ethics*?"
*Review of Metaphysics* 55: 269–96

Cooper, J. M. 1996. "Justice and Rights in Aristotle's *Politics*." *Review of
Metaphysics* 49: 859–72

Gill, D. 1996. "Political Rights in Aristotle: a Response to Fred Miller,
*Nature, Justice, and Rights in Aristotle's Politics*." *Ancient Philosophy*
16: 431–43

Golden, M. 1993. "Aristotelian Ethics and Natural Rights: a Critique." *Reason Papers* 18: 71–78

Keyt, D. 1996. "Fred Miller on Aristotle's Political Naturalism." *Ancient
Philosophy* 16: 425–30

Kraut, R. 1996. "Are there Natural Rights in Aristotle?" *Review of Metaphysics* 49: 755–74

McGrade, A. S. 1996. "Aristotle's Place in the History of Natural Rights."
*Review of Metaphysics* 49: 803–30

Miller, F. D. 1988. "Aristotle and the Natural Rights Tradition." *Reason
Papers* 13: 166–81

1989. "Aristotle's Political Naturalism." *Apeiron* 22: 195–218

1991. "Aristotle on natural law and justice." In Keyt and Miller 1991

1996. "A Reply to David Keyt and David Gill." *Ancient Philosophy* 16:
443–54

2001. "Sovereignty and Political Rights (*Pol.* III.10–13)." In Höffe 2001

2002. "Aristotelian autonomy." In Tessitore 2002

2003 [2001]. "Aristotle's theory of political rights." In *Aristotle and Modern Law*, eds. R. O. Brooks and J. B. Murphy. Burlington, VT: Ashgate Publishing

2006. "Legal and Political Rights in Demosthenes and Aristotle." *Philosophical Inquiry* 28: 27–60

# INDEX LOCORUM

# INDEX OF NAMES AND SUBJECTS